THE RORSCHACH IN MULTIMETHOD FORENSIC ASSESSMENT

This volume demonstrates how multimethod forensic assessment with the Rorschach adds incremental validity, insight, and practical value. Case discussions by leading forensic psychologists illustrate the integration of contemporary Rorschach assessment with the MMPI-2 and MMPI-2-RF, the PAI, and the HCR-20. This text addresses a wide range of forensic applications including child custody, psychological trauma, personal injury, psychotic offenders, competency evaluations, immigration cases, and impression management. It also shows how the recently developed Rorschach Performance Assessment System® (R-PAS®) effectively enhances the use of the Rorschach in forensic cases, while offering guidance for Comprehensive System users as well.

The late **Robert E. Erard, PhD,** was a clinical and forensic psychologist. He was a past president of the Society for Personality Assessment, a Fellow of the American Psychological Association (Divisions, 31, 41, and 42), and a co-author of the R-PAS® manual. He edited the "Clinical Case Applications" section of the *Journal of Personality Assessment* and was Head of the Assessment Section for *Psychological Injury and Law*. Dr. Erard passed away shortly before the publication of this book and will be remembered as an inspirational leader on the Rorschach.

F. Barton Evans, PhD, is professor of psychiatry and director of Psychological and Forensic Assessment Services at James H. Quillen College of Medicine, East Tennessee State University. He is Fellow of the American Psychological Association and the Society for Personality Assessment and author of *Harry Stack Sullivan: Interpersonal Theory and Psychotherapy*.

THE RORSCHACH IN MULTIMETHOD FORENSIC ASSESSMENT
Conceptual Foundations and Practical Applications

Edited by
Robert E. Erard and F. Barton Evans

NEW YORK AND LONDON

First published 2017
by Routledge
711 Third Avenue, New York, NY 10017

and by Routledge
2 Park Square, Milton Park, Abingdon, Oxon, OX14 4RN

Routledge is an imprint of the Taylor & Francis Group, an informa business

© 2017 Taylor & Francis

The right of Robert E. Erard and F. Barton Evans to be identified as the authors of the editorial material, and of the authors for their individual chapters, has been asserted in accordance with sections 77 and 78 of the Copyright, Designs and Patents Act 1988.

All rights reserved. No part of this book may be reprinted or reproduced or utilised in any form or by any electronic, mechanical, or other means, now known or hereafter invented, including photocopying and recording, or in any information storage or retrieval system, without permission in writing from the publishers.

Trademark notice: Product or corporate names may be trademarks or registered trademarks, and are used only for identification and explanation without intent to infringe.

Library of Congress Cataloging in Publication Data
A catalog record for this book has been requested

ISBN: 978-1-138-92507-6 (hbk)
ISBN: 978-1-138-92509-0 (pbk)
ISBN: 978-1-315-68293-8 (ebk)

Typeset in ITC Legacy Serif
by Apex CoVantage, LLC

R. E.
DEDICATES THIS BOOK
TO BARBARA, WITH LOVE.
B. E.
DEDICATES THIS BOOK
TO JUDY MARIS, MY BELOVED
AND
THE LATE GREAT BEN SCHUTZ,
WHO GOT THIS WHOLE THING STARTED.

CONTENTS

List of Contributors — ix
Preface — x
ROBERT E. ERARD AND F. BARTON EVANS

Acknowledgments — xx
About the Editors — xxii

PART I. CONCEPTUAL FOUNDATIONS — 1

1. Toward an Integrative Perspective on the Person: Opportunities and Challenges of Multimethod Assessment — 3
   ROBERT F. BORNSTEIN

2. Psychometric Foundations of the Rorschach Performance Assessment System® (R-PAS®) — 23
   GREGORY J. MEYER, DONALD J. VIGLIONE, AND JONI L. MIHURA

3. Integrating Self-Report and Performance-Based Testing in Detecting Impression Management — 92
   DOUGLAS S. SCHULTZ

PART II. FORENSIC APPLICATIONS — 129

4. Integrating the Personality Assessment Inventory and Rorschach Inkblot Method in Forensic Assessment — 131
   CHRISTOPHER HOPWOOD AND F. BARTON EVANS

5	Multimethod Forensic Assessment Using the Rorschach in Personal Injury Evaluations ROBERT E. ERARD	160
6	The Rorschach in the Differential Diagnosis of Psychotic Offenders ALI KHADIVI	194
7	The Rorschach in Multimethod Custody Evaluations ROBERT E. ERARD, JACQUELINE S. SINGER, AND DONALD J. VIGLIONE	210
8	Madness, Mayhem, and Murder: A Comparative Rorschach Case Study of Methamphetamine Psychosis and Paranoid Schizophrenia MARVIN W. ACKLIN	242

PART III. SPECIAL TOPICS — 295

9	Collaborative/Therapeutic Assessment in Multimethod Forensic Evaluations BRUCE L. SMITH AND F. BARTON EVANS	297
10	Using the CS in an R-PAS World: Multimethod Forensic Assessment with the Exner Comprehensive System F. BARTON EVANS	316

Index — 333

CONTRIBUTORS

Marvin W. Acklin, PhD, John A. Burns School of Medicine, Honolulu, HI

Robert F. Bornstein, PhD, Adelphi University, Garden City, NY

Robert E. Erard, PhD, Psychological Institutes of Michigan, P.C., Bloomfield, MI

F. Barton Evans, PhD, James H. Quillen College of Medicine, Johnson City, TN

Christopher Hopwood, PhD, Michigan State University, East Lansing, MI

Ali Khadivi, PhD, Albert Einstein College of Medicine, Bronx, NY

Gregory J. Meyer, PhD, University of Toledo, Toledo, OH

Joni L. Mihura, PhD, University of Toledo, Toledo, OH

Douglas S. Schultz, PhD, Delaware Psychiatric Center, New Castle, DE

Jacqueline S. Singer, PhD, Private Practice, Sonoma, CA

Bruce L. Smith, PhD, University of California, Berkeley, CA

Donald J. Viglione, PhD, Alliant International University, San Diego, CA

PREFACE

It has been less than ten years since the publication of Gacono and Evans's (2008) groundbreaking work on the use of the Rorschach in forensic practice, and yet the field of Rorschach assessment has advanced further scientifically during this period than perhaps during any other since the original publication of Exner's Comprehensive System (CS: Exner, 1974). These advances include, among others, a) the collection and analysis of the CS international reference samples (Meyer, Erdberg, & Shaffer, 2007; Shaffer, Erdberg, & Meyer, 2007), leading to the Composite International Reference Values (CIRV; see Meyer, Shaffer, Erdberg, & Horn, 2015); b) Mihura, Meyer, Dumitrascu, and Bombel's (2013, 2015) comprehensive meta-analyses of major CS variables; and c) the development of R-Optimized Administration to control the number of Rorschach responses to sharpen the accuracy of interpretation (Dean, Viglione, Perry, & Meyer, 2007; Dean, Viglione, Perry, & Meyer, 2008; Viglione et al., 2015). Resulting from these empirical advances has been the Rorschach Performance Assessment System® (R-PAS®: Meyer, Viglione, Mihura, Erard, & Erdberg, 2011): a Rorschach system developed to incorporate these and other essential scientific improvements, which offers much to forensic psychological assessors.

Concurrently, the field of personality assessment has also undergone a period of greater systematic thinking and research about how to conceptualize and use multiple methods of assessment (Hopwood & Bornstein, 2014; Mihura, 2012). As will be discussed in greater detail in this preface, the systematic integration of self-report measures with performance-based measures offers forensic assessors a clear and comprehensible rationale for psychological assessment within the psycholegal context.

The Rorschach is the most widely used performance-based method in forensic settings. It is used by about a third of forensic psychologists overall (Archer, Buffington-Vollum, Stredny, & Handel, 2006) and in over 40% of personal injury and over 50% of child custody evaluations (Ackerman & Pritzl, 2011; Boccacini & Brodsky, 1999). In view of its continuing importance in forensic practice, it is important to help psychological experts stay abreast of both cutting-edge Rorschach science and the integration of the Rorschach with other tests in multimethod assessment. That is the aim of this book.

We begin with three chapters on Conceptual Foundations. The first is by Bornstein, setting the stage for the book by discussing the opportunities and challenges of multimethod assessment. Next, Meyer, Viglione, and Mihura offer a detailed introduction to the R-PAS and its psychometric foundations. Last, Schultz rounds out this section by describing how the Rorschach can be used in multimethod assessment to address the vexing problem of impression management in forensic assessment.

The next section—Forensic Applications—provides in many ways the meat of the book for forensic practitioners by offering numerous applications of multimethod Rorschach practice. Hopwood and Evans begin with the integration of the Rorschach and the PAI in a case in immigration court. Erard describes the place of the Rorschach in multimethod assessment in personal injury cases, providing a conceptual background and illustrating it with a detailed application of R-PAS in a complex case. Khadivi informs readers on how the Rorschach can be integrated with other data in the forensic assessment of psychotic offenders. Next, Erard, Singer, and Viglione provide a conceptual model for using the Rorschach in multimethod child custody evaluations and present an updated forensic normative study of child custody litigants using R-PAS. Finally, Acklin deeply explores the complex relationship between methamphetamine use and violent offending and illustrates his approach to using R-PAS in multimethod assessment by comparing a high-profile murder case complicated by methamphetamine psychosis to a clinical case of schizophrenia.

The last section, Special Topics, offers perspectives on two issues of topical interest. Smith and Evans push the envelope of forensic practice by discussing the application of collaborative/therapeutic principles in forensic evaluations. The final chapter by Evans examines the continued use of the Exner Comprehensive System in forensic psychological assessment in light of new empirical advances and provides recommendations on how (and why it is essential) to incorporate these advances in a CS-based approach.

This preface closes with a detailed look at conceptualizing and integrating self-report tests and performance-based Rorschach method in multimethod assessment.

SELF-REPORT TESTS

Self-report measures all rely on three sequential processes: a) introspection, b) retrospective memory search, and c) deliberate self-presentation (Bornstein, 2009). Each of these processes presents particular problems for forensic evaluations.

Beginning with introspection, abundant clinical and social psychological research have demonstrated the limitations of deliberate introspection—a process that is often distorted by self-deception, attribution biases, cognitive heuristics (including recency, salience, and availability biases), priming, and personality styles associated with lack of insight (Bornstein, 2009; Cogswell, Alloy, Karpinski, & Grant, 2010; Cyders & Coskunpinar, 2011; Huprich, Bornstein, & Shmitt, 2011; Nisbett & Wilson, 1977; Shedler, Mayman, & Manis, 1993). Recent neuroscience findings also show that important aspects of personality functioning involve right-brain and limbic neuro-pathways that are generally inaccessible to conscious introspection (see Smith & Finn, 2014). Thus test takers' attitudes, motives, and traits are by no means fully captured by what they can recognize through conscious reflection and describe on self-report tests.

Turning to retrospective memory search, self-report tests tap into one kind of memory that may influence personality functioning (Schultheiss, 2007): declarative memory systems (i.e., those that lend themselves to direct recall), rather than non-declarative memory systems (i.e., those that are only recognized or acted upon when prompted in the right circumstances). State-dependent and mood-congruent memory can be distorting factors (Huprich et al., 2011). For example, depressed people tend to exaggerate the seriousness of their failures and infirmities

(Griens, Jonker, Spinhoven, & Blom, 2002). Recollections of experiences and behavior also tend not to discriminate between frequency (how often does this happen?) and chronicity (how long has this been going on?), because memory search is often dominated by heuristic schemas rather than concrete examples (Shiffman, 1999). Research has shown weak correlations between immediate self-reports of state experiences and contemporaneous observer reports of act frequencies, on the one hand, and subjective retrospective summaries of these events on the other (Gosling, John, Craik, & Robins, 1998). One study exploring adult memories of childhood depression and anxiety and of hyperactivity showed that they were correlated at only 0.06 and 0.05, respectively (Henry, Moffitt, Caspi, Langley, & Silva, 1994).

Further, how people present themselves is highly dependent on the interpersonal context and what they wish to achieve with their presentations (Goffman, 1959). Child custody litigants want to be seen to be virtuous, competent, and psychologically mature. Refugees want to be seen as long-suffering and deserving. Defendants in criminal responsibility evaluations want to be seen as having been out of control of their mental processes and behavior. Personal injury litigants want to be seen as unjustly wronged and seriously injured.

In addition to the processing features that may limit or distort the quality of data captured by self-report testing, it is also important to recognize that interviews, checklists, and self-report personality tests all depend on similar cognitive and emotional processes. As a result, convergences among findings from such methods do not necessarily provide meaningful confirmations. By sharing a common methodology, self-report methods pose a risk of spurious correlation (Meyer, 2012).

Performance Assessment with the Rorschach

In contrast to self-report personality tests, stimulus attribution personality tests like the Rorschach do not depend strongly on capacities for introspection, retrospective memory search, or deliberate self-presentation. Attention is focused on the stimulus rather than the self. Associations, feelings, need states, and motives primed by the stimulus are activated, influencing the meanings assigned. Possible interpretations are developed, re-checked against the stimulus, subjected to censorship, and an attribution is made. Each part of this sequence can be a source of clinical information and can be compared to normative expectations. Also, because the Rorschach instructions provide less structure or guidance than self-report methods, the test tends to elicit more self-generated and spontaneous behavior. The situation is somewhat analogous to using essay questions versus multiple choice or fill in the blanks.

Unlike self-report tests, which largely elicit self-descriptions of personality and behavior, the Rorschach affords an opportunity for observing personality in action. How does the respondent go about solving an unfamiliar task, relating to the examiner, responding to frustration or embarrassment, and managing self-disclosure? What locations and features of the inkblots does she focus on? How does she resolve contradictory ideas? What themes does she keep returning to?

The Rorschach task offers an opportunity as well to observe performance under stressful conditions. The respondent likely lacks any detailed schema for how to behave while performing the task and experiences relatively little control over how he presents himself. Also, because the task does not lend itself to many simple solutions, it is inherently frustrating and tends to draw out negative affects and highlights internal conflicts.

Whereas self-report tests ask people to describe themselves in a largely context-free format using pre-set options, the Rorschach offers opportunities to contextualize motives, affects, traits, and coping patterns. For example, one can observe how the quality of perception and thinking vary according to changing conditions (e.g., card pull, emotional reactions, thematic content, reactions to the examiner). With respect to personality traits, the work of Mischel and Shoda (1995) elucidated the importance of determining the kinds of situations in which particular traits are likely to be manifest. For example, the same employee may be domineering with subordinates, polite with peers, and submissive with superiors. Mischel and Shoda recommend that personality be described in "if-then" propositions. For example, "If she starts thinking about sad or gloomy situations, she quickly tries to turn them into something exciting and uplifting," or "If he finds himself in an aggressive interaction, he tends to misunderstand other people's motives," or "If she gets sidetracked by strong feelings, she tends to recover quickly." The Rorschach provides evidence to support such contextualized interpretations.

At the same time, there is no simple and self-evident path from observing how someone goes about making attributions to semi-ambiguous stimuli to generating accurate descriptions of the person making the attributions. Similar behaviors during performance-based testing may have different meanings in different contexts. Also, implicit motives, traits, tensions, and affects suggested by Rorschach scores may not reflect conscious experience or behavior in particular circumstances (see Huprich et al., 2011; McClelland, Koestner, & Weinberger, 1989). Thus, for example, someone may elevate on the R-PAS Suicide Concern Composite (SC-Comp) but not be experiencing any active suicidal ideation.

When Self-Report Tests and Performance Assessment Disagree

It is important to recognize that self-report and performance-based tests often fail to confirm each other (Archer & Krishnamurthy, 1993). This is particularly true in cases where a respondent has been reticent or guarded on one kind of instrument, but not on the other (Meyer, 1999; Meyer, Riethmiller, Brooks, Benoit, & Handler, 2000). Meyer (2012) observed,

> I think the biggest nut to crack remains the heteromethod conundrum. We need to formally recognize the massive influence that the source of information or method of assessment has on our obtained data and thus on the inferences we can draw from our data.

When self-report tests and the Rorschach disagree, it is often the case that the MMPI-2 or PAI (especially when it is invalidly defensive) is insensitive to certain types of pathology, whereas the Rorschach picks it up. But the inverse sometimes also occurs because the respondent "freezes up" on the Rorschach and fails to engage, whereas she is more forthcoming in self-report testing. In a personal injury context, someone may tend to exaggerate suffering or impairment on the MMPI-2, while showing few comparable signs of difficulty on the Rorschach, whereas in a child custody context, the inverse pattern may be manifested (Ganellen, 1994; Hartmann & Hartmann, 2014). In some cases, both the MMPI-2 and the Rorschach, while seemingly yielding different inferences about the degree of pathology, may both be correct in different spheres (Bornstein, 2002). The MMPI-2 may accurately show how someone manages most of the time in familiar situations where prescribed roles and social expectations are fairly clear-cut, whereas the Rorschach may reveal how someone may behave spontaneously in unguarded moments under stress or in intimate settings, such as a close relationship or an intensive psychotherapy (see Finn, 2011).

Because personality and behavior are both influenced by explicit and implicit motives and traits, it is essential to use testing that covers both domains. A multimethod approach to forensic evaluations makes it possible to address both internal, verbalized experience (guiding deliberate action) and unscripted spontaneous behavior.

Situating Psychological Testing in Forensic Evaluations

Even when it covers a broad range of experiences and psychopathology, testing alone cannot usually answer the most important referral questions in forensic evaluations. No contemporary self-report or performance-based test can reliably a) distinguish between emergent, acute and pre-existing, chronic distress or psychopathology, or b) determine on its own what kind of parenting arrangement is best for the children of a divorced couple, or c) establish whether a criminal defendant was legally insane at the time of the crime, or d) determine whether an immigrant seeking asylum will suffer extreme hardship if returned to her home country. In order to form valid opinions about essential legal questions, it is important to use a systematic approach, seeking to confirm and disconfirm alternative narratives. Most importantly, one must integrate test results with multiple sources, including interviews; direct observation; self-reported history; medical, psychiatric, and employment records; and legal discovery documents, such as depositions, interrogatories, and witness statements. Together these sources of information paint a picture of a person within the legal context, which is the heart of multimethod assessment.

Robert E. Erard and F. Barton Evans

References

Ackerman, M. J., & Pritzl, T. B. (2011). Child custody evaluation practices: A 20-year follow-up. Family. *Court Review, 49*(3), 618-628.

Archer, R. P., Buffington-Vollum, J. K., Stredny, R. V., & Handel, R. W. (2006). Survey of psychological test use patterns among forensic psychologists. *Journal of Personality Assessment, 87,* 84-95.

Archer, R. P., & Krishnamurthy, R. (1993). Review of MMPI and Rorschach interrelationships in adult samples. *Journal of Personality Assessment, 61,* 132-140.

Boccacini, M. T., & Brodsky, S. L. (1999). Diagnostic test usage by forensic psychologists in emotional injury cases. *Professional Psychology: Research and Practice, 30*, 253–259.

Bornstein, R. F. (2002). A process dissociation approach to projective-objective test score interrelationships. *Journal of Personality Assessment, 78*(1), 47–68.

Bornstein, R. F. (2009). Heisenberg, Kandinsky, and the heteromethod convergence problem: Lessons from within and beyond psychology. *Journal of Personality Assessment, 91*, 1–8.

Cogswell, A., Alloy, L. B., Karpinski, A., & Grant, D. A. (2010). Assessing dependency using self-report and indirect measures: Examining the significance of discrepancies. *Journal of Personality Assessment, 92*, 306–316.

Cyders, M. A., & Coskunpinar, A. (2011). Measurement of constructs using self-report and behavioral lab tasks: Is there overlap in nomothetic span and construct representation for impulsivity? *Clinical Psychology Review, 31*, 965–982.

Dean, K. L., Viglione, D. J., Perry, W., & Meyer, G. J. (2007). A method to optimize the response range while maintaining Rorschach Comprehensive System validity. *Journal of Personality Assessment, 89*, 149–161.

Dean, K. L., Viglione, D. J., Perry, W., & Meyer, G. J. (2008). A method to optimize the response range while maintaining Rorschach Comprehensive System validity. *Journal of Personality Assessment, 90*, 204.

Exner, J. E. (1974). *The Rorschach: A comprehensive system*. Oxford, UK: John Wiley.

Finn, S. E. (2011). Journeys through the valley of death: Multimethod psychological assessment and personality transformation in long-term psychotherapy. *Journal of Personality Assessment, 93*, 123–141.

Gacono, C. B., & Evans, F. B. (Eds.). (2008). *The LEA series in personality and clinical psychology. The handbook of forensic Rorschach assessment* (N. Kaser-Boyd & L. A. Gacono, Collaborators). New York: Routledge/Taylor & Francis Group.

Ganellen, R. J. (1994). Attempting to conceal psychological disturbance: MMPI defensive response sets and the Rorschach. *Journal of Personality Assessment, 63*(3), 423–437.

Goffman, E. (1959). *The presentation of self in everyday life*. New York: Doubleday.

Gosling, S. D., John, O. P., Craik, K. H., & Robins, R. W. (1998). Do people know how they behave? Self-reported act frequencies compared with on-line codings by observers. *Journal of Personality and Social Psychology, 74*, 1337–1349.

Griens, A. M. G. F., Jonker, K., Spinhoven, P., & Blom, M. B. J. (2002). The influence of depressive states on trait measurement. *Journal of Affective Disorders, 70*, 95–99.

Hartmann, E., & Hartmann, T. (2014). The impact of exposure to Internet-based information about the Rorschach and the MMPI-2 on psychiatric outpatients' ability to simulate mentally healthy test performance. *Journal of Personality Assessment, 96*(4), 432–444.

Henry, B., Moffitt, T. E., Caspi, A., Langley, J., & Silva, P. A. (1994). On the "remembrance of things past": A longitudinal evaluation of the retrospective method. *Psychological Assessment, 6*, 92–101.

Hopwood, C. J., & Bornstein, R. F. (Eds.). (2014). *Multimethod clinical assessment*. New York: Guilford Publications.

Huprich, S. K., Bornstein, R. F., & Schmitt, T. A. (2011). Self-report methodology is insufficient for improving the assessment and classification of Axis II personality disorders. *Journal of Personality Disorders, 25*(5), 557–570.

McClelland, D. P., Koestner, R., & Weinberger, J. (1989). How do self-attributed and implicit motives differ? *Psychological Review, 96*, 690–702.

Meyer, G. J. (1999). The convergent validity of MMPI and Rorschach scales: An extension using profile scores to define response and character styles on both methods and a reexamination of simple Rorschach response frequency. *Journal of Personality Assessment, 72*, 1–35.

Meyer, G. J. (2012). Interview. Retrieved from meyer.personality.org/interview.php

Meyer, G. J., Erdberg, P., & Shaffer, T. W. (2007). Toward international normative reference data for the Comprehensive System. *Journal of Personality Assessment, 89*(Suppl. 1), S201–S216.

Meyer, G. J., Riethmiller, R. J., Brooks, R. D., Benoit, W. A., & Handler, L. (2000). A replication of Rorschach and MMPI-2 convergent validity. *Journal of Personality Assessment, 74*, 175–215.

Meyer, G. J., Shaffer, T. W., Erdberg, P., & Horn, S. L. (2015). Addressing issues in the development and use of the Composite International Reference Values as Rorschach norms for adults. *Journal of Personality Assessment, 97*(4), 330–347.

Meyer, G. J., Viglione, D. J., Mihura, J. L., Erard, R. E., & Erdberg, P. (2011). *Rorschach Performance Assessment System: Administration, coding, interpretation, and technical manual.* Toledo, OH: Rorschach Performance Assessment System, LLC.

Mihura, J. L. (2012). The necessity of multiple test methods in conducting assessments: The role of the Rorschach and self-report. *Psychological Injury and Law, 5*, 97–106.

Mihura, J. L., Meyer, G. J., Dumitrascu, N., & Bombel, G. (2013). The validity of individual Rorschach variables: Systematic reviews and meta-analyses of the Comprehensive System. *Psychological Bulletin, 139*, 548–605.

Mihura, J. L., Meyer, G. J., Dumitrascu, N., & Bombel, G. (2015). Standards, accuracy, and questions of bias in Rorschach meta-analyses: Reply to Wood, Garb, Nezworski, Lilienfeld, and Duke. *Psychological Bulletin, 141*, 250–260.

Mischel, W., & Shoda, Y. (1995). A cognitive-affective system theory of personality: Reconceptualizing situations, dispositions, dynamics, and invariance in personality structure. *Psychological Review, 102*(2), 246–268.

Nisbett, R. E., & Wilson, T. D. (1977). Telling more than we can know: Verbal reports on mental processes. *Psychological Review, 84*(3), 231–259.

Schultheiss, O. C. (2007). A memory-systems approach to the classification of personality tests: Comment on Meyer & Kurtz (2006). *Journal of Personality Assessment, 89*(2), 197–201.

Shaffer, T. W., Erdberg, P., & Meyer, G. J. (2007). Introduction to the JPA Special Supplement on International Reference Samples for the Rorschach Comprehensive System. *Journal of Personality Assessment, 89*(Suppl. 1), S2–S6.

Shedler, J., Mayman, M., & Manis, M. (1993). The illusion of mental health. *American Psychologist, 48*(11), 1117–1131.

Shiffman, S. (1999). Real-time self-report of momentary states in the natural environment: Computerized ecological momentary assessment. In A. A. Stone,

C. A. Bachrach, J. B. Jobe, H. S. Kurzman, & V. S. Cain (Eds.), *The science of self-report: Implications for research and practice* (pp. 277–296). New York: Routledge.

Smith, J. D., & Finn, S. E. (2014). Integration and therapeutic presentation of multimethod assessment results: An empirically supported framework and case example. In C. J. Hopwood & R. F. Bornstein (Eds.), *Multimethod clinical assessment* (pp. 403–426). New York: Guilford.

Viglione, D. J., Meyer, G. J., Jordan, R. J., Converse, G. L., Evans, J., MacDermott, D., & Moore, R. C. (2015). Developing an alternative Rorschach administration method to optimize the number of responses and enhance clinical inferences. *Clinical Psychology and Psychotherapy, 22*, 546–558.

ACKNOWLEDGMENTS

Together, we would like to acknowledge and applaud all the forensic psychologists who have routinely used the Rorschach in their multimethod psychological evaluations—through thick and thin. It has been a tough journey at times, and in this book, we hope to provide you with more sustenance along the way—and maybe even a few more warriors for the battle.

We wish to acknowledge the individual contributors for taking time from their busy forensic and academic practices to offer unselfishly their scholarship and insights into how to think about and conduct multimethod forensic assessment with the Rorschach. We are deeply grateful to be able to work with such a thoughtful, hardworking, and talented group.

Special appreciation is due to our endlessly competent Routledge book editor, George Zimmar. George's belief in and patient support of our work has been invaluable, and his good-hearted approach to the cold reality of business has made him an excellent partner in our venture.

Robert Erard appreciates the friendship, wise counsel, and spirited collaboration of Barton Evans. Barton's gift for spotting live possibilities and his passion for turning them into delightful realities has always been a source of inspiration for me. I had only recently joined the Society for Personality Assessment when Barton encouraged me (twice) to run for its board of trustees; a short while later, only after much nudging by him did I run for election as its president. It was also Barton who decided that this book needed to be written and that I was going to be the one to edit it with him. I have learned much from him about how the idea of such a book becomes a reality. He has been a pleasure to work with and has challenged me to see important parts of the picture I might have missed (and not just Dds). My fellow R-PAS developers, Greg Meyer, Don Viglione, Joni Mihura, and Phil Erdberg, welcomed me into some of the most stimulating experiences of my intellectual life and have taught me much about how to blend scientific scholarship with insightful clinical practice and how to resolve passionate differences of opinion while remaining close friends and collaborators. A great deal of what I know about the legal system and the place experts have in it I learned from my wife, Barbara Erard, who patiently endured much "weekend widowhood" during the preparation of this book.

Barton Evans's appreciations are many, though a few special thanks are in order. I cannot say enough about the great pleasure of working with the late Bob Erard. Knowledgeable, incisive, brilliant, challenging, and forgiving, he always pushed for the best, and it was impossible not to grow as a scholar and a person when working with him. His death leaves a deep hole in my life as well as the field of personality assessment. Personal thanks go to the incomparable Irving Weiner for his ongoing support and careful reading of my work. Irv is the giver of many gifts, perhaps the most important being his rare combination of wisdom, candor, and tact. To Steve Finn, I wish to share my gratitude for his personal support and for introducing me to therapeutic assessment and encouraging me to push my boundaries in developing humane approaches in forensic assessment. I am also grateful to Chris Hopwood for the opportunity to work with such a first-rate scholar and an all-too-rare Harry Stack Sullivan aficionado. And last to Bruce Smith, my compadre of many years for his friendship and support, professionally and personally, and the opportunity to work together yet another time on a controversial project.

ABOUT THE EDITORS

The late **Robert E. Erard, PhD,** was Clinical Director of Psychological Institutes of Michigan, P.C., in Bloomfield, Michigan, where he practiced clinical and forensic psychology. He was one of the developers of the Rorschach Performance Assessment System® (R-PAS®). He was a past President and Fellow of the Society for Personality Assessment and a Fellow of the American Psychological Association (Divs. 31, 41, & 42), from which he received the Karl F. Heiser Presidential Award. He was also a past President and Fellow of the Michigan Psychological Association, from which he received the Distinguished Psychologist Award in 2004. He served as a U.S. delegate and member of the Scientific Review Committee for the International Rorschach Congress and as the Michigan Representative to the APA Council. Dr. Erard was an Editor for the Clinical Case Applications section of the *Journal of Personality Assessment* and Head of the Assessment Section for *Psychological Injury and Law*. He also served on the editorial boards for the *Journal of Child Custody and Practice Innovations*. He published over 50 scientific and professional articles and book chapters on Rorschach assessment, forensic psychological assessment, professional ethics, psychometrics, and other topics along with many national, and international workshops and symposia on these and other topics. He was a forensic psychological expert in personal injury, family law, professional licensing and malpractice, and criminal matters, and as a consultant on clinical and forensic applications of the Rorschach Performance Assessment System. Sadly, Dr. Erard passed away shortly before the publication of this book. He will be remembered by his family as a devoted and loving husband, father, son, and brother and by his colleagues as a brilliant, modest, collaborative, and inspirational leader in personality assessment.

F. Barton Evans, PhD, is Professor of Psychiatry and Director of Psychological and Forensic Assessment Services, James H. Quillen College of Medicine, Eastern Tennessee State University, Johnson City, Tennessee. He is a Fellow of the Society for Personality Assessment and a Fellow of the American Psychological Association (Division 12). He serves on the executive board of the International Society for the Rorschach and Projective Methods and board of directors of the CooperRiis Healing Community. Dr. Evans is the Head of the Practice Matters Section for *Psychological Injury and Law*. He has held faculty appointments in the schools of medicine at George Washington University, University of Washington, and Georgetown University, as well faculty positions at the American University, University of North Carolina-Greensboro, Montana State University, and Lenoir Rhyne University. Dr. Evans has presented over 150 workshops and papers nationally and internationally on a wide variety of topics including psychological trauma, psychological assessment, forensic psychological evaluation, and personality disorder. Dr. Evans has two published books: *Harry Stack Sullivan: Interpersonal Theory and Psychotherapy* (1996) and the *Handbook of Forensic Rorschach Assessment* (with Carl Gacono, 2008). A fourth book on forensic assessment in immigration court (with Giselle Hass) is under preparation. He has published over 40 book chapters and articles on topics including the Rorschach, interpersonal theory and psychotherapy, psychological trauma, forensic and psychological assessment, and other topics. He is a forensic psychological expert for courts in immigration law, family law, personal injury, and criminal matters.

Part I

Conceptual Foundations

Chapter 1

TOWARD AN INTEGRATIVE PERSPECTIVE ON THE PERSON
Opportunities and Challenges of Multimethod Assessment

Robert F. Bornstein

The human mental apparatus is powerful, indeed able to react to changing circumstances in a matter of milliseconds, perceive the faintest of stimuli, carry out multiple tasks simultaneously, and process vast amounts of information with minimal conscious effort. Despite the impressive power of the human mind and brain, we are surprisingly limited when we focus our attention on ourselves. Evidence confirms that we have only modest insight into many of our mental activities (Bargh & Williams, 2006; Wilson, 2009); as a result, we are not very good at reporting accurately on our thoughts, feelings, attitudes, goals, and motives. We are also poor judges of our own behavior: We cannot recall past events accurately, routinely misconstrue ongoing behavior even as we are exhibiting it, and cannot predict how we will behave in the future (Fernandez, 2013; Kahneman, 2003; Slovic et al., 2002). Complicating the situation, even in those areas where we manage to see things somewhat accurately, we do not always choose to provide accurate self-reports, for a variety of reasons (e.g., wanting to appear conscientious and adaptable to impress a potential employer, choosing to present ourselves as maladjusted and dysfunctional to abrogate some unwanted responsibility).

If humans could (and did) report accurately on their behavior and mental life, there would be no need for psychological assessment. Alas, they cannot—and do not—and as a result, psychologists have developed a broad array of assessment tools for use in laboratory, clinical, and forensic settings. These run the gamut from questionnaires and interviews to tests that require the respondent to interpret ambiguous stimuli, tell stories about pictures, copy geometric figures from cards, sort objects into categories, and provide open-ended descriptions of important people in his or her life.

Despite the availability of a broad array of assessment methods, psychologists today tend to rely primarily on self-report tests. When Ready and Veague (2014) surveyed directors of clinical psychology doctoral programs, they found that all but one of the most widely taught instruments were self-report scales, with little attention to integrating data from measures that use contrasting methods to assess a common construct (see also Camara, Nathan, & Puente, 2000; Childs & Eyde, 2002). The increasing reliance on mono-method assessment that characterizes current training in psychology is reflected in the research literature as well. For example, more than 80% of studies published in five leading personality disorder journals between 1991 and 2000 relied exclusively on self-report data, both to select participants and to assess outcome (Bornstein, 2003). During this same period 73% of empirical studies in the American Psychological Association's (APA's) seven most widely subscribed journals relied exclusively on self-report outcome measures (Bornstein, 2001). When Hogan and Agnello (2004) surveyed 696 research reports from the APA's *Directory of Unpublished Experimental Mental Measures*, identifying the types of validity evidence reported for each, they found that for 87% of tests, the only validity evidence involved correlations between test scores and scores on self-report scales. Similar results were obtained by Bornstein (2011) in his survey of construct validity studies in five leading assessment journals. Given people's limited self-awareness and inclination to dissimulate (i.e., to "fake good" or "fake bad"), psychology's reliance on self-report tests is a recipe for failure in the laboratory, clinic, and courtroom.

From Psychological Testing to Multimethod Assessment

Psychologists often use the terms *testing* and *assessment* interchangeably, but in fact, they mean very different things. Meyer et al. (2001, p. 143) provided an excellent summary of the conceptual and practical differences between psychological testing and psychological assessment. They wrote:

Testing is a relatively straightforward process wherein a particular test is administered to obtain a specific score. Subsequently, a descriptive meaning can be applied to the score based on normative, nomothetic findings. In contrast, psychological assessment is concerned with the clinician who takes a variety of test scores, generally obtained from multiple test methods, and considers the data in the context of history, referral information, and observed behavior to understand the person being evaluated, to answer the referral questions, and then to communicate findings to the patient, his or her significant others, and referral sources.

As Cates (1999) wryly observed, he would be at a loss for words if an astute attorney asked him to provide evidence regarding the reliability and validity of psychological assessment results. He went on to note that "the care provided in the development of psychological tests overlooks the use of these techniques in combination in a battery" (Cates, 1999, p. 632). The *Standards for Educational and Psychological Testing* (American Educational Research Association, American Psychological Association, and National Council on Measurement in Education, 2014) does not address this question either, and as Bornstein (2015) noted, because the utility of psychological assessment is reflected in the degree to which assessment data provide clinically or forensically useful information, traditional validation methods (e.g., derivation of indices of reliability and validity) are not useful in this domain. The utility of psychological assessment results can only be evaluated with respect to the question that the assessment is intended to address. Documenting assessment utility is particularly challenging because a broad array of issues are addressed in clinical and forensic assessments. These include questions related to diagnosis, defense style, potential to benefit from treatment, treatment effectiveness/outcome, mental status, competency, parental fitness, fitness for duty, risk management, death penalty mitigation, and employment litigation (see Meyer et al. [2001] and Gacono & Evans [2008] for overviews of issues in this area).

Multimethod assessment (MMA) has several advantages over assessment that uses measures from within a single modality, especially when complex clinical and forensic questions are being addressed. Myriad studies have shown that across a broad array of domains, correlations between scores on measures that use different methods to assess the same construct are typically in the 0.10–0.30 range (Lobbestael, Cima, &

Arntz, 2013; Mihura, Meyer, Dumistrascu, & Bombel, 2013; Zeigler-Hill, Fulton, & McLemore, 2012). Moreover, as the *Standards for Educational and Psychological Testing* (AERA et al., 2014) notes, unless it is specifically aimed at quantifying a single aspect of functioning (e.g., implicit self-esteem, self-attributed narcissism), mono-method assessment yields data that suffer from *construct underrepresentation*, capturing some—but not all— features of the construct it purports to measure. Simply put, mono-method assessment invariably yields an incomplete picture of the person.

A Process-Focused Classification of Psychological Tests

Because different assessment methods engage different psychological processes, they illuminate different aspects of functioning and predict different features of an individual's underlying motives, traits, and behavioral predispositions (Bornstein, 2009, 2011). For example, studies have shown that scores derived from interviews and questionnaires best predict goal-directed behavior exhibited in structured situations, whereas data derived from the Rorschach Inkblot Method (RIM) and Thematic Apperception Test (TAT) tend to better predict spontaneous behavior exhibited in vivo (see Bornstein, 2002a, Jenkins, 2008; McClelland, Koestner, & Weinberger, 1989; McGrath, 2008). Other studies have shown that integrating self-report test data with data derived from indirect measures, such as the RIM, can illuminate underlying personality dynamics (Cogswell, Alloy, Karpinski, & Grant, 2010; Vater et al., 2013). Thus, as long as the validity of each measure within a test battery is reasonably well established, there is strong support for combining scores from diverse measures and methods to yield a more nuanced and accurate set of assessment data.

How is the psychologist to decide which measures and methods to employ in constructing an integrated multimethod battery in clinical and forensic settings? In part to address this question, Bornstein (2007, 2011) provided a preliminary process-based classification of widely used psychological tests. In an updated version of this classification, these measures may be divided into five broad categories.

Self-Report Tests

Self-report test scores reflect the degree to which the person attributes various traits, feelings, thoughts, motives, behaviors, attitudes, and experiences to him- or herself. Because they are efficient and cost-effective, self-report tests are far and away the most widely used type of measure in both research and clinical settings (Bornstein, 2011; Ready & Veague, 2014). In interpreting self-report test data, it is important to keep in mind that self-reports do not represent veridical indices of behavior and mental life, but instead reflect inferences about the self that are subject to a variety of information processing biases (e.g., the fundamental attribution error, self-serving attributional bias, the actor-observer effect; see Bornstein, 2015). The Beck Depression Inventory (Beck, Steer, & Brown, 1996), the Personality Assessment Inventory (Morey, 1990), and the NEO Personality Inventory (NEO-PI; Costa & McCrae, 1985) would all be included in this category.

Stimulus Attribution Tests

Traditionally called *projective tests*, and more recently *performance-based tests*, in stimulus attribution tests, the person attributes meaning to an ambiguous stimulus, with attributions determined in part by stimulus characteristics and in part by the person's cognitive style, emotions, motives, and need states (see McGrath, 2008; Meyer et al., 2011; Weiner, 2004). Like the self-attributions that emerge as respondents complete self-report measures, the stimulus attributions that occur as people interpret ambiguous stimuli are shaped by a broad array of processes, including schema activation, variations in mood and anxiety level, ego defenses, characteristics of the examiner and the setting in which testing takes place, and self-presentation/impression management strategies (Bornstein, 2007; Ganellen, 2007). The RIM is the most widely used and well-known stimulus attribution test; others include the TAT (Murray, 1943) and the Holtzman (1961) Inkblot Test.

Constructive Tests

In constructive tests, generation of test responses requires the person to create or construct a novel image or written description within parameters defined by the tester. The Draw-a-Person Test (and other projective drawings) would be classified in this category, as would various open-ended self-descriptions (e.g., Blatt, Chevron, Quinlan, Schaffer, & Wein's [1981] measure of Qualitative and Structural Dimensions of Object

Representations; Bruhn's [1992a, 1992b] Early Memories Procedure). In contrast to stimulus attribution tests, which require respondents to describe stimuli whose essential properties were determined a priori, in constructive tests, the "stimulus" exists only in the mind of the respondent (e.g., a self-representation or parental image; see Bers, Blatt, Sayward, & Johnston, 1993).

Behavioral Indices

In some behavioral tests, scores are derived from indices of a person's behavior exhibited and measured in vivo, as in ambulatory assessment (a technique wherein researchers sample real-world behavior at randomly selected times, in multiple contexts; Trull & Ebner-Priemer, 2013). Behavior may also be examined in a controlled setting (e.g., using joystick feedback tasks wherein moment-by-moment behaviors are rated as they occur; see Pincus et al., 2014). Other behavioral tests assess the person's unrehearsed performance on one or more structured tasks designed to tap attentional resources, working memory, and other cognitive skills (e.g., the Bender [1938] Visual-Motor Gestalt Test, the Attentional Capacity Test [Weber, 1988]).

Informant Reports

Scores on tests in this category are based on informants' ratings or judgments of a person's characteristic patterns of responding (e.g., the therapist version of the Shedler-Westen Assessment Procedure [Shedler & Westen, 1998], the informant-report version of the NEO-PI [Costa & McCrae, 1988]). In contrast to observational measures, which are based on direct observation of behavior in real time, informant-report tests are based on informants' retrospective, memory-derived conclusions regarding characteristics of the target person. Like self-reports, informant reports are subject to all the biases and distortions that come into play as the informant reconstructs memories of past events.

CONVERGENCES AND DIVERGENCES IN PSYCHOLOGICAL TEST RESULTS

Given the contrasting psychological processes engaged by different tests, it is important to emphasize test score divergences as well as convergences to maximize the utility of MMA data in clinical and forensic settings. For example, researchers have found that patients with borderline pathology often perform quite well on measures with a high degree of structure (e.g., intelligence tests), while performing poorly on less structured instruments (Carr & Goldstein, 1981). Saltzman-Benaiah and Lalonde (2007) found that divergences between highly structured and less structured indices of social competence helped predict teacher ratings of children's ability to mentalize (i.e., to infer the perspective of another person). With respect to differential diagnosis, Bornstein (1998) demonstrated that individuals with dependent personality disorder traits and symptoms scored high on both self-report and RIM measures of interpersonal dependency, whereas individuals with histrionic personality disorder traits and symptoms obtained high RIM dependency scores, but low self-report dependency scores. Valiente et al. (2011) documented characteristic patterns of implicit-explicit self-esteem discrepancies that distinguish patients with paranoid delusions from depressed patients and healthy controls. Along somewhat different lines, Becerra-Garcia et al. (2013) found that performance on Part A of the Trail-Making Test (TMT; Reitan, 1992) predicted Five-Factor Model (FFM) extraversion scores in a sample of male sex offenders, whereas performance on Part B of the TMT predicted FFM openness scores, in part because Parts A and B tap contrasting attentional and self-regulatory processes.

Thus triangulating across methods that engage different psychological processes, both between and within measures, is a central element of MMA (Bornstein & Hopwood, 2015; Hopwood & Bornstein, 2014). With this in mind, a number of investigators have examined the underlying dynamics of personality traits and dimensions of psychopathology by contrasting the results obtained for self-reports and other types of measures (e.g., stimulus attributions, behavioral indices) of parallel constructs (e.g., self-esteem, narcissism, psychopathy; see Lobbestael, et al., 2013; Vater et al., 2013; Zeigler-Hill et al., 2012). From an interpersonal perspective, researchers have explored dispositional and situational variations in inter- and intrapersonal dynamics by contrasting self-reports, reports by knowledgeable others, observational ratings, and ambulatory assessments of core traits (e.g., agency, communion, dominance, nurturance; see Hopwood, Wright, Ansell, & Pincus, 2013; Pincus et al., 2014).

In addition to illuminating underlying dynamics, triangulating across methods that engage different psychological processes can help the assessor understand the role that self-perception and self-presentation effects may play in shaping assessment results. A number of psychological tests include validity indices designed to quantify the patient's approach to the test situation (e.g., certain MMPI-2 validity scale scores [see Butcher, Hass, Greene, & Nelson, 2015]; RIM task engagement and sequence variables that capture changes in cognitive patterns and affective responses as testing proceeds [see Meyer et al., 2011]). These data can be complemented by comparing the results obtained using measures of a particular construct (e.g., narcissism, stress tolerance) that vary with respect to face validity (i.e., test "obviousness"). It may be, for example, that a respondent obtains a low score on a self-report measure of impulsivity, but scores high on an RIM impulsivity index. In such a situation, the discontinuity between self-report and RIM scores suggests that the respondent's self-reports may not reflect his or her underlying dynamics; the factors that account for this divergence can then be interpreted in the context of validity indices embedded in various psychological tests and explored in greater detail by the examiner.

Construct Validity, Clinical Utility, and Legal Admissibility

Criteria used to evaluate the quality of psychological test results vary as a function of the context in which these test results will be used. From a psychometric perspective, the quality of scores derived from psychological tests has traditionally been operationalized as a statistic: the validity coefficient, which reflects the magnitude of the relationship between a predictor (the test score) and some criterion (an outcome measure). A wide variety of criteria are predicted by psychological tests, some overt and readily observable, others hidden and only detectable indirectly. When an observable criterion (e.g., suicide attempts) is assessed, the validity coefficient is said to be an index of criterion validity; when an unobservable construct (e.g., suicidal ideation) is assessed, the validity coefficient is an index of construct validity (see Cronbach & Meehl, 1955). The concept of test score validity has evolved considerably in recent years (see, e.g., Borsboom, Mellenbergh, & van Heerden, 2004; Slaney & Maraun, 2008); contemporary unified models of validity argue that distinctions among various types of validity evidence (e.g., criterion versus construct, concurrent versus predictive) are less sharp than earlier frameworks had suggested and that multiple forms of converging evidence should be used to establish the validity of test scores within a particular context (AERA et al., 2014).

As one moves from laboratory to clinic, the emphasis in evaluating psychological test results shifts from validity to clinical utility (see McGrath, 2001; Meyer et al., 2001; Youngstrom, 2013). Clinical utility goes beyond psychometric rigor, incorporating criteria such as test fairness (i.e., the degree to which a test yields results that lead to equitable outcomes in members of different groups), cost effectiveness (which has become particularly salient given fiscal constraints in contemporary health and mental health care), and the impact of test results in real-world decisions (what Messick [1995] termed *consequential validity*). Inherent in the distinction between validity and clinical utility is the assumption that a valid test score can provide clinically useful data in certain contexts, but less useful data in others, depending on how that score is utilized. For example, intelligence test scores may be interpreted differently in two different schools, and psychopathology scores may be interpreted differently in two different clinics; in both situations, the test score in question might well yield clinically useful information in one setting and not in the other.

Criteria for admissibility of testimony based on psychological test data are in certain ways similar to those used to evaluate clinical utility. In both clinical and forensic settings, test results must have documented empirical rigor, but the criterion of clinical utility that is central in mental health contexts is replaced in the courtroom by an analogous criterion of helpfulness (i.e., "forensic utility"). The test data must not only be based on scientific evidence but also provide useful information regarding the issue at hand (Erard, 2012; McCann & Evans, 2008).

Criteria for documenting forensic utility and admissibility have been shaped by the Frye standard (*Frye v. United States*, 1923), which holds that expert opinion based on a scientific technique is admissible only when the technique in question is generally accepted in the particular field in which it belongs. In most states, the Frye standard has been supplanted by the Daubert standard (*Daubert v. Merrell Dow Pharmaceuticals*, 1993), which instructs judges to evaluate the reliability of expert testimony by considering factors such as whether it 1) has been tested empirically using methods that allow assertions to be falsified/refuted, 2) has been subjected to peer review, 3) has a known potential error rate, 4) has a set of standards regarding its operation and implementation, and 5) has attained general acceptance among members of the scientific community.

Contemporary evidentiary guidelines are codified by Rule 702 (*Testimony by Expert Witnesses*) in the Federal Rules of Evidence (as amended Apr. 17, 2000, eff. Dec. 1, 2000; Apr. 26, 2011, eff. Dec. 1, 2011) and its state equivalents. Rule 702 combines standards of scientific rigor (elements 2 and 3) with concerns regarding forensic utility and relevance (elements 1 and 4), by offering the following requirements for admissible expert testimony:

> A witness who is qualified as an expert by knowledge, skill, experience, training, or education may testify in the form of an opinion or otherwise if: 1) the expert's scientific, technical, or other specialized knowledge will help the trier of fact to understand the evidence or to determine a fact in issue; 2) the testimony is based on sufficient facts or data; 3) the testimony is the product of reliable principles and methods; and 4) the expert has reliably applied the principles and methods to the facts of the case.

Multimethod Forensic Assessment: Opportunities and Challenges

Given the limitations inherent in mono-method assessment, a compelling argument can be made that for a wide variety of constructs and questions, and in most forensic contexts, MMA is preferable to assessment that relies on measures that employ a single method. Much of the literature evaluating the uses of MMA in forensic settings has focused on the ways in which stimulus attribution tests, especially the RIM, can—or cannot—complement and extend the data provided by self-report tests (Erard, 2012; Gacono, Evans, & Viglione, 2002; Hildebrand & de Ruiter, 2008; Mihura, 2012; cf, Borum & Grisso, 1995; Wood et al., 2009, 2010). With this in mind, MMA contrasting RIM and self-report data offers some unique opportunities in forensic settings and presents some unique challenges as well.

Opportunities: Contextualizing Self-Presentation and Enhancing Behavioral Prediction

Stimulus Attribution Tests Are Relatively Immune from Dissimulation Effects

Although descriptions of the RIM as akin to a "psychological x-ray" (Piotrowski, 1980, p. 86) have not held up to empirical scrutiny, a plethora of evidence confirms that it is more difficult to deliberately dissimulate on the RIM and other stimulus attribution tests than on self-report tests with high face validity (Bornstein, Rossner, Hill, & Stepanian, 1994; Ganellen, 2007, 2008; Sartori, 2010; Schultz, Chapter 3 this volume). This may be particularly useful when undesirable traits (e.g., emotional lability, aggressiveness) are being assessed. In addition to illuminating underlying dynamics not easily accessed via self-report, implicit-explicit test score divergences in these (and other) domains can help document particular forms of bias in the respondent's self-perception and self-presentation (e.g., malingering and defensive response sets; see Ganellen, 2008).

Stimulus Attribution Tests Are Particularly Good Predictors of Behavior In Vivo

As noted, evidence indicates that scores derived from self-report tests best predict goal-directed behavior exhibited in structured situations, whereas data derived from stimulus attribution tests like the RIM tend to better predict spontaneous behavior exhibited in vivo (Bornstein, 2002a; McClelland et al., 1989). These patterns have been obtained in a variety of domains, including help seeking, dominance and aggression, achievement-related behavior, narcissism, empathy, and capacity to delay gratification (see, e.g., Bornstein, 1998; Jenkins, 2008; Mihura et al., 2013; Morf, 2006; Spangler, 1992).

Stimulus Attribution Tests Are Good at Predicting Variables Relevant to Forensic Issues

Many of the traits and behavioral predispositions that are predicted by scores on stimulus attribution tests are particularly relevant to forensic issues (e.g., impulsivity, personality pathology, egocentricity, affective lability), and because many of these behaviors are considered to be undesirable, they may not be amenable to assessment via self-report. In this context, it is worth noting that although a great deal of attention has been devoted to the ways in which respondents may underreport these behaviors, the opposite can be true as well: Depending on the circumstances, respondents may be motivated to exaggerate rather than minimize these and other undesirable qualities.

Challenges: Intuition, Reputation, and Test Score Discontinuity

The RIM and Other Stimulus Attribution Tests Are Not Intuitive to Non-Experts

As Meyer (1996) noted, the low face validity of scores derived from the RIM has been an obstacle to broader acceptance of the measure within the scientific community (cf, Wood et al., 2009). Along similar lines, Mihura (2012) pointed out that the low face validity of many RIM scores makes it difficult to explain them to judge and jury—an obstacle to admissibility. Although there is an intuitive link between a person's answer to the true-false question "I often have difficulty controlling my anger" and that person's risk for behaving aggressively, the link between hypervigilance and a weighted sum of RIM structural variables (i.e., texture, complexity, white space) and content variables (i.e., human and animal content, clothing content) is less obvious (however, see Viglione, Giromini, Gustafson, & Meyer, 2014, for evidence supporting this relationship).

The Reputation of Stimulus Attribution Tests Has Suffered From Persistent Attacks by Critics

A history of spotty—sometimes outright shoddy—research (see, e.g., Exner's [1986] estimate of the proportion of adequately designed RIM studies) coupled with strongly worded condemnations of the instrument by critics (e.g., Dawes, 1994; Wood et al., 2009, 2010) have raised the bar for those who use RIM data in forensic settings. To be convincing, empirical evidence regarding the construct validity of RIM scores cannot merely be good, but must be nearly flawless. This may represent an obstacle to admissibility in some forensic settings (see Hilsenroth &

Stricker, 2004), although in actual practice, rejection of Rorschach-based forensic testimony is rare (McCann & Evans, 2008; Meloy, 2008).

Explaining the Meaning and Value of Test Score Discontinuities Is Not Easy

Studies have shown that psychologists and physicians feel more comfortable interpreting test results when different tests yield converging evidence than when these same tests yield evidence that appears on the surface to be inconsistent or contradictory (Sibinga & Wu, 2010). Similar results have emerged in organizational settings (Ruedy & Schweitzer, 2010), and it is likely that the same is true in the courtroom: It will be far easier for an expert to explain to judge and jury the implications of test results that converge than those that yield divergent patterns (however, see Erard [2012], for recommendations regarding how to address these and other challenges when presenting RIM-related evidence in the courtroom).

Conclusion

Multimethod Assessment, Scientific Evidence, and the Adversary System

The criteria used to evaluate argument and evidence within the scientific community differ substantially from those used to evaluate argument and evidence in the courtroom. The former is typically subjected to peer review by experts who act as dispassionate evaluators of conceptual soundness and empirical rigor, and the latter is subjected to challenge by a motivated opponent whose aim it is to refute this evidence, with no pretense of objectivity. As Levine (1974, p. 669) pointed out, however, beneath the surface there is considerable overlap between the scientific and adversary models. He wrote,

> The scientific community, in the form of an editor, a referee, or a program committee, acts as judge in a preliminary hearing, deciding whether there is a sufficient case to be made in the particular study to take it before the scientific community. If published, the particular position asserted in a paper is subject to cross-examination or further probing. The positions that

survive the adversary process, those positions that convince the scientific community, eventually lead to some form of action—the equivalent of a disposition following a legal proceeding. In many respects, then, the *process* of convincing the scientific community and the *consequences* of convincing the scientific community are analogous to and closely resemble the processes one sees in a legal proceeding.

As Bornstein (1991, 2002b) noted, Levine's (1974) argument not only captures a fundamental (but often unacknowledged) underlying dynamic inherent in the evaluation of scientific evidence but also dovetails with the well-established finding that even the most well-trained, well-intentioned evaluator cannot be truly dispassionate and objective. Aside from the unavoidable information processing biases that characterize judgment and decision-making, humans—scientists included—can never fully separate their underlying needs, motives, and affective responses from their judgments and decisions (Fernandez, 2013; Slovic et al., 2002). Nowhere has this confounding of "dispassionate evaluation" and personal belief been more clear than in the decades-long controversy surrounding the RIM, wherein supporters and critics routinely interpret the same data in diametrically opposed ways (compare, e.g., Mihura, Meyer, Bombel, & Dumitrascu [2015] and Wood, Garb, Nezworski, Lilienfeld, & Duke [2015]).

With this in mind, it is clear that in forensic contexts, MMA may have two distinct salutary effects. First, MMA provides a more complete picture of the respondent by complementing self-report data with data capturing other domains of functioning (e.g., affect patterns, defenses, mental representations of significant figures) obtained using multiple methods. In addition, although jurors generally rely on experts to interpret ambiguous and divergent test results, MMA may help jurors engage psychological test data more actively as they integrate information from diverse sources and attempt to reconcile ostensibly discordant findings. Studies have shown that when people are compelled to grapple with information that suggests different possible interpretations, they engage this information more fully and more mindfully, devoting additional cognitive resources to identifying and interpreting convergences and divergences among different data sources (see Bornstein, 2015; Sibinga & Wu, 2010; Ruedy & Schweitzer, 2010). Thus the test score discontinuities that commonly emerge when MMA is used not only provide a unique glimpse into the mind of the respondent but also help shift those who must evaluate this evidence toward more critical, thoughtful processing of psychological test data.

References

American Educational Research Association, American Psychological Association, and National Council on Measurement in Education. (2014). *Standards for educational and psychological testing.* Washington, DC: Author.

Bargh, J. A., & Williams, E. L. (2006). The automaticity of social life. *Current Directions in Psychological Science, 15,* 1-4.

Becerra-Garcia, J. A., Garcia-Leon, A., & Egan, V. (2013). Toward a neuropsychology of personality in sex offenders against children: An exploratory psychometric study. *Journal of Child Sexual Abuse, 22,* 612-623.

Beck, A. T., Steer, R. A., & Brown, G. K. (1996). *Beck depression inventory.* San Antonio, TX: Psychological Corporation.

Bender, L. (1938). *A visual-motor gestalt test and its clinical use.* New York: American Orthopsychiatric Association.

Bers, S. A., Blatt, S. J., Sayward, H. K., & Johnston, R. S. (1993). The Self in Psychoanalysis. *Psychoanalytic Psychology, 10,* 17-37.

Blatt, S. J., Bers, S. A., & Schaffer, C. E. (1993). *The assessment of self-descriptions.* (Unpublished research manual). New Haven, CT: Yale University.

Blatt, S. J., Chevron, E. S., Quinlan, D. M., Schaffer, C. E., & Wein, S. J. (1981). *The assessment of qualitative and structural dimensions of object representations.* (Unpublished research manual). New Haven, CT: Yale University.

Bornstein, R. F. (1991). Manuscript review in psychology: Psychometrics, demand characteristics and an alternative model. *Journal of Mind and Behavior, 12,* 429-468.

Bornstein, R. F. (1998). Implicit and self-attributed dependency needs in dependent and histrionic personality disorders. *Journal of Personality Assessment, 71,* 1-14.

Bornstein, R. F. (2001). Has psychology become the science of questionnaires? A survey of research outcome measures at the close of the 20th century. *The General Psychologist, 36,* 36-40.

Bornstein, R. F. (2002a). A process dissociation approach to objective-projective test score interrelationships. *Journal of Personality Assessment, 78,* 47-68.

Bornstein, R. F. (2002b). Peer review in neuropsychology: Can we increase effectiveness without sacrificing rigor? *Cortex, 38,* 403-405.

Bornstein, R. F. (2003). Behaviorally referenced experimentation and symptom validation: A paradigm for 21st century personality disorder research. *Journal of Personality Disorders, 17,* 1-18.

Bornstein, R. F. (2007). Toward a process-based framework for classifying personality tests: Comment on Meyer and Kurtz (2006). *Journal of Personality Assessment, 89,* 202-207.

Bornstein, R. F. (2009). Heisenberg, Kandinsky, and the heteromethod convergence problem: Lessons from within and beyond psychology. *Journal of Personality Assessment, 91,* 1-8.

Bornstein, R. F. (2011). Toward a process-focused model of test score validity: Improving psychological assessment in science and practice. *Psychological Assessment, 23*, 532-544.

Bornstein, R. F. (2015). Personality assessment in the diagnostic manuals: On mindfulness, multiple methods, and test score discontinuities. *Journal of Personality Assessment, 97*(5), 446-455.

Bornstein, R. F., & Hopwood, C. J. (2015). Evidence based assessment of interpersonal dependency. *Professional Psychology: Research and Practice.*

Bornstein, R. F., Rossner, S. C., Hill, E. L., & Stepanian, M. L. (1994). Face validity and fakability of objective and projective measures of dependency. *Journal of Personality Assessment, 63*, 363-386.

Borsboom, D., Mellenbergh, G. J., & van Heerden, J. (2004). The concept of validity. *Psychological Review, 111*, 1061-1071.

Borum, R., & Grisso, T. (1995). Psychological test use in criminal forensic evaluation. *Professional Psychology: Research and Practice, 26*, 465-473.

Bruhn, A. R. (1992a). The early memories procedure: A projective test of autobiographical memory, Part 1. *Journal of Personality Assessment, 58*, 1-15.

Bruhn, A. R. (1992b). The early memories procedure: A projective test of autobiographical memory, Part 2. *Journal of Personality Assessment, 58*, 326-346.

Butcher, J. N., Hass, G. A., Greene, R. L., & Nelson, L. D. (2015). *Using the MMPI-2 in forensic assessment.* Washington, DC: American Psychological Association.

Camara, W. J., Nathan, J. S., & Puente, A. E. (2000). Psychological test usage: Implications in professional psychology. *Professional Psychology: Research and Practice, 31*, 141-154.

Carr, A. C., & Goldstein, E. G. (1981). Approaches to the diagnosis of borderline conditions by the use of psychological tests. *Journal of Personality Assessment, 45*, 563-574.

Cates, J. A. (1999). The art of assessment in psychology: Ethics, expertise, and validity. *Journal of Clinical Psychology, 55*, 631-641.

Childs, R. A., & Eyde, L. D. (2002). Assessment training in clinical psychology doctoral programs. *Journal of Personality Assessment, 78*, 130-144.

Cogswell, A., Alloy, L. B., Karpinski, A., & Grant, D. A. (2010). Assessing dependency using self-report and indirect measures: Examining the significance of discrepancies. *Journal of Personality Assessment, 92*, 306-316.

Costa, P. T., & McCrae, R. R. (1985). *NEO Personality Inventory manual.* Odessa, FL: Psychological Assessment Resources.

Costa, P. T., & McCrae, R. R. (1988). Personality in adulthood: A six year longitudinal study of self-reports and spouse ratings on the NEO Personality Inventory. *Journal of Personality and Social Psychology, 54*, 853-863.

Cronbach, L. J., & Meehl, P. E. (1955). Construct validity in psychological tests. *Psychological Bulletin, 52*, 281-302.

Daubert v. Merrell Dow Pharmaceuticals, Inc., 113 S. Ct. 2786 (1993).

Dawes, R. M. (1994). *House of cards: Psychology and psychotherapy built on myth.* New York: Free Press.

Erard, R. E. (2012). Expert testimony involving the Rorschach Performance Assessment System in psychological injury cases. *Psychological Injury and the Law, 5*, 122-134.

Exner, J. E., Jr. (1986). *The Rorschach: A Comprehensive System: Vol. 1. Basic foundations* (2nd ed.). New York: Wiley.
Federal rules of evidence. (2015). Seattle, WA: Create Space/Michigan Legal Publishing.
Fernandez, J. (2013). Self-deception and self-knowledge. *Philosophical Studies, 162,* 379–400.
Frye v. United States, 293 F. 1013 (D.C. Cir. 1923)
Gacono, C. B., & Evans, F. B. (Eds.). (2008). *The handbook of forensic Rorschach assessment.* New York: Routledge/Taylor & Francis.
Gacono, C. B., Evans, F. B., & Viglione, D. J. (2002). The Rorschach in forensic practice. *Journal of Forensic Psychology Practice, 2,* 33–54.
Ganellen, R. J. (2007). Assessing normal and abnormal personality functioning: Strengths and weaknesses of self-report, observer, and performance-based methods. *Journal of Personality Assessment, 89,* 30–40.
Ganellen, R. J. (2008). Rorschach assessment of malingering and defensive response sets. In C. B. Gacono & F. B. Evans (Eds.), *The handbook of forensic Rorschach assessment* (pp. 89–119). New York: Routledge/Taylor & Francis.
Hildebrand, M., & de Ruiter, C. (2008). Psychological assessment with the Rorschach and MMPI-2 in a forensic psychiatric hospital. *Rorschachiana, 29,* 151–182.
Hilsenroth, M. J., & Stricker, G. (2004). A consideration of challenges to psychological assessment instruments used in forensic settings: Rorschach as exemplar. *Journal of Personality Assessment, 83,* 141–152.
Hogan, T. P., & Agnello, J. (2004). An empirical study of reporting practices concerning measurement validity. *Educational and Psychological Measurement, 64,* 802–812.
Holtzman, W. (1961). *Inkblot perception and personality.* Austin: University of Texas Press.
Hopwood, C. J., & Bornstein, R. F. (2014). Toward a framework for integrating Multimethod clinical assessment data. In C. J. Hopwood & R. F. Bornstein (Eds.), *Multimethod clinical assessment* (pp. 427–441). New York: Guilford Press.
Hopwood, C. J., Wright, A. G. C., Ansell, E. B., & Pincus, A. L. (2013). The interpersonal core of personality pathology. *Journal of Personality Disorders, 27,* 270–295.
Jenkins, S. R. (Ed.). (2008). *A handbook of clinical scoring systems for thematic apperceptive techniques.* Mahwah, NJ: Erlbaum.
Kahneman, D. (2003). A perspective on judgment and choice: Mapping bounded rationality. *American Psychologist, 58,* 697–720.
Levine, M. (1974). Scientific method and the adversary model. *American Psychologist, 29,* 661–677.
Lobbestael, J., Cima, M., & Arntz, A. (2013). The relationship between adult reactive and proactive aggression, hostile interpretation bias, and antisocial personality disorder. *Journal of Personality Disorders, 27,* 53–66.
McCann, J. T., & Evans, F. B. (2008). Admissibility of the Rorschach. In C. B. Gacono & F. B. Evans (Eds.), *The handbook of forensic Rorschach assessment* (pp. 55–78). New York: Routledge/Taylor & Francis.

McClelland, D. C., Koestner, R., & Weinberger, J. (1989). How do self-attributed and implicit motives differ? *Psychological Review, 96*, 690-702.

McGrath, R. E. (2001). Toward more clinically relevant assessment research. *Journal of Personality Assessment, 77*, 307-332.

McGrath, R. E. (2008). The Rorschach in the context of performance-based personality assessment. *Journal of Personality Assessment, 90*, 465-475.

Meloy, J. R. (2008). The authority of the Rorschach: An update. In Gacono, C. B., & Evans, F. B. (Eds.). (2008). *The LEA series in personality and clinical psychology. The handbook of forensic Rorschach assessment* (N. Kaser-Boyd & L. A. Gacono, Collaborators). (pp. 79-87). New York: Routledge/Taylor & Francis.

Messick, S. (1995). Validity of psychological assessment: Validation of inferences from persons' responses and performances as scientific inquiry into score meaning. *American Psychologist, 50*, 741-749.

Meyer, G. J. (1996). The Rorchach and MMPI: Toward a more scientific understanding of cross-method assessment. *Journal of Personality Assessment, 67*, 558-578.

Meyer, G. J., Finn, S. E., Eyde, L. D., Kay, G. G., Moreland, K. L., Dies, R. R., . . . Reed, G. M. (2001). Psychological testing and assessment: A review of evidence and issues. *American Psychologist, 56*, 128-165.

Meyer, G. J., Viglione, D. J., Mihura, J. L., Erard, R. E., & Erdberg, P. (2011). *Rorschach performance assessment system: Administration, coding, interpretation, and technical manual*. Toledo, OH: Rorschach Performance Assessment System, LLC.

Mihura, J. L. (2012). The necessity of multiple test methods in conducting assessments: The role of the Rorschach and self-report. *Psychological Injury and the Law, 5*, 97-106.

Mihura, J. L., Meyer, G. J., Bombel, G., & Dumitrascu, N. (2015). Standards, accuracy, and questions of bias in Rorschach meta-analyses: A reply to Wood, Garb, Nezworski, Lilienfeld, and Duke (2015). *Psychological Bulletin, 141*, 250-260.

Mihura, J. L., Meyer, G. J., Dumitrascu, N., & Bombel, G. (2013). The validity of individual Rorschach variables: Systematic reviews and meta-analyses of the comprehensive system. *Psychological Bulletin, 139*, 548-605.

Morey, L. C. (1990). *Personality assessment inventory*. Torrance, CA: Western Psychological Services.

Morf, C. C. (2006). Personality reflected in a coherent idiosyncratic interplay of inter- and intrapersonal self-regulatory processes. *Journal of Personality, 74*, 1527-1556.

Murray, H. A. (1943). *Thematic Appreciation Test*. Cambridge, MA: Harvard University Press.

Pincus, A. L., Sadler, P., Woody, E., Roche, M. J., Thomas, K. M., & Wright, A. G. C. (2014). Multimethod assessment of interpersonal dynamics. In C. J. Hopwood & R. F. Bornstein (Eds.), *Multimethod clinical assessment* (pp. 51-91). New York: Guilford Press.

Piotrowski, Z. A. (1980). CPR: The psychological x-ray in mental disorders. In I. B. Sidowski, J. H. Johnson & T. A. Williams (Eds.), *Technology in mental health care delivery systems* (pp. 85-108). Norwood, NJ: Ablex.

Ready, R. E., & Veague, H. B. (2014). Training in psychological assessment: Current practices of clinical psychology programs. *Professional Psychology: Research and Practice, 45*, 278-282.

Reitan, R. M. (1992). *Trail making test: Manual for administration and scoring.* Tucson, AZ: Reitan Neuropsychology Laboratory.

Ruedy, N. E., & Schweitzer, M. E. (2010). In the moment: The effect of mindfulness on ethical decision-making. *Journal of Business Ethics, 95*, 73-87.

Saltzman-Benaiah, J., & Lalonde, C. E. (2007). Developing clinically suitable measures of social cognition for children: Initial findings from a normative sample. *The Clinical Neuropsychologist, 21*, 294-317.

Sartori, R. (2010). Face validity in personality tests: Psychometric instruments and projective techniques in comparison. *Quality and Quantity, 44*, 749-759.

Shedler, J., & Westen, D. (1998). Refining the measurement of Axis II: A Q-sort procedure for assessing personality pathology. *Assessment, 5*, 335-355.

Sibinga, E. M. S., & Wu, A. W. (2010). Clinician mindfulness and patient safety. *Journal of the American Medical Association, 304*, 2532-2533.

Slaney, K. L., & Maraun, M. D. (2008). A proposed framework for conducting data-based test analysis. *Psychological Methods, 13*, 376-390.

Slovic, P., Finucane, M., Peters, E., & MacGregor, D. G. (2002). The affect heuristic. In T. Gilovich, D. Griffin & D. Kahneman (Eds.), *Heuristics and biases: The psychology of intuitive judgment* (pp. 397-420). Cambridge, UK: Cambridge University Press.

Spangler, W. D. (1992). Validity of questionnaire and TAT measures of need for achievement: Two meta-analyses. *Psychological Bulletin, 112*, 140-154.

Trull, T. J., & Ebner-Priemer, U. (2013). Ambulatory assessment. *Annual Review of Clinical Psychology, 9*, 151-176.

Valiente, C., Cantero, D., Vázquez, C., Sanchez, Á., Provencio, M., & Espinosa, R. (2011). Implicit and explicit self-esteem discrepancies in paranoia and depression. *Journal of Abnormal Psychology, 120*, 691-699.

Vater, A., Ritter, K., Schroder-Abe, M., Schutz, A., Lammers, C. H., Bosson, J. K., & Roepke, S. (2013). When grandiosity and vulnerability collide: Implicit and explicit self-esteem in patients with narcissistic personality disorder. *Journal of Behavior Therapy and Experimental Psychiatry, 44*, 37-47.

Viglione, D., Giromini, L., Gustafson, M. L., & Meyer, G. J. (2014). Developing continuous variable composites for Rorschach measures of thought problems, vigilance, and suicide risk. *Assessment, 21*, 42-49.

Wilson, T. D. (2009). Know thyself. *Perspectives on Psychological Science, 4*, 384-389.

Weber, A. M. (1988). A new clinical measure of attention: The Attentional Capacity Test. *Neuropsychology, 2*, 59-71.

Weiner, I. B. (2004). Rorschach Inkblot Method. In M. E. Maruish (Ed.), *The use of psychological testing for treatment planning and outcomes assessment* (pp. 553-588). Mahwah, NJ: Erlbaum.

Wood, J. M., Garb, H. N., Nezworski, M. T., Lilienfeld, S. O., & Duke, M. C. (2015). A second look at the validity of widely used Rorschach indices: Comment on Mihura, Meyer, Dumitrascu, and Bombel (2013). *Psychological Bulletin, 141*, 236-249.

Wood, J. M., Lilienfeld, S. O., Nezworski, M. T., Garb, H. N., Allen, K. H., & Wildermuth, J. L. (2010). Validity of Rorschach Inkblot scores for discriminating psychopaths from non-psychopaths in forensic populations: A meta-analysis. *Psychological Assessment, 22*, 336–349.

Wood, J. M., Nezworski, M. T., Lilienfeld, S. O., & Garb, H. N. (2009). Projective techniques in the courtroom. In J. L. Skeem, K. S. Douglas, & S. O. Lilienfeld (Eds.), *Psychological Science in the Courtroom: Controversies and consensus* (pp. 203–223). New York: Guilford Press.

Youngstrom, E. A. (2013). Future directions in psychological assessment: Combining evidence-based medicine innovations with psychology's historical strengths to enhance utility. *Journal of Child and Adolescent Psychiatry, 42*, 139–159.

Zeigler-Hill, V., Fulton, J. J., & McLemore, C. (2012). Discrepancies between explicit and implicit self-esteem: Implications for mate retention strategies and perceived infidelity. *Journal of Social Psychology, 152*, 670–686.

CHAPTER 2

PSYCHOMETRIC FOUNDATIONS OF THE RORSCHACH PERFORMANCE ASSESSMENT SYSTEM® (R-PAS®)

Gregory J. Meyer, Donald J. Viglione, and Joni L. Mihura

WHY USE THE RORSCHACH?

Before considering the psychometric foundation for the Rorschach Performance Assessment System® (R-PAS®; Meyer, Viglione, Mihura, Erard, & Erdberg, 2011), it is important to consider why one would use the Rorschach task in an assessment. There are several reasons. Most importantly, the task provides a standardized, in vivo sample of problem-solving behavior in response to complex, feature-rich, evocative inkblot stimuli. Each of these elements will be elaborated in the following sections.

A Sample of Problem-Solving Behavior

The problem to solve is posed in the standard introduction to the task with the opening question, "What might this be?" given as the respondent is handed the first of Rorschach's ten inkblots. The task then is to make sense out of the visual stimuli and formulate a response—a statement of what the inkblot or some component of it might be. Despite the seeming simplicity of this task, the solution to it is quite complex, as each inkblot provides multiple response possibilities that vary across many stimulus dimensions. Solving the problem posed in the query invokes a series of perceptual problem-solving operations related to scanning the stimuli, selecting locations to emphasize, comparing potential inkblot images to mental representations of objects, filtering out responses judged as less optimal, and articulating the responses selected for emphasis to the examiner.

The resulting response is a visual attribution—a statement of what the inkblot elements look like to the respondent. The process of generating responses is repeated across all ten inkblots, with respondents encouraged to take their time and offer two or three responses to each of the inkblots. Subsequently, the examiner takes the respondent back through each response, seeking clarification concerning where the responses were located and what features of the inkblot made it look like the object(s) that were seen. The process of explaining to another person how one looks at things against a backdrop of multiple competing possibilities is a novel challenge, as people do not routinely provide a detailed explanation to another person about why something looks the way it does to them.

These visual attributions, the verbal and nonverbal communications that accompany the initial responding and subsequent clarification, and the manner in which the respondent interacts with the task and examiner forms the pool of behaviors that are the yield of the task. These behaviors are then classified along multiple dimensions, including imagery, language, and communication, and subsequently these coded behaviors are quantified and compared to normative data characterizing what people typically see, say, and do when presented with the same problem-solving task.

Complex, Feature-Rich, Evocative Stimuli

Hermann Rorschach first published his carefully selected and artistically enhanced set of ten inkblots in 1921 (Rorschach, 1942). Subsequently, what became known as "the Rorschach" has been in continuous clinical use since it was published, in large part because it is a reasonably brief, portable, behavioral experiment, which can be readily administered in various clinical settings (e.g., a private office, hospital room, jail cell). Although Rorschach referred to his inkblots as "accidental forms," he meant that to signify that they were "non-specific forms" (p. 15), not that they were haphazardly created. To the contrary, based on material stored in the Hermann Rorschach Archives and Museum and what he wrote about general and card-specific rules for composition to make them "suggestive" rather than "inkblots" (p. 15), it is clear that he iteratively refined the design composition of each inkblot, embedding structure, symmetrical visual organization, shading, and recognizable but contradictory partial forms, which he then pilot tested and refined further based on the results he obtained (see pp. 15, 52–53).[1] Discrete visual features of the blots, which have been referred to as "critical bits" (Exner, 1996b), incorporate elements that suggest familiar shapes and objects, while allowing considerable latitude for idiographically unique perceptions. With his training as an artist, Rorschach created inkblot designs that are complex and evocative, using incomplete and imperfect perceptual likenesses that form competing visual images. Thus the question "What might this be?" in reference to these stimuli challenges respondents with a problem to be solved.

A Standardized Task

The task is standardized in the sense of using a fixed set of stimuli and instructions for their administration. In addition, different systems for using the task have developed further standardization associated with specific procedures of administration, including the number of responses to be given and how and when examiners should ask questions for clarification, as well as specific guidelines for coding and classifying responses, and interpreting the summary scores derived from those codes.

Task versus Method versus Test?

In our view, the administration of Rorschach's inkblots in the context of asking the respondent to answer the question "What might this be?" is using the inkblots as a task to be completed by the respondent. As a task, it need not be any kind of formal assessment procedure or method of assessment. However, as it is traditionally used in clinical psychology, this task becomes a method for assessing psychological operations. More technically, the task provides several methods for assessing psychological functions; these methods include obtaining visual attributions, which can be evaluated for their degree of fit to inkblot locations; recording verbal and nonverbal communications, which can be coded for content and themes; classifying the features of the inkblot stimuli that are elements in structuring the perceptions; and assessing the formal structure of the imagery and communications to evaluate their logic and coherence, among others. For the Rorschach to be used as a test, responses have to be systematically coded according to articulated criteria; codes must be tallied across responses and converted into scores and then the scores must be compared to what is typical for other people who also have had their responses coded using the same formal system of classification. So the task can employ several methods of assessment and can be used as a formal psychological test.

An In Vivo Sample of Behavior

Because the Rorschach is a behavioral performance task, it provides a unique means of assessing psychological functioning. Although often called a "personality" assessment measure, the functioning that can be assessed by the task is broader than the sort of Five-Factor Model of normal personality attributes that most people think of these days as defining personality. It encompasses cognitive processes, perceptual representations, and thought organization, among other things. As such, it is better conceptualized as a psychological assessment tool rather than as a personality assessment tool.

As a performance task, Rorschach responding also should be differentiated from other types of performance tasks that are used in psychological assessment, the most important of which are performance tasks of intelligence, academic achievement, and neuropsychological processing. All of the latter are designed as maximal performance measures of cognitive ability and impairment. Maximal performance measures provide test takers with clear guidelines about what is considered "good performance," explicit instructions for how to achieve good or accurate performance, and quiet, non-distracting testing conditions that foster maximal performance output.

In contrast to these maximal performance measures, the Rorschach is a task of typical performance. Typical performance measures evaluate what a person most often does when left to his or her own devices across situations. They do not have clear guidelines with respect to what qualifies as "good performance," they permit a wide range of allowable responses, and they impose minimal demands on the respondent to perform in a particular way. When Cronbach first coined these terms to describe types of assessment measures, he noted that maximal performance measures assess what a person "can do," while typical performance measures assess what a person "will do" (e.g., Cronbach, 1990). Thus, even though responses to the Rorschach task can be evaluated for their degree of cognitive sophistication, synthetic operations, and general complexity, these indicators are obtained from behaviors that are spontaneously offered under conditions in which task demands are minimal.

Because the Rorschach is a task that requires behavioral performance, it allows an examiner to observe what people do, as opposed to learning about how they think of themselves. Unlike interview-based measures or self-report inventories, the Rorschach does not require clients to describe what they are like; rather, it requires them to provide an in vivo illustration of what they are like by repeatedly providing a sample of behavior in the responses generated to each card. Thus it is a performance assessment measure, as opposed to the ubiquitously used self-report inventories, which are introspective measures that are founded on the person's understanding of him or herself relative to others and willingness to report this understanding in an honest and unbiased manner.

Not surprisingly, given their very different natures as sources of information, Rorschach-assessed variables are essentially independent of and minimally correlated with self-reports of seemingly similar constructs (e.g., Meyer, 1997; Meyer, Riethmiller, Brooks, Benoit, & Handler, 2000; Mihura, Meyer, Dumitrascu, & Bombel, 2013). By relying on an actual sample of behavior collected under standardized conditions, the Rorschach is able to provide information about personality that may reside outside of the client's immediate or conscious awareness, much as the formal assessment of memory and other cognitive abilities provides information that people are unable to volunteer reliably or validly in self-report. The value of this divergence is that it allows valid Rorschach scores to be an incrementally valid complement to self-reported characteristics in the context of a multimethod assessment. That is, the Rorschach adds valid information that cannot be obtained from other sources of information. It also means that when Rorschach data are juxtaposed with self-reported characteristics, there regularly are seeming divergences or disagreements that need to be conceptualized and understood in order to have an enhanced understanding of the person being assessed (Meyer, Finn et al., 2001; Mihura, 2012). In fact, because there is so much independence across methods of assessment, any individual method provides an incomplete picture of the person being evaluated and there is growing consensus on the necessity of using multimethod assessment in clinical and forensic practice (Hopwood & Bornstein, 2014). Accessing information obtained from observing a client's personality in action, as is the case with the Rorschach, can be an important resource for clinicians engaged in the idiographic challenge of trying to understand a person in her or his full complexity.

The Rorschach in Clinical and Forensic Practice

There is a long tradition of using Rorschach-derived variables as psychometrically established test scores in both clinical practice (Camara, Nathan, & Puente, 2000) and forensic practice (Erard, 2012; Erard, Meyer, & Viglione, 2014; Gacono & Evans, 2008; Meloy, 2008; Meloy, Hanson, & Weiner, 1997; Ritzler, Erard, & Pettigrew, 2002a, 2002b; Viglione & Hilsenroth, 2001; Weiner, Exner, & Sciara, 1996). This tradition is largely founded on the Comprehensive System (CS; Exner, 1974, 2003), which, more than any of the previous systematized approaches to using Rorschach-based assessment material in clinical practice, brought standardization to the administration, coding, and interpretation of the task so that it could serve as a psychometrically sound tool (Anastasi & Urbina, 1997). The CS provided evidence for the reliable coding of variables, for the validity of summary scores as indicators of psychological constructs, and, over time, extensive normative data to guide inferences about how an individual was similar to or different from others. The initial CS text (Exner, 1974) drew together elements of five systems that had been in use at the time in the United States. These five systems had disparate administration procedures, coded variables, coding guidelines for the same variables, summary scores, and interpretive postulates. Nonetheless, in 1974, Exner made use of the research evidence that had accumulated for these earlier systems as support for the reliability and validity of scores that were included in the CS. Exner continued to cite this pre-CS evidence readily as support for the CS as late as 2003 (see also Exner, 1986, 1993).

Between 1974 and 2003, the CS evolved in major ways, including revised norms for adults, newly developed norms for children and adolescents, revised administration procedures that included guidelines to prompt for additional responses when only one was offered or to request the card back when more than enough had been offered; revised administration procedures to eliminate protocols that were considered too short for reliable interpretation; revised variables to assess perceptual accuracy; revised tables to guide the coding of response objects as being conventional versus distorted; revised coding guidelines, new response-level codes, and new protocol-level variables; revised interpretation strategies; and revised inferences about the meaning or interpretation of some variables. Most of these changes and evolutions were based on data documenting the value of the change—either for correcting a known problem or for integrating something new into the system in order to facilitate clinical practice.

Exner noted that he almost died in 1996 because of a surgical "mishap" (Exner, 1996a, p. 1). After that experience, he realized that he did not have plans in place for allowing the CS to continue evolving without his active guidance. In the following year, because he wanted to ensure the system was addressing new research findings and issues after he retired or passed away, Exner established the Rorschach Research Council to advance Rorschach-based assessment by reviewing recent and historical research and by planning and implementing studies on focused topics. The mission of this group was to identify modifications or additions to existing CS procedures, codes, summary scores, or interpretive postulates to help ensure that the CS remained an empirically sound and useful system for using the Rorschach task in applied practice. Along with John Exner, the initial members of the Rorschach Research Council were Thomas Boll, Mark Hilsenroth, Gregory Meyer, William Perry, Donald Viglione, and Irving Weiner. Exner announced that the Rorschach Research Council ultimately would guide CS developments and changes after his death. As he said in his 1997 annual Alumni Newsletter, distributed to all previous workshop attendees, "the Council will ultimately have the responsibility for the continued development of the Comprehensive System" (Exner, 1997, p. 2).

Nevertheless, when Exner passed away in 2006, he left no explicit instructions for how the Research Council would enact developments while copyright and ownership of his works remained with his family. At the time of his death, besides John Exner, the members of the Research Council were Philip Erdberg, Christopher Fowler, Roger Greene, Gregory Meyer, Joni Mihura, and Donald Viglione. For three years, members of the Research Council explored ways in which it could prepare an updated version of the CS workbook or its foundational textbook. Ultimately, however, Exner's heirs decided that they wanted to honor his memory by preserving the CS as he left it, with no further changes.

Why Use the Rorschach Performance Assessment System?

R-PAS was developed by four people who were members of the Rorschach Research Council when Exner passed away (Erdberg, Meyer, Mihura, & Viglione), who were joined by one other co-author (Erard). R-PAS directly implements many of the corrections, revisions, and enhancements that had been part of the Research Council's work from 1997 to 2006, as well as others that were extensions of work that was begun during that time. These corrections, revisions, and enhancements include addressing problems with the CS norms as well as problems related to excessive variability in the number of responses given to the task, both of which were long-standing concerns actively addressed by the Rorschach Research Council (e.g., Dean, Viglione, Perry, & Meyer, 2007, 2008; Koonce, Meyer, & Viglione, 2008; Meyer, 2002a, 2002c; Meyer, Caracena, Shaffer, & Erdberg, 2002; Meyer & Viglione, 2005, 2006; Meyer, Viglione, Erdberg, Exner, & Shaffer, 2004; Meyer, Viglione, & Exner, 2001; Meyer, Viglione, Exner, et al., 2003; Viglione & Meyer, 2005). Other innovations and enhancements included in R-PAS began with work by the Research Council during this period, including updated tables to classify perceptual distortions, more fully specified administration guidelines, enhanced coding guidelines to increase intercoder agreement within and across training sites, dropping variables that lacked validity evidence or uniqueness, and adding new variables (such as Aggressive Content, the Ego Impairment Index, Mutuality of Autonomy, and Oral Dependency Language), based on contemporary reviews of the Rorschach literature.

Because the CS is no longer evolving or responding to evidence as Exner envisioned it would in 1997 and as it continually did over the years from 1974 to 2003, R-PAS was designed as a replacement for it, not a competitor or alternative to it. During the years when the R-PAS developers were working with Exner on the Rorschach Research Council, and for about three years after his death, their time and energy was directed toward helping the CS evolve and ensuring it did so on a sound scientific foundation. However, this is now no longer possible. The CS remains as it was in 2003; therefore, creating R-PAS was a necessary step to continue to improve the Rorschach based on the available and emerging research.

R-PAS Addresses Key Psychometric Limitations of the CS

Beginning in the mid-1990s, around the same time the Rorschach Research Council was founded, several psychologists published a series of criticisms of the Rorschach, with a focus on the CS. These critiques raised doubts about various aspects of the CS's psychometric foundations (e.g., Lilienfeld, Wood, & Garb, 2000; Wood, Nezworski, Lilienfeld, & Garb, 2003; Wood, Lilienfeld, Garb, & Nezworski, 2000). Many of the criticisms were unfounded (e.g., suggesting that coding reliability may be no better than chance agreement; Wood, Nezworski, & Stejskal, 1996), but some raised legitimate concerns that became more obvious over time as additional data accumulated. These concerns were attended to as part of the Rorschach Research Council's agenda and addressed as well in the forensic psychology literature (see Gacono & Evans, 2008). In what follows, we delineate eight specific ways that R-PAS addresses and rectifies CS limitations.

Limit Error Associated with Variability in the Number of Responses

Variability in the number of responses in a Rorschach protocol, referred to as "R," introduces extraneous variance into Rorschach test data. The degree of variability in R has been noted as a psychometric confound since the early history of the Rorschach's use in the United States (e.g., Cronbach, 1949; Meyer, 1992). CS administration procedures do limit variability in R relative to other systems, such as the Beck system, where it was possible to obtain records with just five or six responses on the low end but 100 or more on the high end. Although the CS produces less extreme variability than this, when CS administration guidelines are used, the respondent has to give at least 14 responses, but the upper limit is not defined, which can result in a large and unwieldy number of responses (e.g., 60 or more). Too few responses causes concerns about the sensitivity of the protocol to detect problems (Dean et al., 2007); too many responses can lead to an excess of administration and scoring time and potential overpathologizing of respondents (Meyer, 1993); both extremes lead to lower stability in protocols (Sultan & Meyer, 2009). In addition, because many scores are correlated with R, variability in responding causes secondary variability in many other scores (Meyer, 1993). R-PAS uses procedures to minimize extraneous variance associated with R by adopting an updated version of the "R-Optimization" procedures that were first tested by Dean et al. (2007) in a project that was designed with guidance from the Rorschach Research Council.

When using R-Optimized procedures, examiners tell respondents before starting the task that they would like two, or maybe three, responses for each card. If respondents provide only one response on a card, the examiner then prompts for a second, though does not require that an additional one be given. Conversely, if respondents spontaneously provide four responses to a card, the examiner thanks them and asks for the card back. In both instances, the examiner also provides a reminder of the instructions to provide two or three responses to each card. Asking for an additional response is called a "prompt," and asking for the card back is called a "pull," both of which are indicators of potentially important performance behaviors. Using R-Optimized administration, examiners can expect a minimum of 16 responses and a maximum of 40 responses, though the latter would be extremely unusual and 17 is the typical minimum. If the respondent produces 15 or fewer responses despite the examiner's prompts, which is also quite rare, the examiner retains the initial responses but goes back through the cards on which fewer than four responses were produced and requests additional responses.

Research across multiple samples has documented that randomly assigning youth or adults to receive R-Optimized administration or standard CS administration has two main effects: R-Optimized administration slightly increases the mean number of responses given and notably decreases the variability of R around that mean, both of which are intended effects (see Dean et al., 2007; Meyer et al., 2011; Reese, Viglione, & Giromini, 2014; Viglione, 2015). It also slightly reduces variability in scores that are correlated with R, though it does not reliably alter the mean reference value for other variables, including a variable examining the proportion of responses that are given to the last three fully chromatic cards relative to the first seven cards containing achromatic color.

Reduce Examiner Variability

A second psychometric goal for R-PAS was to reduce the impact of variability across individual examiners as much as possible. There are two main targets for this reduction in examiner variance: (a) to improve coding reliability within and across sites and (b) to improve administration consistency, including consistency in how and when examiners ask questions when they are at the stage of clarifying examinee responses. The goal is to ensure that, as much as possible, respondents will have a coded and profiled protocol that looks the same no matter who the examiner was. For instance, in the most recent normative data collected by Exner (2007), two examiners collected more than 25 protocols each and had an average R of about 20, while two other examiners collected 6 protocols each with an average R of about 27. These sets of examiners (inadvertently) established different expectations with respondents, leading to large differences in the number of responses their respondents generated in the task. With R-Optimized administration, the goal in R-PAS is to ensure that every examiner collects the same mean number of responses over time and that those responses show the same degree of variability around that mean, with variability dictated by individual differences in the respondents (not the examiners).

Toward this end, in addition to R-Optimized guidelines to control variability in R, R-PAS provides much more detailed guidance on administration than the CS. This guidance is focused on how to complete the Clarification Phase (CP) of administration, as well as how to contend with response ambiguity, including resolving conflicting information between the response phase and CP, deciding whether it is one response or two, and contending with instances when the respondent says that one response could be two different things (a "This or That" response). The R-PAS manual includes a tear sheet that examiners can use to facilitate proper administration, while free online resources include a ten-page examiner checklist for administration and two narrated videos demonstrating proper administration, among other resources.

Probably the most challenging aspects of Rorschach administration are knowing when to ask a question to clarify features of the response and when not to ask any further questions. Examiner variability in the extent of questioning during the CP has been considered the single biggest threat to the psychometric validity of the Rorschach (Exner, 2003;

Gibby & Stotsky, 1953). Exner called the examiner's decision-making processes associated with this clarification "the soft underbelly of the test" (Exner, 1993). Although decision-making about when and what to ask can be challenging to learn, the R-PAS manual provides detailed guidelines for a standardized clarification phase to significantly lessen variability across examiners.

In R-PAS, the primary tasks for the examiner during the CP are to mentally identify (a) what codes are suggested, but not yet confirmed, by the respondent's verbalizations and task behaviors, and (b) whether any of the three coding categories required for each response (what it is, where it is, and what makes it look the way it does) are not yet able to be coded. With the exception of two rather rare situations, clarification questions should only be asked when they address an identifiable coding ambiguity, and the wording of the question should target the specific coding issues. In other words, clarification questions should have the goal of resolving a specific and identifiable coding ambiguity, which may be the presence or absence of a code, differentiating which code is warranted among a number of possibilities, or resolving uncertain codes from more than one coding category. The only two exceptions in which clarification questions do not target specific coding uncertainties are when the response is so confusing it is not clear what the respondent means or when the respondent uses "loaded words" like "scary" or "disgusting-looking," which signify strong but unexplained personal reactions to the inkblots that the examiner needs to understand.

Use Updated Indices of Perceptual Accuracy

A third goal for R-PAS was to have cross-culturally generalizable standards for coding indices of perceptual accuracy (Allen & Dana, 2004). These standards are operationalized in Form Quality (FQ) tables, where inkblot locations are differentiated and within which potential response objects are listed along with one of three codes to designate the extent to which that object represents a perception that is conventional or "ordinary" (FQo), fairly reasonable but unusual (FQu), or a distorted misperception (FQ-). The R-PAS FQ tables were derived from new research on the two primary components of perceptual accuracy—fit and frequency. Fit indicates how well the perceived object matches the inkblot features at the location where it is perceived. Frequency indicates how often the perceived object is spontaneously reported at a particular location by people completing the task. To obtain fit data, a pool of more than 13,000 non-redundant response objects was identified by reviewing existing compilations of form quality codes. These objects were rated for fit to their specified location by an average of 9.9 judges from Brazil, China, Finland, Israel, Italy, Japan, Portugal, Romania, Taiwan, Turkey, and the United States. The judges made their fit ratings on a 5-point dimensional scale ranging from "1= No. I can't see it at all. Clearly, it's a distortion" to "5 = Definitely. I think it looks exactly or almost exactly like that" (Meyer et al., 2011, p. 179).

Frequency data were derived from five adult FQ tables that had been created in Argentina (Lunazzi et al., 2011), Brazil (Villemor-Amaral, Yazigi, Nascimento, Primi, & Semer, 2007), Italy (Parisi, Pes, & Cicioni, 2005), Japan (Takahashi, Takahashi, & Nishio, 2009), and Spain (Miralles Sangro, 1996, 1997). All tables were based on the responses of nonpatients, except for Spain, which were based on responses from outpatients. Across samples, objects that were reported by at least 1.5% of the people were translated into English and matching objects were linked across these data sets and to the 13,031 objects that had been rated for perceptual fit. The average frequency for each percept across samples was obtained, in addition to counting how often each percept showed up across all five FQ tables. Next, in part to make the tables a more manageable size, the fit ratings and frequency data were linked to a subset of 5,060 objects that also had data on their current and previous FQ codes from the CS (Exner, 1974, 1986, 2003). Although of secondary importance, the objects also had the FQ codes that had been assigned by Beck, Beck, Levitt, and Molish (1961) and Hertz (1970) in their FQ tables. As described in the R-PAS manual, the final FQ designations for each of the 5,060 objects contained in the R-PAS tables were assigned by taking into account their historical U.S.-based FQ classification and their internationally derived fit and frequency data. Relative to the current CS FQ tables, approximately 40% of the objects in the R-PAS FQ tables have a different FQ designation.

Initial validity data suggested that the performance of the CS and R-PAS FQ codes were fairly comparable in the detection of psychotic spectrum disorders (Meyer et al., 2011). However, more recent research documented superior validity for the R-PAS FQ codes relative to the CS FQ codes in a Taiwanese study of patients and nonpatients (Su et al., 2015).

Align Interpretation with Current Validity Evidence

A major aim with R-PAS was to ensure that the interpretation of variables in the system was aligned with their validity evidence, with two major considerations: The first was to ensure that all variables included in the system had empirical support in the validity literature, including systematic reviews and meta-analyses (e.g., Mihura et al., 2013) and utility as rated by a large sample of experienced clinicians (Meyer, Hsiao, Viglione, Mihura, & Abraham, 2013). The second was to ensure that there was a transparent logic that linked the psychological operations associated with the variable coded in the microcosm of the task to parallel psychological operations in everyday life. This is referred to as the response process or behavioral representation foundation for interpretation. As part of this effort, R-PAS also brings a strength-based approach to variable interpretation to counter what we consider to be negatively slanted inferences that developed over time as a result of interpreting Rorschach results in mostly clinical settings. A final influence on variable selection was parsimony, with the goal of minimizing overlap among scores and maximizing benefit when pitting effort and time against interpretive yield in cost-benefit considerations.

Recent research has documented that the interpretation of many CS variables is out of step with their empirical evidence base (e.g., Mihura et al., 2013) or normative standards (Meyer, Erdberg, & Shaffer, 2007; Meyer, Shaffer, Erdberg, & Horn, 2015; Viglione & Hilsenroth, 2001; Wood, Nezworski, Garb, & Lilienfeld, 2001), which will lead to faulty inferences about respondents. The validity of Rorschach scores has been a concern repeatedly expressed over the years (e.g., Cronbach, 1949; Jensen, 1965; Lilienfeld et al., 2000; Society for Personality Assessment, 2005). Garb (1999) went so far as to call for a moratorium on the use of the Rorschach in clinical and forensic practice until all variables were subjected to adequate empirical scrutiny to determine their validity. Importantly, based on the extensive series of meta-analyses completed by Mihura, Meyer, Bombel, and Dumitrascu (2015) and Mihura, Meyer, Dumitrascu, and Bombel (2013), this call for a complete moratorium on the Rorschach has been lifted by Garb and his colleagues, the staunchest group of self-described "critics" of the Rorschach (Wood, Garb, Nezworski, Lilienfeld, & Duke, 2015).

All of the variables selected for inclusion in R-PAS have been used in the past either as part of previous systems for using the Rorschach or as stand-alone variables, coded independent of any particular Rorschach system. Because the Rorschach task is best thought of as a set of performance-based personality assessment methods, understanding the range of behaviors that can contribute to each code and to task performance in general is critical to using and interpreting the data derived from it (Viglione & Rivera, 2012). In R-PAS, a premium was placed on aligning interpretive guidelines with the behavioral response process underpinnings of coded Rorschach performance behaviors, as well as their empirical foundation. Thus, even though the codes and variables included in R-PAS have been used before, the interpretation of these variables is often notably different than in the past. Consideration of the response process facilitates generalizations from coded R-PAS task behaviors to real-life behaviors.

The "response process" refers to all the factors that lead to or produce the task behaviors, which are then captured by a particular R-PAS code. They are the psychological elements that are present in the process of generating a response with a particular set of coded attributes. The relevant factors or psychological elements are embedded in the respondent's coded behavior and imagery, which include his or her abilities, organizational efforts, styles of processing, feelings, ideas, motives, and conflicts. These factors include long-standing personality characteristics, current state-like circumstances, and reactions that are present in the context of being assessed by a particular examiner at a particular time. Interpretive guidelines anchored in empirical evidence and response process considerations are offered for each response-level R-PAS code and separately for each protocol-level variable that is profiled.

Primary resources for gauging the published empirical support for variables are the meta-analytic validity review of the CS variables by Mihura et al. (2013, 2015; Wood et al., 2015). Additionally, separate systematic reviews and meta-analyses provide a foundation for several non-CS scores that were added to R-PAS, including the Ego Impairment Index (EII; Diener, Hilsenroth, Shaffer, & Sexton, 2011), Mutuality of Autonomy Scale (MOA; Graceffo, Mihura, & Meyer, 2014), and Rorschach Oral Dependency Scale (ROD; Bornstein, 1996). A systematic review as well as primary research studies formed the base for adding Aggressive Content (AGC; Gacono, Bannatyne-Gacono, Meloy, & Baity, 2005; Katko, Meyer, Mihura, & Bombel, 2010), and individual studies were the foundation for differentiating the overall code in the CS for responses that made use of the background white space (S), which lacked validity in the Mihura et al. (2013) review, into its two very different constituent components of Space Reversal (SR) and Space Integration (SI; e.g., Bandura, 1954a, 1954b; De Koninck & Crabbe-Decleve, 1971; Dumitrascu, Mihura, Meyer, & Onofrei, 2011; Nelson, 1954; Stein, 1973). An itemized listing and description of all the variables in R-PAS, along with the rationale for retaining or dropping them, is provided in Chapter 15 of the R-PAS manual (Meyer et al., 2011). The manual also provides tables that list the historical origins of each code in the system (p. 54) and the CS counterparts to R-PAS variables (p. 494).

Improve Normative Anchors for Accurate Interpretation

Another important goal for R-PAS was to have improved estimates of what is typical or expected performance among nonclinical individuals. Over time, evidence accumulated that the CS normative samples looked notably different than other nonpatient samples for some Rorschach variables; this was true for the United States and other countries (Shaffer, Erdberg, & Haroian, 1999; Viglione & Hilsenroth, 2001; Wood et al., 2001). Although it was initially thought that problems were limited to FQ (Meyer, 2001), in fact, the CS norms erroneously cause nonpatients to appear psychologically unhealthy across a broader number of variables. Beginning in the summer of 1997, Rorschach researchers from various countries around the world started to compile all of the existing efforts to gather nonpatient and normative reference samples for the CS. That project ultimately was published in 2007 as a Special Supplement to the *Journal of Personality Assessment* (JPA) devoted to the International Reference Samples for the Rorschach Comprehensive System (Shaffer, Erdberg, & Meyer, 2007). The internationally collected adult data are cohesive across countries, including the United States, but they differ from the CS norms on a number of notable variables (Meyer, Erdberg, & Shaffer, 2007; Meyer, Shaffer et al., 2015). Thus it is important for CS users to rely on these norms rather than the traditional CS norms to make correct inferences about health and pathology.

After the JPA Supplement was published in 2007, Meyer asked researchers contributing samples if they would donate a random sample of protocols for additional research. Almost all authors from the Supplement offered data, though not all of it could be used for one reason or another. In the end, however, data from 15 adult samples were used to construct what would become the R-PAS normative reference database.

As detailed in the R-PAS manual (Meyer et al., 2011), there are two primary samples of normative reference data. First, up to 100 protocols were selected from each of the 15 donated samples, and these were combined to form a composite sample of 1,396 CS administered protocols. This sample was then used as a base to statistically adjust and model what protocols would look like when using R-Optimized administration procedures. For this step, a target sample of 123 protocols, collected by experienced examiners using the final R-Optimized administration guidelines in diverse nonpatient and clinical settings, was used to generate expectations for how R is distributed across cards when using R-Optimized administration. Statistical modeling procedures were then used to convert the distribution of R obtained under CS administration to the distribution of R obtained under R-Optimized administration. The main goal of the modeling procedure was to ensure that the original CS data had the same distribution of first, second, third, and fourth responses to each card as was found with actual R-Optimized data. Ensuring this match at the level of each card would, secondarily, ensure a match on the distribution of R between the target and modeled records at the protocol level.

The result was that modeled normative data for R matched the actual R-Optimized data for R on a response-by-response, card-by-card, and protocol-by-protocol basis. For instance, in the target sample of protocols collected using R-Optimized procedures, R had M = 24.2 and SD = 4.4; in the final normative sample of statistically modeled records, R had M = 24.2 and SD = 4.7. The latter sample makes use of 640 of the original 1,386 records, with the smaller number of records being due to the fact that fewer people give second or third responses to cards when using CS administration as compared to R-Optimized administration.

Using statistically modeled reference data is a limitation of R-PAS, and new international normative data collection efforts are underway. However, it is noteworthy that when the subsample of 640 records was compared to the original sample of 1,396 records, the primary difference between them was the intended effect, viz., a notable decrease in the SD for R. Pianowski, Meyer, and Villemor-Amaral (2016) recently replicated these findings using normative reference data from a fully Brazilian sample that had no overlap with the R-PAS normative sample. The modeling had virtually identical effects in their norms as in the R-PAS norms, suggesting that the procedures can be reliably applied across cultures and languages. Across studies, besides the reduced variability in R, there also is a small and desirable increase in the mean R, reflecting the fact that R-PAS does not have problematic low R protocols of 14 or 15 responses, as is found with the CS. In addition, research across several studies has shown that when people are randomly assigned to have protocols collected using CS administration or R-Optimized administration guidelines, the same pattern of results is found: There are no reliable differences in normative mean values except for R, which by design consistently has a notably smaller degree of variability and a slightly higher mean (Meyer et al., 2011; Reese et al., 2014; Viglione et al., 2015). In combination, these results highlight how either modeling R-Optimized administration or actually using R-Optimized administration does not have much of an impact on the normative reference values that were in place for the CS.

Thus controlling R during administration can produce substantial practical benefits in terms of reducing its variability, thereby allowing the norms to apply readily to more people. The findings just described also refute objections that have been raised stating that R-Optimized administration is dramatically different from CS administration and that the research literature on the CS would not generalize to R-PAS (e.g., Gurley, Sheehan, Piechowski, & Gray, 2014; Mattlar, 2011; Ritzler, 2011, 2014). To the contrary, differences in summary scores other than R are not discernable, and there is no reason to doubt the existing CS research literature will fully generalize to R-PAS. Stated differently, if the administration procedures of R-PAS and the CS produce different types of response data, there is no evidence for these effects that can be found comparing the distributions of variables between the two systems, other than the intended change in R.

Although some forensic examiners may have reservations about the idea of using R-Optimized modeled reference data (see Erard, 2012; Erard et al., 2014), statistically modeled norms are increasingly standard at the major test publishing companies, including for the Wechsler scales and Stanford-Binet (e.g., Zhu & Chen, 2011). Nonetheless, R-PAS also does provide examiners with norms for protocols administered using CS administration guidelines (i.e., the original sample of 1,396 protocols). Importantly, forensic examiners should recognize that either set of internationally based R-PAS normative data provides a much better reference standard than the traditional CS reference data for characterizing what is typical and atypical nonpatient Rorschach behavior. The R-PAS norms do not make typical nonpatients look disturbed or pathological (Giromini, Viglione, & McCullaugh, 2015; Meyer, Shaffer et al., 2015), and forensic examiners relying on Exner's CS norms will not be able to defend themselves in court from charges that they have overpathologized their clients.

Improve the Psychometrics of Composite Variables

Another goal for R-PAS was to improve the psychometric properties of its composite variables based on statistical advances and empirical findings with regard to the dimensional nature of psychopathology. Consequently, revisions were made for three of the former CS Constellation Indices to make them more fully dimensional (Viglione, Giromini, Gustafson, & Meyer, 2014). The R-PAS Thought and Perception Composite (TP-Comp) is a replacement for the CS Perceptual Thinking Index (PTI), the R-PAS Suicide Concern Composite (SC-Comp) replaces the CS Suicide Constellation (S-CON), and the R-PAS Vigilance Composite (V-Comp) replaces the CS Hypervigilance Index (HVI). The PTI and S-CON were chosen because of their good empirical support. The range of research support for the HVI is not as extensive, but the available data is supportive and its coded response process behaviors transparently generalize to day-to-day behaviors in a face valid manner (Meyer & Archer, 2001; Meyer et al., 2013; Mihura et al., 2013; Viglione, 1999; Viglione & Hilsenroth, 2001; Viglione & Meyer, 2008). The remaining CS Constellations were not incorporated into R-PAS because they were too redundant with other variables or because they lacked sufficient empirical support.

The CS Constellation Indices use a series of dichotomous cutoff items (e.g., Criterion 2 on the PTI is either scored 0 or 1 depending on whether X-% is > 0.29 or not) that then lead to a step-based integer scale rather than a fully dimensional scale (e.g., the PTI can only take integer values from 0 to 5). These CS integer-based scales, relative to fully dimensional, continuous scales, suffer from distributional and reliability problems because they use a limited number of values and do not capitalize on all the available variance. Recent evidence suggests that continuous measures of psychopathology are more valid and reliable than are discrete measures (Dutta, Greene, Addington, McKenzie, Phillips, & Murray, 2007; Markon, Chmielewski, & Miller, 2011).

The fully dimensional Composites for R-PAS were created using multiple regression equations to predict each respective CS Constellation as the target criterion variable. Predictors were fully dimensional revisions of the Constellation's component scores. Predictors that were not significant were removed from the regression equations. All three R-PAS Composites improve interrater reliability and are as valid as or more valid than their CS counterparts, which thus should also improve interpretive accuracy in applied work (Viglione et al., 2014).

The R-PAS Composites are highly similar to their CS counterparts with regard to distributional properties and validity. Furthermore, the R-PAS Composites and CS Indices correlate highly with one another, which supports using the R-PAS Composites as replacements for the CS Indices (Viglione et al., 2014). However, these scores are complicated to generate and require a computer to be generated accurately. They each use some square root transformed variables that give them more optimal statistical properties, even though they make the equations appear particularly uninviting for hand calculations. The Composites are computed automatically by the online R-PAS scoring program (www.r-pas.org) on the basis of response-level codes entered by the examiner. Alternatively, there is a free Excel file that can be downloaded from within the online program and used to compute the Composites if a user is calculating the results by hand.

Thought and Perception Composite (TP-Comp)

As its name implies, the TP-Comp is a composite measure of the R-PAS Thinking and Perception variables. The TP-Comp is derived from perceptual accuracy (Form Quality, FQ) and thought disturbance (Cognitive Codes) variables, including the human movement response with distorted FQ (M-).

FQ has proven to be a valid method of capturing psychotic-like perceptual difficulties (e.g., Dawes, 1999; Kleiger, 1999; Mihura et al., 2013, 2015; Su et al., 2015; Viglione, 1999; Wood et al., 1996, 2015). Individuals with psychotic-like disturbances struggle to translate and interpret environmental stimuli accurately (e.g., Hilsenroth, Eudell-Simmons, DeFife, & Charnas, 2007), and the semi-ambiguous Rorschach inkblots serve as an analogue to the perceptual environment of people, things, and events encountered in day-to-day life. Consequently, individuals with psychotic-like disturbances produce a relatively higher quantity of poor form responses with FQ- codes.

R-PAS Cognitive Codes assess for speech coherence, relevance, logic, and peculiarity. Thinking disturbance is coded when respondents produce responses with any of the following characteristics: (a) a mistaken or inappropriate word or phrase is used to describe a response; (b) confused language, task distortions, or rambling, circumstantial responses that drift from the task; (c) peculiar, strained, confused, or overly concrete reasoning; (d) implausible visual combinations of two or more blot details into a single response object; (e) implausible or impossible visualized relationships between two or more distinct response objects; and (f) the simultaneous perception of two mutually exclusive response objects or subcomponents involving the same blot area. If the respondent has a proclivity toward any of these thinking disturbances, the Rorschach method is likely to elicit them because it requires respondents to provide a verbal description of their perceptions and then explain the logic behind those perceptions. Using the Rorschach has two advantages over using interview-based samples of spontaneous speech to code for behavioral instances in lapses in logic and coherence. First, R-PAS is able to capture illogical or inappropriate visual combinations of objects or object features; spontaneous verbal speech samples cannot. Second, R-PAS has relevant norms for its coded speech samples; spontaneous verbal speech samples do not.

As previously noted, the TP-Comp is based on the PTI (Exner, 2003). The PTI was itself an updated version of its predecessor, the Schizophrenia Index (SCZI; Exner, 1986). The PTI and SCZI are quite highly correlated ($\geq .94$; Hilsenroth et al., 2007; Smith, Baity, Knowles, & Hilsenroth, 2001), and both have excellent research support as indicators of disturbance in thinking and perception that is most commonly seen in psychotic states. This was a strong and stable finding in the Mihura et al. (2013) validity meta-analyses and it is consistent with previous literature reviews (e.g., Jørgensen, Andersen, & Dam, 2000, 2001; Lilienfeld et al., 2000; Wood, Nezworski, & Garb, 2003). The PTI also was among the most highly rated useful and valid variables in the clinician survey (Meyer et al., 2013). The TP-Comp is highly correlated with the PTI ($r = 0.87$ or higher), but it is more reliably scored, and it shows stronger validity with relevant criteria (Dzamonja-Ignjatovic, Smith, Jocic, & Milanovic, 2013; Su et al., 2015; Viglione et al., 2014).

Suicide Concern Composite (SC-Comp)

The SC-Comp is a general measure of suicide risk and self-destructive behavior. Psychologically, it may be related to desperation, but evidence suggests that it is not related to self-mutilation or suicidal gestures that lack lethal intent (Fowler, Piers, Hilsenroth, Holdwick, & Padawer, 2001). High scores represent an implicit risk for suicide that may not be reflected in self-report but should be explored with the respondent, along with assessing other risk factors (e.g., substance abuse, lack of sense of belongingness). Although people who commit suicide or engage in near-lethal suicidal behavior elevate this index, the base rate for suicide in most populations is low, which leads to many false-positive results, and this needs to be kept in mind when interpreting the index.

When simultaneously elevated, the variables included in the SC-Comp together shape and intensify the interpretation of the individual components. Thus overall elevations suggest a negative and potentially inescapable proclivity toward introspection, self-focus, and self-criticism (r, V, V + FD); strong responsivity to emotional or compelling environmental stimuli that may predispose one to rash or impulsive action ([CF + C]−FC); a proneness to vulnerable and mixed affective experiences, whereby negative feelings spoil positive reactions and enjoyment (CBlend); a propensity to view oneself as damaged, flawed, or hurt by life (Morbid); an inability to perceive the world as others do (low FQo%) and a lack of attunement to what is most obvious or conventional to others (Popular); excessive or burdensome mental complexity (LSO/R, the SI component of AnyS); potential oppositionality or strivings for independence or freedom from imposed constraints (the SR component of AnyS); psychologically taxing mental imagery or affective distress that overshadows more organized coping resources (PPD−MC); and a lack of whole or complete representations of people (H) that may inhibit reaching out to others for help.

In one study, the SC-Comp's CS predecessor (i.e., the S-CON) was related to a measure of serotonin turnover in patients hospitalized following a suicide attempt (i.e., CSF 5-HIAA; Lundbäck et al., 2006), and, in another study, a slightly modified version of the index validly incremented over self-report to predict near-lethal suicidal acts among adolescents and young adults (Blasczyk-Schiep, Kazén, Kuhl, & Grygielski, 2011). The correlation between the S-CON and the SC-Comp in its dimensional validation study was 0.79, and the SC-Comp was as valid as the S-CON and more reliable (Viglione et al., 2014).

Vigilance Composite (V-Comp)

The V-Comp is interpreted as a sign of chronic activation and attentiveness to protect oneself from potential threats. When simultaneously elevated, the variables included in the V-Comp are understood to assess a guarded interpersonal stance (low T); effortful focused cognition (sum of responses with W or SI or Sy; LSO/R; AnyS); potential oppositionality or strivings for independence (AnyS); a preoccupation with others (SumH) and a propensity for representations to be incomplete and partial [low H+(H)+A+(A) / All H and A] or imbued with mythic, unreal, or superhuman/subhuman qualities [(H)+(Hd)+(A)+(Ad)]; and attention to clothing and other personalized accessories (Cg), which can suggest a preoccupation with detail and appearances, as well as potential concerns about protection or disguise. V-Comp elevations are associated with vigilantly scanning the environment for threats, but elevations are not specific to paranoid conditions. The index captures a general cognitive style and not necessarily an expectation of malevolence from others and fearfulness.

The V-Comp's predecessor is the CS Hypervigilance Index (HVI; Exner, 2003). In the Viglione et al. (2014) validation sample, the HVI and the V-Comp correlated at 0.86. Despite the absence of support for using this variable as a dichotomous measure to assess paranoid conditions, it does have replicated convergent validity with paranoid criteria using first-factor-aligned Rorschach and MMPI data (Meyer et al., 2000). Nevertheless, it did not fare well in the Mihura et al. (2013) meta-analysis in three studies using criteria of paranoid psychosis, paranoid personality disorder, and child sexual abuse victimization. These criteria might not capture the organized, focused, and effortful cognitive style thought to be associated with the V-Comp, though this newly formulated composite score should be interpreted tentatively until additional research is completed.

Make Learning and Interpretation Easier

R-PAS has taken several important steps to making the interpretive process easier for users and new learners. As Groth-Marnat (2009) noted,

> One of the frequent criticisms of the Rorschach is that it is not user friendly. It takes considerable time to learn, the scores typically seem complex, the names of many of the categories/formulas often sound abstruse (i.e., "Lambda," "Erlebnistypus," "Experience Actual"), and it is difficult to work from the scores to interpretation. Thus an important goal would be to make changes such that it will be more user friendly."
>
> (p. 307)

Relative to other Rorschach systems, R-PAS strives to use more parsimonious and practical terminology, symbols, calculations, and data presentation methods.

Regarding terminology, many of the CS variables that were retained or modified for R-PAS were assigned more transparent names incorporating semantic cues. For example, rather than referring to Rorschach disordered thinking variables as "Special Scores," they are simply called Cognitive Codes. As an example of changes in symbols, rather than designating form quality minus at the response level with "FQ-" but then designating the percentage of form quality minus in a protocol with "X-%," R-PAS uses the more transparent designation of "FQ-" at the response level and "FQ-%" at the protocol level. As another example, instead of using the term "Lambda" to refer to the proportion of responses determined just by form (F) features, R-PAS uses the more transparent calculation and terminology of "F%" to indicate the percent of responses determined just by form features. Similarly, R-PAS also uses the label "Human Movement and Weighted Sum of Color" (MC) rather than "Experience Actual" (EA) to indicate the sum of Human Movement and the Weighted Sum of Color. Finally, although the CS uses the term "Erlebnistypus" (EB) for the balance of Human Movement to Weighted Sum of Color based on the term's historical origins in Rorschach's writings, R-PAS simply refers to this score as the "Human Movement Proportion" (M/MC).

Some of the most notable changes in R-PAS relative to previous systems for using the Rorschach involve the options for presenting data.

In the CS, as with all other previous systems, the response-level codes are aggregated across all responses to form protocol-level scores. Some of these scores are then turned into more complex variables as percentages, ratios, or composites. Historically, all of these scores have then been displayed in raw numeric form. In the CS, the protocol-level calculations were completed on a page called the Structural Summary, where the primary scores were a combination of interval and nominal data. Importantly, the numeric raw scores did not indicate the extent to which a person's score was typical or atypical. Rather, to accomplish this, an examiner would have to mentally compare an examinee's raw scores across approximately 70 variables to a table of normative descriptive statistics. This historical reliance on raw scores for Rorschach interpretation stands in contrast to what is done with other contemporary broadband measures of personality or cognitive ability, all of which make use of normatively based standardized scores to determine the extent to which a particular examinee's results are typical or atypical.

The R-PAS developers sought to facilitate the examiner's ability to make rapid visual comparisons between the results for a particular respondent and the nonpatient reference values. This was done first by putting all R-PAS scores on a common metric, using percentiles to quantify the relative position of every score value in the normative data. These normative percentiles were then converted to their normal curve equivalent Standard Scores, and the results were then profiled in a visual display. In addition to plotting the Standard Score equivalent of the respondent's raw score, the profile pages allow examiners to view the underlying raw score units, which is an essential aid for many of the infrequently assigned scores because it helps ensure accurate inferences for the scores that have irregular and non-normal distributions or low base rates. Providing easily understood standard score profiles facilitates Rorschach interpretation and makes the process similar to what is done in contemporary practice for other broadband psychological measures.

To produce an R-PAS standard score profile, the most convenient option is to enter coding into the secure and encrypted online scoring program, which is available at www.r-pas.org, although hand scoring forms are also available. The Protocol Level Counts & Calculations Page displays raw counts for all R-PAS variables grouped by coding category, as well as calculations that make use of those raw counts. This page is analogous to the Structural Summary in the CS. Next, the Profile Pages contain the raw scores, percentiles, and standard score equivalents for each profiled variable. The Profile Pages include the following domains: Administration Behaviors and Observations, Engagement and Cognitive Processing, Perception and Thinking Problems, Stress and Distress, and Self and Other Representation.

The Standard Scores are displayed on either "Page 1" or "Page 2" according to the degree of evidentiary support for the variable. Variables with strong support are displayed on Page 1. Page 2 variables have some support, but their validity and interpretive significance is more tentative, often due to a lack of good research linking coded task behaviors to their R-PAS interpretive constructs. Thus these scores generally should be considered supplements to the Page 1 variables, particularly in high-stakes testing contexts, such as forensic psychological evaluations for psychological injury claims.

Provide the Ability to Adjust for the Simplicity or Complexity of Protocols

When Rorschach data are factor analyzed using principal components analyses, research has shown that the largest factor is determined by the complexity and number of responses contributing to a protocol (e.g., Meyer, 1992, 1997; Meyer & Viglione, 2006; Meyer et al., 2011). This factor typically accounts for 20% to 25% of the total variance in a CS protocol (Meyer, 1997) and is smaller than the first dimension from the MMPI-2 or MCMI-III (which account for about 50% to 55% of the total variance; see Meyer, 1997). Because R has less variability in R-PAS protocols relative to CS protocols, when examining all the individually assigned count variables in the R-PAS norms, the first principal component accounted for about 12% of the total variance in scores (Meyer et al., 2011, pp. 442–443).

The R-PAS Complexity score is an index that quantifies this primary dimension among the scored variables, having a correlation of 0.95 with it. It does so by taking into account the number of responses given and their complexity as determined by visual representation (considering the location used, incorporation of background white space, and synthesis of response elements), range of ideas that come to mind (as indexed by the number and type of content codes), and the respondent's ability to describe environmental nuances and characteristics that contributed to their understanding of that environment (as indexed by the number and type of determinants identified).

Each component of complexity is weighted and then summed across all responses to produce the total Complexity score. Because the complexity components are summed across all responses, R is an important element of the final Complexity score. However, it is somewhat "invisible," given that it is not a factor identified in the coding scheme applied to each response. Protocol complexity has always influenced nomothetic Rorschach data, with higher complexity being associated with more codes of all types. Because of this and because there is some evidence that complexity acts as a moderator for other variables (Dean et al., 2007; Meyer et al., 2000), "Complexity-Adjusted" Standard Scores are presented as part of the standard R-PAS interpretive output.

As a single variable in its present form, complexity has been studied against criteria of psychological complexity, flexibility, and adaptive capacity in a small body of research. Dumitrascu et al. (2011) found a strong relationship ($r = 0.44$) between complexity and level of education. With a group of older individuals with schizophrenia, Moore, Viglione, Rosenfarb, Patterson, and Mausbach (2013) found that complexity made a unique contribution to both functional (*Beta* = 0.23) and social skills capacity (*Beta* = 0.35), after controlling for neurocognitive functioning and psychopathology. In this study, complexity was negatively associated with negative symptoms of schizophrenia ($r = -0.31$), indicating that low complexity is associated with functional limitations in daily life, including blunted affect and emotional and social withdrawal. In a CS study, Dean et al. (2007) showed, as expected, that adjusting for complexity improved the prediction of psychotic criteria for protocols that were short or lengthy, though it did not make a difference for those in an optimal range of R. Nevertheless, most of the empirical support for the complexity variable lies in the considerable amount of indirect research connecting its subcomponents to age, education, intelligence, adaptation, and various other relevant criteria (Exner, 2003; Mihura et al., 2013; Stanfill, Viglione, & Resende, 2013; Viglione, 1999).

Accordingly, complexity is generally interpreted as both an indicator of the respondent's level of task engagement or motivation and as an indicator of cognitive sophistication. It is an overall index of processing depth and richness, as measured by the degree of differentiation, integration, sensitivity, and productivity in the responses in a given protocol.

High Complexity scores may reflect either a psychological or processing strength (e.g., flexibility in coping) or the presence of disturbance (e.g., losing ideational control due to mania). In some cases, the complexity elevation may also result from attempts by respondents to complicate their record with presumed indicators of disturbance. A low Complexity score may be due to a cognitive or coping deficit or to an emotional factor such as an anxiety-driven conflict, depressive withdrawal, traumatic numbing, or a defensive maneuver to mask psychological disturbance (Ganellen, 1994; Meyer, 1999; Meyer et al., 2011; Viglione, 1999; Viglione, Towns, & Lindshield, 2012). A person's history of adaptive functioning, other assessment information, and clinical observations, as well as the context of the assessment, should be consistent with the direction of the interpretation (i.e., strength vs. weakness). Very low Complexity scores (standard score < 80) necessitate more tentative interpretations across other scores, as there is less personally relevant Rorschach data to aggregate in the protocol. Interpretive inferences with records with marginally low complexity (< 90) might also deserve some caution.

Because other scores tend to rise and fall in conjunction with complexity, when complexity is high or low it can be challenging to determine whether a respondent's other scores are typical or atypical for that level of complexity. The Complexity-Adjusted protocol scores allow clinicians to readily determine what is unusual versus what is to be expected given an examinee's level of complexity. Methodologically, Complexity-Adjusted scores are similar to adjustments that can be made with other types of psychological test data. For instance, they are akin to using the "Negative Impression Management (NIM) predicted" or "Positive Impression Management (PIM) predicted" score profiles for the Personality Assessment Inventory. Those profiles display the respondent's score across all scales alongside the score that he or she would be expected to have on those scales given the NIM or PIM scores. Both the NIM predicted and PIM predicted scores are designed to aid in the interpretation of profiles that may be distorted by overly negative or positive self-presentations (Hopwood, Morey, Rogers, & Sewell, 2007). Similarly, just as Wechsler subscale scores can be identified as relative "strengths" or "weaknesses" when they stand out as higher or lower than expected for a person's overall level of intelligence, Complexity-Adjusted scores identify which variables are higher or lower than expected given the individual's overall level of complexity.

Because some R-PAS variables have non-normal skewed and kurtotic distributions, Complexity-Adjusted Scores were derived via quantile regression, in preference to other more typical, linear statistical procedures (e.g., linear regression or analysis of covariance; see Meyer et al., 2011). The Complexity-Adjusted Score shows what the person's score would look like if complexity was controlled and held constant at its median value. Stated differently, it shows what the person's score on a particular variable would be if he or she had a median or typical level of complexity rather than a high or low level of complexity. The Complexity-Adjusted score also can be thought of as illustrating what this person's score would be if everyone else in the norms had the same level of complexity as this person.

OVERVIEW OF PSYCHOMETRICS

Norms

Adult Norms

The development of the R-PAS norms was described earlier. The 640 normative records are derived from 15 independent samples from 13 countries: Argentina (n = 25), Belgium (55), Brazil (36), Denmark (54), Finland (44), France (47), Greece (34), Israel (26), Italy (38), Portugal (43), Romania (47), Spain (54), and the United States (137; 56 of which were from Exner [2007], 43 from Shaffer, Erdberg, & Haroian [2007], and 38 from Viglione). Although full demographic information was available for each of these samples in their initial publications, this information was not always stored with the protocols that were shared with R-PAS, resulting in variable sample sizes for the demographic information. Nonetheless, the mean age is 37.3 (SD = 13.4; range 17 to 86), the mean years of education is 13.3 (SD = 3.6, range 1 to 22), and 44.7% are male. In terms of ethnic background, 66.8% of the cases are White, followed by mixed-race or other (19.4%), Hispanic (8.7%), and Black or Asian (each 2.6%). For the age variable, 20.2% of the sample was 25 or younger (only one person was 17) and 3.8% were 65 or older. For the variables that are new to R-PAS and not found in the CS or that are derived from the R-PAS form quality tables, norms are based on 118 English full-text normative records from the United States. This subsample is similar to the full sample with respect to demographics, though it is slightly more balanced in gender (48.3% male), slightly older (M age = 40.3) and more educated (M years = 15.0), and has more individuals endorsing Black (8.8%) or Asian (7.9%) ethnic identities (White = 70.3%, Hispanic = 7.0%, mixed-race or other = 3.5%).

Given the countries contributing data to the norms, the international reference sample is quite diverse in terms of culture and geography. About one-fifth of the protocols are from the United States and about two-thirds from nine European countries, with the remainder from Israel, Argentina, and Brazil. Thus the Western Hemisphere and westernized countries, cultures, and languages are well represented in the R-PAS reference samples, whereas Eastern Hemisphere countries, cultures, and languages are currently underrepresented.

As standards for comparison, one can consider three options: worldwide statistics, international statistics for Developed countries, and U.S. Census data. The United Nations (UN) classifies countries as "Developed" and "Developing," with many other countries falling between these two classifications. Developed countries include all of Europe (consisting of 53 countries and territories), Canada, the United States, Australia, New Zealand, and Japan. The UN provides statistics for 2015 (http://esa.un.org/unpd/wpp/), which can be used to obtain worldwide and Developed countries data for the adult female to male gender ratio, the average age for adults who are age 20 and older, and the distribution of people around the world. Other UN data from 2013 provide estimates of the average years of adult education across 187 countries (http://hdr.undp.org/en/content/mean-years-schooling-adults-years). The UN has some data on ethnocultural identity (http://unstats.un.org/unsd/demographic/sconcerns/popchar/default.htm). However, the remarkable diversity of classification schemes used by census bureaus in different countries makes it impossible to consolidate these data into the classification schemes familiar to U.S. readers. U.S. Census data for 2012 can be used to determine the adult gender ratio and average age over 20 years (http://www.census.gov/population/age/data/2012comp.html), while data from 2014 can be used to estimate average years of education among adults aged 25 years or older (http://www.census.gov/hhes/socdemo/education/data/cps/2014/tables.html) and ethnic identification (http://quickfacts.census.gov/qfd/states/00000.html). A summary of data drawn from these sources is provided in Table 2.1.

Table 2.1: Demographic Data for the R-PAS Norms and Comparison Standards

Variable	R-PAS		UN		US Census
	640	118	Global	Developed	
% Male	44.7%	48.3%	49.8%	48.0%	48.2%
M Adult Age	37.3	40.3	43.5	49.5	47.7
M Adult Years Ed	13.3	15.0	7.9	11.1	13.7
Ethnicity (by Region)					
White	66.8%	70.3%	(15.0%)	(89.1%)	62.1%
Hispanic	8.7%	7.0%	(9.0%)		17.4%
Black	2.6%	8.8%	(16.0%)		13.2%
Asian	2.6%	7.9%	(60.0%)	(10.1%)	5.4%
Mixed	19.4%	3.5%			2.5%
Amer Indian/AK Native					1.2%
HI & Pacific Islander					0.2%

Developed = United Nations Developed countries (53 countries of Europe, Canada, United States, Australia, New Zealand, and Japan). The parenthesized values are very rough indicators of ethnic identity based on the country in which people reside.

Relative to a global standard, the R-PAS norms have somewhat fewer men, are younger, and are much more educated. The R-PAS norms also have many more people of White European ancestry and many fewer people of Asian ancestry when using very rough country-based ethnic classifications. Relative to the standard of 58 Developed countries, the R-PAS norms have a similar proportion of men, are notably lower in average age among adults, have about two more years of education, and show more diversity among the roughly categorized country-based ethnic classifications. Relative to U.S. Census data, the R-PAS norms have a similar gender distribution, are younger, have a similar level of education, and have somewhat less diversity in ethnic background.

A key question then is to what extent these demographic variables are associated with variability in R-PAS scores. Consistent with historical research on the influence of gender (Bornstein, 1995; Exner, 1991), adult age (Gross, Newton, & Brooks, 1990; Pertchik, Shaffer, Erdberg, & Margolin, 2007), and race or ethnicity (Meyer, 2002b; Meyer et al., 2007; Presley, Smith, Hilsenroth, & Exner, 2001), the most recent and systematic exploration of these three demographic variables documented their absence of association with R-PAS scores (Meyer, Giromini, Viglione, Reese, & Mihura, 2015) in three large samples (ns from 241 to 640) encompassing nonpatients, patients, youth, and adults. However, consistent with previous research, Meyer, Giromini et al. (2015) documented that there are two demographic factors that do have an important influence on Rorschach responding: level of education (Nascimento, 2004; Pires, 2007) and youth age (Stanfill et al., 2013). Both of these variables are associated with the overall complexity and richness of a protocol in nonpatients, while youth age is also associated with perceptual accuracy and thought organization in clinical and nonclinical samples (Meyer, Giromini et al., 2015; Stanfill et al., 2013). To some extent the use of Complexity-Adjusted scores with adults can adjust for instances when a lower than normative level of education contributes to unsophisticated and simplistic responding, as the data suggest it will. However, it should be recognized that the R-PAS adult norms, with an average of 13.3 years of education, are more applicable to people in the United States and from other Developed countries than to people from countries with much lower standards for education. In addition, given the association of youth age with many facets of Rorschach responding, including those that go beyond typical markers of protocol complexity and extend to the conventionality and accuracy of perception and thought organization, it is important to have age-stratified R-PAS norms available for youth.

Before leaving the issue of adult normative data, it is important to clarify how the internationally collected normative data correct for significant problems with the CS norms. The internationally collected normative data have been criticized as problematic because some of the data collection efforts were completed by relatively inexperienced examiners (Ritzler & Sciara, 2009). Meyer, Shaffer et al. (2015) recently investigated these concerns in three interrelated studies. The first study documented how the international norms were virtually identical when organized into three groups differentiated by the quality of their data collection effort, including an optimal group of four samples that relied on multiple experienced examiners and provided ongoing quality control over administration and coding. Analyses also showed that relative to the group of more optimal samples, the group of less optimal samples did not produce more variability in summary scores within or across samples or lower interrater reliability for coding. The second study used the existing CS reference norms to generate T-scores for the mean scores observed in the international norms. Doing so documented how the CS norms made other samples of healthy nonpatients look psychologically impaired in multiple domains. The third study used example data from four different countries that each had two sets of normative data available as competing reference points to indicate what was typical or expected for that country. This study demonstrated how these contrasting within-country local norms produced notably different results on some variables, which compromises the ability of local norms to be used instead of the composite international norms.

Taken together, these three studies provided strong support for using the international norms in clinical practice as norms that are generalizable across samples, settings, languages, and cultures and that account for the natural variability that is present when clinicians and researchers contend with the ambiguity contained in the standard CS reference materials concerning the proper ways to administer and code. To avoid overpathologizing inferences, the international norms should be used instead of the standard CS norms, not just as is done in R-PAS but also by all CS users.

Giromini, Viglione, and McCullaugh (2015) demonstrated a similar point using a sample of 80 nonpatient protocols collected in San Diego using CS administration and coding guidelines. They used Bayesian statistics to determine the odds ratio associated with the probability of obtaining the San Diego mean scores under the hypothesis that they were a subsample of the CS norms versus the probability of obtaining the San Diego mean scores under the hypothesis they were a subsample of the international norms. In other words, they determined whether the San Diego data were more likely to belong to a population defined by CS norms or a population defined by the international norms. They restricted their analyses to 28 variables that differed notably between the two sets of norms, defined as a Cohen's d value of $|0.50|$ or more. The evidence indicated clearly that the San Diego sample most likely belonged to the international norms for 24 of the 28 variables. For the remaining four variables, neither normative sample provided a better fit. Of the 24 variables that were more likely to have come from a population defined by the international norms, 22 of them showed very strong evidence of belonging to the international norms rather than the CS norms. Even though one might assume that the San Diego sample would show a closer affinity to another U.S.-based sample than to an international standard, this was not the case. In addition, the CS norms made the San Diego nonpatients appear pathological on the same variables that the CS norms made the international sample of nonpatients appear pathological (Meyer, Shaffer et al., 2015).

Child and Adolescent Norms

Expanding on their adult norm study, Viglione and Giromini (2016) conducted a second study comparing (a) the pattern of differences in the CS norms and the international norms for youth to (b) the pattern of differences seen in the adult norms as summarized earlier. Using the same criteria as in the adult study, they identified 43 variables for the child and adolescent norms that differed notably across groups, which is considerably more than the 28 notable differences found with adults. Differences were much larger for FQ variables among youth then they were among adults. As with adults, using the traditional CS norms would result in more pathological interpretations for the nonpatient youths. Also, the pattern of differences was very similar in the youth and adult samples: The correlation between the Cohen's d values for the children and adolescents and the d values for the adults was 0.75, using absolute values, and 0.84, using signed values. Thus, as with adults, there is a similar foundation for needing new norms for children and adolescents.

With this in mind, transitional R-PAS norms for children and adolescents have been developed (Meyer, Viglione, & Giromini, 2014b).[2] These norms will be briefly summarized here; additional details are available at www.r-pas.org/ChildNorms.aspx. The norms make use of a sample of 346 youth protocols primarily from Brazil and the United States, though including some from Italy as well, ranging in age from 6 to 17. Gender was approximately evenly balanced, though sample size varied by age and by country. To anchor the developmental continuum, the R-PAS adult normative sample was used.

Because the individual, age-based subsamples are small in size, two statistical procedures were used to maximize the ability to detect genuine developmental changes. First, rather than estimating normative values by plotting mean scores in age-based bins or silos, continuous inferential norming was used to fit polynomial regression curves to the developmental data (Zachary & Gorsuch, 1985; Zhu & Chen, 2011), which allows all protocols across all ages to identify the most accurate and generalizable normative expectations. Inferential norming with samples of 50 per age group produce norms that are as accurate as norms produced the traditional way (i.e., mean scores calculated for specific ages) with samples of 200 per age group (Zhu & Chen, 2011). Second, because our samples were relatively small and thus affected by fairly substantial sampling error, which is the natural variability that causes the observed data values to depart from the true population values, bootstrap resampling procedures (Efron & Tibshirani, 1993; Howell, 2010) were used to create 100 alternative possible versions of the existing age-based data sets for each variable. These bootstrap samples show 100 equally likely versions of what each age-based sample could have looked like, and they show how much the sample estimate for a variable (e.g., the mean for Sy) could vary by chance alone.

Regression equations were then fit to predict means for all the variables on the Page 1 and Page 2 profiles from age using the linear, quadratic, and cubic functions of age (i.e., Age, Age2, and Age3) as the predictors entered sequentially on separate steps. After predicting the means for each variable, the same process was repeated to predict the standard deviations for each variable. The goal of these regression analyses was to find the best fitting linear or curvilinear model that made developmental sense. In the inferential norming literature, a key step is to review the alternative regression results both to see how much prediction increases when moving from a linear to a quadratic and then a cubic function and, most importantly, to see if the various alternative regression models make developmental sense. For the R-PAS norms, initial judgments about optimal fit were made by one researcher and then independently checked by two others, with disagreements resolved through discussion.

The resulting norms provide developmentally expected scores (i.e., *M*s and *SD*s) for each variable at each age from 6 to 17. For applied use, the age-based normative expectations are superimposed on the adult Profile Pages using overlays that illustrate the broad average range for a youngster of a particular age. These norms are transitional and will ultimately be replaced by larger age-based samples from multiple countries. However, for the time being, they provide reasonable, developmentally sensitive expectations for what youth see, say, and do when completing the task at various ages.

Form Quality

Before leaving the topic of norms, it is worth noting the R-PAS Form Quality tables. Although they do not constitute norms per se, they do establish empirically based standards for what are conventional and unconventional perceptions among adults. The Form Quality tables benefited from significant contributions from Japanese, Chinese, and Taiwanese data, along with data from Europe, West Asia, and North and South America.

Reliability

The type of reliability that is most commonly studied with Rorschach data is interrater reliability, which assesses the consistency of judgments or decisions across raters (Meyer, Viglione, & Giromini, 2014a). For the Rorschach, this type of reliability primarily concerns coding reliability. Because of its importance, Rorschach coding reliability has been studied regularly, and there are a number of meta-analyses summarizing this literature. Two of them were related studies addressing CS reliability (Meyer, 1997; Meyer, Hilsenroth et al., 2002), while others addressed individual variables such as Urist's (1977) Mutuality of Autonomy scale (Bombel, 2006; Bombel, Mihura, Meyer, & Katko, 2005), Elizur's Hostility score and Holt's Aggression variables (Katko, Meyer, Mihura, & Bombel, 2009), the Rorschach Prognostic Rating Scale (Meyer, 2004), and the Rorschach Oral Dependency scale (Meyer, 2004). Other summaries or aggregated interrater reliability studies have also been published (e.g., Gacono et al., 2005; Sahly, Shaffer, Erdberg, & O'Toole, 2011). Taken together, these data indicate that reasonably trained coders achieve good reliability, with average Pearson or intraclass correlations (ICCs) for summary scores above 0.85 and average kappa values for scores assigned to each response above 0.80.

Meyer (2004) compared Rorschach interrater reliability data to all other published meta-analyses of interrater reliability in psychology, psychiatry, and medicine, and the data showed it compared favorably to a wide range of other applied judgments. For instance, Rorschach coders agree more than supervisors evaluating the job performance of employees ($r = 0.57$), surgeons or nurses diagnosing breast abnormalities on a clinical exam (kappa = 0.52), and physicians evaluating the quality of medical care provided by their peers (kappa = 0.31). For many Rorschach variables, coding shows the same degree of reliability as when physicians measure the size of the spinal canal and spinal cord from MRI, CT, or X-ray scans ($r = 0.90$); dentists and dental personnel count decayed, filled, or missing teeth in early childhood (kappa = 0.79); or when physicians or nurses rate the degree of drug sedation for patients in intensive care (r = 0.91, ICC = 0.84). These data show that Rorschach coding for trained examiners is typically fairly straightforward and good agreement is attainable across different coders.

This finding is also consistent with the studies completed so far on the interrater reliability of R-PAS scores (Meyer et al., 2011; Viglione, Blume-Marcovici et al., 2012). Viglione, Blume-Marcovici et al. randomly selected 50 Rorschach records from ongoing research projects and investigated the protocol-level interrater reliability of 60 R-PAS variables found on the Page 1 and Page 2 interpretive profiles. The mean ICC was 0.88, and the median 0.92, indicating that the great majority of R-PAS codes had good to excellent interrater reliability. In the R-PAS manual, Meyer et al. provided interrater reliability data on the six codes that are new to R-PAS relative to the CS (Space Reversal, Space Integration, Aggressive Content, Oral Dependency Language, Mutuality of Autonomy Health, and Mutuality of Autonomy Pathology). Six raters each independently coded a set of 60 protocols from the R-PAS normative sample. The raters varied in their previous experience coding Rorschach protocols, ranging from being highly experienced to having coded just one protocol before the study began. However, all coders were applying the written R-PAS coding guidelines for the first time (and the final guidelines were improved and clarified by coding challenges they encountered). Across the six new codes, the average of the pairwise reliability coefficients was r = 0.83 and ICC = 0.81; as might be expected, for the three most experienced coders, the average ICC was higher at 0.86. In addition, the study developing the R-PAS Composite Scores showed that when compared to the three CS Constellation Indexes, the three R-PAS Composite Scores produced higher ICCs for interrater reliability in four datasets (Viglione et al., 2014). In 10 of the 12 comparisons, the R-PAS Composites were statistically significantly higher than the CS Constellations.

Several other findings from the literature are worth noting. Although they did not statistically compare CS to R-PAS variables, Dzamonja-Ignjatovic et al. (2013) found the R-PAS EII-3 (ICC = 0.96) had higher interrater reliability than the EII-2 (ICC = 0.94) used for the CS, while the TP-Comp from R-PAS and PTI from the CS had equivalently high reliability (ICC = 0.96) in a sample of 20 inpatient protocols. Moore et al. (2013) relied on draft versions of the R-PAS coding guidelines and had two independent coders evaluate 12 protocols from patients with diagnoses of schizophrenia or schizoaffective disorder. They examined four variables and found ICCs of 0.92 for the EII-2, 0.97 for Complexity, 0.89 for the Good Human Representation (GHR) minus Poor Human Representation (PHR) difference score, and 0.83 for the Mutuality of Autonomy Pathology Proportion (MAP/MAHP). Su et al. (2015) examined the reliability of variables to assess severity of disturbance using protocols that were administered and coded either according to R-PAS guidelines or CS guidelines. Their reliability coders worked with sequences of five protocols until a reasonable level of reliability was achieved. It took the two R-PAS coders 20 protocols to reach this level, and it took the CS coders 30 protocols to reach this standard. The ICCs for the R-PAS coders were as follows: FQ-% = 0.71, WD-% = 0.77, TP-Comp = 0.80, and EII-3 = 0.87. The ICCs for the CS coders on parallel variables were as follows: X-% = 0.82, WDA% = 0.78, PTI = 0.69, and EII-2 = 0.86.

Examining different types of variables, Charek, Meyer, and Mihura (2015) had three graduate student coders independently code 21 protocols. Two of the coders were applying R-PAS coding rules for the first time; one had prior experience coding several variables. Using percentage scores to control for slight differences in R in their main analyses, they found exact agreement ICCs across 11 variables ranged from a low of 0.71 (for Synthesis) to a high of 0.94 (for Sum of Human Content). The average ICC was 0.83, and the other variables considered were Synthetic Whole responses, Space Integration, Vagueness, Color Dominance Proportion, Weighted Sum of Color, Level Incongruous Combinations, Level 1 Fabulized Combinations, Personal Knowledge Justification, and Populars. Hsiao, Meyer, and Mihura (2015) used the same database of 21 protocols to document reliability for other variables, with reliability being good for Mutuality of Autonomy Health (MAH; ICC = 0.74) and Mutuality of Autonomy Pathology (MAP; ICC = 0.76) and excellent for Anatomy, Blood, Explosion, Fire, and Sex content (ICCs = 0.93, 1.0, 1.0, 0.83, and 0.83, respectively).

Taken together, the studies designed to systematically assess reliability and the focused investigations of reliability that have taken place within validity studies indicate R-PAS variables can be coded with good to excellent reliability. At the same time, however, there are challenges or difficulties associated with Rorschach coding. Several studies show how the reliabilities for low base rate variables are erratic (e.g., Acklin, McDowell, Verschell, & Chan, 2000; McGrath et al., 2005; Meyer, Hilsenroth et al., 2002; Viglione & Taylor, 2003; Viglione, Blume-Marcovici et al., 2012). Roughly speaking, low base rate variables occur on average no more than once per record (i.e., in < 5% of responses; e.g., sex, reflections, color without form) so that large samples are needed to accurately estimate their reliability. In addition, there are some more common codes that generally show lower reliability and thus appear to be more challenging to code accurately. These variables include differentiating among the subtypes of shading; the extent to which form is primary, secondary, or absent when coded in conjunction with color; classifying specific types of cognitive disorganization; and coding unusual Form Quality (Viglione & Meyer, 2008).

Forensic practitioners using R-PAS (or any system for Rorschach-based assessment) also need to realize that interrater reliability is not a fixed property of the scores or of a particular test manual. Rather, reliability is entirely dependent on the training, skill, and conscientiousness of the examiner. Thus repeated practice and calibration with criterion ratings are essential for good forensic practice.

Another issue is that most reliability research (for the Rorschach and for other instruments) relies on coders who work or train in the same setting. To the extent that local guidelines develop to contend with coding ambiguities, agreement among those who work or train together may be greater than agreement across sites or different workgroups. As a result, existing reliability data may then give an overly optimistic view of coding consistency across sites or across clinicians working independently. Another way to say this is that coding reliability (i.e., agreement among two fallible coders) may be higher than coding accuracy (i.e., correct coding).

This issue was examined for the CS. In a preliminary report of the data, Meyer et al. (2004) examined 40 randomly selected protocols from Exner's new CS nonpatient reference sample (Exner & Erdberg, 2005) and 40 protocols from Shaffer, Erdberg, and Haroian's (1999) nonpatient sample from Fresno, California. Then a third group of advanced graduate students, trained and supervised by Donald Viglione, blindly recoded the 80 protocols. To determine the degree of cross-site reliability, the original scores were compared to the second set of scores. The data revealed an across-site median ICC of 0.72 for summary scores. Although this would be considered "good" reliability according to established benchmarks, it is lower than the value of 0.85 or higher than typically has been generated by coders working together in the same setting.

Findings like this suggest ambiguities in the coding process that are not fully clarified in standard CS training materials (Exner, 2001, 2003). As a result, training sites, such as specific graduate programs, may develop guidelines or benchmarks for coding that help resolve these residual complexities. However, these principles may not generalize to other training sites. To minimize these problems, the R-PAS manual (Meyer et al., 2011) provides much more extensive coding guidelines than Exner, as well as 100 practice responses that are accompanied by an articulated rationale for challenging coding decisions. Thus one would anticipate that R-PAS coding should have less problematic variability across training sites than had been the case for the CS.

Construct Validity of Individual Variables

Application of Research with Previous Systems

One issue that has been raised about R-PAS is the extent to which earlier construct validity research completed with previous Rorschach systems generalizes to R-PAS. That is, is R-PAS different enough in its coding guidelines and administration procedures that it should be considered such a novel instrument that it cannot rely on previous research? This would apply to research from the CS as well as research for R-PAS variables that were not in the CS, such as Space Reversal, Oral Dependency Language, Mutuality of Autonomy, and Aggressive Content. There are several ways to consider this important issue.

First, from a coding perspective, the R-PAS definitions of variables are essentially the same as those used in previous systems. The benchmarks for coding these variables are elaborated more completely in R-PAS than in any previous system, and, with rare exception, they are designed again to target the original definitions while reducing the ambiguity that emerges in applied practice when coding guidelines are incomplete. The biggest change in the R-PAS coding guidelines relative to the CS was for the Art content code. Consistent with its interpretation as indicative of an intellectualized process, it is coded for artistic representations but no longer coded for simple responses of just "paint."

Second, R-PAS administration is different from the CS given its use of R-Optimized administration instructions. As described earlier, optimizing the range of responses was done to correct a known problem with the CS, in which it is not possible for the same norms to adequately apply to a 14-response protocol as to a 50- or 60-response protocol. But to what extent do the R-PAS changes in administration instructions influence the obtained data? The evidence indicates it has a minimal impact. When studies have randomly assigned adults and children to receive R-PAS administration, or early versions of R-Optimized administration, there are no replicable differences in mean scores across samples except for the intended effect of reducing variability in R and slightly increasing its mean by eliminating shorter, low-yield protocols (Dean et al., 2007; Meyer et al., 2011; Reese et al., 2014; Viglione et al., 2015).

It also is important to keep in mind that the CS itself was never a static system. It evolved and changed considerably over the years, and R-PAS extended that trajectory by bringing to fruition numerous projects that the Rorschach Research Council had worked on for years. For example, the original CS (Exner, 1974) did not have any scores to assess thought disorder, did not contain the FQu score, and it accepted fewer than 14 responses as a "valid" record. As noted before, between 1974 and 2003, the CS evolved in major ways, including revised norms for adults, new administration procedures that included what we now call "prompts" and "pulls," new administration procedures to eliminate "invalid" low R protocols, revised Form Quality tables and scores, revised coding guidelines, new norms for children and adolescents, revised interpretation strategies, and revised interpretative postulates for some variables, as well as additions of new codes and deletions of others. Most of these changes were based on data documenting the value of the change—either for correcting a known problem or for integrating something new into the system in order to enhance clinical practice. R-PAS continues this evolution of correcting known problems and incorporating new findings.

The situation with the introduction of R-PAS is similar to the situation in 1974 when Exner published his initial text for administering, scoring, and interpreting the Rorschach according to CS guidelines. As noted before, the CS drew together elements of five U.S.-based systems that had been in use at the time. These systems had disparate administration procedures, coded variables, coding guidelines for the same variables, summary scores, and interpretive postulates. His bringing together the best of these five systems, based on research evidence and clinical utility, is the root for the "comprehensive" term in the CS name. The evidence for the CS in 1974 was largely based on research that had been conducted with these earlier systems, and Exner continued to readily cite this evidence from other systems as support for the CS as late as 2003 (see also Exner, 1986, 1993). In fact, for many key variables, validity evidence from other systems remained the *only* published validity research that Exner cited. In particular, he never cited *any* published CS research for the following variables: AG, An + Xy, EB, FC: CF + C, M, Popular, Pure C, Space, SumH, Pure H, WSumC, and Zf.

Just as a new Rorschach system builds on older versions, so later versions of the MMPI and Wechsler intelligence and achievement tests share items with and rely on research from previous versions. Occasionally there are certain types of interpretations that cannot be applied to the new version of a test, such as the complications of applying the research on MMPI code types to the MMPI-2 code types, but typically validity research with test scales using the same or largely the same items—or even items of the same general kind, as is done with cognitive ability measures—are assumed to apply to subsequent versions of their parent tests.

Validity Meta-Analyses

Construct validity refers to evidence that a test scale is measuring what it is supposed to measure. It is determined by the aggregation of research findings related to both convergent and discriminant validity. Convergent validity refers to expected associations with criteria that theoretically should be related to the target construct, while discriminant validity refers to an expected lack of association with criteria that theoretically should be independent of the target construct. Evaluating the validity of a complex, multidimensional measure like the Rorschach is challenging, because it is difficult to systematically review the full historical pattern of evidence attesting to convergent and discriminant validity for every test score. Here we focus on results from meta-analytic reviews.

Thousands of studies from around the world have provided evidence addressing the validity of the Rorschach. Narrative summaries of the literature for specific variables has been provided in Bornstein and Masling (2005), Exner (2003), Exner and Erdberg (2005), and Viglione (1999). Recent meta-analyses include the comprehensive review of CS variables by Mihura et al. (2013, 2015), focused reviews on the EII by Diener et al. (2011), the Mutuality of Autonomy scale by Graceffo, Mihura, and Meyer (2014) and Monroe et al. (2013), and on the extent to which variables change as a function of treatment by Grønnerød (2004). Meyer and Archer (2001) summarized the evidence from Rorschach meta-analyses that were available at the time, including four that examined the global validity of the test and seven that examined the validity of specific scales in relation to particular criteria. The scales included CS and non-CS variables. For comparison, they also summarized the meta-analytic evidence available on the validity of the MMPI and IQ measures. Subsequently, Meyer (2004) compared the validity evidence for these psychological tests to meta-analytic findings for the medical assessments reported in Meyer, Finn et al. (2001).

Although the use of different types of research designs and validation tasks makes it challenging to compare findings across meta-analyses, the broad review of evidence yielded three primary conclusions. First, psychological and medical tests have varying degrees of validity, ranging from scores that are essentially unrelated to a particular criterion to scores that are strongly associated with relevant criteria. Second, it was difficult to distinguish between medical tests and psychological tests in terms of their average validity; both types of tests produced a wide range of effect sizes and had similar averages. Third, test validity is conditional and dependent on the criteria used to evaluate the instrument. For a given scale, validity is greater against some criteria and weaker against others.

Within these findings, validity for the Rorschach was much the same as it was for other instruments; effect sizes varied depending on the variables considered, but, on average, validity was similar to other instruments. For instance, Meyer and Archer (2001) found that across 523 hypothesized findings, the general validity for the Rorschach was 0.32 and across 533 hypothesized findings, the general validity for the MMPI was also 0.32. Similarly, when considering studies that were not confounded by method variance (Rorschach scores were not correlated with other Rorschach scores; the MMPI was not correlated with another self-report inventory), across 73 studies and 6,520 participants, the average validity for the Rorschach was 0.29, and across 85 studies and 15,985 participants the average validity for the MMPI was 0.29. Thus Meyer and Archer concluded that on average the systematically collected data showed the Rorschach produced good validity coefficients, on par with other tests:

> Across journal outlets, decades of research, aggregation procedures, predictor scales, criterion measures, and types of participants, reasonable hypotheses for the vast array of Rorschach ... scales that have been empirically tested produce convincing evidence for their construct validity.
>
> (p. 491)

Atkinson, Quarrington, Alp, and Cyr (1986) conducted one of the earliest global meta-analytic reviews of the Rorschach and found good evidence for its validity and similar to the validity for the MMPI (Atkinson, 1986). They noted that the test is regularly criticized and challenged despite the evidence attesting to its validity. To understand why, they suggested that "deprecation of the Rorschach is a sociocultural, rather than scientific, phenomenon" (p. 244). Viglione and Rivera (2012) have also addressed this sociopolitical perspective from a conceptual and historical viewpoint. Meyer and Archer (2001) reached a similar conclusion about the evidence base and concluded that a dispassionate review of the evidence would not warrant singling out the Rorschach for particular criticism. However, they also noted that the same evidence would not warrant singling out the Rorschach for particular praise. Its broadband validity appears both as good as and also as limited as that for other psychological tests.

Robert Rosenthal, a widely recognized and highly regarded expert in meta-analysis, was commissioned to conduct a comparative analysis of Rorschach and MMPI validity for a special issue of the journal *Psychological Assessment*. He and his co-authors (Hiller, Rosenthal, Bornstein, Berry, & Brunell-Neuleib, 1999; Rosenthal, Hiller, Bornstein, Berry, & Brunell-Neuleib, 2001) found that on average the Rorschach and MMPI were equally valid. However, they also identified moderators to validity for each instrument. Moderators are factors that influence the size of the validity coefficients observed across studies. The Rorschach demonstrated greater validity against criteria that they classified as objective, while the MMPI demonstrated greater validity against criteria consisting of other self-report scales or psychiatric diagnoses. The criteria they considered objective encompassed a range of variables that were largely behavioral events, medical conditions, behavioral interactions with the environment, or classifications that required minimal observer judgment, such as dropping out of treatment, history of abuse, number of driving accidents, history of criminal offenses, having a medical disorder, cognitive test performance, performance on a behavioral test of ability to delay gratification, or response to medication. Viglione (1999) conducted a systematic descriptive review of the Rorschach literature and similarly concluded that the Rorschach was validly associated with behavioral events or life outcomes involving person-environment interactions that emerge over time. In general, these findings are consistent with the types of spontaneous behavioral trends and longitudinally determined life outcomes that McClelland, Koestner, and Weinberger (1989) showed were best predicted by tests measuring implicit characteristics, as opposed to the conscious and deliberately chosen near-term actions that were best predicted by explicit self-report tests (also see Bornstein, 1998).

In a Rorschach meta-analysis that was not considered in the previous reviews, Grønnerød (2004) systematically summarized the literature examining the extent to which Rorschach variables could measure personality change as a function of psychological treatment. The Rorschach produced a level of validity that was equivalent to alternative instruments based on self-report or clinician ratings. Grønnerød also examined moderators to validity and, consistent with expectations from the psychotherapy literature, found that Rorschach scores changed more with longer treatment, suggesting that more therapy produced more healthy change in personality. Grønnerød also noted that effect sizes were smaller when Rorschach coders clearly did not know whether a protocol had been obtained before versus after treatment but larger in studies that clearly described coding reliability procedures and obtained good reliability results using conservative statistics.

Lastly, the most recent and extensive set of systematic reviews and meta-analyses of the Rorschach has been conducted by Mihura and colleagues (2013; also see Wood et al., 2015 for a challenge to these findings and the reply by Mihura et al., 2015). The authors systematically reviewed the Rorschach CS validity literature, addressing both externally assessed criteria such as psychiatric diagnoses or observer ratings, and introspectively assessed criteria based on self-report measures. Importantly, the previous meta-analytic reviews of the Rorschach focused on its global validity whereas Mihura and colleagues addressed the validity of individual scales. Out of an initial pool of 68 variables under consideration, 53 variables had sufficient relevant research to be considered in the analyses. The final meta-analytic sample drew on 1,156 validity coefficients, 215 independent samples, and 25,795 Rorschach records. Collapsing results across all variables, the mean *r* obtained against the externally assessed criteria was 0.27, an index of good validity support according to Hemphill's (2003) guidelines; the mean *r* using introspectively assessed criteria to provide validity was notably lower—equal to .008. These findings indicate that the Rorschach does not correlate with self-report instruments. However, because the Rorschach is a performance-based test, this result is not surprising, and it is also consistent with previous literature (e.g., Meyer et al., 2000; Viglione, 1999). Instead, the Rorschach contributes to the validity of clinical assessment by providing information from an assessment method that is entirely different from the self-report method. These findings also reveal that the average Rorschach validity effect size largely resembles that seen in meta-analytic reviews of the validity of other psychological assessment instruments, thus confirming again that previous concerns about the general validity of the Rorschach were unfounded. What this study added uniquely, however, was a meta-analytic review of each specific variable, allowing for a focused appraisal of which variables were and which were not working as expected.

The Rorschach variables demonstrating the strongest empirical support were those assessing thought disorder, impaired perceptual processes, psychological resources, cognitive complexity, emotional reactivity, potential suicide risk, implicit distress, mental agitation, morbid dysphoria, cooperative interpersonal interactions, and preoccupations with physical integrity or functioning. The least-supported variables were those with very low base rates or some of the scales recently developed for use in the CS but without a history in previous scoring systems. Out of the 53 variables under investigation, based on externally assessed criterion measures, 13 had excellent support, 17 had good support, 10 had modest support, 13 had little or no support, and 12 had no construct-relevant validity studies. For a further understanding of the methodology and the specific findings for each of the variables, forensic assessors should carefully consult this article.

Generally, variables with less empirical support were not included in R-PAS. Indeed, Mihura et al.'s (2013) meta-analytic validity review was a primary resource utilized by the R-PAS developers when selecting the final variables to be included in the system. Other selection criteria included (a) the extent to which each variable had a good response process foundation; (b) the perceived utility of each variable among clinicians, according to a survey of experienced practitioners; and (c) parsimony. Because of this selection process, one may anticipate that the global validity of R-PAS will be superior to that of the CS. For instance, initial data investigating the validity of R-PAS and CS equivalent measures of schizophrenia-spectrum symptoms and mental disturbance support this hypothesis. Specifically, in a sample of 90 patients and nonpatients from Taiwan, Su et al. (2015) showed that R-PAS variables yielded higher criterion-related validity coefficients in 16 out of 16 comparisons relative to comparable CS variables.

An interesting and important topic associated with the validity of the Rorschach task is the extent to which the support provided for certain variables in the empirical literature converges with the subjective experience of experienced practitioners about which variables work validly in clinical practice. Meyer et al. (2013) addressed this issue by surveying 246 experienced clinicians from 26 countries about their perceived sense of the clinical validity possessed by a large number of Rorschach scores. The aggregated responses from these clinicians could reliably differentiate the variables that were viewed as more valid from those viewed as less valid according to their experience. Importantly, these clinical judgments were not influenced by the findings obtained by Mihura et al.'s (2013) meta-analyses, because that meta-analytic review was not yet completed when the survey was conducted. As one might expect, given the empirical literature reviewed earlier, some of the Rorschach variables that clinicians perceived to be the most valid were measures of thinking disturbance and perceptual accuracy. Other highly rated variables were those related to responsiveness to color, attribution of human contents or movement, and both the comparison between color and human movement responses and the combination of these two variables. Perhaps more importantly, the rank correlation between the aggregated clinical ratings of perceived validity and the empirical validity results from Mihura et al.'s meta-analyses was 0.51. This is a large effect size, and it indicates that aggregated clinical judgments concerning the validity of individual Rorschach variables are strongly associated with the findings emerging from the empirical statistical literature. However, both sources diverge from the definitive source on CS validity, Exner's (2003) text, which essentially endorses the validity of all variables equally (the only exceptions were the Food content code and some equivocation on the Depression Index).

With respect to validity, forensic examiners should recognize how much systematic data has been collected and summarized for the Rorschach, whether using the CS or R-PAS. There is currently no other multiscale psychological test (either cognitive or personality test) with construct validity meta-analyses for so many of its scales. The MMPI-2-RF has no published construct validity meta-analyses for its clinical scales. There are two published meta-analyses for the MMPI or MMPI-2 clinical scales—one on the construct validity of its code types, finding a low effect size of $r = 0.07$ (N = 8,615; McGrath & Ingersoll, 1999a, 1999b), and another finding a medium effect size relationship for two of its depression scales (Scale 2 and DEP) in relation to a diagnosis of depression (Gross, Keyes, & Greene, 2000).

Because R-PAS based its selection of variables on the existing meta-analytic data, it is currently the only multiscale psychological test with published construct validity support for most of its individual scales. Consider just the key variables on Page 1 of the R-PAS output profile in the domains of Engagement and Cognitive Processing, Perception and Thinking Problems, Stress and Distress, and Self and Other Representations. Out of the 32 variables, 29 have published validity meta-analyses and two have meta-analyses that are currently being written for publication. The remaining variable without a meta-analysis is the Complexity score, which has meta-analyses supporting most of its constituent elements, but not the composite measure itself.

Recent R-PAS Validity Studies

In this section, we briefly describe several recent R-PAS research studies. We start with experimental studies and then discuss correlational studies.

Experimental Studies

Charek et al. (2015) examined the impact of ego depletion on a selected subset of Rorschach cognitive processing variables and self-reported affect states. A prominent theory of cognition, accompanied by considerable experimental support, posits that people have a finite pool of cognitive resources for complex mental processing. In addition, acts of effortful self-regulation temporarily deplete this pool of cognitive resources, which then means that performance on subsequent tasks requiring self-regulation are impaired. Charek et al. predicted that relative to a control group, participants who had undergone an ego-depleting letter cancellation task would have Rorschach protocols containing more spontaneous reactivity to color, less cognitive sophistication, and more frequent logical lapses in visualization, whereas self-reports would reflect greater fatigue and less attentiveness.

Their hypotheses were partially supported; despite a surprising absence of self-reported differences, ego-depleted participants had Rorschach protocols with lower scores on two variables indicative of sophisticated combinatory thinking (Synthetic Whole responses and Space Integration), as well as higher levels of color receptivity. The strongest effect was that the depleted participants had lower scores on a composite variable computed across all hypothesized markers of cognitive complexity.[3] Depletion did not affect three R-PAS variables that were hypothesized to be unrelated to cognitive complexity. In addition, baseline levels of self-reported achievement striving moderated the effect of the experimental manipulation on color receptivity. Participants who described themselves as high in achievement striving threw themselves more fully into the depleting tasks, showing higher levels of attentiveness. Subsequently, when completing the Rorschach, they were the ones most likely to mentally coast and provide less global synthetic processing and more color reactivity. This produced a clear interaction effect of achievement striving and the two conditions on color reactivity. As can be seen in Figure 2.1, those people with the highest levels of achievement striving are the least reactive to color in the Control condition. However, after putting greater effort into completing the cognitively depleting task, they are the most reactive to color in the Depletion condition. Overall, this study, though limited by a less potent experimental intervention than planned, provided clear support for SI, Sy with W, WSumC, and the overall degree of complexity that can be found in a protocol. It also indicated an alternative way to compute the Color Dominance Proportion and suggested potential refinements to the Complexity score.

Giromini et al. (2016) examined R-PAS variables in the Stress and Distress domain to determine whether they predicted increased sympathetic arousal during a laboratory, stress-inducing task. During an initial meeting (T1) 52 participants were administered the Rorschach task according to R-PAS guidelines; about one week later (T2), their

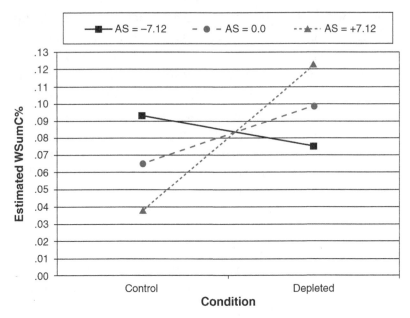

Figure 2.1: The interaction of Achievement Striving (AS) and Condition on Weighted Sum of Color: Simple slopes for Achievement Striving at its centered M and one SD below and above the M

Modified and adapted from Charek, D. B., Meyer, G. J., & Mihura, J. L., 2015. The impact of an ego depletion manipulation on performance-based and self-report assessment measures. *Assessment*. doi:10.1177/1073191115586580. Adapted with permission from SAGE Publications.

electrodermal activity (EDA) was recorded during exposure to a mild laboratory stress-inducing task. Based on literature indicating that exposure to stress and distress tends to increase physiological reactivity to stress, they anticipated that Stress and Distress variables measured at T1 would positively correlate with increased sympathetic reactivity to stress at T2, as indicated by greater electrodermal activity changes from baseline to stress. Results partially confirmed their hypotheses. Morbid Content and Vista both predicted subsequent stress reactivity with medium effect sizes; when both variables were averaged, together they generated a large effect size ($r = 0.50$) for predicting subsequent reactivity.

Hsiao et al. (2015) examined the impact of two brief film clips designed to influence mood and mental sets on R-PAS scores and self-reported experience. The study explored the Rorschach's ability to capture consciously recognized as well as implicitly experienced psychological states. A total of 76 participants were randomly assigned to watch one of the two films. One film clip featured a battle scene of violent aggression and the other clip a scene of compassion and sadness over loss. Both self-report and the Rorschach results indicated that participants watching the violent and aggressive scene had more varied reactions than those watching the compassion and loss scene. Furthermore, the participants who watched the violent and aggressive scene had elevated scores for Aggressive Movement, Aggressive Content, Morbid Content, and Critical Content% when compared to participants who watched the compassion and loss scene. Those who watched the compassion and loss scene, however, had notably lower scores on the Mutuality of Autonomy Pathology Proportion, indicating more positive interpersonal representations among people in that condition. Gender was found to be an important moderator of Aggressive Content, such that males watching the violent and aggressive scene had the highest amount of Aggressive Content and women watching the compassion and loss scene had the lowest amount of Aggressive Content in their protocols. Self-reported reactions showed an expected pattern for the compassion and loss condition, though in the violent condition surprise and pleasurable activation were present rather than the hostility and aggression originally predicted. Overall, the results of this study helped to document the validity of the Rorschach as a task that can capture the concerns and preoccupations on a person's mind, though it does not indicate how people consciously feel about those concerns or preoccupations.

Correlational Studies

In an important study examining the cross-cultural applicability of R-PAS relative to the CS, Su et al. (2015) addressed the validity of R-PAS and CS measures of psychotic characteristics and psychopathology severity in Taiwan using 75 psychiatric patients and 15 nonpatients. They also evaluated the incremental validity of R-PAS scores relative to parallel CS variables. All participants were given a standard R-PAS administration, and their resulting protocols were scored separately according to R-PAS guidelines and CS guidelines. The criterion variables consisted of two measures of general severity of disturbance and two measures of psychosis. The R-PAS scores FQ-%, WD-%, TP-Comp, and EII-3 validly assessed psychotic symptoms and psychopathology severity, producing large effect sizes ($M\ r$ = 0.49) and demonstrating the system's cultural and linguistic adaptability. Although CS scores also were valid, they produced lower effect sizes ($M\ r$ = 0.37), and hierarchical regression analyses demonstrated incremental validity for the R-PAS variables over their CS counterparts. These findings provide support for the belief that the revisions made to R-PAS enhance its psychometric properties relative to the CS. The findings also demonstrate that R-PAS can be used effectively outside the United States in a different language and culture.

Similar evidence was presented by Dzamonja-Ignjatovic et al. (2013) after examining severity of disturbance and psychosis markers from the CS and R-PAS in a sample of 211 Serbian inpatients (100 with schizophrenia and 111 with other diagnoses). They compared the PTI and the EII-2 from the CS with the revised versions of these scales in R-PAS, the TP-Comp and EII-3, with respect to their ability to differentiate the patients with diagnoses of schizophrenia from the remaining patients. Administration and coding followed CS guidelines, including the CS form quality tables. Like Su et al. (2015), Dzamonja-Ignjatovic et al. found all four scales to be valid, though the R-PAS scales were more valid (d values were: TP-Comp = 2.16 vs. PTI = 1.77, and EII-3 = 1.92 vs. EII-2 = 1.58) and had incremental validity over the CS scales, whereas the CS scales did not have incremental validity over the R-PAS scales. Overall, the results supported the use of TP-Comp to aid in the diagnosis of schizophrenia and supported the use of both the TP-Comp and EII-3 in a cross-national context, this time in Europe rather than Asia.

In another correlational study, Moore et al. (2013) used an early version of R-PAS to examine the role of R-PAS assessed thought disorder, psychological complexity, and interpersonal representations to predict functional capacity and social skills capacity in 72 older adult outpatients with schizophrenia. They also examined the ability of these R-PAS variable to explain functioning over and above neurocognitive impairment and negative symptoms. R-PAS complexity was correlated positively with functional capacity (r = 0.30) and social skills capacity (r = 0.34) and negatively with negative symptoms of schizophrenia (r = -0.31). The ability to predict functional capacity was maximized when complexity and the EII-2 were considered together, with higher complexity and lower EII-2 associated with more optimal functioning. Complexity also predicted functional capacity and social skills capacity over and above neurocognitive impairment and clinician-rated negative symptoms. In exploratory analyses, Moore et al. found that PHR and MAP were associated with the positive symptoms of schizophrenia, while healthy interpersonal representations as indexed by MAH, GHR, GHR−PHR, and the Non-Pure Human (NPH) Proportion were correlated with positive social skills (rs = |0.24 to 0.32|; with the NPH Proportion having a negative correlation, as expected). These data highlighted the important role that psychological complexity plays in contributing to functional limitations in schizophrenia, above and beyond the contributions of neuropsychological impairment and negative symptoms. In addition, they provide support for several R-PAS markers of healthy object relations functioning to play a role in everyday social functioning.

Psychometric Considerations Using R-PAS in Forensic Settings

Forensic Articles on R-PAS

A series of articles have appeared in the journal *Psychological Injury and Law* addressing the forensic use of R-PAS. Erard (2012) wrote the initial article, outlining the reasons why R-PAS based testimony should be admissible in state and federal court under either *Frye* or *Daubert* standards, despite R-PAS being a relatively new system for using the Rorschach. Erard also outlined a number of reasons why a forensic examiner would want to use the Rorschach in forensic practice and the advances that R-PAS brings to making Rorschach assessment even more fruitful for forensic practitioners. In terms of using the Rorschach, Erard noted the benefits of behaviorally assessing implicit characteristics as a complement to self-report, which is frequently biased positively or negatively, given the circumstances of the case. In terms of R-PAS benefits, Erard noted the norms that neither underestimate nor overestimate pathology, the optimized range of responding that virtually eliminates the CS challenge of having to re-administer the test due to a low number of responses, the ability to adjust for potential defensiveness via Complexity-Adjusted scores, the review of empirical evidence that led to the selection of R-PAS variables, the differentiation of R-PAS variables by their degree of empirical support, and the intuitive and easy to explain or understand profile pages of results. One could add to this list the interpretive narrative, which provides an in-depth understanding of each variable on the profile pages, along with interpretive postulates for the respondent based on their normative score.

Subsequently, Kvisto, Gacono, and Medoff (2013) and Gurley, Sheehan, Piechowski, and Gray (2014) took issue with a number of Erard's (2012) arguments, questioning whether there was a sufficient evidentiary foundation of psychometric support for R-PAS and sufficient general acceptance among psychologists for R-PAS-based testimony to meet either the *Daubert* or *Frye* criteria for admissibility. However, many of these authors' assertions about R-PAS research, the empirical literature, and the *Frye* and *Daubert* criteria were incorrect, as pointed out by Erard, Meyer, and Viglione (2014). Erard et al. also pointed out in particular how Gurley et al. failed to recognize that R-PAS was a replacement for the CS—one that corrected for known problems with the CS norms, with CS variability in R, and with CS variables that lacked sufficient empirical support for forensic use. Erard et al. noted that these problems with the CS were incapable of being fixed by the CS due to the fact that Exner's death in 2006 meant that the CS would be frozen in time with no way for it to address needed changes on its own.

Another forensically relevant R-PAS article was published by Erard and Viglione (2014). This article focuses specifically on the ways in which the Rorschach, and R-PAS in particular, can be of value for a forensic examiner performing child custody evaluations. R-PAS can reliably and validly help address relevant questions concerning parenting capacity and parental healthiness, as well as areas of concern in child functioning. R-PAS can be particularly helpful in these contexts given that it assesses strengths, resilience, and resources, as well as symptoms and problems.

What You Cannot Know Using R-PAS (or Other Rorschach Systems)

Although using the Rorschach in forensic work according to the R-PAS approach brings with it many benefits and assets, it also has some inherent limitations that are as important to keep in mind. Several key issues are highlighted here. We discuss them from the perspective of R-PAS, but they apply equally to the CS or any other Rorschach-based assessment system.

R-PAS Does Not Indicate the Emotions That a Person Consciously Feels

First, R-PAS codes are assigned to "responses" and behaviors observed in the microcosm of the inkblot task. The responses are attributions that the respondent makes to an external stimulus (see Bornstein, 2011, 2012). As a consequence of this, there is nothing in the database of what is traditionally coded on the Rorschach that indicates the emotions people *consciously* feel or even what they consciously think about themselves. As shown in Mihura and colleagues' (2013) meta-analyses, overall, the Rorschach shows minimal to no association ($r = 0.08$) with a person's self-reported conscious experiences. Although R-PAS considers multiple scores in the domain of Stress and Distress, it is important for forensic examiners to be clear that what is assessed here are implicit qualities, not conscious emotional experiences. Elevated scores in this domain on variables such as the Sum of Shading (YTVC') or inanimate movement (m) or Morbid content (MOR) indicate what respondents are carrying with them as they navigate their way through everyday life. But elevations do not say anything about how these facets of the person's experiential world get represented in conscious awareness. Thus it is not possible to say that a person *feels* affective discomfort based on an elevated YTVC', nor it is not possible to say that a person has dysphoric *feelings* based on an elevated number of MOR responses.

A good variable to consider in this regard is the Suicide Concern Composite (SC-Comp). No matter how elevated this score may be, it does not speak to the respondent's *conscious experience* of affective turmoil, oppositionality, despair, or hopelessness. It is an index of indirect markers that in combination have been linked to increased risk for serious self-harm. But it is silent on many key factors related to suicide risk, including the presence of suicidal ideation, intent, plan, means, rehearsal, reasons to live, sources of social support, and so on.

Most importantly, using different methods of assessment will result in different types of information for the assessor. We can never really know how it consciously feels to be anyone other than ourselves; to know how a person consciously feels at any moment we must ask him or her (i.e., a self-report method), although we also can help a person pay closer attention to experiences and better notice how they feel as a result of them. The strength of the Rorschach method is that, in contrast to the self-report method, it is a performance task that assesses what people do, not what they *say* they do. The Rorschach assesses *behavior*, not introspective reports of symptoms and experiences. Thus as shown in Mihura et al. (2013), Rorschach results correspond more closely to other external methods of assessing a person's behavior than they do to self-reported experiences.

R-PAS Findings Likely Correspond Better with Other External Methods of Assessment

As just mentioned, the Mihura et al. (2013, 2015) meta-analyses documented how Rorschach scores are more likely to correspond to externally assessed characteristics than to introspectively assessed characteristics. That is, what the examiner codes based on what the respondent sees, says, and does while completing the inkblot task is more likely to correspond to what other external assessors perceive the respondent to be like based on what the respondent sees, says, and does in everyday life than to what the respondent will say he or she is like when asked on interview or via a self-report inventory. One consequence of this for the forensic examiner is that she or he will often be faced with multimethod assessment data that do not fit together in a neat and tidy package. The task of the examiner is to synthesize and interpret information from multiple instruments and sources, keeping in mind the strengths and weaknesses of each (Mihura & Graceffo, 2014), to this particular individual in a more complete and multifaceted way. A benefit of such multimethod assessment is that with a valid understanding of both the respondent's self-attributions and also observations of what he or she sees, says, and does during the inkblot task, the examiner is uniquely qualified to help the respondent enhance self-awareness and grow as an individual. Although forensic assessments do not always provide an opportunity for personal feedback with the respondent, enhanced self-knowledge can be a positive by-product of a multimethod assessment with the Rorschach, even in the frequently adversarial context of forensic evaluation (see Evans, 2012; Smith & Evans, Chapter 9, this volume).

R-PAS Does Not Indicate the Specific Criteria Met for a Diagnosis

Finally, although it may go without saying, R-PAS data are not designed to make a formal diagnosis via the *Diagnostic and Statistical Manual* (DSM-5) or *International Classification of Diseases* (ICD-10). The data can certainly help inform thinking about diagnostic issues, but they cannot be used to make a diagnosis. A diagnosis requires knowledge of the person's history, which is not obtained from a Rorschach protocol, and often also requires knowledge of the person's subjective experience of symptoms, which is not obtained from a Rorschach protocol.

Final Thoughts

This chapter has provided an overview of the Rorschach Performance Assessment System. Hermann Rorschach introduced his inkblot "experiment" in 1921, and since that time numerous approaches to administering, scoring, and interpreting the test have been put forth in the United States and in other parts of the world. Some of these approaches had more empirical support than others. For many years, the CS was the approach that embodied the most comprehensive, standardized, reliable, and valid Rorschach practices. However, evidence began to accumulate suggesting that the CS had limitations in some key areas and that it would benefit from revision. Over the years that it met, Exner's Rorschach Research Council identified and began to work on many of these areas of limitation. Ultimately, however, when Exner passed away in 2006, he did not leave behind a mechanism for the Research Council to continue its work, and ultimately his heirs decided that the CS would not evolve further. This prompted four former members of the Research Council to continue their work by initiating a broad reformulation of the task, including its administration, coding, and interpretive procedures, in order to facilitate increased reliability, validity, and utility. Ultimately, with the help of a fifth collaborator, this resulted in the R-PAS manual being published in 2011. R-PAS is designed to appeal to new learners, though given its deep roots in the CS, seasoned forensic examiners accustomed to the CS should find the move to R-PAS to be a fairly easy one. Our hope is that this chapter provides readers with an evidence-based rationale for using the Rorschach in forensic practice and an evidence-based rationale for choosing R-PAS as the best-suited approach to using the Rorschach in practice.

Notes

1 Several sources have said that Rorschach's inkblots originally lacked variation in ink saturation or shading until mistakes were made during the printing process (Ellenberger, 1954; Exner, 1974; Kleiger, 1997). However, the early versions of the published cards that are stored at the Rorschach Archives and Museum contain considerable shading. Thus, while it is possible that the printing process accentuated these shading features (Exner, 2003), they were present at the outset and the printing process did not produce those effects.

2 Data and research contributions to these norms came from Ana Cristina Resende, Carla Hisatugo, Janell Crow, Daria Russo, and Jessica Swanson; scoring help came from Heidi Miller, Vanessa Laughter, and Andrew Williams.

3 Complexity and most other R-PAS variables were not coded in this database to reduce time demands.

References

Acklin, M. W., McDowell II, C. J., Verschell, M. S., & Chan, D. (2000). Interobserver agreement, intraobserver reliability, and the Rorschach comprehensive system. *Journal of Personality Assessment, 74,* 15-47. http://dx.doi.org/10.1207/S15327752JPA740103

Allen, J., & Dana, R. H. (2004). Methodological issues in cross-cultural and multicultural Rorschach research. *Journal of Personality Assessment, 82,* 189-206. http://dx.doi.org/10.1207/s15327752jpa8202_7

Anastasi, A., & Urbina, S. (1997). *Psychological testing* (7th ed.). Upper Saddle River, NJ: Prentice Hall/Pearson Education.

Atkinson, L. (1986). The comparative validities of the Rorschach and MMPI: A meta-analysis. *Canadian Psychology, 27,* 238-247. http://dx.doi.org/10.1037/h0084337

Atkinson, L., Quarrington, B., Alp, I. E., & Cyr, J. J. (1986). Rorschach validity: An empirical approach to the literature. *Journal of Clinical Psychology, 42,* 360-362. 10.1002/1097-4679(198603)42:2<360::AID-JCLP2270420225>3.0.CO;2-R

Bandura, A. (1954a). The Rorschach white space response and "oppositional" behavior. *Journal of Consulting Psychology, 18,* 17-21. http://dx.doi.org/10.1037/h0056911

Bandura, A. (1954b). The Rorschach white space response and perceptual reversal. *Journal of Experimental Psychology, 48,* 113-118. http://dx.doi.org/10.1037/h0063608

Beck, S. J., Beck, A. G., Levitt, E. E., & Molish, H. B. (1961). *Rorschach's test: I. Basic processes* (3rd ed.). New York: Grune & Stratton.

Blasczyk-Schiep, S., Kazén, M., Kuhl, J., & Grygielski, M. (2011). Appraisal of suicidal risk among adolescents and young adults through the Rorschach Test. *Journal of Personality Assessment, 93,* 518-526. http://dx.doi.org/10.1080/00223891.2011.594130

Bombel, G. (2006). *A meta-analysis of interrater scoring reliability for the Rorschach Mutuality of Autonomy (MOA) Scale* (Unpublished master's thesis). University of Toledo, Toledo, OH.

Bombel, G., Mihura, J. L., Meyer, G. J., & Katko, N. J. (2005, March). *A meta-analysis of scoring reliability with the Rorschach Mutuality of Autonomy (MOA) Scale.* Presented at the annual meeting of the Society for Personality Assessment, Chicago, IL.

Bornstein, R. F. (1995). Sex differences in objective and projective dependency tests: A meta-analytic review. *Assessment, 2,* 319-331. http://dx.doi.org/10.1177/1073191195002004003

Bornstein, R. F. (1996). Construct validity of the Rorschach Oral Dependency Scale: 1967-1995. *Psychological Assessment, 8,* 200-205. http://dx.doi.org/10.1037/1040-3590.8.2.200

Bornstein, R. F. (1998). Implicit and self-attributed dependency strivings: Differential relationships to laboratory and field measures of help seeking. *Journal of Personality and Social Psychology, 75,* 778-787. http://dx.doi.org/10.1037/0022-3514.75.3.778

Bornstein, R. F. (2011). Toward a process-focused model of test score validity: Improving psychological assessment in science and practice. *Psychological Assessment, 23*, 532–544. http://dx.doi.org/10.1037/a0022402

Bornstein, R. F. (2012). Rorschach score validation as a model for 21st-century personality assessment. *Journal of Personality Assessment, 94*, 26–38. http://dx.doi.org/10.1080/00223891.2011.627961

Bornstein, R. F., & Masling, J. M. (Eds.). (2005). *Scoring the Rorschach: Seven validated systems*. Mahwah, NJ: Lawrence Erlbaum Associates.

Camara, W. J., Nathan, J. S., & Puente, A. E. (2000). Psychological test usage: Implications in professional psychology. *Professional Psychology: Research and Practice, 31*, 141–154. doi:10.1037/0735-7028.31.2.141

Charek, D. B., Meyer, G. M., & Mihura, J. L. (2015, online first). The impact of an ego depletion manipulation on performance-based and self-report assessment measures. *Assessment*. doi:10.1177/1073191115586580

Cronbach, L. J. (1949). Statistical methods applied to Rorschach scores: A review. *Psychological Bulletin, 46*, 393–429. http://dx.doi.org/10.1037/h0059467

Cronbach, L. J. (1990). *Essentials of psychological testing* (5th ed.). New York: Harper Collins Publishers.

Dawes, R. M. (1999). Two methods for studying the incremental validity of a Rorschach variable. *Psychological Assessment, 11*, 297–302. http://dx.doi.org/10.1037/1040-3590.11.3.297

Dean, K. L., Viglione, D. J., Perry, W., & Meyer, G. J. (2007). A method to optimize the response range while maintaining Rorschach Comprehensive System validity. *Journal of Personality Assessment, 89*, 149–161. doi:10.1080/00223890701468543.

Dean, K. L., Viglione, D. J., Perry, W., & Meyer, G. J. (2008). Correction to: "A method to optimize the response range while maintaining Rorschach Comprehensive System validity." *Journal of Personality Assessment, 90*, 204. doi:10.1080/00223890701845542

De Koninck, J. M., & Crabbe-Decleve, G. (1971). Field dependence and Rorschach white-space figure-ground reversal responses. *Perceptual and Motor Skills, 33*, 1191–1194. http://dx.doi.org/10.2466/pms.1971.33.3f.1191

Diener, M. J., Hilsenroth, M. J., Shaffer, S. A., & Sexton, J. E. (2011). A meta-analysis of the relationship between the Rorschach Ego Impairment Endex (EII) and psychiatric severity. *Clinical Psychology & Psychotherapy, 18*, 464–485. http://dx.doi.org/10.1002/cpp.725

Dumitrascu, N., Mihura, J. L., Meyer, G. J., & Onofrei, C. (2011, March 12). Selected R-PAS variables and their relationship to level of education. In G. Bombel (Chair), *Recent Rorschach Research*. Boston, MA: Symposium presented at the annual meeting of the Society for Personality Assessment.

Dutta, R., Greene, T., Addington, J., McKenzie, K., Phillips, M., & Murray, R. M. (2007). Biological, life course, and cross-cultural studies all point toward the value of dimensional and developmental ratings in the classification of psychosis. *Schizophrenia Bulletin, 33*, 868–876. doi:10.1093/schbul/sbm059

Dzamonja-Ignjatovic, T., Smith, B. L., Djuric Jocic, D., & Milanovic, M. (2013). A comparison of new and revised Rorschach measures of schizophrenic functioning in a Serbian clinical sample. *Journal of Personality Assessment, 95*, 471-478. http://dx.doi.org/10.1080/00223891.2013.810153

Efron, B., & Tibshirani, R. T. (1993). *An introduction to the bootstrap*. New York: Chapman & Hall.

Ellenberger, H. (1954). The life and work of Hermann Rorschach (1884-1922). *Bulletin of the Menninger Clinic, 18*, 173-219.

Erard, R. E. (2012). Expert testimony using the Rorschach Performance Assessment System in psychological injury cases. *Psychological Injury and Law, 5*, 122-134. http://dx.doi.org/10.1007/s12207-012-9126-7

Erard, R. E., Meyer, G. J., & Viglione, D. J. (2014). Setting the record straight: Comment on Gurley, Sheehan, Piechowski, and Gray (2014) on the admissibility of the Rorschach Performance Assessment System (R-PAS) in court. *Psychological Injury and Law, 7*, 165-177. doi:10.1007/s12207-014-9195-x

Erard, R. E., & Viglione, D. J. (2014). The Rorschach Performance Assessment System (R-PAS) in child custody evaluations. *Journal of Child Custody: Research, Issues, and Practices, 11*, 159-180. http://dx.doi.org/10.1080/15379418.2014.943449

Evans, F. B. (2012). Therapeutic assessment alternative to custody evaluation: An adolescent whose parents could not stop fighting. In S. E. Finn, C. T. Fischer, & L. Handler (Eds.), *Collaborative/Therapeutic Assessment: A case book and guide* (pp. 357-378). New York: Wiley.

Exner, J. E. (1974). *The Rorschach: A Comprehensive System, Vol. 1: Basic foundations*. New York: Wiley.

Exner, J. E. (1986). *The Rorschach: A Comprehensive System, Vol. 1: Basic foundations* (2nd ed.). New York: Wiley & Sons.

Exner, J. E. (1991). *The Rorschach: A Comprehensive System, Vol. 2: Interpretation*. (2nd ed.). New York: Wiley.

Exner, J. E. (1993). *The Rorschach: A Comprehensive System, Vol. 1: Basic foundations* (3rd ed.). New York: Wiley.

Exner, J. E. (1996a, August 15). *1996 Alumni Newsletter*. Asheville, NC: Rorschach Workshops.

Exner, J. E. (1996b). Critical bits and the Rorschach response process. *Journal of Personality Assessment, 67*, 464-477.

Exner, J. E. (1997, July 7). Rorschach workshops and the future. *1997 Alumni Newsletter*. Asheville, NC: Rorschach Workshops.

Exner, J. E. (2001). *A Rorschach workbook for the Comprehensive System* (5th ed.). Asheville, NC: Rorschach Workshops.

Exner, J. E. (2003). *The Rorschach: A Comprehensive System, Vol. 1: Basic Foundations* (4th ed.). Hoboken, NJ: Wiley.

Exner, J. E., Jr. (2007). A new U.S. adult nonpatient sample. *Journal of Personality Assessment, 89*, S154-S158. http://dx.doi.org/10.1080/00223890701583523

Exner, J. E., Jr., & Erdberg, P. (2005). *The Rorschach: A comprehensive system. Vol. 2. Advanced interpretation* (3rd ed.). Hoboken, NJ: John Wiley.

Fowler, J. C., Piers, C., Hilsenroth, M. J., Holdwick, D. J., Jr., & Padawer, J. R. (2001). The Rorschach suicide constellation: Assessing various degrees of lethality. *Journal of Personality Assessment, 76*(2), 333-351. http://dx.doi.org/10.1207/S15327752JPA7602_13

Gacono, C. B., Bannatyne-Gacono, L., Meloy, J. R., & Baity, M. R. (2005). The Rorschach Extended Aggression Scores. *Rorschachiana, 27*, 164-190. http://dx.doi.org/10.1027/1192-5604.27.1.164

Gacono, C. B., & Evans, F. B. (Eds.). (2008). *The handbook of forensic Rorschach assessment* (N. Kaser-Boyd & L. A. Gacono, Collaborators). New York: Routledge/Taylor & Francis Group.

Ganellen, R. J. (1994). Attempting to conceal psychological disturbance: MMPI defensive response sets and the Rorschach. *Journal of Personality Assessment, 63*, 423-437. http://dx.doi.org/10.1207/s15327752jpa6303_3

Garb, H. N. (1999). Call for a moratorium on the use of the Rorschach Inkblot Test in clinical and forensic settings. *Assessment, 6*, 313-317. http://dx.doi.org/10.1177/107319119900600402

Gibby, R. G., & Stotsky, B. A. (1953). The relation of Rorschach free association to inquiry. *Journal of Consulting Psychology, 17*, 359-364. http://dx.doi.org/10.1037/h0056821

Giromini, L., Ando, A., Morese, R., Salatino, A., Di Girolamo, M., Viglione, D. J., & Zennaro, A. (2016). *Rorschach Performance Assessment System (R-PAS) and vulnerability to stress: A preliminary study on electrodermal activity during stress.* Manuscript submitted for publication.

Giromini, L., Viglione, D. J., & McCullaugh, J. (2015). Introducing a Bayesian approach to determining degree of fit with existing Rorschach norms. *Journal of Personality Assessment, 97*, 354-363. doi:10.1080/00223891.2014.959127

Graceffo, R. A., Mihura, J. L., & Meyer, G. J. (2014). A meta-analysis of an implicit measure of personality functioning: The mutuality of autonomy scale. *Journal of Personality Assessment, 96*, 581-595. doi:10.1080/00223891.2014.919299

Grønnerød, C. (2004). Rorschach assessment of changes following psychotherapy: A meta-analytic review. *Journal of Personality Assessment, 83*, 256-276. http://dx.doi.org/10.1207/s15327752jpa8303_09

Gross, A., Newton, R. R., & Brooks, R. B. (1990). Rorschach responses in healthy, community dwelling older adults. *Journal of Personality Assessment, 55*(1-2), 335-343. 10.1207/s15327752jpa5501&2_30

Gross, K., Keyes, M. D., & Greene, R. L. (2000). Assessing depression with the MMPI and MMPI-2. *Journal of Personality Assessment, 75*, 464-477. doi:http://dx.doi.org/10.1207/S15327752JPA7503_07

Groth-Marnat, G. (2009). The five assessment issues you meet when you go to heaven. *Journal of Personality Assessment, 91*(4), 303-310. http://dx.doi.org/10.1080/00223890902935662

Gurley, J. R., Sheehan, B. L., Piechowski, L. D., & Gray, J. (2014). The admissibility of the R-PAS in court. *Psychological Injury and Law, 7*, 9-17. doi:10.1007/s12207-014-9182-2

Hemphill, J. F. (2003). Interpreting the magnitudes of correlation coefficients. *American Psychologist, 58*, 78-79. http://dx.doi.org/10.1037/0003-066X.58.1.78

Hertz, M. R. (1970). *Frequency tables for scoring Rorschach responses with code charts, normal and rare details, F+ and F- responses, and popular and original responses* (5th ed.). Cleveland, OH: The Press of Case Western Reserve University.

Hiller, J. B., Rosenthal, R., Bornstein, R. F., Berry, D. T. R., & Brunell-Neuleib, S. (1999). A comparative meta-analysis of Rorschach and MMPI validity. *Psychological Assessment, 11*, 278–296. http://dx.doi.org/10.1037/1040-3590.11.3.278

Hilsenroth, M. J., Eudell-Simmons, E. M., DeFife, J. A., & Charnas, J. W. (2007). The Rorschach Perceptual-Thinking Index (PTI): An examination of reliability, validity, and diagnostic efficiency. *International Journal of Testing, 7*(3), 269–291. http://dx.doi.org/10.1080/15305050701438033

Hopwood, C. J., & Bornstein, R. F. (Eds.). (2014). *Multimethod clinical assessment*. New York: Guilford Press.

Hopwood, C. J., Morey, L. C., Rogers, R., & Sewell, K. (2007). Malingering on the Personality Assessment Inventory: Identification of specific feigned disorders. *Journal of Personality Assessment, 88*, 43–48. http://dx.doi.org/10.1207/s15327752jpa8801_06

Howell, D. C. (2010). *Statistical Methods for Psychology* (8th ed.). Belmont, CA: Wadsworth, Cengage Learning.

Hsiao, W.-C., Meyer, G. J., & Mihura, J. L. (2015). *The impact of film-based cognitive-affective priming on self-reported experience and Rorschach imagery*. Unpublished manuscript.

Jensen, A. R. (1965). Review of the Rorschach Inkblot Test. In O. K. Buros (Ed.), *The sixth mental measurements yearbook* (pp. 501–509). Highland Park, NJ: Gryphon.

Jørgensen, K., Andersen, T. J., & Dam, H. (2000). The diagnostic efficiency of the Rorschach Depression Index and the Schizophrenia Index: A review. *Assessment, 7*, 259–280. http://dx.doi.org/10.1177/107319110000700306

Jørgensen, K., Andersen, T. J., & Dam, H. (2001). The diagnostic efficiency of the Rorschach depression index and the Schizophrenia Index: A review: Erratum. *Assessment, 8*, 355. http://dx.doi.org/10.1177/107319110100800311

Katko, N. J., Meyer, G. J., Mihura, J. L., & Bombel, G. (2009). The interrater reliability of Elizur's hostility systems and Holt's aggression variables: A meta-analytical review. *Journal of Personality Assessment, 91*, 357–364. doi:10.1080/00223890902936116

Katko, N. J., Meyer, G. J., Mihura, J. L., & Bombel, G. (2010). A principal components analysis of Rorschach aggression and hostility variables. *Journal of Personality Assessment, 62*, 594–598. doi:10.1080/00223890902936116

Kleiger, J. H. (1997). Rorschach shading responses: From a printer's error to an integrated psychoanalytic paradigm. *Journal of Personality Assessment, 69*, 342–364. http://dx.doi.org/10.1207/s15327752jpa6902_7

Kleiger, J. H. (1999). *Disordered thinking and the Rorschach*. Hillsdale, NJ: Analytic Press.

Koonce, E. A., Meyer, G. J., & Viglione, D. J. (2008, March 28). The Rorschach research council inquiry guidelines project. In D. J. Viglione & G. J. Meyer (Co-Chairs). *Research to Enhance the Rorschach*. Symposium presented at the annual meeting of the Society for Personality Assessment, New Orleans, LA.

Kvisto, A. J., Gacono, C., & Medoff, D. (2013). Does the R-PAS meet standards for forensic use? Considerations with introducing a new Rorschach coding system. *Journal of Forensic Psychology Practice, 13*, 389–410. http://dx.doi.org/10.1080/15228932.2013.838106

Lilienfeld, S. O., Wood, J. M., & Garb, H. N. (2000). The scientific status of projective techniques. *Psychological Science in the Public Interest, 1*, 27–66. http://dx.doi.org/10.1111/1529-1006.002

Lunazzi, H. A., Urrutia, M. I., García de la Fuente, M., Elías, D., Fernández, F., De La Fuente, S., Bianco, A. S., & Sarachu, A. (2011). *Is Form Quality (FQ) a cultural context related variable? Presentation of the Argentinean FQ Tables*. Unpublished manuscript.

Lundbäck, E., Forslund, K., Rylander, G., Jokinen, J., Nordström, P., Nordström, A.-L., & Åsberg, M. (2006). CSF 5-HIAA and the Rorschach test in patients who have attempted suicide. *Archives of Suicide Research, 10*, 339–345. doi:10.1080/13811110600790942

Markon, K. E., Chmielewski, M., & Miller, C. J. (2011). The reliability and validity of discrete and continuous measures of psychopathology: A quantitative review. *Psychological Bulletin, 137*, 856–879. http://dx.doi.org/10.1037/a0023678

Mattlar, C.-E. (2011). *The issue of an evolutionary development of the Rorschach Comprehensive System (RCS) versus a revolutionary change (R-PAS)*. Retrieved from http://www.rorschachtraining.com/category/articles/

McClelland, D. C., Koestner, R., & Weinberger, J. (1989). How do self-attributed and implicit motives differ? *Psychological Review, 96*, 690–702. http://dx.doi.org/10.1037/0033-295X.96.4.690

McGrath, R. E., & Ingersoll, J. (1999a). Writing a good cookbook: I. A review of MMPI high-point code system studies. *Journal of Personality Assessment, 73*, 149–178. doi:10.1207/S15327752JPA7302_1

McGrath, R. E., & Ingersoll, J. (1999b). Writing a good cookbook: II. A synthesis of MMPI high-point code system study effect sizes. *Journal of Personality Assessment, 73*, 179–198. doi:10.1207/S15327752JPA7302_2

McGrath, R. E., Pogge, D. L., Stokes, J. M., Cragnolino, A., Zaccario, M., Hayman, J., . . . Wayland-Smith, D. (2005). Field reliability of comprehensive system scoring in an adolescent inpatient sample. *Assessment, 12*, 199–209. http://dx.doi.org/10.1177/1073191104273384

Meloy, J. R. (2008). The authority of the Rorschach: An update. In C. B. Gacono & F. B. Evans (Eds.), *The handbook of forensic Rorschach assessment* (pp. 79–87). New York: Routledge/Taylor & Francis Group.

Meloy, J. R., Hansen, T. L., & Weiner, I. B. (1997). Authority of the Rorschach: Legal citations during the past 50 years. *Journal of Personality Assessment, 69*, 53–62. http://dx.doi.org/10.1207/s15327752jpa6901_3

Meyer, G. J. (1992). Response frequency problems in the Rorschach: Clinical and research implications with suggestions for the future. *Journal of Personality Assessment, 58*, 231–244. doi:10.1207/s15327752jpa5802_2

Meyer, G. J. (1993). The impact of response frequency on the Rorschach constellation indices and on their validity with diagnostic and MMPI-2 criteria. *Journal of Personality Assessment, 60*, 153–180. doi:10.1207/s15327752jpa6001_13

Meyer, G. J. (1997). On the integration of personality assessment methods: The Rorschach and MMPI. *Journal of Personality Assessment, 68,* 297-330. doi:10.1207/s15327752jpa6802_5

Meyer, G. J. (1999). The convergent validity of MMPI and Rorschach Scales: An extension using profile scores to define response and character styles on both methods and a reexamination of simple Rorschach response frequency. *Journal of Personality Assessment, 72,* 1-35. doi:10.1207/s15327752jpa7201_1

Meyer, G. J. (2001). Evidence to correct misperceptions about Rorschach norms. *Clinical Psychology: Science and Practice, 8,* 389-396. doi:10.1093/clipsy.8.3.389

Meyer, G. J. (2002a, September 11). A preliminary report on efforts to measure the quality of Rorschach CS administration. In Viglione, D. J., Jr. (chair), *Update from the Rorschach Research Council for the Comprehensive System.* Symposium presented at the XVIIth Congress of the International Rorschach Society, Rome, Italy.

Meyer, G. J. (2002b). Exploring possible ethnic differences and bias in the Rorschach Comprehensive System. *Journal of Personality Assessment, 78,* 104-129. doi:10.1207/S15327752JPA7801_07

Meyer, G. J. (2002c, March 22). Issues for understanding normative standards and potential changes over time. In R. Ganellen (chair), *Norms for the Comprehensive System: Standards and evidence.* San Antonio, TX: Symposium presented at the annual meeting of the Society for Personality Assessment.

Meyer, G. J. (2004). The reliability and validity of the Rorschach and TAT compared to other psychological and medical procedures: An analysis of systematically gathered evidence. In M. Hilsenroth & D. Segal (Eds.), *Personality assessment.* Vol. two in M. Hersen (Ed.-in-Chief), *Comprehensive handbook of psychological assessment* (pp. 315-342). Hoboken, NJ: John Wiley & Sons.

Meyer, G. J., & Archer, R. P. (2001). The hard science of Rorschach research: What do we know and where do we go? *Psychological Assessment, 13,* 486-502. doi:10.1037/1040-3590.13.4.486

Meyer, G. J., Caracena, P., Shaffer, T. W., & Erdberg, P. (2002, March 23). Efforts to examine the quality of protocol administration in the Fresno and Rorschach Workshop nonpatient samples. Paper presented at the annual meeting of the Society for Personality Assessment, San Antonio, TX. Paper presented at the annual meeting of the Society for Personality Assessment, San Antonio, TX.

Meyer, G. J., Erdberg, P., & Shaffer, T. W. (2007). Toward international normative reference data for the Comprehensive System. *Journal of Personality Assessment, 89,* S201-S216. doi:10.1080/00223890701629342

Meyer, G. J., Finn, S. E., Eyde, L., Kay, G. G., Moreland, K. L., Dies, R. R., Eisman, E. J., Kubiszyn, T. W., & Reed, G. M. (2001). Psychological testing and psychological assessment: A review of evidence and issues. *American Psychologist, 56,* 128-165. doi:10.1037/0003-066X.56.2.128

Meyer, G. J., Giromini, L., Viglione, D. J., Reese, J. B., & Mihura, J. L. (2015). The association of gender, ethnicity, age, and education with Rorschach scores. *Assessment, 22,* 46-64. doi:10.1177/1073191114544358

Meyer, G. J., Hilsenroth, M. J., Baxter, D., Exner Jr., J. E., Fowler, J. C., Piers, C. C., & Resnick, J. (2002). An examination of interrater reliability for scoring the Rorschach Comprehensive System in eight data sets. *Journal of Personality Assessment, 78,* 219-274. doi:10.1207/S15327752JPA7802_03

Meyer, G. J., Hsiao, W., Viglione, D. J., Mihura, J. L., & Abraham, L. M. (2013). Rorschach scores in applied clinical practice: A survey of perceived validity by experienced clinicians. *Journal of Personality Assessment, 95,* 351-365. doi:10.1080/00223891.2013.770399

Meyer, G. J., Riethmiller, R. J., Brooks, R. D., Benoit, W. A., & Handler, L. (2000). A replication of Rorschach and MMPI-2 convergent validity. *Journal of Personality Assessment, 74,* 175-215. doi:10.1207/S15327752JPA7402_3

Meyer, G. J., Shaffer, T. W., Erdberg, P., & Horn, S. L. (2015). Addressing issues in the development and use of the Composite International Reference Values as Rorschach norms for adults. *Journal of Personality Assessment, 97,* 330-347. doi:10.1080/00223891.2014.961603

Meyer, G. J., & Viglione, D. J. Jr. (2005, March 2). *An overview of current evidence on the reliability, validity, and utility of the Rorschach.* Workshop presented at the annual meeting of the Society for Personality Assessment, Chicago, IL.

Meyer, G. J., & Viglione, D. J. Jr. (2006, March 23). *The influence of R, Form%, R-Engagement, and Complexity on interpretive benchmarks for Comprehensive System variables.* Paper presented at the annual meeting of the Society for Personality Assessment, San Diego, CA.

Meyer, G. J., Viglione, D. J. Jr., Erdberg, P., Exner, J. E., Jr., & Shaffer, T. (2004, March 11). *CS scoring differences in the Rorschach Workshop and Fresno nonpatient samples.* Paper presented at the annual meeting of the Society for Personality Assessment, Miami, FL.

Meyer, G. J., Viglione, D. J. Jr., & Exner Jr., J. E. (2001). Superiority of Form% over Lambda for research on the Rorschach Comprehensive System. *Journal of Personality Assessment, 76,* 68-75. doi:10.1207/S15327752JPA7601_4

Meyer, G. J., Viglione, D. J., Exner, J. E., Hilsenroth, M. E., Fowler, J. C., Shaffer, T. W., Erdberg, P., & Caracena, P. (2003, March 22). An update on efforts to measure the quality of Rorschach CS inquiry. In Erdberg, P. (chair), *Rorschach Comprehensive System: An update on methods, nonpatient sample, and new variables.* San Francisco, CA: Symposium presented at the annual meeting of the Society for Personality Assessment.

Meyer, G. J., Viglione, D. J., & Giromini, L. (2014a). An introduction to Rorschach assessment. In R. P. Archer and S. R. Smith (Eds.), *Personality Assessment* (2nd ed., pp. 301-369). New York: Routledge.

Meyer, G. J., Viglione, D. J., & Giromini, L. (2014b). *Current R-PAS transitional child and adolescent norms.* Retrieved from the Rorschach Performance Assessment System website: http://www.r-pas.org/CurrentChildNorms.aspx

Meyer, G. J., Viglione, D. J., Mihura, J. L., Erard, R. E., & Erdberg, P. (2011). *Rorschach performance assessment system: Administration, coding, interpretation, and technical manual.* Toledo, OH: Rorschach Performance Assessment System, LLC.

Mihura, J. L. (2012). The necessity of multiple test methods in conducting assessments: The role of the Rorschach and self-report. *Psychological Injury and Law, 5,* 97-106. doi:10.1007/s12207-012-9132-9

Mihura, J. L., & Graceffo, R. A. (2014). Multimethod assessment and treatment planning. In C. J. Hopwood & R. F. Bornstein (Eds.), *Multimethod clinical assessment* (pp. 285-318). New York: Guilford Press.

Mihura, J. L., Meyer, G. J., Bombel, G., & Dumitrascu, N. (2015). Standards, accuracy, and questions of bias in Rorschach meta-analyses: Reply to Wood, Garb, Nezworski, Lilienfeld, and Duke (2015). *Psychological Bulletin, 141*, 250-260. http://dx.doi.org/10.1037/a0038445

Mihura, J. L., Meyer, G. J., Dumitrascu, N., & Bombel, G. (2013). The validity of individual Rorschach variables: Systematic reviews and meta-analyses of the comprehensive system. *Psychological Bulletin, 139*, 548-605. doi:10.1037/a0029406

Miralles Sangro, F. (1996). *Rorschach: Tablas de localización y calidad formal en una muestra española de 470 sujetos [Rorschach: Tables of location and form quality in a Spanish sample of 470 subjects]*. Madrid: Universidad Pontificia Comillas.

Miralles Sangro, F. (1997). Location tables, form quality, and popular responses in a Spanish sample of 470 subjects. *Rorschachiana, 22*, 38-66. doi:http://dx.doi.org/10.1027/1192-5604.22.1.38

Monroe, J. M., Diener, M. J., Fowler, J. C., Sexton, J. E., & Hilsenroth, M. J. (2013). Criterion validity of the Rorschach Mutuality of Autonomy (MOA) scale: A meta-analytic review. *Psychoanalytic Psychology, 30*, 535-566. http://dx.doi.org/10.1037/a0033290

Moore, R. C., Viglione, D. J., Rosenfarb I. S., Patterson, T. L., & Mausbach B. T. (2013). Rorschach measures of cognition relate to everyday and social functioning in schizophrenia. *Psychological Assessment, 25*, 253-263. doi:10.1037/a0030546

Nascimento, R. S. G. F. (2004). The impact of education and/or socioeconomic conditions on Rorschach data in a Brazilian nonpatient sample. *Rorschachiana, 26*, 45-62. http://dx.doi.org/10.1027/1192-5604.26.1.45

Nelson, W. D. (1954). *An evaluation of the white space response on the Rorschach as figure-ground reversal and intellectual opposition*. (Unpublished doctoral dissertation). Michigan State University, East Lansing, MI.

Parisi, S., Pes, P., & Cicioni, R. (2005). *Tavole di localizzazione Rorschach, Volgari ed R+ statistiche [Rorschach location tables, Popular and R+ statistics]*. Arcene, Beragamo, Italy: Disponibili Presso l'Istituto.

Pertchik, K., Shaffer, T. W., Erdberg, P., & Margolin, D. I. (2007). Rorschach comprehensive system data for a sample of 52 older adult nonpatients from the United States. *Journal of Personality Assessment, 89*, S166-S173. http://dx.doi.org/10.1080/00223890701583598

Pianowski, G., Meyer, G. J., & Villemor-Amaral, A. E. (2016). The impact of R-Optimized Administration modeling procedures on Brazilian normative reference values. *Journal of Personality Assessment, 98*, 408-418.

Pires, A. A. (2007). Rorschach comprehensive system data for a sample of 309 adult nonpatients from Portugal. *Journal of Personality Assessment, 89*, S124-S130. http://dx.doi.org/10.1080/00223890701583408

Presley, G., Smith, C., Hilsenroth, M., & Exner, J. (2001). Clinical utility of the Rorschach with African Americans. *Journal of Personality Assessment, 77*(3), 491-507. http://dx.doi.org/10.1207/S15327752JPA7703_09

Reese, J. B., Viglione, D. J., & Giromini, L. (2014). A comparison between Comprehensive System and an early version of the Rorschach Performance Assessment System administration with outpatient children and adolescents. *Journal of Personality Assessment, 96*, 515–522. doi:10.1080/00223891.2014.889700

Ritzler, B. A. (2011). *A critical review of the R-PAS Manual*. Rorschach Training Programs, Inc. Newsletter, Vol. 3, # 5. Retrieved from http://www.rorschachtraining.com/category/newsletters/

Ritzler, B. A. (2014). *Society for Personality Assessment (SPA)*. March/April Newsletter [for Rorschach Training Programs], Vol. 6, # 2. Retrieved from http://www.rorschachtraining.com/category/newsletters/

Ritzler, B., Erard, R., & Pettigrew, G. (2002a). Protecting the integrity of Rorschach expert witnesses: A reply to Grove and Barden (1999) re: The admissibility of testimony under Daubert/Kumho analyses. *Psychology, Public Policy, and Law, 8*, 201–215. http://dx.doi.org/10.1037/1076-8971.8.2.201

Ritzler, B., Erard, R., & Pettigrew, G. (2002b). A final reply to Grove and Barden: The relevance of the Rorschach Comprehensive System for expert testimony. *Psychology, Public Policy, and Law, 8*, 235–246. http://dx.doi.org/10.1037/1076-8971.8.2.235

Ritzler, B., & Sciara, A. (2009). Rorschach comprehensive system international norms: Cautionary notes. Retrieved from http://www.rorschachtraining.com/category/articles/

Rorschach, H. (1942). *Psychodiagnostics: A diagnostic test based on perception*. Bern, Switzerland: Verlag Hans Huber.

Rosenthal, R., Hiller, J. B., Bornstein, R. F., Berry, D. T. R., & Brunell-Neuleib, S. (2001). Meta-analytic methods, the Rorschach, and the MMPI. *Psychological Assessment, 13*, 449–451. http://dx.doi.org/10.1037/1040-3590.13.4.449

Sahly, J., Shaffer, T. W., Erdberg, P., & O'Toole, S. (2011). Rorschach intercoder reliability for protocol-level comprehensive system variables in an international sample. *Journal of Personality Assessment, 93*, 592–596. http://dx.doi.org/10.1080/00223891.2011.608761

Shaffer, T. W., Erdberg, P., & Haroian, J. (1999). Current nonpatient data for the Rorschach, WAIS–R, and MMPI-2. *Journal of Personality Assessment, 73*, 305–316. http://dx.doi.org/10.1207/S15327752JPA7302_8

Shaffer, T. W., Erdberg, P., & Haroian, J. (2007). Rorschach comprehensive system data for a sample of 283 adult nonpatients from the United States. *Journal of Personality Assessment, 89*, S159–S165. http://dx.doi.org/10.1080/00223890701583572

Shaffer, T. W., Erdberg, P., & Meyer, G. J. (Eds.). (2007). International reference samples for the Rorschach comprehensive system [Special issue]. *Journal of Personality Assessment, 89*(Suppl. 1).

Smith, S. R., Baity, M. R., Knowles, E. S., & Hilsenroth, M. J. (2001). Assessment of disordered thinking in children and adolescents: The Rorschach Perceptual-Thinking Index. *Journal of Personality Assessment, 77*, 447–463. http://dx.doi.org/10.1207/S15327752JPA7703_06

Society for Personality Assessment. (2005). The Status of the Rorschach in Clinical and Forensic Practice: An Official Statement by the Board of Trustees of the

Society for Personality Assessment. *Journal of Personality Assessment, 85,* 219-237. http://dx.doi.org/10.1207/s15327752jpa8502_16

Stanfill, M. L., Viglione D. J., & Resende, A. C. (2013). Measuring psychological development with the Rorschach. *Journal of Personality Assessment, 95,* 174-186.

Stein, M. L. (1973). An empirical validation of the relation between Rorschach white-space and oppositionality. *Perceptual and Motor Skills, 37,* 375-381. http://dx.doi.org/10.2466/pms.1973.37.2.375

Su, W.-S., Viglione, D. J., Green, E. E., Tam, W.-C. C., Su, J.-A., & Chang, Y.-T. (2015, May 25). Cultural and linguistic adaptability of the Rorschach Performance Assessment System as a measure of psychotic characteristics and severity of mental disturbance in Taiwan. *Psychological Assessment.* http://dx.doi.org/10.1037/pas0000144

Sultan, S., & Meyer, G. J. (2009). Does productivity impact the stability of Rorschach scores? *Journal of Personality Assessment, 91,* 480-493. doi:10.1080/00223890903088693

Takahashi, M., Takahashi, Y., & Nishio, H. (2009). ロールシャッハ・テスト形態水準表 [*Rorschach Form Quality table*]. Tokyo: Kongo Shuppan.

Urist, J. (1977). The Rorschach test and the assessment of object relations. *Journal of Personality Assessment, 41,* 3-9. http://dx.doi.org/10.1207/s15327752jpa4101_1

Viglione, D. J. (1999). A review of recent research addressing the utility of the Rorschach. *Psychological Assessment, 11,* 251-265. http://dx.doi.org/10.1037/1040-3590.11.3.251

Viglione, D. J., Blume-Marcovici, A. C., Miller, H. L., Giromini, L., & Meyer, G. J. (2012). An initial inter-rater reliability study for the Rorschach performance assessment system. *Journal of Personality Assessment, 94,* 607-612. doi:10.1080/00223891.2012.684118

Viglione, D. J., & Giromini, L. (2016). The effects of using the Composite International Reference Values versus Comprehensive System Rorschach Norms for Children, Adolescents, and Adults. *Journal of Personality Assessment, 98,* 391-397.

Viglione, D. J., Giromini, L., Gustafson, M., & Meyer, G. J. (2014). Developing continuous variable composites for Rorschach measures of thought problems, vigilance, and suicide risk. *Assessment, 21,* 42-49. doi:10.1177/1073191112446963

Viglione, D. J., & Hilsenroth, M. J. (2001). The Rorschach: Facts, fiction, and future. *Psychological Assessment, 13,* 452-471. http://dx.doi.org/10.1037/1040-3590.13.4.452

Viglione, D. J., & Meyer, G. J. (2005, July 27). *Preliminary suggestions for collecting and reporting Comprehensive System reference samples.* Paper presented at the XVIIIth Congress of the International Rorschach Society, Barcelona, Spain.

Viglione, D. J., & Meyer, G. J. (2008). An overview of Rorschach psychometrics for forensic practice. In C. B. Gacono & F. B. Evans with N. Kaser-Boyd & L. A. Gacono (Eds.), *Handbook of forensic Rorschach psychology* (pp. 21-53). Mahwah, NJ: Lawrence Erlbaum Associates.

Viglione, D. J., Meyer, G., Jordan, R. J., Converse, G. L., Evans, J., MacDermott, D., & Moore, R. (2015). Developing an alternative Rorschach administration method to optimize the number of responses and enhance clinical inferences. *Clinical Psychology and Psychotherapy, 22,* 546-558. http://dx.doi.org/10.1002/cpp.1913

Viglione, D. J., & Rivera, B. (2012). Performance assessment of personality and psychopathology. In I. B. Weiner (Ed.-in-Chief), J. R. Graham, & J. A. Naglieri (Vol. Eds.), *Comprehensive handbook of psychology: Assessment psychology* (2nd ed., Vol. 10, pp. 600–621). Hoboken, NJ: John Wiley & Sons.

Viglione, D. J., & Taylor, N. (2003). Empirical support for interrater reliability of Rorschach Comprehensive System coding. *Journal of Clinical Psychology, 59*, 111–121. http://dx.doi.org/10.1002/jclp.10121

Viglione, D. J., Towns, B., Lindshield, D. (2012). Understanding and using the Rorschach inkblot test to assess post-traumatic conditions. *Psychological Injury and Law, 2*, 122–134. doi:10.1007/s12207-012-9128-5

Villemor-Amaral, A. E., Yazigi, L., Nascimento, R. S. G. F., Primi, R., & Semer, N. L. (2007). Localização, Qualidade Formal e Respostas Populares do Rorschach no SC em uma Amostra Brasileira [Location, Form Quality and Popular Responses in the Rorschach CS in a Brazilian sample]. Em: III Congresso Brasileiro de Avaliação Psicológica. João Pessoa, PB, Brasil.

Weiner, I. B., Exner, J. E., & Sciara, A. (1996). Is the Rorschach welcome in the courtroom? *Journal of Personality Assessment, 67*, 422–424. http://dx.doi.org/10.1207/s15327752jpa6702_15

Wood, J. M., Garb, H. N., Nezworski, M. T., Lilienfeld, S. O., & Duke, M. C. (2015). A second look at the validity of widely used Rorschach indices: Comment on Mihura, Meyer, Dumitrascu, and Bombel (2013). *Psychological Bulletin, 141*, 236–249. http://dx.doi.org/10.1037/a0036005

Wood, J. M., Lilienfeld, S. O., Garb, H. N., & Nezworski, M. T. (2000). The Rorschach test in clinical diagnosis: A critical review, with a backward look at Garfield (1947). *Journal of Clinical Psychology, 56*, 395–430. doi:10.1002/(SICI)1097-4679(200003)56:3<395::AID-JCLP15>3.0.CO;2-O

Wood, J. M., Nezworski, M. T., & Garb, H. N. (2003). What's right with the Rorschach? *The Scientific Review of Mental Health Practice, 2*, 142–146.

Wood, J. M., Nezworski, M. T., Garb, H. N., & Lilienfeld, S. O. (2001). The misperception of psychopathology: Problems with norms of the Comprehensive System for the Rorschach. *Clinical Psychology: Science and Practice, 8*, 350–373. http://dx.doi.org/10.1093/clipsy/8.3.350

Wood, J. M., Nezworski, M. T., Lilienfeld, S. O., & Garb, H. N. (2003). *What's wrong with the Rorschach?: Science confronts the controversial inkblot test*. San Francisco: Jossey-Bass.

Wood, J. M., Nezworski, M. T., & Stejskal, W. J. (1996). The comprehensive system for the Rorschach: A critical examination. *Psychological Science, 7*, 3–10. http://dx.doi.org/10.1111/j.1467-9280.1996.tb00658.x

Zachary, R. A., & Gorsuch, R. L. (1985). Continuous norming: Implications for the WAIS-R. *Journal of Clinical Psychology, 41*, 86–94. doi:10.1002/1097-4679(198501)41:1<86::AID-JCLP2270410115>3.0.CO;2-W

Zhu, J., & Chen, H.-Y. (2011). Utility of inferential norming with smaller sample sizes. *Journal of Psychoeducational Assessment, 29*, 570–580. doi:10.1177/0734282910396323

CHAPTER 3

INTEGRATING SELF-REPORT AND PERFORMANCE-BASED TESTING IN DETECTING IMPRESSION MANAGEMENT

Douglas S. Schultz

As mental health professionals, we are trained to try to see things through our clients' eyes. Guided by what they tell us, we attempt to see the world as they do. However, there may be many situations in which our clients do not present themselves genuinely. In forensic evaluations, for example, examinees often have very tangible motivations to present themselves as either exceptionally free from psychological problems (e.g., in child custody evaluations) or to exaggerate mental health symptoms (e.g., in disability evaluations or assessments of criminal responsibility).

As assessors, we must always consider the possibility that an examinee may not be honestly reporting his or her experiences and symptoms. Research has indicated that, for example, in some instances, clients may attempt to prepare for psychological tests (Rogers, Bagby, & Chakraborty, 1993). In a forensic evaluation, attorneys might "coach" their clients by providing them with information about the tests they are likely to encounter, including the presence and mechanics of validity scales (Lees-Haley, 1997).

Indeed, the possibility that an examinee might be coached on a psychological test in advance of a forensic evaluation should not be underestimated. In a survey of 70 practicing attorneys and 150 law students, Wetter and Corrigan (1995) found that 36% of law students and almost 50% of practicing attorneys reported that they believe they should always discuss validity scales with clients referred for psychological evaluations.

In addition, motivated clients could also coach themselves by studying information about psychological tests from professional materials available in libraries or bookstores (Baer, Wetter, & Berry, 1995).

In addition to good clinical interviewing, examining psychological test data can be helpful in detecting impression management, particularly when including tests with specific validity scales or those that were designed to detect "faking good" or "faking bad" response sets. Before we can detect attempts at impression management, however, we must first understand the different ways in which examinees may misrepresent themselves.

Dimensional Models of Impression Management

Malingering—exaggerating or feigning psychological problems in order to achieve some secondary gain—is often considered on an all-or-none, dichotomous level. That is, an examinee is either determined to be malingering or he/she is not. This conceptualization of malingering is overly simplistic, however, and fails to recognize that there are some contexts in which individuals may present certain aspects of themselves honestly, while exaggerating or feigning other problems. Thus, when considering the problem of malingering, we must distinguish between an examinee who outright fabricates symptoms that do not exist and one who exaggerates the severity of symptoms that he or she truly experiences.

Based on this conceptualization, Rogers (1997) proposed three different levels of malingering: *mild malingering*, characterized mainly by exaggeration of symptoms rather than fabrication; *moderate malingering*, characterized by gross exaggeration of symptoms, as well as some fabrication (mostly focused on a few key symptoms rather than widespread fabrication); and *severe malingering*, characterized by extensive and severe fabrications of symptoms, which overshadow any exaggerations.

Consistent with this model, Walters et al. (2008) also found support for a continuous—rather than dichotomous—conceptualization of malingering. Based on their analysis of the latent structure of feigned psychopathology as measured by the MMPI-2 (Butcher, Graham, Ben-Porath, Tellegen, Dahlstrom, & Kaemmer, 2001) and the Structured Interview of Reported Symptoms (SIRS; Rogers, Bagby, & Dickens, 1992), Walters et al. concluded, "Malingering might therefore be more accurately conceptualized as levels of exaggeration or fabrication rather than as a response style that is categorically distinct from honest responding" (p. 243). They also noted that "psychopathology and malingering, rather than being opposing categories of behavior, may actually be interdependent or partially interdependent dimensions, such that many individuals with genuine mental disorders also exaggerate or fabricate symptoms for internal and/or external gain" (p. 244).

Resnick, West, and Payne (2008) also proposed recognizing three dimensions of malingering, though their categories differed from the model proposed by Rogers (1997). Resnick et al. first differentiated *pure malingering* from *partial malingering*. Pure malingering, they argued, involved feigning symptoms of a disorder that the patient does not genuinely have, whereas partial malingering was characterized by exaggerating or embellishing symptoms that the patient does experience. They also identified a third type of malingering, termed *false imputation*. In this category, a patient attributes causality for psychological problems or emotional distress to an event or trigger that, in reality, the individual knows is not the cause of the symptoms. For example, an examinee who is suing another driver after being injured in an automobile accident may claim that the accident induced severe anxiety, whereas in truth, the anxiety predated the automobile accident.

Less attention has been devoted in the research to developing dimensional models of "faking good," or socially desirable responding. However, there have been some attempts to categorize the varying motivations for an individual to "fake good." Morey (1993, as cited in Peebles & Moore, 1998) noted that socially desirable responding may arise from deliberate intentions to deceive, from self-deception, or from limited insight into one's own problems. Paulhus (1984) identified similar categories in his two-factor model of socially desirable responding. The first factor involved perceived desirability or self-deception, while the second factor was characterized by deliberate defensiveness or deception of others.

Prevalence of Malingering

Research has generally shown that the prevalence of malingering can vary widely, particularly depending upon the evaluation context. In their survey of practitioners recruited from postdoctoral forensic psychology workshops, for example, Rogers, Sewell, and Goldstein (1994) found that the proportion of examinees classified as malingering in forensic evaluations was nearly double that of non-forensic examinees (15.7% vs. 7.4%).

Even within forensic evaluations, prevalence rates can vary by the specific type of legal case. Mittenberg, Patton, Canyock, and Condit (2002) surveyed psychologists on over 33,000 legal cases and found varying rates of malingering by referral type. They found that 29% of plaintiffs in personal injury cases, 30% of disability claimants, 19% of criminal defendants, and 39% of individuals with mild closed head injuries were identified as malingering or exaggerating symptoms to some extent.

Notably, individuals in different forensic assessment contexts may present with diagnostically distinct symptoms. For example, feigned psychosis may be observed more often in the criminal forensic arena (Cornell & Hawk, 1989), whereas feigned posttraumatic stress disorder (PTSD) and affective disorders may be more prevalent in the civil forensic domain (Douglas, Huss, Murdoch, Washington, & Koch, 1999; Landon & Almer, 2002; Lees-Haley, 1997; McGuire, 1999; Resnick, 1997).

Motivations to Malinger

There are a multitude of reasons why examinees might not present themselves honestly, in addition to simply desiring some external gain from presenting themselves as psychologically impaired. Perhaps there is a poor working alliance, and the examinee does not fully trust the examiner. Another possibility is that they desire the attention gained from being in the patient role, as can be seen in the case of a factitious disorder. Thus, in addition to determining that an examinee may not be reporting his or her symptoms in an honest manner, it is also important to understand his or her motivation for doing so.

Rogers (1990) described three models of malingering that attempt to explain why an individual may exaggerate or feign psychological symptoms. According to the *pathogenic model*, malingering is considered a form of ineffective coping. In this model, the patient is thought to be struggling to control emerging psychological symptoms, which he or she genuinely experiences. However, as part of their struggle to maintain control over psychopathology, they consciously fabricate symptoms that they are aware they do not experience.

The second model of malingering described by Rogers (1990) is the *criminological model*. This model postulates that individuals feign mental disorders as part of a larger antisocial character disorder. According to this model, the sole motivation to feign psychopathology is to further the individual's own interests.

Lastly, Rogers (1990) proposed an *adaptational model* of malingering. This model is based on three main assumptions. First, the model assumes that the examinee perceives the evaluation to be involuntary and adversarial. Second, the examinee must perceive that either he or she has something to lose by presenting honestly or has something to gain by feigning symptoms. Finally, the examinee must perceive that there is not a more effective strategy to achieve his or her desired goal. This final assumption is considered the *cost-benefit analysis assumption*.

The adaptational model was reviewed and streamlined by Rogers, Salekin, Sewell, Goldstein, and Leonard (1998). From the original three assumptions proposed by Rogers (1990), the authors delineated two main components in the model: the cost-benefit analysis (assumption 3) and the adversarial setting (assumption 1). Rogers et al. then used prototypical analysis to examine the support for the adaptational model. They found that the first component—the cost-benefit analysis—was more prototypical for forensic cases, whereas the adversarial setting was more prototypical for non-forensic cases. In other words, in forensic evaluations, examinees may be more likely to feign or exaggerate psychopathology because they believe they have something to gain by doing so.

In non-forensic evaluations, however, examinees may be dishonest in response to a perception that they are being forced to undergo this assessment and have little or no autonomy. This certainly has implications for clinicians conducting evaluations in non-forensic settings. These conclusions seem to indicate a potential to enhance honest responding in non-forensic cases by paying particular attention to developing a solid, positive working alliance before proceeding with the bulk of the evaluation.

Coaching on Psychological Tests

There is increasing evidence that if an examinee is motivated to exaggerate or feign psychological symptoms during an evaluation, he or she may have attempted to research testing instruments and/or psychological symptoms prior to the evaluation (Baer, Wetter, & Berry, 1995). The literature also seems to indicate that, particularly in forensic evaluations, some examinees may have been coached on tests or on psychological symptoms by their attorneys (e.g., Youngjohn, 1995; Wetter & Corrigan, 1995).

Powell, Gfeller, Hendricks, and Sharland (2004) described two types of coaching that examinees may have experienced prior to an evaluation: symptom coaching and test coaching. *Symptom coaching* refers to learning about the symptoms of the disorder or disorders that the examinee is attempting to feign. *Test coaching* describes an examinee learning about the psychological test or tests that he or she will take and may include information about validity scales and detection strategies. As we shall see when we discuss the research on coaching effects, being familiar with validity scales seems to compromise our ability to detect impression management the most.

Unfortunately, information about psychological tests is readily available, both online and in easily accessible books. Attempts to quantify how much information about popular psychological tests is available online have generally found that only a small minority of websites present enough detailed information to pose a significant threat to test security (Ruiz, Drake, Glass, Marcotte, & van Gorp, 2002; Schultz & Loving, 2012). However, these studies have found a larger number of websites that include less-detailed—but still potentially troublesome—information about psychological test instruments, including suggestions for how to respond. The Wikipedia article on the Rorschach, for example, not only provides full-color replications of the inkblots but also suggestions for "popular responses" (Rorschach test, n.d.).

Even without the Internet, however, information about psychological tests can easily be found in readily available books. In the 1980s, William Poundstone published *Big Secrets*, which included reproductions of all ten inkblots, along with advice as to how to "cheat" the test (Poundstone, 1983). Textbooks describing the use of psychological tests can also easily be accessed in libraries and bookstores. Sliter and Christiansen (2012) found that examinees who self-coached using information from readily available books in pre-employment personality testing were able to raise their scores associated with desirable traits on testing. Furthermore, those who read information about avoiding lie-detection items were able to score lower, on average, on the Balanced Inventory of Socially Desirable Responding (Paulhus, 1988). Thus the utility of validity scales on self-report instruments may be decreased if an examinee has been coached on these detection strategies. Exactly how well a test can detect efforts at impression management, though, depends on the precise instrument being used.

Detecting Impression Management with Self-Report Instruments

There have been a multitude of empirical studies examining the ability of various psychological tests to detect efforts at both over- and under-reporting of psychological problems. Before turning our attention to these studies, however, a general word of caution regarding the generalizability of their results is warranted. Rogers (2008) notes that much of the research that has been conducted in this area has utilized "normal" participants instructed to feign psychopathology. However, examinees who undergo these evaluations in real-world contexts likely have greater motivation and may be more sophisticated in their attempts to feign than those instructed to feign for research purposes. As such, the results may not always generalize completely to real-world examinees. As an example, Edens, Poythress, and Watkins-Clay (2007) found that suspected malingerers were much less likely to be detected on certain psychological tests than were research participants instructed to simulate a mental disorder.

Malingering-Specific Instruments

SIRS & SIRS-2

The Structured Interview of Reported Symptoms (SIRS; Rogers, Bagby et al., 1992), arguably one of the most widely used forensic measures of malingering (Archer, Buffington-Vollum, Stredny, & Handel, 2006), utilizes a structured interview format and empirically derived methods of malingering detection to assess the likelihood that an examinee is not reporting his or her symptoms honestly. The SIRS focuses on feigned psychopathology (rather than feigned cognitive impairment).

The original SIRS contains eight scales, each based on a distinct detection strategy: Rare Symptoms (symptoms rarely endorsed among genuine patients), Symptom Combinations (common symptoms that rarely occur together), Improbable and Absurd Symptoms (highly unusual or fantastical symptoms that are extremely unlikely to occur in genuine patients), Blatant Symptoms (obvious symptoms that are easily recognized as signs of severe psychopathology), Subtle Symptoms (common symptoms among bona fide patients that are not immediately recognizable by untrained persons), Selectivity of Symptoms (indiscriminately endorsing symptoms across diagnostic categories), Severity of Symptoms (the proportion of symptoms identified as unbearable or incapacitating), and Reported versus Observed (comparing what the examinee reports with his/her actual behavior during the evaluation). Each scale is scored and may fall in the range of *definite feigning, probable feigning, indeterminate*, or *honest responding*.

A second edition of the SIRS, the SIRS-2 (Rogers, Sewell, & Gillard, 2010) was published several years ago, containing the same test items but new scoring and interpretive criteria. Supplemental scales, based on the same test items, were also added. The SIRS-2 utilizes a decision tree, based on the examinee's combination of scores, which provides five possible outcomes: Feigning, Indeterminate-General, Indeterminate-Evaluate, Disengagement, or Genuine Responding. When an examinee is identified in one of the Indeterminate categories, it indicates that their results do not conclusively indicate either that they were attempting to feign or responding honestly. Disengagement refers to an examinee who does not respond in the affirmative to a majority of the SIRS-2 items—even those commonly endorsed by most people—suggesting that he or she was not adequately engaged with the evaluation.

There has been some controversy among researchers as to whether the SIRS-2 represents an improvement over the original SIRS. For example, while Green, Rosenfeld, and Belfi (2013) found an improved specificity rate over the original SIRS (94.3% vs. 92.0%, respectively), they lamented that the new criteria resulted in significantly lower sensitivity rates (36.8% among forensic psychiatric patients and 66.7% among simulators, as compared to 47.4% and 75.0%, respectively). Consistent with these results, Brand, Tursich, Tzall, and Loewenstein (2014) found that the SIRS-2 possessed very high specificity for detecting feigned Dissociative Identity Disorder (nearly 96%). However, they also found fairly low sensitivity, such that many knowledgeable feigners of DID were able to successfully avoid detection.

Generally, the original SIRS was considered to be accurate in detecting feigning across different diagnostic categories, including psychotic disorders, mood disorders, and posttraumatic stress disorder (Rogers, Kropp, Bagby, & Dickens, 1992). Rogers, Kropp et al. asked 45 psychologically knowledgeable correctional residents to attempt to feign schizophrenia, a mood disorder, or PTSD and found that the SIRS was relatively robust in its ability to distinguish diagnostically mixed groups of bona fide patients from simulators of each of the three diagnostic conditions. However, a recent meta-analysis revealed that research since the initial validation studies of the SIRS found higher sensitivity but lower specificity rates than those reported in the SIRS manual (Green & Rosenfeld, 2011). This meta-analysis noted that studies in which feigners were composed of simulators yielded higher classification rates than studies sampling actual suspected malingerers. Furthermore, genuine patient samples were significantly more likely than nonclinical samples to be misclassified as feigning.

Regarding coaching effects, Rogers, Gillis, Bagby, and Monteiro (1991) found that, while coached simulators were able to lower their scale scores on the SIRS, the SIRS was still able—as a whole—to discriminate between coached simulators and genuine psychiatric patients. However, this research was conducted on the original version of the SIRS. As we will see later in this chapter, the original SIRS appears to be more immune to coaching effects than broadband self-report personality instruments. Thus it may be prudent to consider including the SIRS as part of the test battery (or the SIRS-2, if it turns out that resistance to coaching transfers to this version as well) when clinicians are concerned about coaching effects. While false negatives may be a potential concern, if an examinee is classified as malingering on the SIRS or SIRS-2, there is an extremely high likelihood that he or she is, in fact, attempting to feign or exaggerate symptoms.

SIMS

The Structured Inventory of Malingered Symptomatology (SIMS; Widows & Smith, 2005) is a 75-item self-report true/false test that is designed to screen for feigned psychopathology and feigned cognitive impairment. The SIMS is based on the idea that naïve examinees are likely to endorse bizarre, rare, atypical, or extreme responses when they attempt to feign or exaggerate symptoms. Thus the majority of the 75 items on the SIMS consist of highly unlikely or implausible symptoms. The SIMS covers five specific categories of feigned psychopathology: Atypical depression, improbable memory problems, pseudo-neurological symptoms, doubtful claims of psychotic experiences, and hyperbolic signs of mental retardation. The authors recommend using a cutoff score of 15 to identify possible feigning. Since the SIMS is designed as a screener, if an examinee scores above the cutoff, a more in-depth assessment of feigning is recommended.

A recent meta-analysis was conducted of studies that used the SIMS to detect feigned psychopathology (van Impelen, Merckelbach, Jelicic, & Merten, 2014). The authors reviewed 31 studies, consisting of 61 subsamples and 4,009 SIMS protocols. Based on their review, they offered several conclusions regarding the SIMS ability to detect feigning. First, they concluded that the SIMS is, overall, effective at discriminating between feigners and honest responders. They also found that the SIMS results in elevated scores in groups that are known to have a higher prevalence of feigning (e.g., offenders who claim crime-related amnesia).

However, van Impelen et al. (2014) argued that the SIMS may overestimate feigning in patients with schizophrenia, intellectual disability, or psychogenic non-epileptic seizures. They found that the recommended cutoff scores resulted in adequate sensitivity, but substandard specificity, misclassifying genuine patients as feigning. To correct this, the authors suggested combining the SIMS with other measures, or raising the cutoff score to improve specificity. Specifically, they offered possible cutoff scores of greater than 19, or—to increase specificity further—greater than 24. How high the cutoff score is set would be determined by how confident the examiner needed to be in his or her determination of feigning. If using the SIMS for diagnostic certainty, rather than just as a screener, a higher cutoff score would be more appropriate. This would result in fewer, yet safer, identifications of feigning using the SIMS.

Based on their meta-analysis, van Impelen et al. (2014) also argued that the SIMS may be more sensitive in criminal settings because it includes a number of extreme symptoms. These extreme symptoms, they postulate, may be endorsed by defendants in criminal settings, but are less likely to be endorsed by those in non-criminal settings. As an example, in civil forensic cases, where claims of mild or moderate impairment are more common, the SIMS may be less sensitive. The authors additionally stated that the reliance on bizarre and pseudo-symptoms may also make the test more easily recognizable to examinees as a measure of feigning rather than a test of true psychopathology.

Overall, van Impelen et al.'s (2014) meta-analysis revealed that the SIMS is fairly robust against coaching. A review of some recent individual studies seems to support this finding. Jelicic, Merkelbach, Candel, and Geraerts (2007), for example, examined the effect of symptom coaching on the ability of the SIMS to identify feigning of cognitive dysfunction and found that 90% of coached participants were correctly classified as feigning. Jelicic, Ceunen, Peters, and Merkelbach (2011) also tested samples of students, alumni, and employees of an undergraduate university using the SIMS. Participants were divided into three groups: A control group, a symptom-coached group, and a symptom- and test-coached group. The SIMS correctly classified 93% of the symptom-coached participants and 86% of the symptom/test-coached participants as feigning. Although coaching resulted in slightly lower classification rates, the authors concluded that the SIMS appeared to be relatively resistant to coaching effects.

M-FAST

The Miller Forensic Assessment of Symptoms Test (M-FAST; Miller, 2001) is a 25-item structured interview—similar to the SIRS-2, though much briefer—which was developed to screen for feigned psychopathology in a forensic setting. Like the SIRS-2, the detection strategies are empirically derived. The M-FAST consists of seven scales: Reported versus Observed Symptoms, Extreme Symptomatology, Rare Combinations, Unusual Hallucinations, Unusual Symptom Course, Negative Image, and Suggestibility.

Validation studies of the M-FAST have reported sound psychometric properties (Guy & Miller, 2004; Jackson, Rogers, & Sewell, 2005; Miller, 2004; Veazey, Wagner, Hays, & Miller, 2005), and research using simulator and clinical comparison samples (Guy & Miller, 2004; Jackson et al., 2005; Miller, 2001, 2004) supported the validity of the M-FAST as a screen for malingered mental illness. The studies reported that a cutoff score of 6 for the total score (of a possible 25) was most effective for correct classification of malingering in forensic and clinical samples. Guy and Miller (2004) also found that the recommended cutoff score of 6 was optimal for a correctional sample, and the results were generalizable across African-American, Hispanic, and Caucasian inmates. However, Veazey, Wagner, Hays, and Miller (2005) argued that a cutoff score of 8 had the best balance of sensitivity, specificity, positive predictive power (PPP), and negative predictive power (NPP) in a sample of psychiatric inpatients. Additional studies have validated the use of the M-FAST with other forensic samples, including defendants undergoing competency to stand trial evaluations, patients involved in personal injury litigation, and examinees in workers' compensation cases (Vitacco, Rogers, Gabel, & Munizza, 2007; Christiansen & Vincent, 2012; Alwes, Clark, Berry, & Granacher, 2008).

Guy, Kwartner, and Miller (2006) examined the ability of the M-FAST to differentiate between simulators and honest patients with respect the four different disorders: schizophrenia, major depressive disorder, bipolar disorder, and PTSD. Overall, they found that the simulators obtained higher M-FAST total scores relative to genuine patients, with the largest effect size shown for schizophrenia. In addition, one scale in particular (Rare Combinations) significantly differentiated the simulators from the comparison group of bona fide patients, regardless of the disorder under consideration. However, the authors cautioned that individual M-FAST scales were not intended to be used in isolation for diagnostic purposes.

There has been considerably less research on the effects of coaching on the M-FAST. Only one study seems to have examined this topic, with results suggesting that coaching may decrease the ability of the M-FAST to identify feigners. In a study of feigned PTSD, fewer coached simulators were classified as feigning by the M-FAST than naïve simulators when using a cutoff score of 6 (52% vs. 84%; Guriel-Tennant & Freemouw, 2006).

Self-Report Broadband Personality Measures

In order to identify possibly impression management, many broadband personality instruments include one or more validity scales, which are typically designed to detect inconsistent or unusual response patterns, underreporting of problems, or feigning/exaggeration of symptoms. However, as a general word of caution, self-report instruments are limited by examinees' self-awareness and insight, as well as their capacity and willingness to describe themselves and their problems accurately and honestly (Meyer, 1997; Westen & Shedler, 2007). Self-report personality tests also tend to have high face validity, meaning that it is fairly easy for an examinee to guess what the test is trying to measure. Instruments with high face validity are generally considered to be more vulnerable to efforts at impression management than performance-based tests, which have lower face validity (Ganellen, 2008).

MMPI-2

The Minnesota Multiphasic Personality Inventory—2 (MMPI-2) is arguably the most widely known and researched broadband personality assessment measure. The MMPI-2 consists of 567 true-or-false items and contains several validity scales. The Lie (L) Scale contains items that are highly desirable, but rarely true. A high score on the L scale thus reflects defensiveness. The K Scale was developed as a less obvious measure of defensiveness. The F and Fb scales contain items that are infrequently endorsed and thus, indicative of potential malingering. The Fp scale specifically contains items infrequently endorsed by a patient population. Finally, the VRIN and TRIN scales are measures of inconsistency in response patterns across the test.

A meta-analysis of feigning on the MMPI-2 indicated that overreporting of some specific disorders may be more difficult to detect than others (Rogers, Sewell, Martin, & Vitacco, 2003). The authors found that the effect sizes of the F, Fb, and Fp scales were smaller when comparing feigners of PTSD with genuine PTSD patients than when comparing feigners of schizophrenia with genuine schizophrenia patients. These results suggest that feigned PTSD may be more difficult to detect on the MMPI-2 than feigned schizophrenia, possibly because feigning PTSD involves endorsing more moderate, less dramatic symptoms than feigning a psychotic disorder.

In a study of defensiveness on the MMPI-2, Bagby, Rogers, Nicholson, Buis, Seeman, and Rector (1997) asked healthy students and patients with schizophrenia to complete the MMPI-2 first under standard instructions, then a second time with specific instructions to attempt to conceal their problems. The authors found that both groups were able to minimize their problems during the second administration, but both were detected on the validity scales. In particular, the L scale was the best at distinguishing between honest reporting and dissimulation in the clinical sample.

With regard to symptom coaching effects on the MMPI-2, Veltri and Williams (2012) best summarized the available research in this area:

> Most studies examining the impact of symptom knowledge on the MMPI-2 have concluded that symptom information does not improve the ability of most individuals to avoid being identified as overreporters of psychiatric disorders such as schizophrenia (Bagby, Rogers, & Buis, 1994; Bagby, Rogers, Nicholson, et al., 1997; Rogers, Bagby, & Chakraborty, 1993; Wetter, Baer, Berry, Robison, & Sumpter, 1993) and posttraumatic stress disorder (PTSD; Arbisi, Ben-Porath, & McNulty, 2006; Bury & Bagby, 2002; Elhai, Frueh, Gold, Gold, & Hamner, 2000; Elhai, Gold, Frueh, & Gold, 2000; Elhai, Gold, Sellers, & Dorfman, 2001; Lange, Sullivan, & Scott, 2010, Marshall & Bagby, 2006; Moyer, Burkhardt, & Gordon, 2002; Wetter et al., 1993).
> (p. 200)

However, Veltri and Williams noted that there is some evidence to suggest that feigning of somatoform disorders and depression may be somewhat less likely to be detected if examinees are coached on symptom information.

Studies examining the impact of test coaching effects—specifically, informing subjects about the validity measures—indicate that test coaching may undermine the ability of the MMPI-2 to detect feigning. Viglione, Wright, Dizon, Moynihan, DuPuis, and Pizitz (2001) administered the MMPI-2 to a sample of psychology graduate students who were given a realistic life predicament designed to increase their motivation to feign a mental disorder. They were told that they should feign impairment in order to obtain disability payments for an on-the-job injury. Some of these participants were cautioned against presenting themselves too dramatically so that they do not look fake, whereas the rest were not given this warning. The authors found that participants who received the caution scored significantly lower on malingering indices, resulting in unacceptably low sensitivity for detecting the cautioned feigners.

With regard to underreporting, the available research again suggests that when examinees are given information about the MMPI-2's validity scales, they are more likely to be able to successfully avoid detection than naïve underreporters (Baer, Wetter, & Berry, 1995; Baer & Sekirnjak, 1997). In their meta-analysis of the ability of the MMPI-2 to detect underreporting, Baer and Miller (2002) suggested that the L and K scales seem to be the most effective for detecting "faking good" response sets.

Recently, Hartmann and Hartmann (2014) examined the ability of the MMPI-2 to detect underreporting among psychiatric outpatients when coached with information that is available online about the test. Some patients were given Internet information about the test and instructed to fake good, others were instructed to fake good without coaching materials, and a third group was instructed to respond honestly. While the Internet-faking and the faking patient groups were both able to conceal problems on the clinical scales, there were significant differences between the two groups on the validity scales. The L scale was the most robust in identifying both faking groups. It was effective at detecting the faking patients, but only moderately so at detecting the Internet-faking group. The K scale was also able to detect the non-Internet faking patients. Interestingly, the Internet-faking patients scored significantly higher on the F scale than standard nonpatients and the non-Internet faking patients and similarly to standard patients, indicating that they did acknowledge some personal problems, despite their instructions to appear healthy.

Across the research, the L scale seems to be the most consistent and the most robust in its ability to detect underreporting, even in instances in which examinees have been coached. In response to coaching effects, Bacchiochi and Bagby (2006) developed the malingering discriminant function index (M-DFI) for the MMPI-2 as a supplemental feigning scale that was designed to be less vulnerable to the impact of coaching. However, a study by Toomey, Kucharski, and Duncan (2009) found that the M-DFI was relatively poor at differentiating between malingerers and non-malingerers in a correctional sample. The authors concluded that the F scale had much better predictive utility in identifying malingerers in their sample.

With the restructuring of the MMPI-2 scales in the shorter 338-item MMPI-2-RF (Ben-Porath & Tellegen, 2008), clinicians now have a choice as to whether to utilize the original MMPI-2 or the restructured version. The validity scales are quite similar (though, again, their contents have been restructured), with a few notable exceptions. The Fb scale is not included on the MMPI-2-RF, and the restructured version includes a new validity scale: the Infrequent Somatic Responses scale (Fs). This scale consists of somatic complaints that are rarely endorsed by bona fide medical patients. Research suggests that, like the MMPI-2, the restructured validity scales are effective at identifying both malingering (Rogers, Gillard, Berry, & Granacher, 2011; Sellbom, Toomey, Wygant, Kucharski, & Duncan, 2010) and underreporting (Sellbom & Bagby, 2008).

PAI

The Personality Assessment Inventory (PAI; Morey, 1991) is a 344-item broadband measure of psychiatric symptomatology and personality functioning. It is shorter and has a slightly lower recommended reading grade level than the original MMPI-2. Unlike the simple true/false format of the MMPI-2, however, the PAI contains four answer choices for each item. Examinees may choose whether they feel an item is *false* in describing them, or whether it is *slightly true, mainly true*, or *very true*.

Like the MMPI-2, the PAI was developed with several built-in validity scales. Two scales are included to assess for random responding. Infrequency (INF) contains items that are rarely endorsed by most people. As an example, one test item asks the examinee whether his/her favorite hobbies are stamp collecting and archery. Given that these two hobbies are highly dissimilar and would attract different types of personalities, it is highly unlikely that they would be someone's two favorite hobbies (Morey, 2003). Inconsistency (ICN) contains item-pairs that should be endorsed in a similar manner. For example, one item in the pair might read something like, "I feel sad most of the time," while the corresponding item reads, "I rarely feel happy." If an examinee marks these items in a dissimilar manner, their score on ICN increases.

The PAI includes three validity scales for assessing possible overreporting of psychiatric symptoms. The Negative Impression Management (NIM) scale contains symptoms that are rarely endorsed in community samples and psychiatric patients (Morey, 1996). However, Morey (2003) notes that this scale may be elevated in some patients with severe psychopathology. The Malingering Index (MAL) consists of eight PAI profile characteristics that are associated with attempting to feign a mental disorder (Morey, 1996). For each characteristic that is present in an examinee's PAI profile, he or she is given one point on the MAL, with scores of 3 or greater raising questions about possible malingering. Scores of 5 or more tend to be highly specific to malingering (Morey, 2003). Lastly, the Rogers Discriminant Function (RDF) is based on a weighted combination of 20 PAI scores and a constant value (Morey, 1996), with scores above 0 being indicative of overt efforts to malinger psychopathology. While the NIM may be influenced by true psychopathology, Morey (2003) suggests that the RDF is relatively free from this influence, with the MAL falling somewhere in between.

Edens et al. (2007) found that MAL and RDF were significantly predictive of malingering status in a sample of prison inmates. However, a meta-analysis of overreporting on the PAI by Hawes and Boccaccini (2009) found that effect sizes for all three symptom exaggeration scales (NIM, MAL, and RDF) were smaller when participants were instructed to feign mood or anxiety disorders, as compared to participants instructed to feign psychotic conditions. Similar to research findings on the MMPI-2, it seems that the validity scales of the PAI may be less sensitive to detecting malingering of more subtle conditions than feigning of severe psychopathology.

The PAI also contains three validity scales designed to assess defensive responding. The Positive Impression Management (PIM) scale contains negatively worded items that describe common shortcomings to which most people will admit (Morey, 1991). High scores on the PIM (defined by Morey as 23 or higher) indicate that the examinee endorsed items which are infrequently selected by most people and that the examinee may be claiming to be excessively virtuous. The Defensiveness Index (DEF) is based on eight PAI profile characteristics associated with defensive responding. Like the MAL, for every profile characteristic that an examinee matches, he or she receives one point on the DEF. Morey (2003) suggests that scores above 6 indicate overt attempts at defensiveness. However, Morey cautions that scores below 6 do not necessarily rule out defensiveness, particularly if the examinee has been coached. Finally, the Cashel Discriminant Function (CDF) is a discriminant function consisting of six PAI scales that best differentiate between defensive and "normal" response sets. Morey (2003) indicates that scores above 145 may indicate some efforts at positive impression management, while scores above 160 suggest overt defensiveness.

In their study examining simulated defensiveness in a college sample, however, Peebles and Moore (1998) found that a PIM score of 18 (down from Morey's more conservative cutoff of 23) accurately classified 85% of college students instructed to "fake good" from a control group instructed to respond honestly. The authors also found that a lower cutoff score of 5 on DEF resulted in a correct classification rate of 83.3%.

As the three PAI scales designed to assess for symptom exaggeration, the three defensiveness scales also vary in their specificity. Morey (2003) indicates that if the PIM is elevated, but the other two scores are average, the examinee may simply be underreporting due to a lack of insight or awareness rather than due to defensiveness. However, if the CDF is high, or all three scores are elevated, Morey notes that the examinee is likely making overt efforts to respond defensively.

Several studies have examined the ability of the PAI to detect impression management when examinees have been coached. However, the results have not always been consistent. While some studies did not find significant differences in mean scores on PAI validity scales between coached feigners and comparison groups (e.g., Bagby, Nicholson, Bacchiochi, Ryder, & Bury, 2002; Eakin, Weathers, Benson, Anderson, & Funderbunk, 2006), other studies have found that coached feigners produced lower mean scores on the PAI validity scales than uncoached feigners (Guriel-Tennant & Fremouw, 2006). As such, the evidence is inconclusive at this point whether test coaching decreases the sensitivity of the PAI validity indices when feigners have been coached.

Veltri and Williams (2012) investigated whether symptom coaching would improve the ability of feigners to successfully malinger on the PAI and found mixed results. They concluded that when malingerers were attempting to feign schizophrenia, being provided with symptom information did not improve their ability to avoid detection on the validity scales. However, feigners were somewhat less likely to be detected on the PAI when feigning nonpsychotic disorders (e.g., PTSD, depression, generalized anxiety disorder). Again, as we have seen with the MMPI-2, coached feigners may be more successful when attempting to malinger mild or moderate dysfunction, as compared to severe psychosis.

Baer & Wetter (1997) examined the ability of the PAI validity scales to detect coached underreporting using samples of college students. They divided subjects into three groups: standard responders, uncoached "fake good" responders, and coached "fake good" responders. They found that the standard PAI validity scales were able to distinguish between uncoached "fake good" responders and honest reporters, but they were much less effective at identifying coached "fake good" responders. The uncoached "fake good" group scored lower on NIM than the standard responders and higher on the PIM and DEF than both the standard responders and the coached group. The authors also found large effect sizes on PIM and DEF between the uncoached group and standard responders, but very small effect sizes on these scales between the coached group and standard responders, suggesting that coaching allowed them to evade detection more successfully.

MCMI-III

The Millon Clinical Multiaxial Inventory-III (MCMI-III; Millon, Davis, & Millon, 1997) was developed to measure personality pathology consistent with Millon's personality typology, as well as assess features of DSM-IV Axis I disorders. Unlike the MMPI-2 and the PAI, which have community normative samples, the MCMI-III was normed on a clinical population and is intended to be used to discriminate among different clinical groups (Craig, 1999).

The MCMI-III contains four validity scales. The Validity Index (V scale) assesses for random responding and carelessness and is composed of items that are highly unlikely to be true (e.g., "I have not seen a car in ten years"). Endorsing two or more statements in this scale invalidates the test protocol (Craig, 1999). The Disclosure Scale (X scale) is interpretively useful at both the high and low ends. High scores on the X scale indicate indiscriminate symptom endorsement and may be indicative of possible feigning or carelessness. Low scores, in contrast, represent likely defensive responding (Craig, 1999). The Desirability Scale (Y scale) is also designed to detect defensiveness. High scores on this scale are correlated with overreporting of virtuous attitudes and underreporting of psychological problems (Craig, 1999). Lastly, the Debasement Scale (Z scale) is designed to be a measure of symptom exaggeration. However, Craig (1999) notes that high Z-scale scores can also be indicative of acute distress and may be influenced by true psychopathology.

Overall, there are far fewer studies examining impression management on the MCMI-III, as compared to the research on the MMPI-2 and the PAI. In particular, there are no current studies examining the impact of symptom or test coaching on the MCMI-III's ability to detect impression management. Two studies regarding the MCMI-III's ability to detect malingering both produced similar results. Daubert and Metzler (2000) and Schoenberg, Dorr, and Morgan (2003) both found that the best way to identify feigning on the MCMI-III was an elevated score on the X scale (defined as a score of 80 or higher in the former and above 84 in the latter). As a word of caution, though, Daubert and Metzler found acceptable positive predictive power (PPP) and negative predictive power (NPP) only when the base rate of malingering was 50%. They noted that PPP would decline with decreasing base rates in the population being evaluated. Schoenberg et al. also noted that their PPP and NPP were fairly low

(55.6 and 72.1, respectively), with a hit rate of only 63.1%. Taken together, these studies seem to support a tentative conclusion that elevations on the X scale may be the best method of identifying feigners on the MCMI-III, but this may not always be a reliable indicator of feigning, particularly when base rates of malingering are low in the population being evaluated.

Daubert and Metzler (2000) also examined the ability of the MCMI-III to detect underreporting of psychological problems. They concluded that the best method of identifying defensive profiles was a single cutoff of less than 38 on the Z scale. They found that using all three scales did not improve detection over using the single cutoff. Other studies have found that low scores on the X scale and high scores on the Y scale are also indicative of defensive responding (Bagby, Gillis, Toner, & Goldberg, 1991; Lenny & Dear, 2009). Interestingly, several studies have also found differences on the clinical scales of profiles in examinees who respond defensively. These studies have consistently found elevated scores on scales 4, 5, and 7 among examinees who attempt to "fake good" (Fals-Stewart, 1995; Lampel, 1999; Lenny & Dear, 2009; McCann et al., 2001).

Hanlon (2001), however, noted that elevations on clinical scales—particularly scales 4, 5, and 7—may be the result of built-in corrections on the MCMI-III when a "defensive" response set is detected. This "Denial/Complaint Adjustment" is an adjustment upwards of the three highest scales. Hanlon also indicated that, due to some item overlap of scales 4, 5, and 7, they sometimes tend to move in a set. Furthermore, since the MCMI-III was normed on a patient population and is not suitable for nonpatient test takers, the test may interpret "normal" responding by a nonpatient examinee as defensive responding. The resulting Denial/Complaint Adjustment could very well then lead to a clinical profile with elevations on scales 4, 5, and 7—suggesting that the examinee has significant problematic personality traits, when in fact, these elevations are simply the result of overcorrection. Other research has indicated that corrections for defensiveness make it almost impossible for the test to be invalidated due to overreporting of symptoms. These examples illustrate the importance of only selecting tests that are appropriate to the referral question and the individual examinee.

Of note, a new version of the MCMI—the MCMI-IV (Millon, Grossman, & Millon, 2015)—has just been released. However, because of its newness, there are currently no independent studies assessing its performance in examinees who overreport or underreport their symptoms.

Summary

Based on the available research, it seems reasonable to conclude that when examinees attempt to feign psychiatric symptoms or respond in a defensive manner, the MMPI-2, the PAI, and the MCMI-III are generally able to detect these efforts at impression management using standard validity scales. However, the efficacy of these validity scales seems to decrease when examinees have been coached on the test—specifically, the presence of the validity scales. In addition, there is also some evidence to suggest that these measures are more effective at detecting feigning of severe psychopathology, such as psychosis, and may be less effective at detecting feigning of more moderate impairments, such as depression or anxiety.

Detecting Impression Management with Performance-Based Testing

Much of the research on performance-based-testing and impression management focuses on the Rorschach, possibly because it is arguably the most popular performance-based method of personality assessment in clinical and forensic practice (Piotrowski, 1996; Quinnell & Bow, 2001). There are many differences between the Rorschach and self-report personality instruments that can provide crucial information that may only be revealed through performance-based testing. As Erard (2012) notes, the Rorschach, unlike self-report instruments, represents an in vivo, more indirect, and less controllable performance-based approach to assessing what examinees do in response to a new, challenging, and stressful task. Rather than asking examinees how they react to novel situations (as we might in a self-report measure), we instead present them with a novel situation and observe firsthand what they do.

Because of the drastic difference in how we measure personality constructs with the Rorschach as compared to self-report instruments, how we attempt to detect impression management will obviously be distinct. Unlike self-report instruments, in general, there are no built-in "validity scales" that were designed solely to measure possible symptom exaggeration or defensiveness. However, of note, the Rorschach Performance Assessment System® (R-PAS®; Meyer, Viglione, Mihura, Erard, & Erdberg, 2011) includes the Complexity score, which is expected to be low in examinees who attempt to conceal psychopathology and is expected to be high in examinees who attempt to exaggerate psychopathology

(Meyer et al.; Meyer, Viglione, & Mihura, this volume). In such cases, the R-PAS provides Complexity-Adjusted scoring to predict how the test results would look if the examinee had approached the test with an appropriate set. However, further research is needed to determine how well the Complexity score works in cases of malingering and defensive responding. For the time being, we must examine how examinees who intentionally try to present themselves in a spurious manner perform on measures that were designed to assess clinical constructs.

The Rorschach may be scored using a number of different scoring systems. The two most prominent systems at present are Exner's (2003) Comprehensive System and the Rorschach Performance Assessment System® (R-PAS®; Meyer, Viglione, Mihura, Erard, & Erdberg, 2011). Both systems use structural variables to score the examinee's responses to the inkblots and behavior during testing, though a full description of scoring and interpretive procedures is beyond the scope of this chapter (see Meyer et al., 2011; Meyer, Viglione, & Mihura, Chapter 2, this volume).

Meyer et al. (2011) argue that it's likely easier for examinees to consciously alter the thematic content of their responses—which is more explicit and controllable—than to alter their ultimate scores on structural variables, as these reflect more implicit processes. Consistent with this view, Holmes (1974) and Orpen (1978) found that subjects could indeed consciously manipulate their thematic projections when administered the Thematic Apperception Test (TAT), which is also a performance-based measure of personality functioning.

Research on Feigning on the Rorschach

As the Rorschach scoring systems do not contain any pure "validity indices" specifically designed to detect malingering, it can be difficult upon first glance for clinicians to identify malingered Rorschach protocols. An early study by Albert, Fox, and Kahn (1980) found that expert judges (composed of fellows of the Society for Personality Assessment) were unable to reliably distinguish between Rorschach protocols of genuine inpatients and those of simulators. Perry and Kinder (1990) concluded that while some individual studies found Rorschach index scores that were related to malingering, when examining the literature to date at that time, no specific malingering pattern on the Rorschach was evident across the research.

Ganellen, Wasyliw, Haywood, and Grossman (1996) studied a group of examinees with high motives to malinger—individuals accused of serious crimes. They divided subjects into two groups (honest responders and malingerers), based on their scores on the MMPI validity scales. Ganellen et al. found that those classified as malingering did not differ from honest responders on Comprehensive System structural variables that distinguish psychotic patients from nonpsychotic patients. However, consistent with the theory that thematic content is more easily manipulated than structural variables, they noted that those classified as malingering produced a higher number of responses with dramatic content, which would qualify for scoring on Perry and Kinder's (1992) Dramatic Content index.

In contrast, Netter and Viglione (1994) found that at least one structural variable was significantly impacted by examinees' attempts to malinger psychopathology. They found that approximately one-third of subjects instructed to simulate schizophrenia were able to do so, as demonstrated by a score of 4 or higher on the SCZI. According to a post-experiment questionnaire, the most frequently utilized strategy to simulate schizophrenia was to pretend that the response was alive (e.g., on Card IV: "a prehistoric animal . . . it's scary . . . it's going to get me" [p. 54]). Subjects also reported giving rambling or circumstantial responses, trying to appear withdrawn, aloof, nervous, or uncomfortable, or trying to pretend they were hearing voices (e.g., by talking to an "imaginary friend") during the assessment in order to try to appear psychotic.

Perry and Kinder (1992) also found that participants were able to alter structural variables when given information about schizophrenia and asked to simulate this condition on the Rorschach. Participants who received this instruction produced elevations on SCZI and WSum6 as well as evidence of impairments in reality testing (elevated X-%, low Pop and X+%) and elevations on M-. When combined with Netter and Viglione's (1994) results, this suggests that informed examinees may be able to simulate indicators of psychosis on some structural variables.

Meisner (1988) found different results, however, during a study of simulated depression on the Rorschach. Participants were given information about symptoms of depression and offered a cash incentive to try to successfully feign these symptoms. However, while participants produced elevated scores on the Beck Depression Inventory, they failed to produce significant elevations on Rorschach variables associated with emotional distress. Labott and Wallach (2002) also failed to find significant differences between Rorschach protocols of individuals instructed to feign dissociative identity disorder and those told to respond honestly.

Frueh and Kinder (1994) conducted a study with 40 participants who were assigned to either a control group or a role-informed malingering group, who where given a brief description of the symptoms and experiences of Vietnam veterans with PTSD and offered a cash reward as incentive to simulate this condition on the Rorschach. Their scores were then compared to the Rorschach protocols of 20 Vietnam veterans with PTSD. Malingerers tended to produce more dramatic responses (e.g., with violence, bloodshed), more color responses (less emotionally constrained), and longer and more complicated answers than the Vietnam veterans with PTSD. Moreover, malingerers also produced some scores more often associated with schizophrenia (e.g., scores reflecting poor reality testing or social ineptness), which were not consistent with the examinees with PTSD. This suggests that malingerers tended to go too far in their attempts to feign PTSD.

Summary

There is some overlap across studies to suggest that protocols with high dramatic content and excessively long, rambling—even circumstantial—responses in the absence of structural scores indicating poor reality testing (e.g., high X-%, low populars) and cognitive slippage (e.g., low WSum6) may be indicative of malingering. However, there is some evidence to suggest that malingerers informed about the symptoms of schizophrenia may be able to alter their structural variables such that they appear to be genuinely psychotic on some of these variables.

As a word of caution, it is important to note that some of the dramatic responses that malingerers may produce could load onto the Traumatic Content Index (Armstrong & Loewenstein, 1990), which is a measure designed to assess for a history of trauma on the Rorschach. As such, one should take care not to assume that dramatic content in Rorschach responses is surely indicative of malingering. Clinicians should be sure to assess for a history of trauma in these cases to explore alternate explanations. Research from Frueh and Kinder (1994) suggests that—at least for war veterans with PTSD—true trauma patients may be more constricted (both in the amount of emotionally laden/color responses and in their verbosity when giving responses) than malingerers.

Research on Defensiveness on the Rorschach

Some have suggested that defensive examinees tend to produce Rorschach protocols characterized by a low number of responses, high Lambda, and a high number of popular responses (Ganellen, 1994; Weiner, 2003). While these variables would make theoretical sense in defensive examinees, the research is, unfortunately, inconsistent in supporting these hypotheses.

Ganellen (1994) studied airline pilots who were being assessed as part of an evaluation to assess fitness to return to work after having completed a program for substance abuse treatment. These examinees had a very real motive to try to present themselves as psychologically healthy. However, on the whole, these subjects still produced Rorschach protocols with indicators of emotional distress, self-critical ideation, and difficulties in relationships, all of which were denied during interviews and on the MMPI-2. These pilots also produced three times as many Personalized (PER) responses and a greater number of high-Lambda protocols than Exner's (1991) sample.

In contrast, Wasyliw, Benn, Grossman, and Haywood (1998) found no significant differences on Comprehensive System variables between two groups of sex offenders, classified as "minimizing" and "nonminimizing" based on their MMPI-2 validity scales. They concluded that none of the variables that they studied could detect a minimizing response style on the Rorschach. In a follow-up study, Grossman, Wasyliw, Benn, and Gyoerkoe (2002) found that minimizers produced normal MMPI-2 clinical profiles, but still produced evidence of psychological problems on the Rorschach. Taken in combination with Ganellen's (1994) findings, these results suggest that, despite motivations to "fake good" and attempts to conceal problems during interviewing and self-report testing, examinees may be unable to alter their Rorschach structural variables to minimize psychological problems.

Research on Test Coaching on the Rorschach

Given that, as previously discussed, information about the Rorschach can readily be found online and in easily accessible books, recent studies have begun to examine how reading information about the test—including scoring and interpretive procedures—may impact examinees' responses. Unfortunately, at present, only two major studies have tackled this topic.

Schultz and Brabender (2013) used a community-based sample of parents, who were given a simulated child custody situation and instructed to present themselves as free from psychological problems on the Rorschach in order to retain custody of their children. Prior to administration, half of the subjects received a summary of Internet information about the Rorschach, while the remainder had no prior exposure to the test. The results indicated that those who read information about the Rorschach produced, on average, fewer responses overall, but more popular responses than the control group. Initially, Schultz and Brabender found higher scores on variables related to perceptual accuracy (e.g., FQo, XA%). However, these significant differences disappeared when the difference in popular responses was statistically controlled.

Hartmann and Hartmann (2014) utilized a sample of psychiatric outpatients in Norway to examine whether exposure to test information about the Rorschach would impact their results. Participants were divided into three groups: uncoached "fake good" patients, Internet "fake good" patients (who were given information from the Internet about the Rorschach and the MMPI-2, including how to appear healthy, prior to testing), and a standard control group. A comparison group of nonpatients were also recruited from the University of Oslo.

The researchers found that neither the faking patients nor the Internet faking patients were able to portray themselves as mentally healthy on the Rorschach. The profiles of the faking patients could not be distinguished from the profiles of standard patients. In contrast to results from Schultz and Brabender (2013), those patients who received Internet information about the test showed poorer results with regard to perceptual accuracy (e.g., higher X-%) than those who had not received this information. Internet-faking patients also scored higher on F% and low on movement and color responses. In addition, they produced fewer aggressive and dramatic responses than the other groups. Again, this appears to be consistent with the theory that patients may more easily manipulate the thematic content of Rorschach responses when attempting to dissimulate, rather than change their scores on structural variables.

Advantages and Challenges of Utilizing a Multimethod Approach

With any psychological evaluation, an approach that uses multiple methods of assessment, including both self-report measures and performance-based testing is ideal. While self-report measures appear to be the most popular method of psychological assessment (Archer et al., 2006), utilizing this method alone can have many limitations. For example, as Mihura (2012) points out, what people report about themselves and what they do in the real world may be quite different. A meta-analysis conducted by Greenwald, Poehlman, Uhlmann, and Banaji (2009) found only a small association between self-reported characteristics and implicitly assessed personality traits. As Meyer (1997) notes, there may be a disparity between the characteristics that an examinee consciously recognizes and is willing to report and those traits that are actually present on an implicit level. Thus it would be wise to include evaluation methods as part of a comprehensive assessment that do measure these constructs through means other than just self-report.

Mihura (2012) also argues that utilizing a multimethod approach to assessment can provide incremental validity for obtaining a full, coherent picture of the area or referral question that one is trying to assess. Because no one test can fully capture the range and depth of experiences of everyone with a given disorder or personality trait, it is crucial to include multiple methods of assessing the same construct in order to try to capture the breadth of experience of the person in front of us. As Meyer (1997) notes, different tests capture different types of information. He argues that while self-report measures can provide specific information about symptoms and experiences, the Rorschach can deliver rich information about personality characteristics, propensities, and mental representations. Trying to pigeonhole an examinee's personality functioning by using only one measure would rob us of the richness of a full picture of their worldview and history, which is necessary if we as assessors are going to provide useful and individualized recommendations.

Using a multimethod approach to assessment is particularly important when attempting to detect efforts at impression management. As we have seen through a review of available research, different methods of assessment have unique advantages in detecting efforts to malinger or respond defensively. Many self-report methods have built-in validity scales, which provide specific cutoff scores based on empirical data to help decide if an examinee might be attempting to present him or herself dishonestly. However, because self-report measures are higher in face validity, they may be easier for examinees to consciously manipulate, particularly if they have been coached. Performance-based measures, such as the Rorschach, on the other hand, are low in face validity. Research seems to generally support the theory that, while examinees may be able to consciously alter the thematic content of their responses, it tends to be much more difficult for them to alter their scores on structural variables. As such, performance-based testing offers a unique perspective when an examinee may be making efforts to manage how they present themselves in an evaluation.

When using multiple methods of assessment (e.g., self-report measures and performance-based testing), it is inevitable that, much of the time, the results from these tests will not converge—particularly if an examinee is making efforts at impression management. Meyer (1997) demonstrated that when examinees are open and engaged on one method of assessment (e.g., the MMPI), but guarded and defensive on another type (e.g., the Rorschach), the results from the two tests on the same construct (e.g., depression) may very well not be correlated. That is, an examinee may approach different methods of assessment differently, and as such, each test may show something different about the same construct of interest. Thus it is always advantageous to use multiple methods when available, as one method alone may not provide a great deal of information, particularly if the examinee is guarded when responding to that measure.

Using multiple methods of assessment is not without its challenges. Because of the aforementioned differences between self-report and performance-based testing, the clinician is likely to encounter different results on different tests assessing the same characteristic. The clinician will then have to examine seemingly discrepant pieces of information to determine why different tests produced different results. Could it be—as Meyer (1997) observed—that the examinee approached the tests with different degrees of openness?

Alternatively, one test may focus more on a certain aspect or cluster of symptoms of a diagnostic category, while another method could capture an entirely unique perspective. As an example, an examinee may not view herself as particularly distant from others, but on the Rorschach, she provided no Texture responses and few responses with Human content or cooperative movement. Perhaps, in this case, the examinee is simply not aware of her detached interpersonal style, or it may be that the examinee wants to portray herself as someone warm and friendly, even if she is not in everyday life. Making sense of this discrepancy in the data would certainly be important if the examinee was attempting to portray herself in a more positive light for the purposes of the assessment.

Summary and Conclusions

Regardless of the context—be it a routine clinical personality assessment or a high-stakes forensic evaluation—we must be vigilant regarding the possibility that examinees have motivations to present themselves differently from how others see them during a psychological evaluation. Given high enough stakes, they may be motivated to present themselves in a defensive manner or attempt to exaggerate or feign psychological symptoms that they do not truly experience. While good clinical interviewing skills are a must in helping to discern whether an examinee might be defensive or malingering, examination of psychological test data can be a valuable tool in detecting impression management.

A clear advantage of using self-report personality measures or instruments specifically designed to detect symptom feigning in these cases is that these tests generally have reliable, well-researched validity scales that give clear indications and cutoff scores to detect impression management. However, it is important to remember that with commonly used broadband personality measures (e.g., MMPI-2, PAI, MCMI-III), the ability of these validity scales to detect impression management may be compromised when examinees have been coached about the test. Research also suggests that validity scales may be better at detecting malingering when examinees are attempting to feign psychosis or other severe form of psychopathology. The validity scales may be less effective at detecting milder forms of psychopathology.

In some cases, instruments specifically designed to detect malingering—such as the SIRS, the SIMS, or the M-FAST—may be helpful in making a determination that an examinee is intentionally trying to exaggerate his or her psychological problems. However, it is important to remember that these instruments tend to be more useful in clear-cut cases. For example, the SIRS-2 has high specificity, but unfortunately much more modest sensitivity in detecting malingering. Furthermore, while these instruments may be able to confirm that an examinee is feigning, they do not tell the examiner anything about the motivation behind the feigning. In addition, as they do not assess genuine psychiatric symptoms or personality traits, these tests cannot rule out the possibility that the examinee may be experiencing some genuine problems. They are not designed to discern between genuine and feigned symptoms—only to detect when an examinee is attempting to feign at least some of their reported problems.

Regarding performance-based testing, it is widely believed that thematic content is more easily manipulated than structural variables. In general, the research on the Rorschach seems to support this notion. However, given the limited research available on how coaching with Internet information about the test may impact performance, caution should be exercised, and examinees should always be questioned about their prior exposure to information about the Rorschach. Furthermore, there have been studies that indicate that examinees can sometimes alter structural variables when instructed to malinger—particularly, when they are instructed to feign psychosis. In cases where an examinee is suspected of malingering a depressive disorder, the available research indicates that he or she has been less effective at manipulating structural variables associated with this diagnosis. Given that there is some indication that validity scales on self-report measures may falter when examinees attempt to feign milder forms of mood or anxiety disorders, it may be helpful to include the Rorschach as part of one's test battery to further evaluate whether the examinee also presents with evidence of the disorder on performance-based testing.

REFERENCES

Albert, S., Fox. H. M., & Kahn, M. W. (1980). Faking psychosis on the Rorschach: Can expert judges detect malingering? *Journal of Personality Assessment, 44*, 115–119.

Alwes, Y. R., Clark, J. A., Berry, D. T. R., & Granacher, R. P. (2008). Screening for feigning in a civil forensic setting. *Journal of Clinical and Experimental Neuropsychology, 30*(2), 1–8.

Arbisi, P. A., Ben-Borath, Y. S., & McNulty, J. (2006). The ability of the MMPI-2 to detect feigned PTSD within the context of compensation seeking. *Psychological Services, 3*, 249–261.

Archer, R. P., Buffington-Vollum, J. K., Stredny, R. V., & Handel, R. W. (2006). A survey of psychological test use patterns among forensic psychologists. *Journal of Personality Assessment, 87*, 84–94.

Armstrong, J. G., & Loewenstein, R. J. (1990). Characteristics of patients with multiple personality and dissociative disorders on psychological testing. *Journal of Nervous and Mental Disorders, 178*, 448–454.

Bacchiochi, J. B., & Bagby, R. M. (2006). Development and validation of the malingering discriminant function index for the MMPI-2. *Journal of Personality Assessment, 87*, 51–61.

Baer, R. A., & Miller, J. (2002). Underreporting of psychopathology on the MMPI-2: A meta-analytic review. *Psychological Assessment, 14*, 16-26.

Baer, R. A., & Sekirnjak, G. (1997). Detection of underreporting on the MMPI-2 in clinical population: Effects of information about validity scales. *Journal of Personality Assessment, 69*, 555-567.

Baer, R. A., & Wetter, M. W. (1997). Effects of information about validity scales on underreporting symptoms on the Personality Assessment Inventory. *Journal of Personality Assessment, 68*, 402-413.

Baer, R. A., Wetter, M., & Berry, T. R. (1995). Effects of information about validity scales on underreporting of symptoms on the MMPI-2: An analogue investigation. *Assessment, 2*, 189-200.

Bagby, M. R., Gillis, J. R., Toner, B. B., & Goldberg, J. (1991). Detecting fake-good and fake-bad responding on the Millon Clinical Multiaxial Inventory-II. *Psychological Assessment: A Journal of Consulting and Clinical Psychology, 3*, 496-498.

Bagby, M. R., Nicholson, R. A., Bacchiochi, J. R., Ryder, A. G., & Bury, A. S. (2002). The predictive capacity of the MMPI-2 and the PAI validity scales and indices to detect coached and uncoached feigning. *Journal of Personality Assessment, 78*, 69-86.

Bagby, R. M., Rogers, R., & Buis, T. (1994). Detecting malingered and defensive responding on the MMPI-2 in a forensic inpatient sample. *Journal of Personality Assessment, 62*(2), 191-203.

Bagby, M. R., Rogers, R., Nicholson, R. A., Buis, T., Seeman, M. V., & Rector, N. A. (1997). Does clinical training facilitate feigning schizophrenia on the MMPI-2? *Psychological Assessment, 9*, 106-112.

Ben-Porath, Y. S., & Tellegen, A. (2008). *Minnesota Multiphasic Personality Inventory-2 Restructured Form (MMPI-2-RF): Manual for administration, scoring, and interpretation.* Minneapolis: University of Minnesota Press.

Brand, B. L., Tursich, M., Tzall, D., & Loewenstein, R. J. (2014). Utility of the SIRS-2 in distinguishing genuine from simulated Dissociative Identity Disorder. *Psychological Trauma: Theory, Research, Practice, and Policy, 6*(4), 308-317.

Bury, A. S., & Bagby, R. M. (2002). The detection fo feigned uncoached and coached posttraumatic stress disorder with the MMPI-2 in a sample of workplace accident victims. *Psychological Assessment, 14*, 472-484.

Butcher, J. N., Graham, J. R., Ben-Porath, Y. S., Tellegen, A., Dahlstrom, W. G., & Kaemmer, B. (2001). *Minnesota Multiphasic Personality Inventory—2: Manual for administration, scoring, and interpretation* (Rev. ed.). Minneapolis: University of Minnesota Press.

Christiansen, A. K., & Vincent, J. P. (2012). Assessment of litigation context, suggestion, and malingering measures among personal injury litigants. *Journal of Forensic Psychology Practice, 12*(3), 238-258.

Cornell, D. G., & Hawk, G. L. (1989). Clinical presentation of malingerers diagnosed by experienced forensic psychologists. *Law and Human Behavior, 13*, 375-383.

Craig, R. J. (1999). Essentials of MCMI-III assessment. In S. Strack (Ed.), *Essentials of Millon Inventories assessment* (pp. 1-51). New York: Wiley.

Daubert, S. D., & Metzler, A. E. (2000). The detection of fake-bad and fake-good responding in the Millon Clinical Multiaxial Inventory III. *Psychological Assessment, 12*, 418-424.

Douglas, K. S., Huss, M. T., Murdoch, L. L., Washington, D. O., & Koch, W. J. (1999). Posttraumatic stress disorder stemming from motor vehicle accidents: Legal issues in Canada and the United States. In E. J. Hickling (Ed.) *The international handbook of road traffic accidents & psychological trauma: Current understanding, treatment, and law* (pp. 271-289). New York: Elsevier.

Eakin, D. E., Weathers, F. W., Benson, T. B., Anderson, C. F., & Funderbunk, B. (2006). Detection of feigned posttraumatic stress disorder: A comparison of the MMPI-2 and PAI. *Journal of Psychopathology and Behavioral Assessment, 28*, 145-155.

Edens, J. F., Poythress, N. G., & Watkins-Clay, M. M. (2007). Detection of malingering in psychiatric unit and general population prison inmates: A comparison of the PAI, SIMS, and SIRS. *Journal of Personality Assessment, 88*(1), 33-42.

Elhai, J. D., Frueh, B. C., Gold, P. B., Gold, S. N., & Hamner, M. B. (2000). Clinical presentations of posttraumatic stress disorder across trauma populations: A comparison of MMPI-2 profiles of combat veterans and adult survivors of child sexual abuse. *The Journal of Nervous and Mental Disease, 188*(10), 708-713.

Elhai, J. D., Gold, P. B., Frueh, B. C., & Gold, S. N. (2000). Cross-validation of the MMPI-2 in detecting malingered posttraumatic stress disorder. *Journal of Personality Assessment, 75*(3), 449-463.

Elhai, J. D., Gold, S. N., Sellers, A. H., & Dorfman, W. I. (2001). The detection of malingered posttraumatic stress disorder with MMPI-2 fake bad indices. *Assessment, 8*(2), 221-236.

Erard, R. E. (2012). Expert testimony using the Rorschach performance. *Psychological Injury and Law, 5*, 122-134.

Exner, J. E. (1991). *The Rorschach: A comprehensive system. Vol. 2: Interpretation* (2nd ed.). New York: Wiley.

Exner, J. E. (2003). *The Rorschach: A comprehensive system: Vol. 1. Basic foundations and principles of interpretation* (4th ed.). Hoboken, NJ: Wiley.

Fals-Stewart, W. (1995). The effect of defensive responding by substance abusing patients on the Millon Clinical Multiaxial Inventory. *Journal of Personality Assessment, 64*, 540-551.

Frueh, B. C., & Kinder, B. N. (1994). The susceptibility of the Rorschach inkblot test to malingering of combat-related PTSD. *Journal of Personality Assessment, 62*, 280-298.

Ganellen, R. J. (1994). Attempting to conceal psychological disturbance: MMPI defensive set and the Rorschach. *Journal of Personality Assessment, 63*, 423-437.

Ganellen, R. J. (2008). Rorschach assessment of malingering and defensive response set. In C. B. Gacono & F. B. Evans (Eds.), *The handbook of forensic Rorschach assessment* (pp. 89-119). New York: Routledge, Taylor & Francis Group.

Ganellen, R. J., Wasyliw, O. E., Haywood, T. W., & Grossman, L. S. (1996). Can psychosis be malingered on the Rorschach? An empirical study. *Journal of Personality Assessment, 66*, 65-80.

Green, D., & Rosenfeld, B. (2011). Evaluating the gold standard: A review and meta-analysis of the Structured Interview of Reported Symptoms. *Psychological Assessment, 23*(1), 95-107.

Green, D., Rosenfeld, B., & Belfi, B. (2013). New and improved? A comparison of the original and revised versions of the Structured Interview of Reported Symptoms. *Assessment, 20*, 210-218.

Greenwald, A. G., Poehlman, T. A., Uhlmann, E. L., & Banaji, M. R. (2009). Understanding and using the Implicit Association Test: III. Meta-analysis of predictive validity. *Journal of Personality and Social Psychology, 97*, 17–41.

Grossman, L. S., Wasyliw, O. E., Benn, A. F., & Gyoerkoe, K. L. (2002). Can sex offenders who minimize on the MMPI conceal psychopathology on the Rorschach? *Journal of Personality Assessment, 78*, 484–501.

Guriel-Tennant, J., & Freemouw, W. (2006). Impact of trauma history and coaching on malingering of posttraumatic stress disorder using the PAI, TSI, and M-FAST. *The Journal of Forensic Psychiatry & Psychology, 17*(4), 577–592.

Guy, L. S., Kwartner, P. P., & Miller, H. A. (2006). Investigating the M-FAST: Psychometric properties and utility to detect diagnostic specific malingering. *Behavioral Sciences & the Law, 24*, 687–702.

Guy, L. S., & Miller, H. A. (2004). Screening for malingerd psychopathology in a correctional setting: Utility of the Miller Forensic Assessment of Symptoms Test (M-FAST). *Criminal Justice and Behavior, 31*(6), 695–716.

Hanlon, R. L. (2001). The Millon Clinical Multiaxial Inventory-III: The normal quartet in child custody cases. *American Journal of Forensic Psychology, 19*, 57–75.

Hartmann, E., & Hartmann, T. (2014). The impact of exposure to Internet-based information about the Rorschach and the MMPI-2 on psychiatric outpatients' ability to simulate mentally healthy test performance. *Journal of Personality Assessment, 96*, 432–444.

Hawes, S. W., & Boccaccini, M. T. (2009). Detection of overreporting of psychopathology on the Personality Assessment Inventory: A meta-analytic review. *Psychological Assessment, 21*, 112–124.

Holmes, D. S. (1974). The conscious control of thematic projection. *Journal of Consulting and Clinical Psychology, 42*, 323–329.

Jackson, R. L., Rogers, R., & Sewell, K. W. (2005). Forensic applications of the Miller Forensic Assessment of Symptoms Test (MFAST): Screening for fringed disorders in competency to stand trial evaluations. *Law and Human Behavior, 29*, 199–210.

Jelicic, M., Ceunen, E., Peters, M. J. V., & Merckelbach, H. (2011). Detecting coached feigning using the Test of Memory Malingering (TOMM) and the Structured Inventory of Malingered Symptomatology (SIMS). *Journal of Clinical Psychology, 67*(9), 850–855.

Jelicic, M., Merckelbach, H., Candel, I., & Geraerts, E. (2007). Detection of feigned cognitive dysfunction using special malinger tests: A simulation study in naïve and coached malingerers. *International Journal of Neuroscience, 117*, 1185–1192.

Labott, S. M., & Wallach, H. R. (2002). Malingering dissociative identity disorder: Objective and projective assessment. *Psychological Reports, 90*, 525–538.

Lampel, A. (1999). Use of the Millon Clinical Multiaxial Inventory-III in evaluation child custody litigants. *American Journal of Forensic Psychology, 17*, 10–31.

Landon, R. I., & Almer, E. R. (2002). Characteristics of compensable disability patients who choose to litigate. *Journal of the American Academy of Psychiatry and the Law, 30*, 400–404.

Lange, R. T., Sullivan, K. A., & Scott, C. (2010). Comparison of MMPI-2 and PAI validity indicators to detect feigned depression and PTSD symptom reporting. *Psychiatry Research, 176*(2), 229-235.

Lees-Haley, P. R. (1997). Attorney's influence on expert evidence in forensic psychological and neuropsychological. *Assessment, 4*, 321-326.

Lenny, P., & Dear, G. E. (2009). Faking good on the MCMI-III: Implications for child custody evaluations. *Journal of Personality Assessment, 91*, 553-559.

Marshall, M. B., & Bagby, R. M. (2006). The incremental validity and clinical utility of the MMPI-2 Infrequency Posttraumatic Stress Disorder Scale. *Assessment, 13*(4), 417-429.

McCann, J., Flens, J., Campagna, V., Collman, P., Lazzaro, T., & Connor, E. (2001). The MCMI-III in child custody evaluations: A normative study. *Journal of Forensic Psychology, 1*, 27-44.

McGuire, B. E. (1999). The assessment of malingering in traumatic stress claimants. *Psychiatry, Psychology and Law, 6*, 163-173.

Meisner, S. (1988). Susceptibility of Rorschach distress correlates to malingering. *Journal of Personality Assessment, 52*, 564-571.

Meyer, G. J. (1997). On the integration of personality assessment methods: The Rorschach and MMPI. *Journal of Personality Assessment, 68*, 297-330.

Meyer, G. J., Viglione, D. J., Mihura, J. L., Erard, R. E., & Erdberg, P. (2011). *Rorschach Performance Assessment System: Administration, coding, interpretation, and technical manual*. Toledo, OH: Rorschach Performance Assessment System, LLC.

Mihura, J. L. (2012). The necessity of multiple test methods in conducting assessments: The role of the Rorschach and self-report. *Psychological Injury and the Law, 5*, 97-106.

Miller, H. A. (2001). *M-FAST: Miller Forensic Assessment of Symptoms Test professional manual*. Odessa, FL: Psychological Assessment Resources.

Miller, H. A. (2004). Examining the use of the M-FAST with criminal defendant incompetent to stand trial. *International Journal of Offender Therapy and Comparative Criminology, 48*, 268-280.

Millon, T., Davis, R., & Millon, C. (1997). *The Millon Clinical Multiaxial Inventory—III manual* (2nd ed.). Minneapolis, MN: National Computer Systems.

Millon, T., Grossman, S., & Millon, C. (2015). *The Millon Clinical Multiaxial Inventory—IV manual*. Minneapolis, MN: Pearson Assessments.

Mittenberg, W., Patton, C., Canyock, E. M., & Condit, D. C. (2002). Base rates of malingering and symptom exaggeration. *Journal of Clinical and Experimental Neuropsychology, 24*, 1094-1102.

Morey, L. C. (1991). *The Personality Assessment Inventory: Professional manual*. Odessa, FL: Psychological Assessment Resources.

Morey, L. C. (1996). *An interpretive guide to the Personality Assessment Inventory (PAI)*. Odessa, FL: Psychological Assessment Resources.

Morey, L. C. (2003). *Essentials of PAI assessment*. Hoboken, NJ: Wiley.

Moyer, D. M., Burkhardt, B., & Gordon, R. M. (2002). Faking PTSD from a motor vehicle accident on the MMPI-2. *American Journal of Forensic Psychology, 20*(2), 81-89.

Netter, B. E. C., & Viglione, D. J. (1994). An empirical study of malingering schizophrenia on the Rorschach. *Journal of Personality Assessment, 62,* 45-57.

Orpen, C. (1978). Conscious control of projection in the Thematic Apperception Test. *Psychology: A Journal of Human Behavior, 15*(2), 67-75.

Paulhus, D. L. (1984). Two-component models of socially desirable responding. *Journal of Personality and Social Psychology, 46*(3), 598-609.

Paulhus, D. L. (1988). *Assessing self-deception and impression management in self-reports: The Balanced Inventory of Desirable Responding* (Unpublished manual). Vancouver, Canada: University of British Columbia.

Peebles, J., & Moore, R. J. (1998). Detecting socially desirable responding with the Personality Assessment Inventory: The Positive Impression Management Scale and the Defensiveness Index. *Journal of Clinical Psychology, 54*(5), 621-628.

Perry, G. G., & Kinder, B. N. (1990). The susceptibility of the Rorschach to malingering: A critical review. *Journal of Projective Techniques and Personality Assessment, 54*(1-2), 47-57.

Perry, G. G., & Kinder, B. N. (1992). Susceptibility of the Rorschach to malingering: A schizophrenia analogue. In C. D. Spielberger & J. Butcher (Eds.), *Advances in personality zssessment,* (Vol. 9, pp. 127-140). Hillsdale, NJ: Lawrence Erlbaum Associates, Inc.

Piotrowski, C. (1996). The status of Exner's comprehensive system in contemporary research. *Perceptual and Motor Skills, 82,* 1341-1342.

Poundstone, W. (1983). *Big secrets: The uncensored truth about all sorts of stuff you are never supposed to know.* New York: HarperCollins.

Powell, M. R., Gfeller, J. D., Hendricks, B. L., & Sharland, M. (2004). Detecting symptom- and test-coached simulators with the Test of Memory Malingering. *Archives of Clinical Neuropsychology, 19,* 693-702.

Quinnell, F., & Bow, J. (2001). Psychological tests used in child custody evaluations. *Behavioral Sciences and the Law, 19,* 491-500.

Resnick, P. J. (1997). Malingered psychosis. In R. Rogers (Ed.) *Clinical assessment of malingering and deception* (pp. 47-67). New York: Guilford Press.

Resnick, P. J., West, S., & Payne, J. W. (2008). Malingering of posttraumatic disorders. In R. Rogers (Ed.), *Clinical assessment of malingering and deception* (3rd ed., pp. 109-127). New York: Guilford.

Rogers, R. (1990). Models of feigned mental illness. *Professional Psychology: Research and Practice, 21,* 182-188.

Rogers, R. (Ed.). (1997). *Clinical assessment of malingering and deception* (2nd ed.). New York: Guilford.

Rogers, R. (2008). *Clinical assessment of malingering and deception.* (3rd ed.) New York: Guilford.

Rogers, R., Bagby, R. M., & Chakraborty, D. (1993). Feigning schizophrenic disorders on the MMPI-2: Detection of coached simulators. *Journal of Personality Assessment, 60,* 215-226.

Rogers, R., Bagby, R. M., & Dickens, S. E. (1992). *Structured Interview of Reported Symptoms (SIRS) and professional manual.* Lutz, FL: Psychological Assessment Resources.

Rogers, R., Gillard, N. D., Berry, D. T. R., & Granacher, R. P. (2011). Effectiveness of the MMPI-2-RF validity scales for feigned mental disorders and cognitive impairment: A known-groups study. *Journal of Psychopathology and Behavior Assessment, 33*, 355–367.

Rogers, R., Gillis, J. R., Bagby, R. M., & Monteiro, E. (1991). Detection of malingering on the Structured Interview of Reported Symptoms (SIRS): A study of coached and uncoached simulators. *Psychological Assessment: A Journal of Clinical and Consulting Psychology, 3*(4), 673–677.

Rogers, R., Kropp, R. P., Bagby, R. M., & Dickens, S. E. (1992). Faking specific disorders: A study of the Structured Interview of Reported Symptoms (SIRS). *Journal of Clinical Psychology, 48*(5), 643–648.

Rogers, R., Salekin, R. T., Sewell, K. W., Goldstein, A., & Leonard, K. (1998). A comparison of forensic and nonforensic malingerers: A prototypical analysis of exploratory models. *Law and Human Behavior, 22*(4), 353–367.

Rogers, R., Sewell, K. W., & Gillard, N. D. (2010). *Structured Interview of Reported Symptoms-2 (SIRS-2) and professional manual.* Lutz, FL: Psychological Assessment Resources.

Rogers, R., Sewell, K. W., & Goldstein, A. (1994). Explanatory models of malingering: A prototypical analysis. *Law and Human Behavior, 18*, 543–552.

Rogers, R., Sewell, K. W., Martin, M. A., & Vitacco, M. J. (2003). Detection of feigned mental disorders: A meta-analysis of the MMPI-2 and malingering. *Assessment, 10*(2), 160–177.

Rorschach test. (n.d.). In *Wikipedia*. Retrieved from https://en.wikipedia.org/wiki/Rorschach_test

Ruiz, M., Drake, E., Glass, A., Marcotte, D., & van Gorp, W. (2002). Trying to beat the system: Misuse of the Internet to assist in avoiding the detection of psychological symptom dissimulation. *Professional Psychology: Research and Practice, 33*, 294–299.

Schoenberg, M. R., Dorr, D., & Morgan, C. D. (2003). The ability of the Millon Clinical Multiaxial Inventory—Third edition to detect malingering. *Psychological Assessment, 15*(2), 198–204.

Schultz, D. S., & Brabender, V. M. (2013). More challenges since Wikipedia: The effects of exposure to Internet information about the Rorschach on selected Comprehensive System variables. *Journal of Personality Assessment, 95*, 149–158.

Schultz, D. S., & Loving, J. L. (2012). Challenges since Wikipedia: The availability of Rorschach information online and Internet users' reactions to online media coverage of the Rorschach-Wikipedia debate. *Journal of Personality Assessment, 94*, 73–81.

Sellbom, M., & Bagby, M. R. (2008). Validity of the MMPI-2-RF (restructured form) L-r and K-r scales in detecting underreporting in clinical and nonclinical samples. *Psychological Assessment: A Journal of Consulting and Clinical Psychology, 20*, 370–376.

Sellbom, M., Toomey, J. A., Wygant, D. B., Kucharski, T. L., & Duncan, S. (2010). Utility of the MMPI-2-RF (Restructured Form) validity scales in detecting malingering in a criminal forensic setting: A known groups design. *Psychological Assessment, 22*, 22–31.

Sliter, K. A., & Christiansen, N. D. (2012). Effects of targeted self-coaching on applicant distortion of personality measures. *Journal of Personnel Psychology, 11*(4), 169–175.

Toomey, J. A., Kucharski, L. T., & Duncan, S. (2009). The utility of the MMPI-2 Malingering Discriminant Function Index in the detection of malingering. *Assessment, 16*(1), 115–121.

van Impelen, A., Merckelbach, H., Jelicic, M., & Merten, T. (2014). The Structured Inventory of Malingered Symptomatology (SIMS): A systematic review and meta-analysis. *The Clinical Neuropsychologist, 28*(8), 1336–1365.

Veazey, C. H., Wagner, A. L., Hays, J. R., & Miller, H. A. (2005). Validity of the Miller forensic assessment of symptoms test in psychiatric inpatients. *Psychological Reports, 96*(3), 771–774.

Veltri, C. O. C., & Williams, J. E. (2012). Does the disorder matter? Investigating a moderating effect on coached noncredible overreporting using the MMPI-2 and PAI. *Assessment, 20*(2), 199–209.

Viglione, D. J., Wright, D. M., Dizon, N. T., Moynihan, J. E., DuPuis, S., & Pizitz, T. D. (2001). Evading detection on the MMPI-2: Does caution produce more realistic patterns of responding? *Assessment, 8*, 237–250.

Vitacco, M. J., Rogers, R., Gabel, J., & Munizza, J. (2007). An evaluation of malingering screens with competency to stand trial patients: A known-groups comparison. *Law and Human Behavior, 31*, 249–260.

Walters, G. D., Rogers, R., Berry, D. T. R., Miller, H. A., Duncan, S. A., McCusker, P. J., . . . Granacher, R. P. (2008). Malingering as a categorical or dimensional construct: The latent structure of feigned psychopathology as measured by the SIRS and MMPI-2. *Psychological Assessment, 20*(3), 238–247.

Wasyliw, O. E., Benn, A. F., Grossman, L. S., & Haywood, T. W. (1998). Detecting of minimization of psychopathology on the Rorschach in cleric and noncleric alleged sex offenders. *Assessment, 5*, 389–397.

Weiner, I. B. (2003). *Principles of Rorschach interpretation* (2nd ed.). Mahwah, NJ: Erlbaum.

Westen, D., & Shedler, J. (2007). Personality diagnosis with the Shedler-Westen assessment procedure (SWAP): Integrating clinical and statistical measurement and prediction. *Journal of Abnormal Psychology, 116*, 810–822.

Wetter, M. W., Baer, R. A., Berry, D. T. R., Robison, L. H. & Sumpter, J. (1993). MMPI-2 profiles of motivated fakers given specific symptom information: A comparison to matched patients. *Psychological Assessment, 5*, 317–323.

Wetter, M. W., & Corrigan, S. K. (1995). Providing information to clients about psychological tests: A survey of attorney and law student attitudes. *Professional Psychology: Research and Practice, 26*, 474–477.

Widows, M., & Smith, G. P. (2005). *Structured Inventory of Malingered Symptomatology (SIMS) and professional manual*. Odessa, FL: Psychological Assessment Resources.

Youngjohn, J. R. (1995). Confirmed attorney coaching prior to neuropsychological evaluation. *Assessment, 2*, 279–283.

Part II

Forensic Applications

CHAPTER 4

INTEGRATING THE PERSONALITY ASSESSMENT INVENTORY AND RORSCHACH INKBLOT METHOD IN FORENSIC ASSESSMENT

Christopher Hopwood and F. Barton Evans

The Personality Assessment Inventory (PAI; Morey, 1991) and Rorschach Inkblot Method (RIM; Rorschach, 1921) are two of the most commonly used and well-validated instruments used in forensic settings (see Gacono & Evans, 2008, Morey & Meyer, 2013). Both instruments have been found to meet standards necessary for use in court (PAI: Mullen & Edens, 2008; Rorschach: McCann & Evans, 2008, Meloy, 2008, Erard, 2012). Furthermore, several aspects of these tests make them highly complementary for clinical and forensic assessment. However, thus far there are currently few resources in the literature on how to combine these instruments for clinical practice (Charnas, Hilsenroth, Zodan, & Blais, 2010; Klonsky, 2004), let alone forensic practice. In this chapter, we first review the PAI in terms of its development, validity, and interpretation in forensic settings. We will then discuss a case example highlighting the value of synthesizing PAI and Rorschach data in forensic practice. We will conclude with the integration of the PAI with the Rorschach for forensic personality assessment.

DEVELOPMENT OF THE PAI

The PAI is a 344-item self-report questionnaire with 22 scales as well as a variety of supplemental indicators. The development of the PAI was based on the construct validation framework as articulated by Loevinger (1957) and Jackson (1970). From a construct validation perspective, tests represent theories about behavior that are instantiated in test content. Thus the first step in construct validation is carefully articulating the theory that will be operationalized by the test. This theory provides the basis for evaluating content validity, or the degree to which test content matches the constructs that the test endeavors to measure. The underlying theory of the PAI was preeminently practical. The goal was to provide clinicians working in a wide range of settings and from a variety of perspectives with scales that they would be interested in for most cases. Thus the focus was on well-validated constructs with an extended legacy in the clinical lexicon across a variety of theoretical orientations (Morey, 1996).

Having articulated the constructs that the PAI would measure, a large number of items were written for each construct. These items were then trimmed based on a variety of factors. The overarching principle during the process of item trimming and scale validation was that no single psychometric parameter should take priority; rather, the intent was to develop scales that were strong across a range of features. A multitude of features were considered.

Items were written to be as readable and straightforward as possible, given research showing that straightforward items tend to contribute to better reliability and validity than wordy, complicated, or double-barreled items (Holden & Fekken, 1990). This issue can be particularly important in forensic settings, where respondents may be relatively more likely to have reading issues. Indeed, the fourth-grade reading level of the PAI makes it easier to read than similar multiscale inventories.

Once items were written, a bias panel with individuals from a variety of religious, racial, and other groups reviewed the items. Any item that any member of the panel identified as potentially biased against their groups were discarded. Next, experts in personality and psychopathology were asked to sort the items into bins based on the various scales that the PAI was designed to measure. Any item that was sorted into the incorrect bin by these experts was discarded.

The remaining items were then administered in order to establish their psychometric properties. The items were anchored using a four-point Likert-type scale ranging from False to Very True. The use of Likert scaling was intended to provide more true score variance per item than

True-False tests, which allows for briefer scales. The administration of the beta version of the PAI initiated the second stage of construct validation, which focuses on evaluating the internal structure of the test, including scale reliability and inter-scale structure. Items were trimmed based on a variety of characteristics in these data. For instance, items that correlated more strongly with a scale it was not intended to measure than the items of the scale it was intended to measure were discarded.

Content validity was a central focus in PAI scale development and item selection. Items were scaled to tap the full range of measured constructs. Take antisocial behavior as an example. Antisocial symptoms might range from relatively mild behaviors such as truancy or dishonesty to severe symptoms that are dangerous to others. By sampling items across this range, as indicated by variability in Item Response Theory (IRT) threshold parameters, the PAI is able to distinguish mild to severe symptomatology and thus make discriminations between the mildly dishonest individual and person with diagnosable antisocial personality as well as between diagnosable but moderate and dangerous and severe individuals. Thus tapping item content across this range ensured that the scales measured PAI scales provided adequate *depth* in the assessment of various clinical constructs.

A related concern is *breadth*, or the degree to which scales measure the various features that are associated with clinical phenomena. For instance, aggression can take a variety of forms ranging from hostile attitudes to verbal outbursts to physical violence. Scales that focus exclusively on internal consistency or unidimensional factor pattern coefficients may tend to overselect items at the core of certain constructs and miss important content at the periphery (Loevinger, 1954). Ten of the PAI full scales have subscales that are designed to assess the full range of issues related to broad constructs. For instance, the Aggression scale has subscales measuring aggressive attitudes, verbal aggression, and physical aggression. The structural validity of the subscales was tested via confirmatory factor analysis; these models fit the data well for all 11 constructs with subscales.

Discriminant validity is one of the most challenging aspects of clinical assessment, because most problems tend to correlate with most other kinds of problems. Several steps were taken to enhance the discriminant validity of the PAI scales. First, no items were allowed to be indicators of more than one scale. Items that overlap across scales increase correlations between those scales and thus compromise discriminant validity. Second, IRT was used to evaluate the degree to which items effectively discriminated individuals at different levels of the underlying trait being measured. IRT was also used to evaluate bias, or the degree to which items designed to measure clinical constructs were unintentionally measuring demographic features.

As it turns out, PAI scales show relatively few mean differences between various demographic groups. The differences that do exist tend to be small and likely represent true between-population differences on certain characteristics. For instance, men tend to have higher scores on aggression and antisocial behavior scales than women. Importantly, these differences will be apparent in clinical assessment because the PAI does not use separate norms for men and women. In other words, women and men will have the same score on these scales given the same propensity for aggressive behavior, a pattern that is obscured when gendered norms are used.

These procedures and others described more fully in the PAI Professional Manual (1991; 2007) led to a test that covers a wide range of content relevant to clinical and forensic assessment, with easy to read items and scales that have excellent psychometric properties. Scale reliabilities are satisfactory in terms of both inconsistency and retest stability, and the PAI tends to show a three-factor structure that maps well onto contemporary models of the structure of psychopathology. The third step of construct validation has to do with the ability of the PAI scales and indicators to predict clinically relevant criterion variables effectively. Overall, a large body of research supports validity in clinical, forensic, and other contexts (Morey, 2007), but this work continues for the life of a test.

Further aiding interpretation is the availability of both clinical and forensic interpretive software packages and the use of large community, clinical, and forensic normative samples against which to standardize scale scores (Edens & Ruiz, 2005; Morey, 2007; see Blais, Baity, & Hopwood, 2010 for norms in more specific populations). It is typical in PAI interpretation to consider both normative and clinical or forensic populations when making interpretations. This allows the assessor to characterize the degree to which a given client is different from average, as well as the degree to which they are different from average within a specialized population. This is important in a variety forensic settings, where many clients are likely to be higher than population norms on externalizing behavior characteristics, but may be below average in a given group (e.g., inmates).

PAI Scale and Supplemental Indicators

Figure 4.1 lists the PAI Full Scales and Table 4.1 lists the PAI supplemental indicators (see below), which can be divided into five groups: validity scales, clinical scales, treatment consideration scales, interpersonal scales, and supplemental indicators.

Validity Scales

Two validity scales measure random, inconsistent, or careless responding. The Inconsistency (ICN) scale consists of pairs of items that are highly correlated in the normative sample. Discrepancies on these items may suggest that the respondent was not fully attending to item content, which elevates the scale. The Infrequency (INF) scale includes items that ask about odd interests or behaviors that are unrelated to psychopathology. Thus it provides a relatively clean distinction between carelessness or inattention and severe psychopathology, a distinction which is sometimes confounded in scales of this type. Morey and Hopwood (2007) also developed an indicator of back-random responding, which can be useful for evaluating that possibility that a respondent answered the first part of the PAI genuinely but began answering inattentively at some point during their completion of the protocol. In cases where back-random responding exists, a short form is available which consists of the first 160 items of the test.

There are three indicators of underreporting on the PAI. The first is the Positive Impression Management (PIM) scale, which consists of items that emphasize unlikely virtues or a tendency to minimize distress or dysfunction. The second is the Defensiveness Index (DEF), which is a configuration of PAI scale combinations that are unlikely and may reflect defensiveness. For instance, grandiosity and irritability are typically correlated with one another, because people with elevated self-esteem tend to be relatively impatient with others. An individual who endorses grandiosity but not irritability appears to be reporting high self-esteem without the accompanying impatience, suggesting perhaps a lack of insight or an intentional minimization of negative attributes. Finally, the Cashel Discriminant Function (CDF) is an empirical algorithm developed to detect differences between genuine responders and individuals instructed to "fake good" on the PAI, which has been cross-validated in a number of samples.

Overall, the underreporting scales tend to have moderate to large effect sizes in studies comparing genuine and feigning responders (Morey, 2007). However, they also show some interesting differences that are interpretively useful. Specifically, PIM tends to be negatively correlated with psychopathology and to show differences between clinical and nonclinical groups, whereas the CDF does not tend to have a relationship with mental health. DEF tends to show a pattern somewhat in between these indicators. Morey and Hopwood (2007) interpreted this pattern as suggesting that PIM is somewhat more related to more covert forms of underreporting, such as naiveté or lack of insight, whereas CDF is more associated with overt manipulation of responses and denial of problems. They also developed an algorithm to distinguishing between these forms of underreporting and showed that this algorithm is able to distinguish between groups with different motivations to underreport.

There are four PAI indicators validated to detect overreporting. Three of them have very similar developmental strategies and psychometric properties as the underreporting indicators. The Negative Impression Management (NIM) scale is composed of items that ask about unlikely and severe mental health problems that are not specifically associated with any particular kind of psychopathology, such as not having any good childhood memories. The Malingering Index (MAL) is a set of PAI scales configurations that are unlikely and may suggest exaggeration, such as reporting being severely depressed but denying interest in treatment. The Rogers Discriminant Function (RDF) is an empirical function developed and cross-validated for distinguishing between genuine responders and individuals instructed to feign various forms of psychopathology. Similar to the positive responding indicators, these scales show a pattern that permits hypotheses about overt as opposed to covert overreporting, as described in Morey and Hopwood (2006). The Negative Distortion Scale (NDS; Mogge et al., 2010) is a newer indicator that includes the most severe items from multiple PAI clinical scales. The logic of this scale is that individuals who report the most severe symptoms, but not the more moderate or mild symptoms, would likely do so in order to emphasize or exaggerate the severity of their problems. In general, the PAI overreporting scales tend to show large effect sizes for distinguishing between genuine responders and individuals instructed to feign psychopathology (Hawes & Boccaccini, 2009).

Clinical Scales

There are 11 clinical scales on the PAI, nine of which have three or four subscales. The first four full scales measure internalizing issues. The Somatization (SOM) full scale includes measures of conversion (SOM-C), or bizarre and unlikely neurological problems, Somatization (SOM-S), or the tendency to be focused on and complain about health issues, and Health Problems (SOM-H), or the presence of genuine medical issues. The Anxiety (ANX) scale measures cognitive (ANX-C), affective (ANX-A), and physiological (ANX-P) anxiety features. The Anxiety-Related Disorders (ARD) scale measures obsessive-compulsive (ARD-O), phobic (ARD-P), and traumatic (ARD-T) anxiety symptoms. The Depression (DEP) scale is similar to the Anxiety scale in having measures of cognitive (DEP-C), affective (DEP-A), and physiological (DEP-P) features.

Three full scales measure constructs on the thought dysfunction spectrum. The Mania (MAN) full scale includes measures of hyperactivity (MAN-A), grandiosity (MAN-G), and irritability (MAN-I). The Paranoid Features (PAR) full scale has two measures of personological aspects of paranoia, including hypervigilant mistrust (PAR-H) and resentful anger (PAR-R), as well as a scale measuring psychotic persecutory delusions (PAR-P). The Schizophrenia full scale has indicators of thought dysfunction and confusion (SCZ-T), social withdrawal (SCZ-S), and acute psychotic experiences (SCZ-P).

Finally, four clinical full scales measure more externalizing features. The Borderline Features (BOR) full scale has four subscales, including affective lability (BOR-A), identify problems (BOR-I), a history of difficult and negative relationships (BOR-N), and impulsivity and self-harming behavior (BOR-S). The Antisocial (ANT) full scale includes measures of sensation-seeking (ANT-S), lack of empathy, egocentricity and callousness (ANT-E), and antisocial or criminal behaviors (ANT-A). The Alcohol (ALC) and Drug (DRG) problems scales do not have subscales.

Treatment Consideration Scales

The Treatment Consideration scales of the PAI assess features that are often clinically important but do not align with any particular form of psychopathology. The first is Aggression (AGG), which has three scales measuring aggressive attitudes and the belief in the instrumental utility of intimidation (AGG-A), verbal aggression (AGG-V), and physical aggression or violence (AGG-P). There are also scales measuring suicidal ideation (SUI), environmental stress (STR), the lack of a social support system (NON), and disinterest or lack of motivation for treatment (RXR).

Interpersonal Scales

Two scales measure normally distributed personality constructs as conceptualized in interpersonal theory (Wiggins, 1979). Dominance (DOM) assesses the tendency to be controlling and assertive versus passive and meek, whereas Warmth (WRM) measures the tendency to be friendly and kind-hearted versus cold, aloof, or cruel. A number of studies have shown that individuals with psychopathology tend to be distributed around these interpersonal dimensions, suggesting that the Interpersonal scales are useful for understanding heterogeneity in patient presentation that might be important for case conceptualization and the individualization of treatment.

Supplemental Indicators

Morey (1996) developed several supplemental indicators that can facilitate the interpretation of the PAI. The Suicide Potential Index (SPI) is a set of risk factors for suicidal behavior, independent of ideation, such as a lack of social support or depressive affect. Similarly, the Violence Potential Index (VPI) is a list of features that are associated with violent or aggressive behavior apparent in the PAI profile, such as paranoia or substance use problems. The Treatment Process Index (TPI) is a set of risk factors for poor treatment engagement or outcome, such as lack of insight or mistrust. Finally, the Drug and Alcohol predicted scores are regression-based algorithms that predict scores on the DRG and ALC scales. These scales can be compared to the actual ALC and DRG scales to provide an indication of the honesty of responding regarding substance use.

INTERPRETIVE GUIDELINES FOR THE PAI IN FORENSIC PRACTICE

Diagnosis

There are several approaches to developing diagnostic hypotheses using the PAI. The first approach is to simply evaluate the scales that reflect the diagnosis of interest. The problem with this approach is that it fails to take into account the complexity of psychiatric diagnoses, and the fact that the PAI scales were designed to assess basic psychopathology constructs, which sometimes differ from disorder syndromes as depicted in diagnostic manuals. For instance, major depressive disorder involves features of depression as indicated by the DEP full scale, but criteria for that disorder also include suicidal ideation as indicated by SUI, low self-esteem as suggested by low scores on MAN-G, and social withdrawal as indicated by SCZ-S.

A second approach to PAI interpretation involves considering the configuration of the overall PAI profile. This is analogous to the code type approach that is common in the interpretation of the MMPI-2, in that it assumes that individuals with certain kinds of profiles tend to be homogeneous with respect to key clinical or interpretive features. However, unlike that approach, the PAI uses profile correlations that capture scale scores across the entire profile. Correlations are given between a given client's profile and those of several diagnostic and other groups (e.g., psychotic, suicidal, criminal) from the normative sample as routine output in the PAI software.

A third approach also makes use of diagnostic groups in the normative data to make predictions about the likelihood of a given diagnosis. Specifically, scores from a client's profile on the scales that are most strongly related to diagnoses in the normative data are entered into a logistic regression to provide a risk estimate for the individual client. This method is the basis for the diagnostic hypotheses that are given at the end of the PAI clinical report.

The final approach is to use the Structural Summary (Morey & Hopwood, 2007), which is a conceptual mapping of various PAI scales onto various diagnoses and other issues. The Structural Summary approach to PAI diagnosis considers scale scores that are elevated or suppressed relative to the average elevation of scores on a given profile. As an example, social phobia would be suggested by a configuration involving relative elevations on ARD-P, ANX, and SCZ-S and suppressions on WRM and DOM. This configuration implies someone who is fearful, anxious, and socially detached, and who has difficulties with self-assertion and becoming close to others.

The PAI Structural Summary also provides a framework for thinking about a number of other issues relevant to forensic assessment. For example, there is an estimate of what the ALC and DRG scores would be based on other aspects of the profile, which can help cue the assessor to the possibility that a client is not disclosing substance abuse issues. There are also configural guidelines for the assessment of self-concept, risk to self, risk to others, and treatments that may be indicated or counterindicated.

The PAI and the Rorschach

Above all else, the guiding priority in the development of the PAI was content validity. That means that knowledgeable professionals should be able to readily identify what constructs a given item is designed to measure. Decades of research with self-report questionnaires has shown that content valid items generally have stronger psychometric properties than "subtle" items with an oblique conceptual relationship to constructs of interest, which is why it is unusual for contemporary test developers to try to create items that attempt to fool respondents into endorsing something that is true but which they would like to deny.

It is important to note that content validity is not necessarily the same thing as face validity. For instance, most respondents may not realize, as professionals would, that high self-esteem (MAN-G) and irritability (MAN-I) often co-occur, because self-esteem has a generally positive connotation, whereas irritability is generally thought of as negative. The PAI MAL and DEF Indexes take advantage of this distinction between face and content validity by including the configuration such that people whose MAN-I is significantly greater than MAN-G are suspected of malingering, whereas the opposite pattern suggests defensiveness. Nevertheless, the general goal of the PAI is to provide the respondent with a straightforward way of describing her or his experience, symptoms, and personality. With some exceptions (e.g., Rogers and Cashel Discriminant Functions, Substance Abuse Estimated scores), this means that a respondent can consciously choose to provide an inaccurate picture, or that picture can be distorted by lack of insight, distress, or other factors.

The PAI attempts to identify distorted profiles via validity scales. When validity scale data suggests that response distortion may have affected the clinical profile, techniques are still available to interpret the individual's clinical picture, but this is also often the kind of situation where multimethod data can be particularly helpful. The Rorschach, in particular, can be valuable in such situations, for two reasons. First, the Rorschach stimuli were never designed to be content valid, because the developmental logic of the test rests on completely different assumptions than is the case for a questionnaire (Bornstein, 2011). This leads to a different kind of cognitive process involving the visual perception of ambiguous stimuli. To the extent that respondents may attempt to filter their responses, they are often unlikely to be aware of how the responses will be scored, so their filtering may have a limited effect on the results relative to an instrument such as the PAI.

Second, the Rorschach is interpreted based on a large body of empirical research that shows how certain kinds of responses reliably relate to important criteria (Mihura et al., 2013). The combination of these two instruments, both of which have substantial validity support, but which use very different means of collecting information and vary in their sensitivity to distortion, provides forensic assessors with a powerful tool for understanding their clients. Next, we describe a case with PAI and Rorschach data that illustrates the value of using these instruments in conjunction for clinical assessment.

A PAI AND RORSCHACH FORENSIC CASE STUDY

The following case illustrates how the PAI and Rorschach can be used in a complementary fashion to elucidate complex forensic cases. In this assessment, neither instrument alone would have provided the necessary information to get a full picture of this client's psychological state. The identity of the client was protected using the guidelines recommended by Clifft (1986) for disguising case material for publication.

Forensic Referral Question and Legal Issues

Mrs. BY was referred by her immigration attorney to author (FBE) for an independent psychological evaluation of exceptional hardship to the U.S. citizen. Her claim as a U.S. citizen was that she would experience exceptional hardship as a result of enforcement of the J-1 Visa foreign residency requirement on her foreign national physician husband, Dr. Y. Under this strict law (see Hake, 2002; Hake, 2003), the requirements of a J-1 Visa oblige that a foreign national physician who marries a U.S. citizen during his U.S. residency must return to his country for two years before applying for reentry into the United States. There is no guarantee that readmission to the United States will be granted, and the process itself may take many years. This process is unlike other foreign nationals on other legitimate visas who marry a U.S. citizen. Usually the U.S citizen can apply for permanent resident status for her spouse after a year and the foreign national can remain in the United States during this period. This is not the case with the J-1 Visa.

To have a waiver granted for the two-year form residency required, the U.S. citizen must prove exceptional hardship as a result of this requirement. Among the valid reasons for such an exceptional hardship include psychological hardships to spouse or child, career or educational disruptions to spouse or child, and/or sociocultural hardships upon relocation to the home country. Hake & Banks (2005) have developed an empirically sturdy scale to quantify the role of various factors in determining exceptional hardship. They note, while immigration officials are likely to be skeptical about such evidence, psychological hardships can play a highly significant role in the overall decision-making process for granting a waiver exception. Such psychological hardships require a serious risk of mental breakdown or suffering that would be unconscionable to inflict.

Among the interesting aspects of the exceptional hardship J-1 waiver is the necessity to assess the impact of the two alternatives open to the U.S. respondent: 1) The psychological hardship of traveling to the country of origin of the foreign resident physician *and* 2) The psychological hardship of the U.S. citizen remaining in the United States while her spouse returns to his native country for the two-year residence requirement.

Background

Mrs. Y was a 38-year-old white female presently living in a large city and working as a health-care consultant. She was born in Canada in 1965 and became a naturalized U.S. citizen after attending college in the United States. She was married to Dr. Y, a physician and native and citizen of El Salvador, who is a fellow in obstetrics at a university-based school of medicine. After a courtship of approximately 20 months, they married.

Mrs. Y was the oldest of five siblings. Her siblings were all married. Both of her parents were alive and live in Western Canada. Mrs. Y stated that she has enjoyed a close relationship with her parents throughout her life. Mrs. Y reported that both of her parents suffer from chronic medical problems, which was a source of worry and concern for her. Additionally, she stated that there is a significant history of mental disorder in her family. Both her mother and her sister had suffered from depression and there was a history of severe mental disorder in two of her father's uncles.

Mrs. Y reported that, starting in childhood, she developed life-threatening pulmonary problems and had been treated for them all her life. As a child, she was hospitalized multiple times for these problems, and her physicians were eventually forced to treat her with powerful drugs for a year, because all other measures had failed. At that time, Mrs. Y's medical condition was so dire that her physicians recommended to her parents that they move the family to a drier, warmer climate, if she did not improve. Fortunately, Mrs. Y did improve enough for her parents, well-established professionals, to stay in Canada, though she continued to have ongoing medical difficulties. Mrs. Y reported that moving to her current home had improved her illness because of the lower pollution, lower level of allergens, and milder winters as compared to her hometown. She nevertheless remained vigilant about any indications of pulmonary problems and continued to be monitored closely by her physicians. Since she married Dr. Y, Mrs. Y visited El Salvador three times. Her asthma deteriorated during those visits due to the exceptional pollution there.

In terms of relationship history, Mrs. Y stated that she did not date until late into her college years. Mrs. Y's academic achievements were stellar, and she attended a highly competitive, co-educational college. During her senior year, she had her first steady relationship, which was sporadic and emotionally distant. When this relationship ended, Mrs. Y did not date again until after she completed graduate school, over five years later. Mrs. Y began treatment with a psychiatrist over seven years prior to the assessment, who provided both intensive psychotherapy and medication for depression and relationship issues. Prior to meeting her husband, Mrs. Y had only distant or painful relationships with men.

Mrs. Y met Dr. Y, an El Salvadoran national who had just begun his obstetrics fellowship at a nationally prominent medical center. She noticed that he was hardworking, sincere, and very intelligent. In October, Mrs. Y stated that she spoke with Dr. Y at length, because he had grown depressed about the obstacles he faced in his program. In a separate interview, Dr. Y also reported that he was undergoing a difficult time and that Mrs. Y "was taking care of me, while also being very tough. I had lots of respect for her ability."

Both Mrs. Y and Dr. Y stated that soon after they went to a party together they found that they had many common interests aside from medicine. Soon afterward, they began seeing each other on a regular basis and married after a six-month courtship. With regard to the soundness of the marriage, Mrs. Y's best friend noted, "He loves her very much and is very affectionate with her and she with him, unlike in her past relationships. This is not what she has had in life. He has an easygoing demeanor, very loving, but firm, a very good mix for her. He has deep respect for her as a professional and her kindness." Mrs. Y's psychiatrist stated, "This series of destructive relationships ended only when Mrs. Y began a relationship with Dr. Y. As their friendship gradually moved from friendship to marriage, each began to help the other learn trust and intimacy. For the first time in her life, Mrs. Y let herself rely on another person."

When Mrs. Y was asked about her reactions to the possibility of going to El Salvador for two years with Dr. Y, she stated that going to El Salvador would be impossible for her because she is American and she would be unsafe. She reported that she would be instantly recognized. It should be noted that Mrs. Y has a distinct accent, reddish hair, and fair skin, and would be easily identified as a non-Latin. Dr. Y also confirmed that it would be highly dangerous for her to accompany him to El Salvador. He noted, "She's an American." He further explained that some El Salvadorans are looking to kidnap Americans. As she does not speak Spanish, she could not work as a health consultant during her time in El Salvador. Mrs. Y and Dr. Y agreed that there was no choice for them if Dr. Y is not granted a hardship waiver. Mrs. Y cannot go to El Salvador. Dr. Y is adamant on this issue that Mrs. Y would be in grave danger if she lived in El Salvador and that this option is not open to her.

When Mrs. Y was asked about her reactions to the possibility of Dr. Y going to El Salvador for two years, she became acutely and highly distressed—a significant departure from her more matter-of-fact demeanor in the interview. She stated plaintively, "He is the only person who has ever been nice to me." She reported that she ruminates excessively about his leaving to the degree that it interferes with her work. When I asked how she might feel if he had to leave, Mrs. Y's distress heightened and she said hauntingly, "I cannot articulate it. It is too awful to think about!" Her psychiatrist related, "In my professional opinion, a prolonged separation where visiting and telephone conversation would be limited will precipitate a severe depression in Mrs. Y. The depression would compromise her ability to work as well as her interpersonal functioning. This would constitute a psychiatric crisis." Mrs. Y's best friend stated, "If they were separated? It would be beyond devastating. She would become dysfunctional, lost and bereaved. B opened something that was never there. She would be very depressed and withdrawn and could not function."

Psychological Assessment Findings

PAI Findings

Overall, Mrs. Y's PAI results suggest that she sees herself as an independent, socially friendly individual. She is likely to be self-confident and function well in stress-free environments with a large social support network. Validity scales provide strong counter-support for the possibility that she might have been exaggerating symptoms or feigning psychopathology. There were no elevated clinical scales, and her overall profile suggests a well-adjusted individual (Figure 4.1; MCE = 39T).

However, these findings need to be tempered because of several indications of positive impression management. Her Coefficient of Fit with Profiles of Known Clinical Groups was highest on PIM predicted. Her PIM score was 59T (Figure 4.1), which is above the score of 57, which tends to be the most reliable cut score for distinguishing honest and feigning responders in studies in which feigners are asked to deny psychopathology. This score, which is somewhat surprising in this assessment context and given the referral question where an indication of psychological problems would support the legal claim, suggests that the rest of the scales on the profile are likely to be suppressed. Indeed, all of the clinical full scales and most of the subscales (Figure 4.2) are below 50T. Furthermore, as noted earlier, her two strongest profile correlations were with groups defined by positive impression management.

Two steps follow the observation of positive response distortion on the PAI. The first step involves trying to determine the nature of that distortion. The Cashel Discriminant Function and Defensiveness Index are not elevated (Table 4.1), which is inconsistent with the hypothesis that the client intentionally denied difficulties or exaggerated strengths. Furthermore, her MAN-G and RXR scores were low (Figure 4.2), suggesting relatively low self-esteem and some desire for personal change. It is quite unusual for people who are "faking good" to have this profile. Thus the most likely interpretation is that she may be somewhat naïve, lack insight, or have a somewhat fragile but optimistic veneer covering up some inner vulnerability.

The second step involves trying to interpret the substantive scales, despite distortion. The PAI software provides a modified profile in cases of elevated PIM scores, in which the client's scores are recalibrated against individuals in the normative sample who also had elevated PIM scores. Because this sample is smaller than the total normative sample and

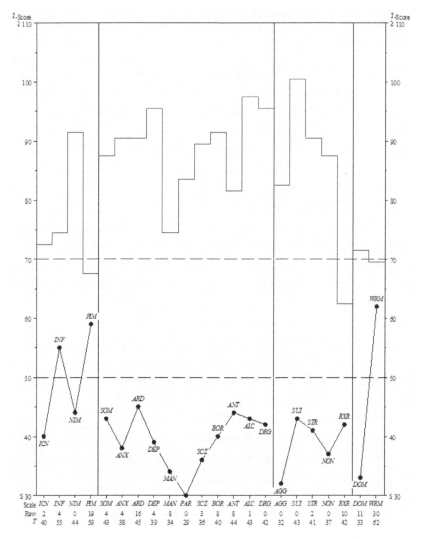

Figure 4.1: PAI full scales

Reproduced with special permission of the publisher, Psychological Assessment Resources, Inc., 16204 North Florida Avenue, Lutz, Florida 33549 from the Personality Assessment Inventory Software Portfolio (PAI-SP) by Leslie C. Morey, PhD and PAR Staff, Copyright 1992, 1998, 2000, 2005, 2008. Further, reproduction is prohibited without permission of PAR.

comes from questionable responders, the scores on this profile should be interpreted with caution. Nevertheless, this recalibration provides a profile that allows some tentative inferences about the client's personality and difficulties. This PIM-specific profile (Figure 4.3) suggests that the

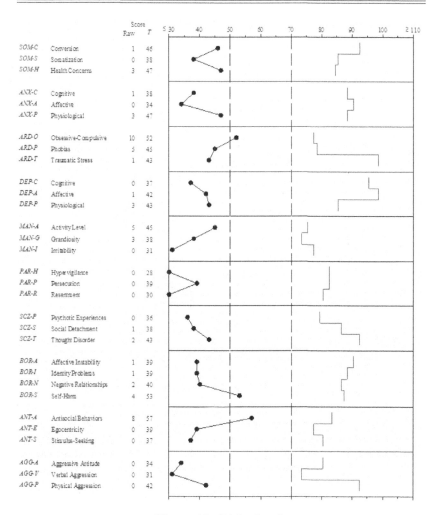

Figure 4.2: PAI subscales

Reproduced with special permission of the publisher, Psychological Assessment Resources, Inc., 16204 North Florida Avenue, Lutz, Florida 33549 from the Personality Assessment Inventory Software Portfolio (PAI-SP) by Leslie C. Morey, PhD and PAR Staff, Copyright 1992, 1998, 2000, 2005, 2008. Further, reproduction is prohibited without permission of PAR.

client is very warm (WRM) and trusting (low PAR), but also may be somewhat impulsive (BOR-S, ANT-A). Relative to other respondents with elevated PIM scores, she has relatively low self-esteem (MAN-G) and a desire for personal changes (RXR), perhaps suggesting inner vulnerability that could be more readily detected by an instrument such as the Rorschach.

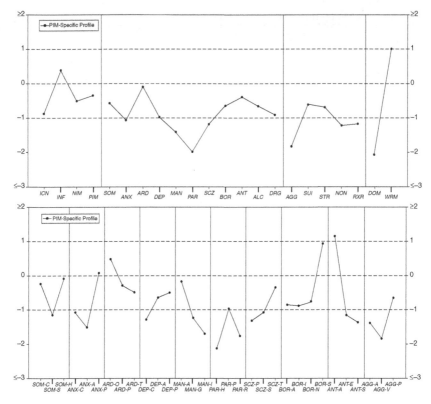

Figure 4.3: PAI PIM-specific profiles

Reproduced by special permission of the publisher, Psychological Assessment Resources, Inc., 16204 North Florida Avenue, Lutz, Florida 33549 from the Personality Assessment Inventory Software Portfolio (PAI-SP) by Leslie C. Morey, PhD and PAR Staff, Copyright 1992, 1998, 2000, 2005, 2008. Further reproduction is prohibited without permission of PAR.

Table 4.1: PAI Supplementary Indexes

Scale/Index	T score
Defensiveness Index (DEF)	51
Cashel Discriminant Function (CDF)	40
Malingering Index (MAL)	57
Rogers Discriminant Function (RDF)	39
Suicide Potential Index (SPI)	43
Violence Potential Index (VPI)	43
Treatment Process Index (TPI)	44
ALC Estimated Score	51
DRG Estimated Score	49
Mean Clinical Elevation (MCE)	39

* Reproduced with special permission of the publisher, Psychological Assessment Resources, Inc., 16204 North Florida Avenue, Lutz, Florida 33549 from the Personality Assessment Inventory Software Portfolio (PAI-SP) by Leslie C. Morey, PhD and PAR Staff, Copyright 1992, 1998, 2000, 2005, 2008. Further, reproduction is prohibited without permission of PAR.

Rorschach Findings

Mrs. Y was also administered the Rorschach Inkblot Method (Comprehensive System), a personality test comprised of the subject's interpretation of ten standard inkblot stimuli. Scores from Exner Comprehensive System (Exner, 2003; Exner & Erdberg, 2005) are linked by research to various personality characteristics, styles, and attributes. The more ambiguous Rorschach is a performance-based method, which allows for the assessment of personality variables in a way not as readily accessible on self-report measures such as the PAI.

Mrs. Y's results on the Rorschach (Table 4.2) suggest a markedly more troubled picture of her underlying psychological state than was cautiously hinted at in the earlier interpretation of the PAI. Her scores on the Depression Index suggest that she has a chronic vulnerability to feeling depressed and unhappy, which is consistent with her family history of individuals suffering from affective disorder. Interestingly, her Rorschach findings suggest she may not report or even acknowledge that she feels this way, in part because she does not pay attention to her inner feelings (es = 1; D/AdjD = +2/+2) and avoids emotional complexity (Blends: R) as well as situations that can trigger strong emotion (Afr). She will prefer clearly defined and well-structured situations, and her tolerance for uncertainty and ambiguity is limited (Lambda). On one hand, consistent with her PAI results, Mrs. Y will likely see herself as relatively untroubled by anxiety, tension, nervousness, and irritability and will handle much of her life with considerable self-assurance (D/AdjD = +2/+2). On the other hand, consistent with van der Kolk & Ducey's (1989) concept of the biphasic psychological trauma response on the Rorschach, Mrs. Y's Rorschach results are also consistent with an avoidant/numbing style that is often found in individuals with a history of repeated exposure to severe psychological trauma (Lambda, Afr). Such avoidance and emotional numbing may be the primary way for Mrs. Y to cope with terrifying memories of past experiences.

Further confirming the aforementioned concern about psychological trauma, Mrs. Y's score on the Trauma Content Index (Armstrong & Lowenstein, 1990) of 0.38 suggests that she is likely to rely on the process of dissociation to defend against traumatic experiences. Dissociation is a mental process in which certain thoughts, emotions, sensations, or memories are repressed, because they are too overwhelming for the conscious mind to hold together. Dissociation can lead to

Table 4.2: Rorschach Structural Summary and Supplemental Scores

Index	Score
R	21
L	1.33
EB	3:3.5
EA	6.5
eb	0:1
es	1
D	+2
Adj es	1
Adj D	+2
FM	0
SumC'	0
SumT	0
m	0
SumV	0
SumY	1
FC:CF+C	1:3
Pure C	0
SumC' : WSumC	0:3.5
Afr	0.40
S	6
Blends:R	0:21
CP	0
COP	2
AG	1
GHR:PHR	5:5
a:p	2:1
Ma:Mp	2:1
Food	0
SumT	0
Human Content	10
Pure H	4
PER	0
Isolation Index	0.10
2AB+(Art+Ay)	5
MOR	4
Sum6	5
Lvl-2	0
WSum6	11
M-	0
M none	0
XA%	0.81
WDA%	0.93
X-%	0.19

Index	Score
S-	2
P	7
X+%	0.52
Xu%	0.29
Zf	12
W:D:Dd	5:9:7
W:M	5:3
Zd	-1.5
PSV	1
DQ+	6
DQv	0
3r+(2)/R	0.19
Fr+rF	0
FD	1
An+Xy	2
MOR	4
H:(H)+Hd+(Hd)	4:6
PTI	0
DEPI	5
CDI	1
S-CON	5
HVI	Yes
OBS	No
TCI/R = AG+MOR+AN+SX+BL	0.38
ROD	0.24
AgC	2 (soft)
MOA	none

seriously ineffective patterns of coping with psychological distress in specific areas of functioning, which for Mrs. Y appears to involve close emotional relationships. Also, consistent with this picture, when Mrs. Y is unable to avoid stressful, emotion-laden situations, she is vulnerable to feel overwhelmed and to express emotions in angry and overly intense ways that undercut her interpersonal effectiveness. Additionally, Mrs. Y's otherwise excellent ability to accurately interpret the world (XA%, WDA%) around her become compromised when she feels angry (S-), and she likely becomes dysregulated and overwhelmed by emotion (FC: CF+C). Also, Mrs. Y exhibited a hypervigilant personality style (HVI+), suggesting that she sees the world around her as a dangerous place in which she needs to be cautious and hyperalert to danger. This form of anxious insecurity is another common symptom that often typifies the long-term impact of psychological trauma. As a result, Mrs. Y showed significant limitations in her ability to form close attachments to other people (H: (H)+Hd+ (Hd)), even though she might deeply long for closeness (ROD = 0.24).

Integration of the PAI and the Rorschach

As stated earlier, the strength of PAI is the straightforward quality of interpretation using empirically validated, content-oriented scales, along with easily understood and well-stated test items. While Mrs. Y's PAI had indications of positive bias, a subtler look at the findings revealed hypotheses of someone who was somewhat naïve and lacking insight, or having a somewhat fragile but optimistic veneer covering up some inner vulnerability. Because these aspects of functioning where unavailable to Mrs. Y due to her lack of awareness or defensive structure, the forensic assessor is left with a significant gap in empirically assessing, to a reasonable degree of psychological certainty, Mrs. Y's report that she would suffer psychologically if separated from Dr. Y. Certainly, on self-report inventory alone, the forensic assessor's opinion on this matter would be speculative.

As noted by Bornstein (2002, 2011), self-report methods are frequently insufficient by themselves in improving assessment of important, often implicit, psychological processes. This can be particularly true in forensic psychological assessment. Clearly, the PAI in Mrs. Y's evaluation indicates that "there is a pony in there somewhere," but a performance-based method such as the Rorschach is necessary to fully elucidate the clinical picture (see Evans & Schutz, 2008 for an application to child custody evaluations).

Models for integration of self-report tests and the Rorschach are well represented in the literature, most specifically the MMPI-2 and the Rorschach (see Ganellen, 2013, Finn, 1996). In particular, Finn's model (Figure 4.4), especially Cell B, offers a clear conceptual way to integrate seemingly disparate findings. In Cell B cases, the Rorschach and the self-report method on the surface seemingly disagree. Finn (1996) conceptualizes these cases as follows:

> Clients with this pattern have underlying pathology that emerges in emotionally arousing, regressive, interpersonal, unstructured situations (such as the Rorschach administration). However, they function relatively well

	High Degree of Disturbance on MMPI-2	Low Degree of Disturbance on MMPI-2
High Degree of Disturbance on Rorschach	Cell A[a]	Cell B[a]
Low Degree of Disturbance on Rorschach	Cell C, Case 1[a] Cell C, Case 2[b]	Cell D[a]

Figure 4.4: Patterns of MMPI-2 and Rorschach results (Finn, 1996)

Note: MMPI-2 profiles in all cases are considered to be consistent (i.e., VRIN and TRIN within normal limits), valid, and unguarded (i.e., with no significant elevations on L, K, Fp, and S).

[a]Rorschach protocol shows adequate engagement on the part of the client (i.e., R is average or above and Lambda is < 1.0); [b]Rorschach protocol is constricted (with low R's and/or Lambda's greater than 1.0).

Reproduced with permission of the author and *Journal of Personality Assessment*. Finn, S. E. (1996). Assessment feedback integrating MMPI-2 and Rorschach findings. *Journal of Personality Assessment*, 67, 543–557.

in familiar, structured situations when they can use intellectual resources to deal with anxiety (such as when taking the MMPI-2). Such clients are often unaware of the full nature of their difficulties and hence, are unable to report them on the MMPI-2.

(p. 546)

This description matches the PAI-Rorschach findings of Mrs. Y and should lead the forensic assessor to explore the hypothesis of disowned psychological distress.

Extended Inquiry

In line with the BETAssessment™ principles later elaborated in this book by Smith and Evans (Chapter 9, this volume), an extended inquiry about hypotheses from the testing results was conducted in this evaluation. The forensic assessor (FBE) asked Mrs. Y about any recent psychological trauma she experienced beyond her childhood illnesses and hospitalization. After puzzling over this, she matter-of-factly stated, "Well, there was 911." She then described that she was temporarily assigned by her firm to an office on one of the upper floors of the World Trade Centers (WTC) and had a meeting on the morning of 9/11/2001. At the last minute, the meeting was rescheduled to a different location, though in sight of the WTC. She vividly recalled hearing the loud boom, when the first plane hit near where her WTC office was, followed later by the explosion from the second plane. With an eerie calm, Mrs. Y shared seeing bodies falling from the WTCs and the clouds of dust from the devastating collapse of the buildings. She then became increasingly upset as she relayed that she wandered around New York City in deep shock, unable to contact parents, family, or friends because cellular telephone service was unavailable. She stated that she could not leave the city because all transportation was shut down. Approaching a state of panic, Mrs. Y then remembered that her college friend lived in Manhattan and walked miles to reach her friend's apartment. Fortunately, her friend was at home and housed Mrs. Y for several days until she could arrange transportation home to her parents. She reported that she was sick with anxiety that her parents did not know she was safe, until she was eventually was able to call them. This extended inquiry provided an essential context for the psychological testing results and clinical presentation puzzle.

Psychological Opinions Regarding Exceptional Hardship

As stated earlier, in this case, Dr. Y must prove that his U.S.-citizen wife would suffer exceptional hardships if he must return to El Salvador for two years or more. The evidence of the psychological evaluation for Mrs. Y was reviewed in the light of that legal standard. The following conclusions were reached based on individual interviews, psychological treatment records, and psychological testing of Mrs. Y, corroborated by third-party information.

The results of the psychological testing were highly consistent with Mrs. Y's report of the distress that she was experiencing and the likelihood that she would experience debilitating levels of psychological anguish if she were separated from her husband. The results of the evaluation suggested that Mrs. Y suffered from a powerful fear of abandonment and separation anxiety arising from her childhood illnesses and parental separation, as well as the devastating experience of 9/11. Having now opened herself for the first time to true intimacy, Mrs. Y was deeply attached to Dr. Y, but did not have the emotional resilience to weather the two-year period of separation that is the only conceivable outcome of enforcement of the J-1 waiver requirement. This level of vulnerability is likely in spite of Mrs. Y external presentation, where she superficially appears highly competent and untroubled by psychological issues. The psychological test findings strongly supported the interpretation that Mrs. Y was a chronically psychologically vulnerable individual with a risk for depression and separation anxiety, especially if she were to experience the loss of Dr. Y.

In the independent psychological evaluation of exceptional hardship to the U.S. citizen, it was necessary to assess the impact of the two alternatives open to her. First, in terms of the prospective psychological impact on Mrs. Y if she accompanied Dr. Y to El Salvador, both Mrs. Y and Dr. Y agreed that there was no choice for them if Dr. Y was not granted a hardship waiver. She could not go to El Salvador, as the country was physically dangerous with significant air pollution, which essentially offered limited police protection and health treatment needed by Mrs. Y. Mrs. Y spoke no Spanish and did not have the personal resources to tolerate living in hiding with a daily fear of danger to her life. It should also be pointed out that a similar danger existed for Dr. Y if it were found out that he was married to a U.S. citizen. As such, both Mrs. Y and Dr. Y would live in fear of reprisal for their interfaith marriage.

Second, while the exceptional hardships that Mrs. Y would endure by going to El Salvador were clear and compelling, Dr. Y's and Mrs. Y's adamant decision that she could not go to El Salvador put Mrs. Y on a collision course for severe psychological trouble. As stated earlier, Mrs. Y was an individual highly vulnerable to increased depression and separation anxiety if she were separated from her husband for an extended period of time with little or no ability to visit with him or communicate with him on a regular basis. If her husband were not allowed to remain in the United States with her, Mrs. Y's psychological distress would likely become agonizing. This independent forensic psychological evaluation, along with her psychiatrist's assessment, strongly supported the conclusion that Mrs. Y was an acutely psychologically vulnerable individual with a high risk for depression should she experience the loss of Dr. Y. While seeming on the surface to be a highly competent individual, the loss of her husband could be reasonably expected to precipitate severe psychological consequences well in excess of the normal stress of such separation. This hardship would be an especially cruel psychological imposition on Mrs. Y.

Another exceptional hardship that Mrs. Y would endure if she stayed in the United States for the two-year foreign residence requirement of her husband was the risk to the stability of her marriage. Mrs. Y suffered from significant fear of abandonment and separation anxiety common among adults with severe medical problems and hospitalizations as children. She was preoccupied with her fear of losing her husband to the degree that it negatively impacted on her life. For her husband to return to his county and family where real pressures would have been exerted on him to remain in El Salvador would only give reality to what was only a fear. Her decision to marry a person with whom she was so well matched in her current social and professional world in the United States was in many ways the kind of reparation in adulthood of past difficulties one sees in highly intelligent and resourceful individuals. The imposition of the foreign residence requirement of her husband would cut short this important life development reparation and thereby create an exceptional hardship on her emotionally.

Outcome

Based on expert legal representation, assisted by the comprehensive and supportive forensic psychological assessment, the Immigration and Naturalization Service granted Dr. Y a waiver of this J-1 residency requirement based heavily on the exceptional hardship to his U.S. citizen wife. A follow-up indicated that the couple moved to a large suburb, where Dr. Y established a successful medical specialty practice, and the Y family established a stable marriage. Mrs. Y decided to take time from her career and they had three children together. There was no indication of long-term psychological difficulties.

Conclusion

In conclusion, as stated in the literature (see Hopwood & Bornstein, 2014; Mihura, 2012) and throughout this book, this forensic assessment case provides compelling evidence about value of comprehensive multimethod assessment using an integration of self-report and performance-based methods. Especially in forensic settings, while the Rorschach has long-proven valuable (see Gacono & Evans, 2008), the combination of PAI and Rorschach offers broad applicability given the PAI's user-friendly characteristics such as a more accessible reading level and strong content-driven clinical scales that are can be straightforwardly presented in court. This case illustrates the incremental utility of both instruments at arriving at objective findings of probative value for the court. It is probably not too strong a statement that, in the case of Dr. and Mrs. Y, these assessment methods offered a key to understanding a critical psycholegal question before the Immigration Court. Without this multimethod approach, important data regarding Mrs. Y's vulnerability to separation may not have been objectively determined to a degree that met the high bar required in J-1 residency requirement waiver cases.

This case demonstration of the value of multimethod forensic assessment with the PAI and the Rorschach arises against a background where U.S. graduate training in psychological assessment moves increasingly away from preparation in performance-based methods such as the Rorschach (see Ready & Veague, 2014; Piotrowski, 2015). This is particularly disturbing as the science of these performance-based methods, especially of the Rorschach, demonstrates strong empirical support (see Mihura, Meyer, Dumitrascu, & Bombel, 2013; Mihura, Meyer, Bombel, & Dumitrascu, 2015). It is hoped that this case will generate greater interest in the multimethod use of the Rorschach and PAI in forensic settings, clinical practice, and professional training.

References

Armstrong, J., & Lowenstein, R. (1990). Characteristics of patients with multiple personality and dissociative disorders on psychological testing. *Journal of Nervous and Mental Disease, 174,* 448–454.

Blais, M. A., Baity, M. R., & Hopwood, C. J. (2010). *Clinical applications of the personality assessment inventory.* New York: Routledge.

Bornstein, R. F. (2002). A process dissociation approach to objective-projective test score interrelationships. *Journal of Personality Assessment, 78,* 47–68.

Bornstein, R. F. (2011). From symptom to process: How the PDM alters goals and strategies in psychological assessment. *Journal of Personality Assessment, 93,* 142–150.

Charnas, J. W., Hilsenroth, M. J., Zodan, J., & Blais, M. A. (2010). Should I stay or should I go? Personality Assessment Inventory and Rorschach indices of early withdrawal from psychotherapy. *Psychotherapy: Theory, Research, Practice, Training, 47,* 484–499.

Clifft, M. A. (1986). Writing about psychiatric patients: Guidelines for disguising case material. *Bulletin of the Menninger Clinic, 50,* 511–524.

Edens, J. F., & Ruiz, M. A. (2005). *Personality assessment inventory interpretive report for correctional settings*. Odessa, FL: Psychological Assessment Resources.

Erard, R. E. (2012). Expert testimony using the Rorschach Performance Assessment System in psychological injury cases. *Psychological Injury and Law, 5*, 122-134.

Evans III, F. B., & Schutz, B. M. (2008). The Rorschach in child custody and parenting plan evaluations: A new conceptualization. In C. B. Gacono, F. B. Evans (Eds.) & N. Kaser-Boyd, L. A. Gacono (Collaborators), *The LEA series in personality and clinical psychology. The handbook of forensic Rorschach assessment* (pp. 233-254). New York: Routledge/Taylor & Francis Group.

Exner, J. E., Jr. (2003). *Basic foundations and principles of interpretation. The Rorschach: A comprehensive system* (4th ed.). Hoboken, NJ: John Wiley.

Exner, J. E., Jr., & Erdberg, P. (2005). *Advanced interpretation, Vol. 2. The Rorschach: A comprehensive system* (3rd ed.). Hoboken, NJ: John Wiley.

Finn, S. E. (1996). Assessment feedback integrating MMPI-2 and Rorschach findings. *Journal of Personality Assessment, 67*, 543-557.

Gacono, C. B., & Evans III, F. B. (Eds.). (2008). *The LEA series in personality and clinical psychology. The handbook of forensic Rorschach assessment* (N. Kaser-Boyd & L. A. Gacono, Collaborators). New York: Routledge/Taylor & Francis Group.

Ganellen, R. J. (2013). *Integrating the Rorschach and the MMPI-2 in personality assessment*. New York: Routledge/Taylor & Francis Group.

Hake, B. A. (2002). Hardship is hardship: The equivalency of hardship standards in U.S. immigration law. In Randy Auberbach (Ed.), *2001-2002 Immigration and Nationality Law Handbook* (Vol. 2, pp. 384-393), Washington, DC: American Immigrations Lawyers Association.

Hake, B. A. (2003). J-1 Visas. In Martin J. Lawler (Ed.), *Professionals: A Matter of Degree* (4th ed.). Washington, DC: American Immigrations Lawyers Association.

Hake, B. A., & Banks, D. L. (2005). The Hake hardship scale: A quantitative system for assessment of hardship in immigration cases based on a statistical analysis of AAO decisions, *Bender's Immigration Bulletin, 10*, 403-420.

Hawes, S. W., & Boccaccini, M. T. (2009). Detection of overreporting of psychopathology on the Personality Assessment Inventory: A meta-analytic review. *Psychological Assessment, 21*, 112-124.

Holden, R. R., & Fekken, G. C. (1990). Structured psychopathological test item characteristics and validity. *Psychological Assessment: A journal of consulting and clinical psychology, 2*, 35-40.

Hopwood, C. J., & Bornstein, R. F. (Eds.). (2014). *Multimethod clinical assessment*. New York: Guilford Publications.

Jackson, D. N. (1970). A sequential system for personality scale development. In C. D. Spielberger (Ed.), *Current topics in clinical and community psychology* (Vol. 2, pp. 62-97). New York: Academic Press.

Klonsky, E. D. (2004). Performance of Personality Assessment Inventory and Rorschach Indices of Schizophrenia in a Public Psychiatric Hospital. *Psychological Services, 1*, 107-110.

Loevinger, J. (1954). The attenuation paradox in test theory. *Psychological Bulletin, 51*, 493-504.

Loevinger, J. (1957). Objective tests as instruments of psychological theory. *Psychological Reports, 3*, 635-694.

McCann, J. T., & Evans, F. B. (2008). Admissibility of the Rorschach. In C. B. Gacono, F. B. Evans (Eds.) & N. Kaser-Boyd, L. A. Gacono (Collaborators), *The LEA series in personality and clinical psychology. The handbook of forensic Rorschach assessment* (pp. 55-78). New York: Routledge/Taylor & Francis Group.

Meloy, J. R. (2008). The authority of the Rorschach: An update. In C. B. Gacono, F. B. Evans (Eds.) & N. Kaser-Boyd, L. A. Gacono (Collaborators), *The LEA series in personality and clinical psychology. The handbook of forensic Rorschach assessment* (pp. 79-87). New York: Routledge/Taylor & Francis Group.

Mihura, J. L. (2012). The necessity of Multiple Test Methods in conducting assessments: The role of the Rorschach and self-report. *Psychological Injury and Law, 5*, 97-106.

Mihura, J. L., Meyer, G. J., Dumitrascu, N., & Bombel, G. (2013). The validity of individual Rorschach variables: Systematic reviews and meta-analyses of the comprehensive system. *Psychological Bulletin, 139*, 548-605.

Mihura, J. L., Meyer, G. J., Bombel, G., & Dumitrascu, N. (2015) Standards, accuracy, and questions of bias in Rorschach meta-analyses: Reply to Wood, Garb, Nezworski, Lilienfeld, and Duke (2015). *Psychological Bulletin, 141*, 250-260.

Mogge, N. L., Lepage, J. S., Bell, T., & Ragatz, L. (2010). The negative distortion scale: A new PAI validity scale. *The Journal of Forensic Psychiatry and Psychology, 21*, 77-90.

Morey, L. C. (1991). *Personality Assessment Inventory Professional Manual*. Odessa, FL: Psychological Assessment Resources.

Morey, L. C. (1996). *An interpretive guide to the Psychological Assessment Inventory*. Odessa, FL: Psychological Assessment Resources.

Morey, L. C. (2007). *Personality Assessment Inventory Professional Manual*, (2nd ed.). Lutz, FL: Psychological Assessment Resources.

Morey, L. C., & Hopwood, C. J. (2004). Efficiency of a strategy for detecting back random responding on the Personality Assessment Inventory. *Psychological Assessment, 16*(2), 197-200.

Morey, L. C., & Hopwood, C. J. (2007). *Personality assessment inventory casebook: A structural summary approach*. Odessa, FL: Psychological Assessment Resources.

Morey, L. C., & Meyer, J. K. (2013). Forensic assessment with the Personality Assessment Inventory. In R. P. Archer & E. M. A. Wheeler (Eds.), *Forensic uses of clinical assessment instruments* (2nd ed.) (pp. 140-174). New York: Routledge/Taylor & Francis Group.

Mullen, K. L., & Edens, J. F. (2008). A case law survey of the Personality Assessment Inventory: Examining its role in civil and criminal trials. *Journal of Personality Assessment, 90*, 300-303.

Piotrowski, C. (2015). On the decline of projective techniques in professional psychology training. *North American Journal of Psychology, 17*, 259-265.

Ready, R. E., & Veague, H. B. (2014). Training in psychological assessment: Current practices of clinical psychology programs. *Professional Psychology: Research and Practice, 45*, 278-282.

Rorschach, H. (1921). *Psychodiagnostics*. New York: Grune & Stratton, 1942.

van der Kolk, B. A., & Ducey, C. P. (1989). The psychological processing of traumatic experience: Rorschach patterns in PTSD. *Journal of Traumatic Stress, 2*, 259-274.

Wiggins, J. S. (1979). A psychological taxonomy of trait descriptive terms: The interpersonal domain. *Journal of Personality and Social Psychology, 37*, 395-412.

Chapter 5

MULTIMETHOD FORENSIC ASSESSMENT USING THE RORSCHACH IN PERSONAL INJURY EVALUATIONS

Robert E. Erard

Introduction to Personal Injury Litigation

Personal injury litigation is a type of civil action based on the law of tort. A tort consists of an injury arising out of the breach of some duty other than a contractual obligation that creates legal liability for the defendant. The existence of such a duty may be established by statute or by common law and is generally dependent on what a "reasonable person" would have done in similar circumstances (Kane & Dvoskin, 2011).

A tort involves several essential elements. First, there must be a legally recognized duty. Second, that duty must have been breached, either intentionally or due to negligence. Third, the breach must have proximately caused an injury. Proximate cause is a complex doctrine, incorporating elements of "but for" causation, foreseeability, and public policy. Finally, the injury must result in compensable damages.

Breaches of duty in tort litigation may be either intentional or negligent. In intentional torts, there is a breach of an obligation not to engage in wrongful harmful behavior on purpose (e.g., defamation, assault, sexual harassment, intentional infliction of emotional distress). Negligent torts involve breaches of duties to protect people from reasonably foreseeable, but unintentional, harm. The nature and scope of such duties depends on the nature of the relationship between the parties. Thus a landlord's duty to provide a safe environment for her tenants differs from any duty of an owner of a vacant building to provide an environment safe from obvious hazards to trespassers. If the evidence shows that a duty was breached, this creates a liability. But liability is not enough—the breach of duty must have been the proximate cause of an injury, resulting in compensable damages. Liability is largely a legal question, whereas causation is partly legal and partly factual, and damages are usually factual but may sometimes be established by statute.

Throughout most of the twentieth century, psychological or emotional harm was not compensable independent of the physical injury. It had to be associated with some kind of physical impact, such as emotional harm accompanying a physical injury or having been in the "zone of danger" in which a physical injury occurred. For the last few decades, compensation for emotional injuries alone has been permitted in all U.S. states (Kane & Dvoskin, 2011), but the rules and criteria vary widely by jurisdiction. Although psychologists may be consulted regarding duty and liability in cases involving psychological malpractice, in most personal injury cases, they are likely to be brought in only when the claimed injuries are alleged to include a significant psychological component. A psychological injury usually needs to include some loss or impairment of function, not mere emotional upset, in order to be compensable. Also, in order to make a plaintiff "whole," one must only compensate him or her up to the point of his or her condition prior to the injury.

Psychological Evaluations in Personal Injury Litigation

Forensic psychological experts are often called upon by either the plaintiff's or defendant's counsel to conduct an independent psychological evaluation of the plaintiff. The word, "independent," as used here does not indicate that the expert has not been retained by one side or the other, but only that the expert has not been involved in the care and treatment of the litigant. Of course, all experts have an ethical and legal duty to be fair and objective in forming their opinions, regardless of who has retained them.

Typical elements of an independent psychological evaluation in a personal injury matter include efforts to answer the following questions: 1) What was the plaintiff's condition prior to the claimed injuries? 2) What injuries, if any, have occurred? 3) What is the nature and extent of the injuries? 4) What actions or events caused the injuries? 5) What can be done to heal or ameliorate the injuries? 6) What is the prognosis? (see also Greenberg, 2003).

Much of the challenge of conducting such evaluations involves ascertaining whether there are valid and measurable differences between the conditions of the plaintiff before and after the alleged injury and how such differences may have come about. What factors might have contributed to the risk of harm or protections against it? To what degree do observed impairments reflect pre-existing personality problems and psychopathology versus recent impairment or loss of function?[1] How can the interplay between the stressful or traumatic events and the individual's coping capacities be described? Does the current distress or impairment represent a temporary disruption of functioning or a lasting breakdown? What kinds of interventions may result in an improved prognosis?

Some of these questions can be addressed by taking a comprehensive and detailed history; conducting structured or unstructured clinical interviews, including mental status examinations; and reviewing pertinent documentary evidence (such as the complaint and answer, interrogatories, depositions, police reports, academic and employment records, medical and psychiatric records) and applying standard diagnostic criteria. In order to form valid opinions about the sequence and causation of symptoms and impairment, it is important to use a systematic approach, seeking to confirm and disconfirm alternative narratives. The construction of time lines is often illuminating. Such sources of hypotheses and factual evidence are so important that some well-regarded authors on the subject of conducting psychological evaluations in personal injury cases largely ignore or at least minimize the utility of psychological testing (e.g., Melton, Petrila, Poythress, & Slobogin, 2007).

Still, psychological experts who are retained to conduct such evaluations are expected to do something more than offer their personal interpretations of evidence that can, for the most part, be gathered by attorneys and their assistants and often be effectively presented to the trier of fact through legal argument. Forensic psychologists add value and assist the court or jury not merely by offering diagnostic formulations and citations to the pertinent psychological literature but also by using their understanding of personality and psychological dynamics to add an element of depth and coherence to the story of the case. By exploring the history of how the events surrounding the complaint have interacted and describing the psychological resources and vulnerabilities personal characteristics of the party claiming injury, a psychological evaluator can help the jury interpret the relevant evidence in a more person-centered and thus, ultimately, more relevant fashion while it strives to determine the applicable damages. In this way, psychological evaluators can advance the ideal, inherent in our legal system, of *individualized* justice.

Where Multimethod Personality Testing Fits In

Personality testing offers the psychological expert a standardized, measurable, and empirically supported means of evaluating the psychological status of the plaintiff. It often serves as the key to understanding both the probability and the nature of the claimed injury. It also helps to make sense of causation within a nexus of personal meaning.

Forensic personality testing also offers a quantifiable foundation for a) judgments about the credibility of a litigant's self-presentation (using validity scales and other markers of presentation style), b) determinations of levels of explicitly claimed and implicitly indicated distress (using scales normed to nonpatient and clinical populations and performance variables that are empirically linked to such distress), and c) assessments of the match or mismatch between a litigant's claims about his or her functional capacities and impairments and those that are demonstrated in measurable performance on standardized tasks.

Self-Report Testing

The most commonly used broadband clinical personality tests in personal injury evaluations are self-report instruments (Boccaccini & Brodsky, 1999), such as the Minnesota Multiphasic Personality Inventory (MMPI-2 or MMPI-2-RF; Butcher, Dahlstrom, Graham, Tellegen, & Kaemmer, 1989; Ben-Porath & Tellegen, 2011), the Millon Clinical Multiaxial Inventory-IV (MCMI-IV; Millon, Grossman, & Millon, 2015), and the Personality Assessment Inventory (PAI; Morey, 1991). These measures are well researched and normed and provide a wealth of information relevant to psychological distress and impairment and about how people habitually view themselves and their experiences. They are widely accepted in the courts. Other self-report tests are useful in evaluating specific syndromes that are commonly claimed in personal injury litigation, such as PTSD (e.g., the Posttraumatic Stress Diagnostic Scale; PDS, Foa, 1995 and the Trauma Symptom Inventory-2nd ed.; TSITM-2, Briere, 2011).

Because the emotional distress component of personality distress claims is necessarily about a subjective experience, it is essential to ask people about how they are feeling. Self-report tests provide a means of not only capturing essential features of psychological distress and claimed psychosocial impairment but also of providing quantitative comparisons with published norms for nonpatient, clinical, and forensic groups.

Most of the major self-report tests include validity scales that are usually effective in detecting efforts to malinger or exaggerate symptoms. The validity scales can also be supplemented by structured interviews that have been developed to detect feigning (e.g., the Structured Interview of Reported Symptoms, 2nd ed.; SIRS-2, Rogers, Sewell, & Gillard, 2010 and the Structured Interview for Malingered Symptoms, Smith & Burger, 1997).

But, as discussed in detail throughout this book (see especially, Erard & Evans, this volume; Bornstein, this volume), self-report testing is limited by its dependence on what people are able and willing to report about themselves. Personal injury plaintiffs have a strong incentive to advocate for the seriousness of their psychological injuries and to place themselves in a favorable light, and some deliberately feign or exaggerate their symptoms. Even for those who do not do so, the process of litigation itself tends to shape the way that psychological problems are understood and described. In a sense, the plaintiff's self-presentation sits on the Procrustean bed of the legal complaint. For example, if the complaint alleges that a tort has caused major depressive disorder or posttraumatic stress disorder, it is more than likely that the plaintiff has some conception of what symptoms are expected to be consistent with such diagnoses. Further, the stress of litigation and the increasing sense of personal grievance that is aggravated by the litigation process may create symptoms of its own and sharpen those that had appeared previously (Lees-Haley, 1988).

In cases in which evidence of symptom exaggeration or malingering has been detected, it is difficult to glean much useful information concerning the true condition and level of distress of litigants who are being forensically evaluated. After all, one cannot safely rule out the existence of some significant emotional damages just on the basis of a finding that suffering or impairment has been exaggerated.

Rorschach Testing

The particular advantages of using the Rorschach in personal injury evaluations and the groundwork for its admissibility in court have been addressed in many previous publications (Erard, 2012; Erard, Meyer, & Viglione, 2014; Kaser-Boyd & Evans, 2008; McCann & Evans, 2008; Meyer & Eblin, 2012; Smith, 2008). Among the most important is that the Rorschach assesses the litigant's performance in an unscripted, moderately stressful situation. Formal observation and normative comparisons of this performance offer insights into an individual's functional capacity and degree of impairment based on what he or she actually does.

As an entirely different kind of task than completing a self-report measure, the Rorschach offers incremental validity to self-report testing. In addition, because it is difficult for most litigants to know what constitutes a particularly healthy or unhealthy self-presentation on the Rorschach, it provides not only another useful check against exaggerated symptom presentation (see Ganellen, 1994; Schultz, this volume) but also an independent method of quantifying functional impairment that does not depend as much on honest descriptions of one's experience. In this way, the evaluator gets a "second bite at the apple" in determining how well or poorly the respondent is managing in everyday life.

As will be illustrated in the case example that follows, the Rorschach is also very sensitive to indications of compromised functioning due to trauma, which may not always be directly evident from a litigant's self-report and interview demeanor (see also Smith & Evans, this volume). Also, because the Rorschach provides contextualized information about the particular circumstances in which psychological functioning is enhanced or compromised (see Erard & Evans, this volume), it can be particularly helpful in drawing inferences about two aspects of personal injury reports that necessarily extend beyond the diagnostic impression: causation and prognosis.

Case Illustration

In the following case, the MMPI-2 and the Rorschach Performance Assessment System™ (R-PAS™; Meyer, Viglione, Mihura, Erard, & Erdberg, 2011) were used, along with other, more narrow-band instruments.

Case Background and Interview Highlights

Sylvia Moore,[2] a 25-year-old married woman, sued a major teaching hospital and several of her treating physicians for medical malpractice resulting in and aggravating complications surrounding the birth of her second child. Her complaint detailed a number of serious physical and emotional injuries.

Immediately following the birth of the child, she experienced an unexpected sense of fullness and abdominal distention. She described these symptoms to her obstetrician and requested an ultrasound to see whether anything had been "left inside" her. Her doctors refused the procedure, deeming it unnecessary. The symptoms persisted and were accompanied by bleeding over several days. The bleeding intensified into hemorrhaging, accompanied by intense pain and an intermittent fever. Again, she requested an ultrasound and was refused, and the medical significance of her fever was minimized. Finally, she went to the emergency room seeking treatment, where she was finally given an ultrasound, which confirmed her belief that something had been "left inside"—a large amount of retained intrauterine products, consisting of placental tissue or possibly the remains of an unviable twin.

She underwent a dilation and curettage procedure on an emergency basis. The source of her fever turned out to be a systemic Streptococcus A infection, an extremely lethal condition. She later learned that this had been diagnosed on a prior doctor visit but was ignored and not reported to her. Adding to her sense of peril was the fact that she was allergic to penicillin, the usual antibiotic used to treat this condition.

She had a lengthy hospitalization, during which she felt close to death. Being a devout Roman Catholic, she received the sacrament of Last Anointing. She wanted to hold and breastfeed her newborn daughter, but this was medically contraindicated. She began to prepare herself emotionally for death.

Ultimately, she was able to regain her health, but with considerable uterine scarring and adhesions, presenting a major barrier to future childbearing. She and her husband had always wanted a large family. Following her return home from the hospital, she experienced a wide range of symptoms associated with posttraumatic stress disorder (PTSD), including nightmares, intrusive memories, panic attacks, periods of emotional numbing and shutdown with poor concentration, and experiences of sudden fearfulness and agitation.

In her interview for her forensic evaluation, she remarked that a lawsuit was "not on my list of things to do." Her initial reaction had been, "It's okay; people make mistakes." But as her medical and other expenses piled up, she thought again about suing. "Also, if I can't have kids, I shouldn't have to pay for that."

As she described the experiences of not being believed, of nearly dying, and of not being able to hold and breastfeed her newborn daughter, she often broke down in tears. She said that she had been advised not to get pregnant again, because with her uterine adhesions, it could be fatal. She was given an option of having a very difficult surgery to repair her uterus, but she was still very leery about going back in a hospital.

She reported that she had been out kayaking down a river that passed the hospital. When she spotted it, she began to feel really tight and had trouble breathing. It was as if her eyes went straight to her room. She felt like she was back there and started crying. If she sees an advertisement for the hospital or something that reminds her of her experiences, she sometimes starts crying hysterically. Sometimes she imagines that there is Strep A all over objects in the household, and she insists that people wash their hands.

Psychosocial History

Sylvia Moore described a reasonably happy childhood in which she felt loved by her parents. She had an older brother. She considered herself a sensitive observer of her family while growing up. Her biggest challenge in childhood was the chronic marital strife between her parents, who divorced during her late adolescence. Her best friend died in an automobile accident around the time of her parents' divorce. She had some college and had worked as a medical secretary and dental assistant.

She was happily married to a skilled tradesman and hunter and had two young children.[3] She and her husband wanted a large family—maybe seven or eight children. Both were outdoorsy and religious and were attracted to a "natural" lifestyle. There was no mental health treatment history and no history of alcohol or drug misuse.

She described herself as somebody who is "not all mushy. I don't like admitting this, but my personality—I don't like admitting I'm in pain or can't do something." Her family of origin always made fun of her when she cried. She never wanted to do ballet or "girly things." Her family warned her years ago to be careful who she cries in front of. Yet every time she talks about the lawsuit, she cries.

Referral Questions for Testing

When interpreting test results, it is important to consider the primary questions one hopes that the testing may help to answer in the context of the particular case. As in most personal injury matters, it is central in this case to evaluate the plaintiff's description of herself in her complaint as having been psychologically damaged by her experiences, the hospital, and her doctors. What can the tests tell us about whether there are signs of psychological injury or impairment? Does the testing support the patient's descriptions of the nature and extent of her injuries or does it point to either less or more damage than she acknowledges? Does the testing indicate any effort to exaggerate or (as is less common in these cases) minimize her problems? In the context of the specific claimed injury, does the testing offer us any insight into particular strengths or vulnerabilities that might help us understand her reaction to the events in question and their meaning to her? Do the problems indicated in the testing appear likely to be amenable to treatment of some kind?

Usually, personality testing will provide considerably more information than just what might be relevant to these questions. It is usually a good idea to review all of the clinically significant findings during the initial interpretive process, because some may open new areas of inquiry or disconfirm preconceived notions. However, at the stage of integrating and summarizing the findings, the emphasis should be on those findings that are most pertinent to the questions at hand.

Self-Report Testing

Sylvia Moore was administered the Posttraumatic Stress Diagnostic Scale (PDS), the MMPI-2, and the MMPI-2-RF.

PDS

On the PDS, she scored positive on all the DSM-IV-TR (American Psychiatric Association, 2000) criteria for PTSD. She also scored at the moderate level of symptom severity and at the severe level of functional impairment. Although it is important to recognize that her claimed symptoms are highly consistent with serious posttraumatic distress, it must also be borne in mind that the questions on this test have high face validity and that many plaintiffs become familiar with the usual symptoms of PTSD early in the course of litigation. Simply looking up PTSD in an online search or completing a checklist of possible symptoms provided by a plaintiff's attorney is enough to teach a litigant what she should be experiencing if she is suffering from this disorder.

MMPI-2

Consistent with her self-presentation style in interviews in which she worked hard not to be self-pitying and downplayed her sensitivity, which she disparaged as "girly" feelings, and with her highly orthodox religious beliefs, her MMPI-2 L-scale was extreme (T = 90) and K was also elevated (K = 70), raising serious doubts about interpretive validity. Other scores appeared to confirm a reaction formation against feminine feelings and efforts to minimize and ignore painful emotions (elevations on 5 and 3). While her defensive, underreporting response style rendered the test results largely uninterpretable, the fact that she seemed to try to conceal her personal problems and symptoms rather than accentuate them is itself a finding of some value.

MMPI-2-RF

After due consideration, I decided to administer the MMPI-2-RF, using a modified version of Butcher, Morfitt, Rouse, and Holden's (1997) special instructions for defensive profiles (explaining in my report the non-standard nature and risks to validity of this approach). This yielded a more meaningful profile. Her validity scales fell within acceptable limits for a litigation context (F-r = 56; FBS-r = 70; L-r = 66; K-r = 59), although they remained suggestive of a naively virtuous self-presentation. Her Higher-Order Scales, Emotional/ Internalizing Dysfunction (EID; 51) and Thinking Dysfunction (THD; 39), were within normal limits, and Behavioral/Externalizing Dysfunction (BXD; 32) was quite low. The latter, along with a submerged Disconstraint-Revised (DISC-r; 35) score, suggested considerable behavioral constraint and a conservative approach to expressing her thoughts and feelings. Among her

Restructured Clinical scales, only Low Positive Emotion (RC2; 69) was elevated. Other elevated scales included Malaise (MLS; 69) and Introversion/Low Positive Emotionality-Revised (INTR-r; 70). Taken together, these scores indicate that she may be pessimistic, socially disengaged, lacking in energy, and showing anhedonia and vegetative signs of depression or psychic numbing. Cynicism (RC3; 34), Antisocial Behavior (RC4; 34), and Hypomanic Activation (RC9; 31) were submerged, suggesting, respectively, that she is somewhat naïve (particularly for a personal injury plaintiff), that she does not appear to be particularly angry or antisocial, and that (along with MLS), she reports a below-average level of activation and engagement with her environment and may be feeling weak or tired.

My interpretation of the self-report findings emphasized that when asked directly about PTSD symptoms, she showed clear indications of posttraumatic stress and problems in daily functioning. On the other hand, when asked in more general terms about how she was doing, she tended to downplay her emotional difficulties, apart from acknowledging a general sense of malaise and feeling low and somewhat disconnected from other people. She appeared to be somewhat emotionally overcontrolled and behaviorally inhibited, perhaps a reflection of psychic numbing. There were no indications of problems in thinking or reality testing.

Even with a measurable reduction in her defensiveness following the modified instructions for the MMPI-2-RF, the overall results were somewhat contradictory and not very informative. It would be difficult to offer a clear picture to the jury of the nature and extent of her difficulties based on the self-report testing. The most likely reason for this, which tended to be confirmed by the interview and mental status data, was that in spite of being a litigant in a personal injury case, she was highly resistant to viewing herself as a victim or even as an impaired person. Acknowledgment of such vulnerability was a threat to her preferred self-image as a strong, independent, and resilient person.

R-PAS Testing and the Interpretive Process

The interpretive process for Sylvia Moore's R-PAS findings will be described in considerable (albeit not exhaustive) detail in order to demonstrate the interpretive process and illustrate the richness of the clinical yield from this Rorschach system, which is still novel to many forensic psychologists.

Nomothetic Findings

While reading this section, it may be helpful to follow along on the R-PAS Summary Scores pages in Appendixes A and B. All variables are assigned Standard Scores with a mean of 100 and a standard deviation of 10.

Validity Check

Ms. Moore offered an average number of responses (R; SS = 102) and showed a very high degree of engagement with the task (Complexity; SS = 119). This supports an expectation that her results should reflect the full range of any difficulties she may have. However, her high score on Complexity also indicates that there may be much going on beneath the surface and that to some degree, her behavior may be difficult for others to predict and understand. At times it may be helpful to consider the impact of Ms. Moore's psychological complexity on the other scores and to consider how some of them may have varied if she were compared to other people with similar levels of complexity (using Complexity-Adjusted scores, shown in Appendix B).

In general, complexity measures differentiation, integration, and productivity in the responses. An elevated score means that a person has demonstrated a high level of psychological activity and energy in her approach to the response process. In everyday life, people who can invest such energy and engagement in their activities are usually sophisticated, flexible, and intelligent in how they think about and cope with challenges they encounter. However, in a person who has recently been exposed to psychological trauma, high complexity can also be an indication of being flooded with poorly controlled and upsetting emotions, ideas, and memories. In such circumstances, high complexity reflects a need to apply a great deal of effort—more than should ordinarily be necessary—just to get through the day. Sorting out to what extent complexity is reflecting a strength or a liability in this case will require a closer look at Ms. Moore's adaptive capacities as the R-PAS results are further explored.

In some rare cases, a high Complexity score can result from a tendency to offer many complex, dramatic, grotesque, or violent responses. Such behavior, in the absence of serious decompensation or thought disorder, may indicate an effort to malinger or exaggerate one's problems. Usually in such cases, this is accompanied by a marked elevation in the Critical Contents Percent (CritCont%), because of a high number of responses with dramatized contents. In the present case, the CritCont% falls within normal limits (SS = 93). This observation, taken together with the absence of any apparent effort to exaggerate her problems and suffering in the interview or self-report testing (far from it!), militates against such an interpretation of her elevated Complexity score.

Initial Scan

After looking at R and complexity to determine whether the overall results are likely to be valid, it is recommended that one briefly scan any extreme results (indicated by the black and red icons at the extreme ends of the scoring range) to gain an initial impression of what stands out about the results. This initial scan of salient features of her personality is provisional until the assessor subjects it to further scrutiny in the ensuing steps in the interpretive process. Results with black icons (which are shown as completely filled in for black-and-white display) fall more than three standard deviations from the mean and those with red icons (which are shown as mostly filled in for black-and-white display) fall more than two standard deviations from the mean (roughly equivalent to MMPI-2 scales above 80 and 70, respectively).

In Ms. Moore's case, there are black icons for pure Human representations (H) and Cooperative Movement (COP) on Page 1 (the page which contains those R-PAS variables with the greatest empirical support and response process rationales) and on Personal Justification Responses (PER) on Page 2 (which contains R-PAS variables that are given less interpretive weight). There are also red icons for Human Movement (M), M Proportion (MProp), and Space Reversal (SR) on Page 1 and for Vista (V), Sum of all Human Representations (SumH), Non-Pure H Proportion (NPH/SumH; low), Vigilance Composite (V-Comp), and Reflections (r) on Page 2.

The results of this scan point to some notable strengths and problem areas. The strengths include an advanced capacity to represent and understand self and others in realistic, comprehensive ways (H; NPH/SUMH); a greater than average interest in other people (SumH); and a strong inclination to view interactions as supportive, helpful, and collaborative (COP). There are also indications of a high capacity to think before acting (M; MProp) and to use her imagination to plan constructive solutions and empathize with others (M; H). She appears to experience a high sense of personal agency, viewing herself as in charge of her life and the initiator of her experiences and resisting control by other people or surrender to her circumstances (MProp; SR). Consistent with her sense of herself as in charge of her own life, she demonstrates a capacity for critical self-reflection and perspective taking (V).

Areas of potential difficulty include possible insecurity about having her beliefs challenged by others and a tendency to justify herself (PER; SR). She also evinces a heightened vigilance toward possible sources of danger, such as injury or attack by others (V-Comp). In addition, she seems to ruminate on feelings of unworthiness or inadequacy (V), which appears to dovetail with a strong, unsatisfied need for approval and recognition (r).

It may be noted in passing that M would only be slightly above average and that SumH and V-Comp would actually fall within the average range if her complexity was only at the average level. In other words, the elevations on these variables are strongly driven by her overall complexity, which as noted earlier, may be elevated in reaction to trauma.

Sifting and Synthesizing

The next steps in R-PAS interpretation more closely examine and integrate findings associated with each of the scores. The nomothetic findings are organized into five domains, consisting of Administrative Behaviors and Observations, Engagement and Cognitive Processing, Perception and Thinking Problems, Stress and Distress, and Self and Other Representations. In this phase, one sifts through and synthesizes the findings from each domain of the Summary Scores pages, again giving greater emphasis to the empirically sturdier results on Page 1 than on Page 2.

Administrative Behaviors and Observations

She required three reminders, known as Prompts (Pr), to give more than one response, as requested in the instructions: more prompts than are usually needed. A review of the responses in which she required prompting (6, 16, and 23) suggests that she tended to become absorbed in her responses to the extent that it was difficult for her to change her "set."

Two of these responses were related to her daughters and to interests she was prone to dismiss as too "girlie," and one involved a frightening scene in a hospital. These may be areas of particular sensitivity for her. She also turned the cards (CT) seven times, somewhat more often than usual. This may reflect an above average degree of curiosity, but it can also reflect anxiety or serve the defensive purpose of removing from view a scene or object that she finds disturbing. Such frequent card turning increases the likelihood of Reflection (r) responses, raising some doubt about the interpretive weight of that variable (Horn, Meyer, & Mihura, 2009).

Engagement and Cognitive Processing

We have already noted that her Complexity score is unusually high and that she gave an average number of responses. Here we should consider that given her level of complexity, we would expect her to have given a higher number of responses. Taken together with the elevated score on Prompts (Pr), it appears that she may have become emotionally absorbed with many of the responses she gave, to the extent that it reduced her productivity from what it might have been. Her Simplicity or F% score (SS = 90) was just below average, suggesting that she is slightly more attuned to subtleties and nuances of her experience than most people, but this is to be expected given her complexity. Similarly she gave more Blend responses (7), and used more multiple determinants than average, showing that she can identify multiple features of her environment in a flexible manner, but predictably so for her level of complexity. However, taking a closer look at her actual Blends, one finds that four of them included three determinants and one of them, four determinants. So many exceptionally complex Blends raise a question of trauma-related affective flooding as one of the components of her complex response style (see van der Kolk & Ducey, 1989). She offered a large number of Synthesis (Sy) responses (SS = 120), indicating that she is very attentive to how different features of her environment relate to one another, again at a level typical for her complexity. Her Human Movement and Weighted Color (MC) score (SS = 114) is above average, indicating substantial cognitive and emotional resources for interacting meaningfully with the world, also as expected for her complexity. This is particularly important, in that it suggests she currently has adequate adaptive resources for managing such a high level of complexity without usually becoming overwhelmed by it. Her MC-PPP score (SS = 114) shows that these resources are also well matched to her everyday stresses, but also suggests that she is under more strain than would be expected if her complexity were functioning only as a source of strength and resilience. As noted earlier, her Human Movement (M) score is quite high (SS = 125), which may indicate a resource to help her maintain a sense of agency and autonomy even when experiencing emotional pain. At the same time, it may also signal an unbridled or poorly controlled imagination (such as might manifest in intrusive images and flashbacks).

On Page 2 under the same domain, she gives an average number of Whole (W) responses (SS = 102), suggesting a typical degree of capacity to see the "big picture," and an average proportion of Dd responses (SS = 109), suggesting a notable but normal interest in making fine discriminations. Her number of Space Integration (SI) responses (SS = 111) was in the upper end of average, again indicating a capacity for flexible thinking. She shows a lower than average score (SS = 81) on Intellectualized Content (IntCont), which suggests a dearth of intellectualizing defenses, as is common among individuals who are flooded by traumatic images. Her Vagueness% (Vg%) is unremarkable (SS = 100), supporting an inference that she rarely falls into impressionistic and imprecise thinking. She gave a high number of Vista (V) responses (SS = 122), as already noted, indicating a capacity for self-criticism and perspective taking. She gave no Form Dimension (FD) responses, a finding that has little interpretive significance in the presence of multiple V responses. She gave an average number of responses (SS = 92) to the last three colored cards (R8910%), showing a typical level of interest in compelling or vibrant stimuli and emotional situations. However, her Weighted Sum of Color responses (WSumC) was low average (SS = 88) and exceptionally low for her level of complexity (Complexity-Adjusted SS = 70), probably suggesting some blunting in her emotional responsiveness and psychic numbing (Scroppo, Weinberger, Drob, & Eagle, 1998). She gave no Pure Color responses, which is not unusual. Her Passive Human Movement Proportion (Mp/(Mp+Ma) falls within the average range (SS = 92), suggesting that she does not engage in passive fantasy and escapist ideation more than most people.

Perception and Thinking Problems

We find that her Ego Impairment Index (EII-3) is elevated above average (SS = 114). The EII-3 is a broadband measure of thinking disturbance and severity of psychopathology. A score in this range indicates a moderate degree of disturbance that is likely to interfere with healthy psychological functioning. The Thought and Perception Composite (TP-Comp) falls just above average (SS = 110), demonstrating some mild problems in thinking clearly and seeing things accurately. The Weighted Sum of Cognitive Codes (WSumCog) is also elevated (SS = 116), suggesting some moderate impairment in the clarity of her thinking. Drilling down into the data, one finds that all of the Cognitive Codes are low-level Deviant Responses (DR1s) rather than more serious codes. Probably problems with the clarity of her thinking are related to circumstantial and idiosyncratic ways of expressing herself or loss of task focus based on emotional preoccupations, such as intrusive images rather than serious mental confusion. Her Severe Cognitive Codes (SevCog) fall within the average range (SS = 94), showing no significant breaks from rational thinking. Her average-level Form Quality scores—FQ-% (SS = 107), WD-% (SS = 92), and FQo% (SS = 96)—show that she is generally capable of perceiving objects and events realistically and conventionally. She also gave an average number of Popular (P) responses (SS = 103), showing that in obvious situations, she responds as most people do.

On Page 2, her percentage of responses with Unusual Form Quality (FQu%) is average (SS = 104). This confirms the inference that she tends to understand the world in conventional ways most of the time.

Stress and Distress

Her score on Sum of Shading and Achromatic Color (YTVC') is above average (SS = 112), pointing to implicit distress associated with anxiety, irritation, sadness, depression, loneliness, or helplessness. She scores quite high (SS = 119) on Inanimate Movement (m), which is likely indicative of a struggle with a sense of inner tension or things going on her mind outside her control. Elevations on m have been associated with PTSD (van der Kolk & Ducey, 1989). Ms. Moore's score on Diffuse Shading (Y) is within normal limits (SS = 99), perhaps suggesting that she has managed not to surrender to a sense of helplessness. Her Morbid

Content (MOR) is also average (SS = 100), showing that she is not giving up on her future or perceiving herself as having sustained irreparable damage. Her average score (SS = 101) on the Suicide Concerns Composite (SC-Comp) does not point to suicidal propensities.

Turning to Page 2, her score on Potentially Problematic Determinants (PPD) is slightly elevated (SS = 116), representing pressing irritating feelings or upsetting needs or a sense of agitation. Even though, as noted earlier, she has an unusual number of complex Blends, none of them involves Color Blended with Shading and Achromatic Color (CBlend), suggesting that she is probably still able to have positive experiences that are not spoiled by traumatic distress. As noted earlier, her score on Vista (V) is very high (SS = 126), indicating (within the Stress and Distress domain) fault-finding and critical ruminations about the self, perhaps associated with a trauma-induced sense of shame. Her Critical Contents (CritCont%) are average (SS = 98). A score in this range tends to rule out overly dramatized self-presentation of the sort commonly seen in malingerers. Some people with posttraumatic stress, particularly from repeated experiences of abuse in childhood, elevate substantially on this score (see Armstrong and Loewenstein, 1990, on the closely related Trauma Content Index), but other sufferers present their trauma-related representations in a more personalized, idiographic manner (Meyer et al., 2011; Viglione, Towns, & Lindshield, 2012), which as we shall see is the case for Sylvia Moore.

Self and Other Representations

Sylvia Moore's Oral-Dependent Language Percent (ODL%) is average (SS = 105), indicating an ordinary degree of interest in receiving care and support from others.[4] As noted earlier, her Space Reversal (SR) score is very high (SS = 122), suggesting a strong impulse toward autonomy and mastery and a dogged resistance to being controlled by others. (This very likely served her well in her stubborn refusal to take "No" for an answer from her doctors.) Her Human Representations codes, as indicated in the PHR Proportion (PHR/GPHR; SS = 103), indicate a probably normal degree of appealing sociability. She has one Human Movement response with poor Form Quality (M-), suggesting that emotional preoccupations can sometimes interfere with an accurate understanding of other people's intentions and motives. She has an ordinary number of responses with

Aggressive Contents (AGC; SS = 94), which tends to rule out an unusual preoccupation with aggressive or violent preoccupations or identifications. As previously noted, she produced an extraordinarily high number of pure Human responses (SS = 135), indicating an advanced capacity to conceive of oneself and other people in complex, integrated ways rather than just as caricatures or sources of need satisfaction. It should be noted, however, that sometimes she thinks she understands other people but really does not (M-). Also, it is interesting that the majority of her human representations were of babies and children. This probably reflects greater comfort in interacting with children than adults and may underscore how central in her life procreation and nurturing are for her. As previously mentioned, she scored very high (SS = 128) on Cooperative Movement (COP), indicating a strong preference for viewing and experiencing interactions as supportive, rewarding, and harmonious. She produced one Mutuality of Autonomy Health (MAH) response, which adds a dimension of potential depth and intimacy to some of her close relationships.

On Page 2, as previously noted, she produced many more Human Content (SumH) responses than expected (SS = 122), suggesting a strong interest in people and much attentiveness to human interactions. Also as described earlier, her Non-Pure H Proportion (NPH/SumH) is unusually low (SS = 74), suggesting that her ideas about people are generally based on mature, straightforward, and informed understanding of what they are like (although again, we should remember how many of these H responses are of babies and children). As previously discussed, her Vigilance Composite (V-Comp) is very high (SS = 121), signaling hyperalertness to potential threats, which could lead her to become wary of other people, a stance very much at odds with her strong preference for harmonious and collaborative relationships. Such hypervigilance has been directly linked to traumatic hypersensitivity (Levin, Lazrove, & van der Kolk, 1999). As described previously, she produced an exceptionally high number of Reflections (r; SS = 138), which raises a question about a possibly high level of self-involvement. On the other hand, it should be noted that two or three responses involved card turning and landscape content; both of these characteristics may cast doubt on the interpretive meaning of the score (Horn et al., 2009). Moreover, other scores previously noted evincing her strong interpersonal skills and interest in intimate and harmonious relationships with other people militate against an interpretation of these responses as pointing to her being self-centered and insensitive to the feelings of others. It is probably best to interpret the elevated r score as a need for mirroring recognition and approval from others. We should also note that such a need may be currently unsatisfied, as suggested by her elevated V score. Her average score (SS = 102) on the Passive Proportion (p/p+a) suggests a typical balance between inclinations to be the center of initiative versus allowing others to take the lead. She gave no Aggressive Movement (AGM) responses, indicating that aggression and competition are not particularly on her mind. She also gave no Texture (T) responses, which, although a normal-range response, may go along with her vigilance and caution with respect to becoming vulnerable to others. As noted previously, she gave an exceptionally large number (SS = 136) of Personal Knowledge Justification (PER) responses. A closer review of these responses shows that they lack the know-it-all, superior attitude of the classic PER response and are more oriented toward engaging the examiner on a personal level in drawing him into her experiences. She seems to be much more at ease in informal, confessional interactions than in the enactment of formal roles. Finally, her score on Anatomy content (An) was somewhat surprisingly in the average range (SS = 99), given that elevations on this score are often associated with a sense of physical vulnerability. Perhaps she tries defensively to deflect her attention from direct bodily awareness.

Idiographic Findings

Now that all of the formal scores have been sifted through, the inferences drawn so far may be enriched or modified by notable idiographic information from the sequence of responses and their elements, permitting further synthesis.

One major theme that runs through her protocol has to do with babies and their care. Her responses include "a mom changing a baby's diaper" (R4), a response that was so compelling that she found it difficult to give a second one; "a baby in a blanket . . . about to be swaddled" (R11); "kind of like a baby crawling . . . it sounds kind of stupid" (R17); and "a baby's head . . . holding the baby" (R14). These "baby" responses were so obviously frequent that she became flustered at one point, exclaiming, "I'm not doing it on purpose! That's why I'm not saying it—it sounds kind of stupid." There are also several direct references to her own daughters (on Responses 11, 12, and 16). It is unusual to give so many responses focusing on babies and children. But keeping in mind that at the heart of this case is a childbirth with terrible complications, deprivation of the chance to hold and nurse her newborn daughter, and major concerns about her future fertility. Such a narrow focus might be explicable.

It may be recalled from prior observations that Sylvia Moore, while having strong maternal longings, thought of herself as a resourceful, outdoorsy person and was highly resistant to viewing herself as overly sensitive, dependent, or preoccupied with feminine interests (see again her elevated Scale 5 on the MMPI-2). One sees this as a source of insecurity on R7, which she said could be fairies, when held upside down and then added, "I'm usually not this girlie!" in her sense of embarrassment about having given too many responses featuring babies. Her preference to see herself as having some masculine qualities is suggested by R19, a percept of a young man driving fast on a "quad" (all-terrain vehicle), and even more explicitly when she notices the Batman symbol during clarification on R12 and comments, "That's the boy in me." It is perhaps important to note that both of her Rorschach responses featuring adult males show them engaged in pleasant recreation (fishing, four-wheeling), whereas both responses featuring adult females involve illness and injury.

According to Labott, Leavitt, Braun, & Sachs (1992), when responses start off pleasantly but suddenly shift and become upsetting, this is often a sign of traumatic dissociation. Here is an example from Ms. Moore's protocol:

> **VIII. 18. RP: That's pretty . . . Hm . . . I said this was pretty but it kind of looks like a lot of blood too—looked pretty at first, but now kind of doesn't look pretty anymore. This looks like some kind of scary animal walking on something. I don't like that.**
> **CP: (ERR) Scary one. Looked really pretty at first. Just like the way it was splotched—kind of like blood. Here like blood coming off its feet or something. Animal walking through it. Coming off of its foot, here and here. (What made it look like blood?) Because it's red, pinkish red, the way it spilled like that. It makes me feel like I'm crazy!**

Most important, she was reluctant to describe in detail three anxiety-ridden responses, all of which can easily be linked to medical trauma:

VII. 14. RP: This looks like someone laying down. This is kind of weird.

CP: (ERR) Here. I didn't want to say it because I didn't want that to seem all... It looks like a sick woman changing the channel[5] on a hospital bed. Was kind of getting bad. Am I supposed to be seeing this? It looks like a baby's head (sheepish tone), holding the baby, changing the channel. I really didn't want to say it. TV control and wall button. Hospital gown. Pushing a button.

X. 23. v RP: It this supposed to work like this because of all the stuff I just took a test on—all the hospital questions? [a reference to the Posttraumatic Stress Disorder Scale]. Well that looks like nurses and those are their gloves. The big light overhead and the wheels on the bed. Looks like people. I can see their head and everything.

CP: (ERR) I don't like this one. Nurses. I'm on the bed. They're pushing me. (Bed?) Blue is gloves, holding the bed. I don't see the bed, but I see the wheels. This is their scrubs. Heads. Wearing their masks. Facing the other way. Those creepy hospital lights—long. (People?) Nurses.

X. 24. RP: Those look like pliers—like a hemostat—something. I don't like that one.

CP: Right here—handles and tweezer-looking part.

These responses raise certain important questions. One is whether they are being offered manipulatively, as the respondent's way of making her case that she was damaged by the events in the hospital. We know that the content of Rorschach responses (more so than the formal scoring) can often be manipulated by respondents who want to show themselves in a certain light (Viglione, 1999). For instance, in child custody cases, one often gets responses featuring children, children's art productions, and children's toys.

Although it might be conjectured that Sylvia Moore could have been a gifted and highly manipulative actress, seeking to exhibit herself on the Rorschach as caught in the grip of serious trauma, this does not square very well with her tendency to minimize and be embarrassed by her distress and personal difficulties through much of the interviews and in the MMPI-2. The opportunity for such cross-checking is an important advantage of the multimethod approach.

Moreover, unlike manipulative responses, which are usually given directly and frankly, in this case one has the sense that Ms. Moore was resisting giving them and providing the painful details. To review, several of the responses have this quality: "I'm not doing it on purpose! That's why I'm not saying it—it sounds kind of stupid"; "looked pretty at first but it doesn't look pretty any more ... I don't like it"; "I really didn't want to say it"; "I don't like that one." The effort to resist such intrusive imagery and failure to do so is suggestive of failed traumatic avoidance. Although she is sometimes aware of the connection between her responses and her hospital experiences ("Is this supposed to work like this because of all the stuff I just took a test on—all the hospital questions?"), she appears naïve about the extent to which she might have some choice about what she sees. Also, it is important to note that it is unlikely that she knew that she would be questioned during a subsequent Clarification Phase about her initial vague response (R14) during the earlier Response Phase: "This looks like someone laying down. This looks kind of weird," which left unspoken a highly elaborated hospital scene that was latent behind this brief verbalization.

But why should the Rorschach particularly lend itself to such graphic and disturbing portrayals and thematic resonances with previous trauma? That it does so has long been observed by evaluators. Numerous clinical examples, many of them quite powerful, have been offered by Briere and Elliott (1997), Franchi and Andronikoff-Sanglade (1993), Kaser-Boyd (1993), Kaser-Boyd and Evans (2008), Levin (1993), Overton (2012), Salley and Teiling (1984), van der Kolk and Ducey (1984, 1989), and Viglione, Towns, and Lindshield (2012). The answer seems to be that the moderately stressful testing situation, combined with stimuli that can be assimilate to what is already on one's mind, tends to "trigger trauma memories and feelings," almost like inducing a flashback (van der Kolk & Ducey, 1989) Further, the lack of structure and guidance offered by the test instructions and procedures gives respondents few opportunities to focus on neutral stimuli and distract themselves from intrusive affects and imagery related to trauma (Viglione et al., 2012).

Brett and Ostroff (1985) describe reactions to trauma as involving two dimensions: repetition and defense. They write, "The first dimension is the repetition of the trauma in images, affective and somatic states and action. The second is defensive attempts to deny the trauma, including psychogenic amnesia, emotional numbing, and suppressive and avoidant behavior." In a similar vein, Viglione et al. (2012) observe,

> Crucial to the understanding of the psychological issues related to post-traumatic reaction is an appreciation of the struggle between loss of control and over-control. For example, cognitive intrusions and loss of affective control are opposed by cognitive constriction, avoidance tactics, and emotional numbing.
>
> (p. 136)

Both dimensions can be observed *in vivo* in the responses described earlier and, indeed, throughout the testing.

Summarizing

The final stage in R-PAS interpretation is to organize the results into a meaningful summary in a way that is relevant to the referral questions and consistent with the evidence from other sources. Focusing here on the principal R-PAS results alone, the evidence supports a finding that Sylvia Moore is not feigning or exaggerating her anxiety and intrusive ideation. On the contrary, she is embarrassed by her symptoms and striving valiantly to contain and suppress them with a great deal of energy and effort, but still at times quite ineffectively. Her difficulties manifest primarily in the form of hypervigilance against potential dangers and threats, internal tension and worry, mental preoccupations and occasional disruptions in her train of thought, and distressing flooding of traumatic memories. Her highly complex Rorschach shows evidence of a kind of traumatic hyperarousal with some dissociative features (see Armstrong & Loewenstein, 1990).

At the same time, the Rorschach evidence indicates that she has considerable psychological resources for coping with even an extraordinary degree of stress and distress. Thus, although there is some moderate and intermittently severe compromise to her everyday functioning, she is holding up reasonably well so far. A particular source of strength is her ability to use close relationships with others as a source of emotional support and sense of purpose, and this shows up particularly in her intense concern about and devotion to her children. It is likely that her prognosis with trauma-oriented outpatient psychotherapy is good, albeit it will probably be quite difficult for her to come to terms with infertility, should this turn out to be a permanent consequence of her uterine adhesions.

Conclusions from the Multimethod Testing

Returning to the questions posed at the outset of this case, it seems clear that in addition to her physical injuries and potential loss of future fertility, the psychological testing (particularly the PDS and R-PAS, but also to a lesser extent the MMPI-2-RF) supports the presence of symptoms and functional impairments consistent with posttraumatic stress disorder. Although the plaintiff was willing on the self-report testing to describe posttraumatic symptoms and functional impairment, she tended to minimize their seriousness. R-PAS testing brought into clear relief the cracks in her composure and even provided *in vivo* demonstrations of the breakthrough of traumatic memories and her struggle to contain them.

The multimethod assessment also helped clarify how her sense of vulnerability over the course of her hospital experiences and their aftermath specifically threatened her self-image of herself as a strong, self-reliant, resilient person. In addition, it tended to confirm impressions from the interviews of the centrality for her of her relationships with her children (and by extension, of her fertility).

At the same time, there was test evidence that her functional impairment is usually only moderate and that she has considerable psychological resources and strong interpersonal skills. These findings support a good prognosis with trauma-oriented outpatient treatment that helps her to face her feelings of loss and helplessness more squarely, while also highlighting her high emotional and interpersonal intelligence to help her cope with them.

Notes

1 Pre-existing vulnerability (the proverbial "thin skull") that leads to worse than expected consequences of the injury does not mitigate damages, but a prior deteriorating condition that would likely have continued to get worse regardless of the injury in question (a "crumbling skull"; *Athey v. Leonati*, 1996, cited in Kane & Dvoskin, 2011) can be mitigating.

2 The plaintiff's name and some minor details of her history have been changed for the sake of anonymity.

3 Her husband, who was interviewed separately, largely confirmed her history.

4 Because Page 2 variables have weaker evidentiary support than Page 1 variables, the threshold for below average is reduced from 90 to 85 and for above average is increased from 110 to 115.

5 Given the traumatically salient nature of this response content, it seems peculiar at first that she would focus on an aspect of the scene as mundane as the patient using a remote control to change a television channel. However, from a psychodynamic viewpoint, one might speculate that this behavior is a kind of condensed representation or symbolic shorthand for dissociation, a kind of "switching" of one's mental "channel" to ward off intolerable experiences.

References

American Psychiatric Association (2000). *Diagnostic and statistical manual of mental disorders: DSM-IV-TR.* Washington, DC: Author.

Armstrong, J. G., & Loewenstein, R. J. (1990). Characteristics of patients with multiple personality and dissociative identity disorders on psychological testing. *Journal of Nervous and Mental Disease, 178,* 448–454.

Athey v. Leonati (1996). 3 S.C.R. 458.

Ben-Porath, Y. S., & Tellegen, A. (2011). *Minnesota Multiphasic Personality Inventory-2-RF (MMPI-2-RF) manual for administration, scoring, and interpretation.* Minneapolis: University of Minnesota Press.

Boccaccini, M. T., & Brodsky, S. L. (1999). Diagnostic test usage by forensic psychologists in emotional injury cases. *Professional Psychology: Research and Practice, 30*(3), 253.

Brett, E. A., & Ostroff, R. (1985). Imagery and posttraumatic stress disorder: An overview. *The American Journal of Psychiatry, 142,* 417–424.

Briere, J. (2011). *Trauma Symptom Inventory-2 (TSI-2).* Lutz, FL: Psychological Assessment Resources.

Briere, J., & Elliott, D. M. (1997). Psychological assessment of interpersonal victimization effects in adults and children. *Psychotherapy: Theory, Research, and Practice, 34,* 353–364.

Butcher, J. N., Dahlstrom, W. G., Graham, J. R., Tellegen, A., & Kaemmer, B. (1989). *Minnesota Multiphasic Personality Inventory–2 (MMPI-2): Manual for administration and scoring.* Minneapolis: University of Minnesota Press.

Butcher, J. N., Morfitt, R. C., Rouse, S. V., & Holden, R. R. (1997). Reducing MMPI-2 defensiveness: The effect of specialized instructions on retest validity in a job applicant sample. *Journal of Personality Assessment, 68*(2), 385–401.

Erard, R. E. (2012). Expert testimony using the Rorschach Performance Assessment System in psychological injury cases. *Psychological Injury and Law, 5*(2), 122–134.

Erard, R. E., Meyer, G. J., & Viglione, D. J. (2014). Setting the record straight: Comment on Gurley, Sheehan, Piechowksi, and Gray (2014) on the admissibility of the Rorschach Performance Assessment program (R-PAS) in court. *Psychological Injury and Law, 7*(2), 165–177.

Foa, E. B. (1995). *Posttraumatic Stress Diagnostic Scale (PDS) manual/user's guide.* New York: Pearson Assessments.

Franchi, V., & Andronikof-Sanglade, H. (1993). Methodological and epistemological issues raised by the use of the Rorschach Comprehensive System in cross-cultural research. *Rorschachiana, 18,* 118–133.

Ganellen, R. J. (1994). Attempting to conceal psychological disturbance: MMPI defensive response sets and the Rorschach. *Journal of Personality Assessment, 63,* 423–437.

Greenberg, S. A. (2003). Personal injury examinations in torts for emotional distress. In I. B. Weiner (Series Ed.) & A. M. Goldstein (Vol. Ed.), *Handbook of Psychology,* Vol. 11, *Forensic psychology* (pp. 233–257). New York: Wiley.

Horn, S. L., Meyer, G. J., & Mihura, J. L. (2009). Impact of card rotation on the frequency of Rorschach reflection responses. *Journal of Personality Assessment, 91,* 346–356.

Kane, A. W., & Dvoskin, J. A. (2011). *Evaluation for personal injury claims.* New York: Oxford University Press.

Kaser-Boyd, N. (1993). Rorschachs of women who commit homicide. *Journal of Personality Assessment, 60,* 458–470.

Kaser-Boyd, N., & Evans, F. B. (2008). Rorschach assessment of psychological trauma. In C. B. Gacono & F. B. Evans (Eds.), *The handbook of forensic psychological assessment* (pp. 255–278). New York: Routledge.

Labott, S. M., Leavitt, F., Braun, B. G., & Sachs, R. G. (1992). Rorschach indicators of multiple personality disorder. *Perceptual and Motor Skills, 75,* 147–158.

Lees-Haley, P. (1988). Litigation response syndrome. *American Journal of Forensic Psychology, 6*(1), 3–12.

Levin, P. (1993). Assessing posttraumatic stress disorder with the Rorschach technique. In J. P. Wilson & P. Raphael (Eds.), *International handbook of traumatic stress syndromes* (pp. 189–200). New York: Plenum.

Levin, P., Lazrove, S., & van der Kolk, B. (1999). What psychological testing and neuroimaging tell us about the treatment of posttraumatic stress disorder by eye movement desensitization and reprocessing. *Journal of Anxiety Disorders, 13,* 159–172.

McCann, J. T., & Evans, F. B. (2008). Admissibility of the Rorschach. In C. B. Gacono & F. B. Evans (Eds.), *The handbook of forensic psychological assessment* (pp. 55–78). New York: Routledge.

Melton, G. B., Petrila, J., Poythress, N. G., & Slobogin, C. (2007). *Psychological evaluations for the courts: A handbook for mental health professionals and lawyers.* New York: Guilford Press.

Meyer, G. J., & Eblin, J. J. (2012). An overview of the Rorschach Performance Assessment System (R-PAS). *Psychological Injury and Law, 5,* 107–121.

Meyer, G. J., Viglione, D. J., Mihura, J. L., Erard, Robert E., & Erdberg, P. (2011). *Rorschach Performance Assessment System: Administration, coding, interpretation, and technical manual.* Toledo, OH: Rorschach Performance Assessment System, LLC.

Mihura, J. L., Meyer, G. J., Dumitrascu, N., & Bombel, G. (2013). The validity of individual Rorschach variables: Systematic reviews and meta-analyses of the comprehensive system. *Psychological Bulletin, 139,* 548–605. doi:10.1037/a0029406

Millon, T., Grossman, S., & Millon, C. (2015). *The Millon Clinical Multiaxial Inventory-IV*. Minneapolis, MN: Pearson Assessments.

Morey, L. C. (1991). *The Personality Assessment Inventory professional manual*. Odessa, FL: Psychological Assessment Resources.

Overton, C. G. (2012). Therapeutic assessment of severe abuse: A woman living with her past. In S. E. Finn, C. T. Fischer, & L. Handler (Eds.), *Collaborative/Therapeutic Assessment: A casebook and guide*. Hoboken, NJ: Wiley.

Rogers, R., Sewell, K. W., & Gillard, N. D. (2010). *Structured Interview of Reported Symptoms (SIRS), 2nd Edition, professional manual*. Lutz, FL: Psychological Assessment Resources, Inc.

Salley, R., & Teiling, P. (1984). Dissociated rage attacks in a Vietnam veteran: A Rorschach study. *Journal of Personality Assessment, 48*, 98-104.

Scroppo, J. C., Weinberger, J. L., Drob, S. L., & Eagle, P. (1998). Identifying dissociative identity disorder: A self-report and projective study. *Journal of Abnormal Psychology, 107*, 272-284.

Smith, B. L. (2008). The Rorschach in tort and employment litigation. In C. B. Gacono & F. B. Evans (Eds.), *The handbook of forensic psychological assessment* (pp. 279-300). New York: Routledge.

Smith, G. P., & Burger, G. K. (1997). Detection of malingering: Validation of the Structured Interview of Malingered Symptomatology (SIMS). *Journal of the American Academy of Psychiatry and Law, 25*(2), 183-189.

van der Kolk, B. A., & Ducey, C. P. (1984). Clinical implications of the Rorschach in posttraumatic stress disorder. In B. A. van der Kolk (Ed.), *Psychological trauma* (pp. 31-42). Washington, DC: American Psychiatric Press.

van der Kolk, B. A., & Ducey, C. P. (1989). The psychological processing of traumatic experience: Rorschach patterns in PTSD. *Journal of Traumatic Stress, 2*, 259-274.

Viglione, D. J. (1999). A review of recent research addressing the utility of the Rorschach. *Psychological Assessment, 47*, 150-154.

Viglione, D. J., Towns, B., & Lindshield, D. (2012). Understanding and using the Rorschach inkblot test to assess post-traumatic conditions. *Psychological Injury and Law, 5*(2), 135-144.

APPENDIX A

Table 5.1: Reproduced from the Rorschach Performance Assessment System® (R-PAS®) Scoring Program (© 2010–2016) and excerpted from the Rorschach Performance Assessment System: Administration, Coding, Interpretation, and Technical Manual (© 2011) with copyrights by Rorschach Performance Assessment System, LLC. All rights reserved. Used by permission of Rorschach Performance Assessment System, LLC. Further reproduction is prohibited without written permission from R-PAS.

R-PAS Code Sequence

C-ID: SM—P-ID: 68—Age: NA—Gender: Female—Education: NA

Cd	#	Or	Loc	Loc #	SR	SI	Content	Sy	Vg	2	FQ	P	Determinants	Cognitive	Thematic	HR	ODL (RP)	R-Opt
I	1		W				(H),Cg				o		F			GH		
	2		W				A				o		F					
II	3		W				H	Sy		2	o		Ma		COP,MAH	GH		
	4		W				A	Sy		2	o	P	FMp		PER			
III	5		D	1			H,Cg,Sx,NC	Sy		2	u	P	Ma		COP	GH	ODL	Pr
	6		Dd	99	SR	SI	A,NC	Sy			u		FMa,mp,C',V					
	7	v	D	2			(H),Cg			2	u		F	DR1	PER	PH		
IV	8	@	Dd	99			An				-		V		PER			
V	9		W		SR		A,NC	Sy		2	-		FMp,C'					
	10		W				A				o	P	F					
	11		W				H,Cg	Sy			o		Mp	DR1	PER	PH	ODL	
	12		D	7			(A)				o		F		PER			
VI	13		W				NC				o		F					
	14	>	D	4			H,Cg,NC	Sy			u		Ma		COP,MOR	GH		
	15	<	W				H,NC	Sy			o		Mp,r	DR1		PH		

VII	16	W		H,Cg	Sy	o	P Ma,mp,r			GH	
	17	D	2	H,Cg		2 u	Ma	DR1		GH	
VIII	18	Dd	1,2,25	A,Bl	Sy	u	P FMa,mp,CF		AGC		Pr
	19	D	8	SI NC		u	V		AGC		
IX	20 >	Dd	99	H,NC		o	Ma,ma,Y	DR1		GH	
	21 <	D	5	NC	Sy Vg	o	r				
	22	D	8	SI Ad		o	C'				
X	23 v	Dd	22	SR SI H,Cg,NC	Sy	2 -	Ma-p,FC		COP	PH	ODL Pr
	24	D	10	NC		u	F				

Tables 5.2–5.5 are reproduced from the Rorschach Performance Assessment System® (R–PAS®) Scoring Program (© 2010–2016) and excerpted from the Rorschach Performance Assessment System: Administration, Coding, Interpretation, and Technical Manual (© 2011) with copyrights by Rorschach Performance Assessment System, LLC. All rights reserved. Used by permission of Rorschach Performance Assessment System, LLC. Further reproduction is prohibited without written permission from R-PAS.

R-PAS Summary Scores and Profiles – Page 1

C-ID: SM   P-ID: 68   Age: NA   Gender: Female   Education: NA

Domain/Variables	Raw Scores	Raw %ile	Raw SS	Cplx. Adj. %ile	Cplx. Adj. SS	Abbr.
Admin. Behaviors and Obs.						
Pr	3	90	119			Pr
Pu	0	40	96			Pu
CT (Card Turning)	7	75	110			CT
Engagement and Cog. Processing						
Complexity	109	91	120			Cmplx
R (Responses)	24	55	102	14	83	R
F% [Lambda=0.41] (Simplicity)	29%	24	90	56	102	F%
Blend	7	83	114	44	98	Bln
Sy	12	91	120	55	102	Sy
MC	10.5	82	114	38	96	MC
MC - PPD	-4.5	29	92	36	95	MC-PPD
M	9	95	125	79	112	M
M/MC	[9/10.5]	86%	94	123	93	121	M Prp
(CF+C)/SumC	[1/2]	NA				CFC Prp
Perception and Thinking Problems						
EII-3	0.5	82	114	76	111	EII
TP-Comp (Thought & Percept. Com...)	1.1	75	110	61	104	TP-C
WSumCog	15	86	116	76	110	WCog
SevCog	0	35	94	35	94	Sev
FQ-%	12%	69	107	58	103	FQ-%
WD-%	5%	31	92	16	85	WD-%
FQo%	54%	38	96	45	98	FQo%
P	6	59	103	56	102	P
Stress and Distress						
YTVC'	7	78	112	52	101	YTVC'
m	4	90	119	68	107	m
Y	1	48	99	17	85	Y
MOR	1	51	100	31	91	MOR
SC-Comp (Suicide Concern Comp.)	4.5	52	101	23	89	SC-C
Self and Other Representation						
ODL%	12%	63	105	43	97	ODL%
SR (Space Reversal)	3	92	122	92	122	SR
MAP/MAHP	[0/1]	NA				MAP Prp
PHR/GPHR	[4/11]	36%	58	103	58	103	PHR Prp
M-	1	81	113	81	113	M-
AGC	2	34	94	23	89	AGC
H	9	99	135	97	128	H
COP	4	97	128	92	122	COP
MAH	1	64	105	26	90	MAH

© 2010–2016 R-PAS

Table 5.3

R-PAS Summary Scores and Profiles – Page 2

C-ID: SM P-ID: 68 Age: NA Gender: Female Education: NA

Domain/Variables	Raw Scores	Raw %ile	Raw SS	Cplx. Adj. %ile	Cplx. Adj. SS	Abbr.
Engagement and Cog. Processing						
W%	42%	56	102	34	94	W%
Dd%	21%	73	109	78	111	Dd%
SI (Space Integration)	4	77	111	68	107	SI
IntCont	0	11	81	11	81	IntC
Vg%	4%	46	99	49	100	Vg%
V	3	96	126	92	122	V
FD	0	21	88	21	88	FD
R8910%	29%	29	92	36	95	R8910%
WSumC	1.5	21	88	2	70	WSC
C	0	36	95	36	95	C
MP/(Ma+Mp) [3/10]	30%	29	92	29	92	Mp Prp
Perception and Thinking Problems						
FQu%	33%	61	104	46	99	FQu%
Stress and Distress						
PPD	15	86	116	56	102	PPD
CBlend	0	28	91	28	91	CBlnd
C'	3	77	111	56	103	C'
V	3	96	126	92	122	V
CritCont% (Critical Contents)	17%	46	98	30	92	CrCt
Self and Other Representation						
SumH	11	93	122	74	109	SumH
NPH/SumH [2/11]	18%	4	74	7	78	NPH Prp
V-Comp (Vigilance Composite)	5.3	92	121	72	109	V-C
r (Reflections)	3	97	128	97	128	r
p/(a+p) [8/18]	44%	55	102	56	103	p Prp
AGM	0	31	93	31	93	AGM
T	0	28	91	28	91	T
PER	5	99	136	99	136	PER
An	1	47	99	47	99	An

© 2010-2016 R-PAS

APPENDIX B
Complexity-Adjusted Scores

Table 5.4

R-PAS Summary Scores and Profiles – Page 1

C-ID: SM   P-ID: 68   Age: NA   Gender: Female   Education: NA

Domain/Variables	Raw Scores	Raw %ile	Raw SS	Cplx. Adj. %ile	Cplx. Adj. SS	Abbr.
Admin. Behaviors and Obs.						
Pr	3	90	119			Pr
Pu	0	40	96			Pu
CT (Card Turning)	7	75	110			CT
Engagement and Cog. Processing						
Complexity	109	91	120			Cmplx
R (Responses)	24	55	102	14	83	R
F% [Lambda=0.41] (Simplicity)	29%	24	90	56	102	F%
Blend	7	83	114	44	98	Bln
Sy	12	91	120	55	102	Sy
MC	10.5	82	114	38	96	MC
MC - PPD	−4.5	29	92	36	95	MC-PPD
M	9	95	125	79	112	M
M/MC [9/10.5]	86%	94	123	93	121	M Prp
(CF+C)/SumC [1/2]	NA					CFC Prp
Perception and Thinking Problems						
EII-3	0.5	82	114	76	111	EII
TP-Comp (Thought & Percept. Com...)	1.1	75	110	61	104	TP-C
WSumCog	15	86	116	76	110	WCog
SevCog	0	35	94	35	94	Sev
FQ-%	12%	69	107	58	103	FQ-%
WD-%	5%	31	92	16	85	WD-%
FQo%	54%	38	96	45	98	FQo%
P	6	59	103	56	102	P
Stress and Distress						
YTVC'	7	78	112	52	101	YTVC'
m	4	90	119	68	107	m
Y	1	48	99	17	85	Y
MOR	1	51	100	31	91	MOR
SC-Comp (Suicide Concern Comp.)	4.5	52	101	23	89	SC-C
Self and Other Representation						
ODL%	12%	63	105	43	97	ODL%
SR (Space Reversal)	3	92	122	92	122	SR
MAP/MAHP [0/1]	NA					MAP Prp
PHR/GPHR [4/11]	36%	58	103	58	103	PHR Prp
M-	1	81	113	81	113	M-
AGC	2	34	94	23	89	AGC
H	9	99	135	97	128	H
COP	4	97	128	92	122	COP
MAH		64	105	26	90	MAH

© 2010–2016 R-PAS

Table 5.5

R-PAS Summary Scores and Profiles – Page 2

C-ID: SM P-ID: 68 Age: NA Gender: Female Education: NA

Domain/Variables	Raw Scores	Raw %ile	SS	Cplx. Adj. %ile	Cplx. Adj. SS	Abbr.
Engagement and Cog. Processing						
W%	42%	56	102	34	94	W%
Dd%	21%	73	109	78	111	Dd%
SI (Space Integration)	4	77	111	68	107	SI
IntCont	0	11	81	11	81	IntC
Vg%	4%	46	99	49	100	Vg%
V	3	96	126	92	122	V
FD	0	21	88	21	88	FD
R8910%	29%	29	92	36	95	R8910%
WSumC	1.5	21	88	2	70	WSC
C	0	36	95	36	95	C
MP/(Ma+Mp) [3/10]	30%	29	92	29	92	Mp Prp
Perception and Thinking Problems						
FQu%	33%	61	104	46	99	FQu%
Stress and Distress						
PPD	15	86	116	56	102	PPD
CBlend	0	28	91	28	91	CBlnd
C'	3	77	111	56	103	C'
V	3	96	126	92	122	V
CritCont% (Critical Contents)	17%	46	98	30	92	CrCt
Self and Other Representation						
SumH	11	93	122	74	109	SumH
NPH/SumH [2/11]	18%	4	74	7	78	NPH Prp
V-Comp (Vigilance Composite)	5.3	92	121	72	109	V-C
r (Reflections)	3	97	128	97	128	r
p/(a+p) [8/18]	44%	55	102	56	103	p Prp
AGM	0	31	93	31	93	AGM
T	0	28	91	28	91	T
PER	5	99	136	99	136	PER
An	1	47	99	47	99	An

© 2010-2016 R-PAS

CHAPTER 6

THE RORSCHACH IN THE DIFFERENTIAL DIAGNOSIS OF PSYCHOTIC OFFENDERS

Ali Khadivi

Establishing the accurate diagnosis of a psychotic disorder is essential in many types of criminal forensic psychological examinations. In some cases, such as insanity evaluations, the diagnosis of psychotic disorder constitutes crucial evidence that directly relates to the psycholegal questions (Goldstein, Morse, & Packer, 2013). In other types of examinations, such as sentencing evaluations, the identification of psychosis serves as an indirect, albeit important, mitigation and is an additional source of evidence in support of the forensic opinion.

Psychologists who practice in criminal forensic mental health evaluations utilize a multimethod assessment that includes clinical interviews, record reviews, review of relevant legal documents, and collateral information (Heilbrun, Marczyk, DeMatteo, & Mack-Allen, 2007). Depending on the case, the forensic practitioner may also use traditional clinical psychological tests (see Archer, 2006) and/or specialized forensic instruments (see Heilbrun, Rogers, & Otto, 2002; Grisso, 2003) in order to assist in measuring psychological constructs that are relevant to the psycholegal issue at hand.

The purpose of this chapter is to examine the role of the Rorschach in assessment and the differential diagnosis of psychosis in offender populations. This chapter will first examine the unique role of the Rorschach in assessing psychosis, followed by a discussion of the use of the Rorschach in the multimethod psychological assessment of offenders. Lastly, the chapter concludes with a discussion of the use of the

Rorschach in assessing psychosis in the criminal forensic evaluation of competency to stand trial, criminal responsibility, violence risk assessment, sentencing, and court diversion.

The Unique Role of the Rorschach in Assessment of Psychosis

At the present time, there are two evidence-based Rorschach systems: The Comprehensive System (CS; Exner, 2003) and the more empirically robust Rorschach Performance Assessment System® (R-PAS®; Meyer, Viglione, Mihura, Erard, & Erdberg, 2012). Although there are conceptual differences between the two systems in the indexes and variables that measure psychosis, there is also significant overlap (Meyer et al., 2012) A recent meta-analysis by Mihura, Meyer, Dumitrascu, and Bombel (2013) demonstrated that the Rorschach's measures of thought disorder and reality testing impairment have the most robust empirically validated evidence. Even the most prolific critics of the Rorschach have argued that the instrument has diagnostic utility in detecting thinking disorder and reality testing (see Lilienfeld, Wood, & Garb, 2000; Wood, Nezworski, Lilienfeld & Garb, 2003).

In assessing psychotic disorder with the Rorschach, it is important to understand and follow the contemporary perspectives and changes in diagnosis of psychosis. With the publication of DSM-5 (American Psychiatric Association, 2013), important changes were made in the diagnostic criteria of psychotic disorders. These changes are both conceptual as well as empirical (see Black & Grant, 2014). A major change that has significant implications for forensic psychological evaluation is that the diagnosis of psychosis can now only be made by positive symptoms, which are limited to disorganized speech, hallucination, and delusions. In contrast to the DSM-IV-TR (American Psychiatric Association, 2000), the DSM-5 outlines that the diagnosis of psychosis cannot be made solely on the basis of negative symptoms or abnormal or grossly disorganized behavior. The DSM-5 also removed the special status of bizarre delusions and "first-rank" hallucinations (hearing two or more voices conversing) in diagnostic classification. However, one can now diagnose a psychotic disorder even in cases where there is a short duration of positive symptoms. Furthermore, even attenuated psychosis syndrome, which was not included as a diagnosis in DSM-5, can now be diagnosed under other specified schizophrenia spectrum and other psychotic disorder.

In short, psychological tests including the Rorschach must focus on assessing and detecting core positive symptoms. However, the nature of delusion or hallucination reported in testing or interview do not contribute to the differential diagnosis; the diagnosis of psychosis can now be made with only one positive symptom in absence of any other features or symptoms. Finally, individuals with transient, less severe psychotic-like symptoms that are below a threshold for full psychosis can now be diagnosed. It remains an empirical question as to whether the aforementioned changes in the DSM-5 will lead to an increased prevalence of diagnosis of psychosis in clinical and forensic settings or whether it will further restrict it.

The following are two recent forensic case examples illustrating the DSM-5 diagnostic changes and their impact.

> Case #1: *Mr. X, a male defendant with a history of multiple psychiatric hospitalizations and documented diagnosis of schizophrenia, killed his father. Following his arrest, his attorney requested an insanity evaluation. In examining the evidence, which included collateral information from his family, his psychiatrist, post-arrest mental status exam, and record review, it became evident that Mr. X was taking his medication; he had no active positive psychotic symptoms, and he was only experiencing marked negative symptoms. Psychological testing, including the Rorschach that was done shortly after his arrest, did not show any thought disorder or any reality testing impairment.*
>
> Case #2: *Mr. B, a 59-year-old male with no prior psychiatric history or any cognitive impairment, physically assaulted a family member with a hammer causing severe injuries. Following his arrest, he reported that he had a transient auditory hallucination lasting a few days just prior to, and during, the alleged crime. After ruling out malingering, a retained defense expert used the DSM-5 criteria to diagnose Mr. B as having other specified schizophrenia-spectrum disorder and suggested further evaluation for the insanity defense.*

In the first case, the defendant clearly has a major psychotic illness, but he did not demonstrate positive symptoms of psychosis such as hallucination, delusion, or disorganized speech at the time of the alleged crime. As a result, there is no evidence that Mr. X had a break from reality, even though he had the negative symptoms of schizophrenia. On the other hand, Mr. B met the threshold for having psychosis as evidenced by positive hallucinations, albeit short in duration, despite no other psychotic symptoms and no prior history of diagnosis of psychotic disorder.

Assessing Core Psychotic Symptoms with the Rorschach

The Rorschach assesses two important and separate dimensions of psychosis: 1) a break from reality, as measured by form quality level, and 2) disordered thinking, as measured by cognitive scores (see Kleiger, 1999). In assessing core psychotic symptoms, the Rorschach has the most empirically supported indices that directly assess disorganized thinking or speech. The instrument is especially sensitive in detecting disorganized speech resulting from impaired focusing or cognitive filtering.

In contrast, the Rorschach does not have empirically valid indices that directly measure hallucinations or delusions. However, there may be several ways that the Rorschach can assess these indirectly. For example, an assessment of hallucination-marked impairment in reality testing, as measured by form quality, may indicate that the person has the proclivity to see things that are not there or perceptually distort what is there. Similarly the Rorschach can provide information as to the degree of illogical thinking and errors in reasoning that can potentially lead to delusional thinking (see Kleiger & Khadivi, 2015).

Going Beyond Self-report and Clinical Interview: The Strengths and Limitations of the Rorschach in Assessing Psychosis

Both the CS and the R-PAS are especially sensitive in detecting a variety of thought disturbances that go beyond clinical interview and self-report measures. It can assess peculiar verbalization (DV) or it can detect derailments (DR), illogical thinking (ALOG or Peculiar logic), perceptual incongruences (INC and FABCOM) and perceptual boundary disturbances (CONTAM). Similarly, both Rorschach systems assess perceptual accuracy and the extent of reality testing impairment (X-%, XA%, WDA% for the CS and FQ-%, WD-%, FQo% for the R-PAS) that in some cases cannot be detected in the clinical interview or by the self-report psychological measures such as the PAI or the MMPI-2.

In fact, recent studies have demonstrated that the Rorschach is a sensitive measure in detecting early signs of psychosis with patients at risk for developing a psychotic disorder (Lacoua, Koren, & Rothschild-Yakar, 2015; Rothschild-Yakar, Lacoua, Brener, & Koren, 2015). For example, Inoue and her colleagues (2014) found that poor form quality was a better diagnostic indicator than Rorschach indices of disordered thinking in high-risk patients. Furthermore, although research has shown that anti-psychotic medication can reduce the severity of thought disorder and diminish the gross distortion of reality on the Rorschach, some degree of impairment in reality testing and less overt thought disorder can still be detected (Gold & Hurt, 1990; Hurt, Holzman, & Davis, 1983).

Use of the Rorschach in a Multimethod Forensic Assessment of Psychotic Offenders

Assessment and differential diagnosis of psychosis is a challenging task for a number of reasons: 1) psychosis can present with a varying degree of signs and symptoms, which each require a different method of assessment; 2) psychosis can impact the level of insight and capacity for self-reflection; 3) psychosis can impair an individual's ability to communicate logically and coherently; and 4) psychosis can impact alliance and degree of trust (Fuji & Ahmed, 2007; Skodol, 1989; Kleiger & Khadivi, 2015). Furthermore, in addition to the aforementioned challenges, defendants with actual mental illness who are undergoing forensic psychological evaluation may also be motivated to engage in gross exaggeration and feigning of symptoms (Rogers & Bender, 2013).

As a result of these challenges, a multimethod psychological evaluation is not only essential, but it is the most effective approach to assessing psychosis (Kleiger & Khadivi, 2015). The recommended multimethod assessment battery for the assessment of psychosis in a forensic context includes several key approaches. Primarily, the evaluation should include an unstructured clinical interview, which gives the most flexibility and allows the forensic examiner to directly inquire, observe, illicit, and explore core positive psychotic symptoms. The battery should also include a multiscale self-report inventory to assess response style and severity of reported psychotic symptoms, such as the PAI (Morey, 1991, 2007), the MMPI-2 (Butcher et al., 1989), or the MMPI-2-RF

(Ben-Porath & Tellegen, 2008). The assessment should also include a performance-based broad personality measure, such as the Rorschach, to detect thought disorder and/or reality testing impairment. Finally, the battery should include structured interview-based measures of malingering to screen for, or assess, gross symptom exaggeration or feigning, such as the Miller Forensic Assessment of Symptom Test (M-FAST; Miller, 2001) and/or the Structured Interview of Reported Symptoms-2nd Edition (SIRS-2; Rogers, Sewell, & Gillard, 2010).

For some individuals, the presentation of psychosis is such that it is not detected in the self-report psychological testing and in the Rorschach. Therefore, single methods of evaluation in assessing psychosis may be ineffective, and clinical interviews are always necessary. Case #3 provides an example of this:

> *Case #3: Mr. J is a 27-year-old man with a history of several psychiatric hospitalizations due to violent behavior. His record indicated that he was diagnosed at age 21 with schizophrenia. He is now being evaluated for violence risk assessment following his arrest and incarceration. During the clinical interview, Mr. J presented with no overt positive symptoms except for an encapsulated delusional belief that a chip had been placed in his brain by his former girlfriend for the purpose of controlling him. When queried in the clinical interview, he could not, or would not, elaborate on the reason or evidence for this delusional belief. He also reported no history of hallucinations. The PAI was not defensive, and his profile was within normal range, except for elevation on scales measuring stress and perceived lack of support. His Rorschach showed no evidence of thought disorder or problems with reality testing.*

This case illustrates a limitation of using single methods of evaluation in assessing psychosis. For example, the Rorschach is unable to effectively assess individuals with well-encapsulated delusions who have organized thought processes. Similarly, the multiscale personality inventories do not capture all types of delusions, and it also requires individuals to have the capacity to be self-reflective and to be open to answer test questions. In this case, the clinical interview was necessary to elicit and assess the extent of Mr. J's delusional thinking.

CRIMINAL RESPONSIBILITY EVALUATION

The assessment of criminal responsibility focuses on determining if at the time of the alleged crime the defendant was legally sane (Goldstein, Morse, & Packer, 2013). Although jurisdictions vary in the definition of insanity, the focus of this type of examination is to determine if the defendant was unable as a result of mental illness to appreciate the wrongfulness of his action (cognitive impairment) or he was unable to refrain (volitional impairment) from the alleged crime (Goldstein et al., 2013).

The assessment of psychosis in a criminal responsibly evaluation is essential, as research suggests that defendants who are found not guilty by reason of insanity (NGRI) are much more likely to be diagnosed with a psychotic disorder (Packer, 2009). Although the focus of the evaluation is the defendant's mental state at the time of alleged crime, many legal professionals do not believe psychological testing is essential. However, the majority of forensic practitioners recommend using it. For example, Packer (2009) has argued for the potential usefulness of using the Rorschach in such insanity evaluations. He indicated that the Rorschach might be helpful in detecting psychosis in cases where the defendants are not forthcoming or are guarded during the clinical interviews. In addition, in cases where there is diagnostic ambiguity regarding the nature and extent of psychosis, the use of the Rorschach might be a helpful tool for the forensic practitioner. Furthermore, when used with multiscale inventories such as the MMPI-2, the Rorschach can add a unique contribution when attempt to identify possible feigning. For example, Ganellen (1996) described a pattern of responding indicative of feigning when individuals report significant psychotic symptoms on the MMPI, but show no evidence of impaired reality testing or thought disorder on the Rorschach. In forensic practice, this pattern of responding can be used to develop a hypothesis that an offender might be feigning symptoms of psychosis, which then can be further evaluated using specialized measures of malingering.

Case #4: Mr. Z is a 22-year-old male with no prior psychiatric history who was arrested after being found naked screaming on the street and

> swinging a knife at a stranger passing by. Following his arrest, he was taken to the psychiatric hospital and his toxicology screen was positive for cannabis. After five weeks of treatment, he was released to jail with the diagnosis of psychotic disorder not otherwise specified. While incarcerated, the defendant stopped taking his medication, but did not show any overt psychotic symptom other than an "odd way of relating." Six months later, during the course of a criminal responsibility evaluation, the question remained as to what extent his psychotic symptoms at the time of the alleged crime were drug induced. That is, it was not clear whether the drugs triggered an already existing psychiatric condition or if his psychotic symptoms were the direct result of his drug use and that he would not have any symptoms in the absence of drugs. Depending on the jurisdiction, purely drug-induced psychotic symptoms do not constitute mental defects and therefore it can be used as an insanity defense. In this case, psychological testing including the Rorschach was used. The results showed highly defensive PAI, but marked thinking disorder and impaired reality on the Rorschach. In conjunction with his odd behavior in jail in the clear absence of drug use (based on random toxicology results), the Rorschach's findings were used to form the hypothesis that the defendant had a proclivity toward developing a psychotic condition independent of drug use.

COMPETENCY TO STAND TRIAL EVALUATION

In contrast to the assessment of criminal responsibility, which is retrospective in nature, competency to stand trial evaluation focuses on the defendant's present state of mind. As such, the presence of active positive psychotic symptoms can potentially impact the defendant's understanding of the legal proceedings and can potentially impair his ability to participate rationally or meaningfully in his defense. In fact, active psychotic symptoms are most frequently found in defendants who are incompetent to stand trial, and defendants with diagnoses of psychosis are much more likely to be found incompetent than defendants without such diagnoses (see Pirelli, Gottdiener, Zapf, 2011; Stafford & Wygant, 2005).

There are no traditional psychological tests, including the Rorschach, that can directly answer the question of competency. Furthermore, the findings of thought disorder or marked impairment in reality testing on the Rorschach do not necessary mean that the defendant is incompetent to stand trial, as exemplified in Case #5.

> Case #5: *Ms. M is a 35-year-old woman with a history of mental illness including psychotic episodes and hospitalization. She had been charged with burglary. In the course of examining her for competency to stand trial, she had overly elaborated paranoid delusions that centered on a family member. She believed that a family member was sending electromagnetic waves in order to kill her. The psychological testing, including the PAI and the Rorschach, were consistent with the diagnosis of psychosis. On the Rorschach, she demonstrated illogical thinking, errors in reasoning, and diminished reality testing. However, during the clinical interview, despite the presence of delusions, she displayed no disorganized thinking: she had rational understanding of the charges against her and the legal proceedings. She also knew the role of various participants in the courtroom: She was actively working with her attorney and had no paranoia or delusions about her lawyer or the outcome of her case. She also did not believe that electromagnetic waves were impacting her legal case or the parties involved.*

The use of the Rorschach is most valuable in cases where there is evidence from the clinical interview or specialized competency measures that the defendant is not competent due to his or her psychotic symptoms. In such cases, the findings of psychotic processes from the Rorschach provide additional support and converging evidence for the forensic opinion, and they further clarify the nature of psychological impairment (Weiner, 2006). Case #6 is an example of such a case.

> Case #6: *Mr. P is a 25-year-old defendant following his first episode of psychosis. He indicated during the competency trial evaluation that he had "special powers," and he was convinced that the mayor of the city would alter the outcome of the court so he would be found not guilty and would be free to join the mayor's office and do "great things for the city."*

> *In addition to the grandiose delusion, he displayed elated mood and pressured speech. Psychological testing was requested that included testing for malingering, self-report inventories, and the Rorschach. The test findings were not consistent with feigning, and the Rorschach indicated gross reality testing problems and severe thought disorder—symptoms that are consistently seen in manic psychotic individuals.*

VIOLENCE RISK ASSESSMENT EVALUATION

Although most individuals with psychosis do not engage in violence, there is consensus in the literature that the presence of psychosis increases the risk of violence (Scott & Resnick, 2013). A recent meta-analysis (Douglas, Guy, & Hart, 2009) demonstrated that "psychosis was significantly associated with 49–68% increase in odds of violence" (p. 679). More recently, a large-scale study using multi-regression methodology demonstrated that positive psychotic symptoms and lack of insight were significantly associated with violence (Witt, van Dorn, & Fazel, 2013).

There are two distinct approaches that are predominantly used in violence risk assessment and the assessment of violence risk in a criminal forensic context: actuarial violence risk assessment and Structured Professional Judgment approach (SPJ). The actuarial violence risk assessment tool is often developed for use with males. In general, psychological testing is not incorporated into the actual measure, and the focus of this type of measure is on the long-term prediction of violence.

In contrast, the SPJ approach differs from actuarial measures in which clinicians, rather than numeric algorithms, make the final determination of the level of risk. Furthermore, the goal of SPJ is not the prediction of violence, but it is the identification of case-specific risk factors for violence and the development of individualized risk management strategies (Heilbrun, 2009)

An example of a SPJ instrument is the Historical-Clinical-Risk Management-20 (HCR-20V3; Douglas, Hart, Webster, Belfrage, Guy, & Wilson, 2014), which includes a Historical scale, comprised of ten past risk factors such as previous violence, age at first violence, problems with employment, early maladjustment, relationship instability, substance use, psychopathy, personality disorder, and major mental illness.

The measure also includes a Clinical scale comprised of five factors relevant to current functioning, including lack of insight, negative attitudes, active symptoms of mental illness, impulsivity, and treatment compliance/responsiveness. Finally, a Risk Management scale includes five factors relevant to anticipated future risk, such as lack of social support, non-compliance, stress, lack of feasibility, and exposure to destabilizers.

The HCR-20 was recently revised and is now in its third edition. The most recent version of the HCR-20 makes such considerations even more explicit, by allowing clinicians to rate the relevance of each risk factor for individual patients. Furthermore, due to the dynamic nature of the measure and inclusion of mental disorder, including psychosis as a violence risk factor, psychological testing in particular, including the Rorschach, can be used to clarify the presence and assess the extent of psychotic symptoms.

> *Case #7: Mr. Y a 24-year-old male who was arrested for assaulting a stranger. He was evaluated at the request of the court for a violence risk assessment. Mr. Y had no past psychiatric hospitalization. He had been seen earlier for mental health evaluation at the jail and the clinician noted guardedness and an odd way of thinking; however, no psychotic symptoms were elicited or reported. As a result, the forensic examiner sought to clarify the presence of psychotic symptoms and added psychological tests, including the PAI and the Rorschach, to facilitate the use of the HCR-20^{V3}. Mr. Y produced a highly guarded PAI; however, on the Rorschach, he demonstrated marked impairment in reality testing and numerous ALOG, suggestive of illogical thinking. As a result of the Rorschach finding, the clinical interview was extended to establish better alliance and to carefully assess for possible delusional thinking. After several hours of clinical interview, Mr. Y revealed elaborate paranoid delusions including delusions of reference.*

In Case #7, the findings from the PAI and the Rorschach helped to guide the clinical interview and led to the identification of underlying psychotic symptoms, which were then incorporated into Mr. Y's violence risk assessment to develop more effective risk-reducing strategies.

Sentencing Evaluation

Forensic psychologists may be asked to consult on cases in which the defendant has entered a plea and is awaiting sentencing by the court. In this type of assessment, the focus of psychological evaluation is to assess for mitigating factors that could potentially impact the length of the sentence. For example, forensic psychologists are assessing for any factors that may negatively affect the defendant's psychological functioning, including cognitive, reality testing, emotional regulation, impulse control, interpersonal and moral development (Cunningham, 2010). As a result, psychological disorders, including psychosis, are considered significant mitigating factors, because the severity of psychotic symptoms can potentially impact multiple areas of functioning.

The use of the Rorschach is particularly helpful in sentencing evaluations, because it can assess the degree of reality testing impairment and the extent of thought disorder. Furthermore, since the focus of the evaluation is on the identification of mitigating factors, the most comprehensive approach is to use a multimethod assessment, which includes evaluation of the eight multidimensional model of psychosis (Barch et al., 2013). Developed by the DSM-5 Psychotic Disorder Work group, this multidimensional approach identifies eight symptom domains that are assessed in any individual presenting with psychosis (Heckers et al., 2013). In addition to the positive symptoms of psychosis, the presence of negative symptoms, mood, and degree of cognitive impairment are also assessed. The eight domains include 1) hallucinations, 2) delusions, 3) disorganized speech, 4) abnormal psychomotor behavior, 5) depression, 6) mania, 7) cognitive impairment, and 8) negative symptoms including avolition and restricted emotional expressiveness. A multimethod assessment approach that includes a clinical interview, multiscale personality inventory, the Rorschach, the Wechsler Intelligence Scale IV (WAIS-IV), and Repeatable Battery for Assessment of Neuropsychological Status (RBANS), which screen cognitive impairment in psychosis (Gold et al., 1999) is likely to assess each of the eight domains (see Kleiger & Khadivi, 2015).

Court Diversion and Treatment Planning

Individuals with mental illness are over-represented in correctional settings (James & Glaze, 2006). As a result, the criminal justice system has become a primary mental health provider, and the courts are overwhelmed by cases of individuals with mental illness (Denckla & Berman, 2001). In response to these changes, the criminal justice system is increasingly beginning to implement court diversion programs for mentally ill offenders. These court diversion programs exemplify the process of therapeutic jurisprudence, whereby the courts act as therapeutic agents. The main objective of these diversion programs is to help the mentally ill offenders enter treatment and avoid prison time. That is, court and judicial practices have been redesigned to be more therapeutic and restorative (Munetz & Teller, 2004) rather than simply punitive. In these cases, the offenders are mandated by the criminal court to attend mental health or addiction programs. Forensic psychologists offer consultation regarding the mental health need of the patient and develop appropriate treatment planning.

Depending on the case, psychological tests, and in particular the Rorschach, are utilized to assess the extent of psychotic symptoms in order to aid in treatment planning. In this type of evaluation, both the presence and the degree of psychotic symptoms are essential, as untreated psychosis can potentially increase the risk of violence (Keers et al., 2014), and delay in receiving treatment for psychosis is associated with poorer outcomes (Marshall et al., 2005).

This type of forensic consultation tends to be less adversarial since both prosecution and defense must agree on the court diversion as the final disposition. As a result, depending on the referral, the forensic consultant has more flexibility in choosing a multimethod assessment battery. In this type of evaluation, the Rorschach, in conjunction with the clinical interview, multiscale personality inventories, and selected cognitive tests, can help not just to assess the extent of thought disorder or the extent of reality testing impairment. Furthermore, in this type of evaluation, the referral questions often go beyond clarification of diagnosis or the extent of psychosis and instead focus on the identification of case-specific areas of psychological functioning that can be detected for development of individualized interventions. As such, the Rorschach can be used to identify other areas of psychological functioning, such as stress tolerance or cognitive processing, which can be the target of treatment interventions.

References

American Psychiatric Association (2000). *Diagnostic and statistical manual of mental disorders* (4th ed., text rev.). Washington, DC: American Psychiatric Association.

American Psychiatric Association (2013). *Diagnostic and statistical manual of mental disorders* (5th ed.). Washington, DC: American Psychiatric Association.

Archer, R. P. (Ed.). (2006). *Forensic uses of clinical assessment instruments.* Mahwah, NJ: Lawrence Erlbaum Associates, Inc.

Barch, D. M., Bustillo, J., Gaebel, W., Gur, R., Heckers, S., Malaspina, D., ... Carpenter, W. (2013). Logic and justification for dimensional assessment of symptoms and related clinical phenomena in psychosis: Relevance to DSM-5. *Schizophrenia Research, 150*(1): 15–20.

Ben-Porath, Y. S., & Tellegen, A. (2008). *Minnesota Multiphasic Personality Inventory-2-RF (MMPI-2-RF).* Minneapolis: University of Minneapolis Press.

Black, D. W., & Grant, J. E. (2014). *DSM-5 guidebook: The essential companion to the Diagnostic and Statistical Manual of Mental Disorders.* Washington, DC: American Psychiatric Publishing.

Butcher, J. N., Dahlstrom, W. G., Graham, J. R., Tellegen, A. M., & Kaemer, B. (1989). *The Minnesota Multiphasic Personality Inventory-2 (MMPI-2) manual for administration and scoring.* Minneapolis: University of Minneapolis Press.

Cunningham, M. D. (2010). Evaluation for capital sentencing. In A. Goldstein, T. Grisso & K. Heilbrun (Series Eds.), *Oxford best practices in forensic mental health assessment.* New York: Oxford University Press.

Denckla, D., & Berman, G. (2001). *Rethinking the revolving door: A look at mental illness in the courts.* New York: Center for Court Innovation. Retrieved from http://www.courtinnovation.org/sites/default/files/rethinkingtherevolvingdoor.pdf

Douglas, K. S., Guy, L. S., & Hart, S. D. (2009). Psychosis as a risk factor for violence to others: A meta-analysis. *Psychological Bulletin, 135*(5): 679–706.

Douglas, K. S., Hart, S. D., Webster, C. D., Belfrage, H., Guy, L. S., & Wilson, C. (2014). Historical-Clinical-Risk Management-20 Version 3 (HCR-20[V3]): Development and overview. *International Journal of Forensic Mental Health, 13*(2): 93–108.

Exner, J. E. (2003). *The Rorschach: A Comprehensive System: Vol. 1. Basic foundations* (4th ed.). New York: Wiley.

Fuji, D., & Ahmed, I. (Eds.). (2007). *The spectrum of psychotic disorders: Neurobiology, etiology, and pathogenesis.* New York: Cambridge University Press.

Ganellen, R. J. (1996). Comparing the diagnostic efficacy of the MMPI, MCMI and Rorschach: A review. *Journal of Personality Assessment, 67,* 219–243.

Gold, J. M., & Hurt, S. W. (1990). The effects of haloperidol on thought disorder and IQ in schizophrenia. *Journal of Personality Assessment, 54,* 390–400.

Gold, J. M., Queern, C., Iannone, V. N., & Buchanan, R. W. (1999). Repeatable battery for the assessment of neuropsychological status as a screening test in schizophrenia,

I: Sensitivity, reliability, and validity. *American Journal of Psychiatry, 156,* 1944-1950.

Goldstein, A. M., Morse, S. J., & Packer, I. K. (2013). Evaluation of criminal responsibility. In R. K. Otto & I. B. Weiner (Eds.), *Handbook of psychology: Volume 11: Forensic Psychology* (2nd ed., pp. 440-472). Hoboken, NJ: John Wiley & Sons, Inc.

Grisso, T. (2003). *Evaluating competencies: Forensic assessments and instruments* (2nd ed.). New York: Kluwer.

Heckers, S., Barch, D. M., Bustillo, J., Gaebel, W., Gur, R., Malaspina, D., ... Carpenter, W. (2013). Structure of the psychotic disorders classification in DSM-5. *Schizophrenia Research, 150*(1), 11-14.

Heilbrun, K. (2009). *Evaluation for risk of violence in adults.* In A. Goldstein, T. Grisso, & K. Heilbrun (Series Eds.), *Oxford best practices in forensic mental health assessment.* New York: Oxford University Press.

Heilbrun, K., Marczyk, G., DeMatteo, D., & Mack-Allen, J. (2007). A principles-based approach to forensic mental health assessment: Utility and update. In A. M. Goldstein (Ed.), *Forensic psychology: Emerging topics and expanding roles.* Hoboken, NJ: John Wiley and Sons.

Heilbrun, K., Rogers, R., & Otto, R. (2002). Forensic assessment: Current status and future directions. In J. Ogloff (Ed.), *Psychology and law: Reviewing the discipline* (pp. 120-147). New York: Kluwer Academic/Plenum.

Hurt, S. S., Holzman, P. S., & Davis, J. M. (1983). Thought disorder: The measurement of its changes. *Archives of General Psychiatry, 40,* 1281-1285.

Inoue, N., Yorozuya, Y., & Mizuno, M. (2014). Identifying comorbidities of patients at ultra-high risk for psychosis using the Rorschach Comprehensive System. Paper presented at the XXI International Congress of Rorschach and Projective Methods, Istanbul, TR.

James, D. J., & Glaze, L. (2006). *Mental health problems of prison and jail inmates* (Bureau of Justice Statistics Special Report NCJ 213600). Washington, DC: U.S. Department of Justice, Office of Justice Programs.

Keers, R., Ullrich, S., DeStavola, B., & Coid, J. W. (2014). Association of violence with emergence of persecutory delusions in untreated schizophrenia. *American Journal of Psychiatry, 171*(3), 332-339.

Kleiger, J. H. (1999). *Disordered thinking and the Rorschach.* Hillsdale, NJ: The Analytic Press.

Kleiger, J. H., & Khadivi, A. (2015). *Assessing psychosis: A clinician's guide.* New York: Routledge Publishing.

Lacoua, L., Koren, D., & Rothschild-Yakar, L. (2015). Poor awareness of problems in thought and perception and risk indicators of schizophrenia-spectrum disorders. A correlational study of nonpsychotic adolescents in the community. Paper presented at the annual meeting of the Society for Personality Assessment, Brooklyn, NY.

Lilienfeld, S. O., Wood, J. M., & Garb, H. N. (2000). The scientific status of projective techniques. *Psychological Science in the Public Interest, 1,* 27-66.

Marshall, M., Lewis, S., Lockwood, A., Drake, R., Jones, P., & Croudace, T. (2005). Association between duration and untreated psychosis and outcome in cohorts of first episode patients—A systematic review. *Archives of General Psychiatry, 62,* 975-983.

Meyer, G. J., Viglione, D. J., Mihura, J. L., Erard, R. E., & Erdberg, P. (2012). *Rorschach Performance Assessment System: Administration, coding, interpretation, and technical manual.* Toledo, OH: Rorschach Performance Assessment System.

Mihura, J. L., Meyer, G. J., Dumitrascu, N., & Bombel, G. (2013). The validity of individual Rorschach variables: Systematic reviews and meta-analyses of the comprehensive system. *Psychological Bulletin, 139*(3), 548–605.

Miller, H. A. (2001). *Miller-Forensic Assessment of Symptoms Test (M-FAST): Professional manual.* Odessa, FL: Psychological Assessment Resources.

Morey, L. C. (1991). *The Personality Assessment Inventory professional manual.* Odessa, FL: Psychological Assessment Resources.

Morey, L. C. (2007). *Personality Assessment Inventory: Professional manual* (2nd ed.). Lutz, FL: Psychological Assessment Resources.

Munetz, M. R., & Teller, J. L. (2004). Challenges of cross-disciplinary collaborations: Bridging the mental health and criminal justice systems. *Capital University Law Review, 32*(4), 935–950.

Packer, I. A. (2009). *Evaluation of criminal responsibility.* New York: Oxford University Press.

Pirelli, G., Gottdiener, W. H., & Zapf, P. A. (2011). A meta-analytic review of competency to stand trial research. *Psychology, Public Policy and Law, 17,* 1–53.

Rogers, R., & Bender, S. D. (2013). Evaluation of malingering and related response styles. In R. K. Otto & I. B. Weiner (Eds.), *Handbook of psychology: Volume 11: Forensic Psychology* (2nd ed.) (pp. 517–540). Hoboken, NJ: John Wiley & Sons, Inc.

Rogers, R., Sewell, K. W., & Gillard, N. D. (2010). *Structured Interview of Reported Symptoms 2nd Edition (SIRS-2): Professional manual.* Lutz, FL: Psychological Assessment Resources, Inc.

Rothschild-Yakar, L., Lacoua, L., Brener, A., & Koren, D. (2015). Impairments in interpersonal representations and deficits in social cognition as predictors of risk for schizophrenia in nonpatient adolescents. Paper presented at the annual meeting of the Society for Personality Assessment, Brooklyn, NY.

Scott, C. L., & Resnick, P. J. (2013). Evaluating psychotic patients' risk of violence: A practical guide. Investigating persecutory delusions and command hallucinations. *Current Psychiatry, 12*(5), 29–32.

Skodol, A. E. (1989). *Problems in differential diagnosis: From DSM-III to DSM-III-R in clinical practice.* Washington, DC: American Psychiatric Press.

Stafford, K. P., & Wygant, D. B. (2005). The role of competency to stand trial in mental health courts. *Behavioral Sciences and the Law, 23*(2), 245–258.

Weiner, I. B. (2006). The Rorschach inkblot method. In R. P. Archer (Ed.), *Forensic uses of clinical assessment instruments.* Mahwah, NJ: Lawrence Erlbaum Associates.

Witt, K., van Dorn, R., & Fazel, S. (2013). Risk factors for violence in psychosis: Systematic review and meta-regression analysis of 110 studies. *PLOS ONE, 8,* e55942.

Wood, J. M., Nezworski, M. T., Lilienfeld, S. O., & Garb, H. N. (2003). *What is wrong with the Rorschach? Science confronts the controversial inkblot test.* New York: Wiley & Sons.

CHAPTER 7

THE RORSCHACH IN MULTIMETHOD CUSTODY EVALUATIONS

Robert E. Erard, Jacqueline S. Singer, and Donald J. Viglione

> Author Note:
> In addition to the first two authors, the following individuals generously contributed protocols from their forensic practices to the custody litigant sample for the R-PAS reference data in this chapter: Larry M. Friedberg, S. Margaret Lee, Nancy W. Olesen, Daniel B. Pickar, Neil Ribner, and Alissa Sherry.

Child custody evaluations (CCEs) are most commonly ordered in family court cases in which potentially serious questions have been raised about relative (and sometimes absolute) parental psychological fitness. These questions often involve allegations about past events involving matters such as neglectful parenting, domestic violence, deliberate alienation of a child from a parent, substance abuse, inappropriate discipline, and child sexual abuse. Many of the investigative tools relevant to addressing such allegations are no more proprietary to psychologists than they are to historians, journalists, detectives, or lawyers.

Admittedly, personality assessment cannot directly supply the answers to any of these questions. Indeed, although personality testing is all but universally used in child custody evaluations by psychologists (Ackerman & Pritzl, 2011), it is not actually a required element (APA, 2010), and its utility in CCEs is not without controversy (see Brodzinski, 1993; Emery, Otto, & O'Donahue, 2005; Melton, Petrila, Poythress, & Slobogin, 2007).

Still, there are good reasons why psychologists and their assessment skills are highly valued by those requesting CCEs. For the most part, this is because family courts (in contrast to criminal courts and, to some degree, child protective services agencies) are not really as concerned with determining what has happened in the past as what is likely to happen in the future. They want to know how various proposals for custody and parenting time and for various possible interventions with family members may affect the best interests of the minor children at issue. To answer *these* questions, it is important to know what the parents and children are like. What kinds of personal strengths, interpersonal skills, and emotional and behavioral dispositions can be observed in the parents, and how do they interact with the particular characteristics and needs of the children?

In conducting CCEs, psychologists must use a multimethod approach to assessment. A multimethod approach provides data from various sources that not only can be checked against each other but can also enhance the evaluator's understanding of the individuals being assessed. Both the "Guidelines for Child Custody Evaluations in Family Law Proceedings" (American Psychological Association, 2007) and the "Model Standards of Practice for Child Custody Evaluation" (Association of Family and Conciliation Courts, 2006) recommend utilizing diverse data gathering methods "with the circumstances of the evaluation in mind" (APA, 2010, p. 14). Multimethod approaches to CCEs should include information from interviews, observations, third-party or collateral reports, and some kind of standardized observation to understand the psychological functioning of the litigants and their children. While each source of data may have its own limitations, an overall approach that uses more than one method maximizes the validity of the assessment (Hopwood & Bornstein, 2014; Meyer, Finn, Eyde, Kay, Moreland, Dies et al., 2001).

The Contribution of Personality Testing

Psychological testing is the most advanced, most scientifically defensible form of standardized observation available to psychological evaluators. It uses standardized administration procedures and tasks, systematic and reliable scoring, statistical comparisons to appropriate norms to quantify constructs of interest, and external validity studies to compare test scores to relevant criteria and constructs. In child custody evaluations, personality testing has, in our opinion, played an essential role. As Evans and Schutz (2008) have observed, it can effectively contribute to constituent factors such as

- Affectivity and its regulation
- Stress and coping
- Psychopathology
- Conflict styles/tactics
- Capacity for non-defensive introspection
- Interpersonal relatedness and responsiveness

Thus it is not surprising that psychologists have routinely used personality testing as part of their data gathering methods (Bow, 2006; Ackerman & Pritzl, 2011).

The Case for a Multimethod Approach to Personality Testing Including the Rorschach

Unfortunately, even though the Rorschach remains the third most widely used clinical personality test in CCEs (Ackerman & Pritzl, 2011; Bow, 2006), many evaluators limit their personality testing to self-report instruments (Erard, 2005; Siegel, 1996). As a result, there is a heavy reliance on what amounts to a single source of data—namely, what individual litigants are able and willing to say about themselves, whether in psychosocial histories, interviews, or self-report personality inventories. What may appear to be consistent findings from the results from these sources of data may in effect be spurious correlations based on shared mono-method variance (Erard & Viglione, 2014; Meyer, 1999). In other words, people are likely to report similar things about themselves across various self-report modalities, but this does not confirm the accuracy of what they say. Information from multiple instruments that rely on the same method can quickly become redundant and may lead to underrepresesentation of important constructs that are being assessed.

Moreover, there is reason to suspect a strong bias toward underreporting personal problems and unflattering characteristics in child custody evaluations in particular. Such evaluations occur in a highly adversarial context, with high stakes and major investments of emotional and financial resources. Research has consistently shown that validity scales associated with social desirability, underreporting, and self-favorable and self-serving misrepresentations are significantly elevated in the MMPI-2 (Bagby, Nicholson, Buis, Radovanovic, & Fidler, 1999; Bathurst, Gottfried, & Gottfried, 1997; Strong, Greene, Hoppe, Johnston, & Olesen, 1999), the MMPI-2-RF (Archer, Hagen, Mason, Handel, & Archer, 2012; Kauffman, Stolberg, & Madero, 2015; Sellbom & Bagby, 2008), and the MCMI-III (Kauffman et al., 2015; McCann, Flens, Campagna, Collman, Lazzaro, & Connor, 2001). Hence this unsurprising conclusion of the APA Psychological Assessment Working Group: "The evidence indicates that clinicians who use a single method to obtain patient information regularly draw faulty conclusions" (Meyer et al., 2001; p. 150).

What is needed is not just a multimethod approach to CCEs, but a multimethod approach to personality testing in CCEs, which includes systematic observation of performance in stressful circumstances—personality in action, in addition to what people say about themselves (Meyer, Viglione, Mihura, Erard, & Erdberg, 2011; Viglione & Rivera, 2003; 2012). The Rorschach is particularly well-suited for this purpose (Erard, 2005; Erard & Viglione, 2014; Evans & Schutz, 2008). It is less amenable to impression management than self-report tests (Ganellen, 2008; Schultz, this volume; Viglione, 1999) and adds incremental validity to self-report findings (Blais, Hilsenroth, Castelbury, Fowler, and Baity, 2001; Ganellen, 1996; Bornstein, this volume; Erdberg, 2008; Gacono, Evans, & Viglione, 2002; Hildebrand & de Ruiter, 2008; Mihura, 2012; Mihura, Meyer, Dumitrascu, & Bombel, 2013; Viglione & Hilsenroth, 2001; Weiner, 1999; 2005).

Self-report test results tend to be correlated with deliberate, conscious decisions to behave in a particular manner or to follow a certain guideline or rule, whereas Rorschach findings more often tap into unacknowledged, unreflective, peremptory inclinations and reactions. Sometimes, this self-report versus performance distinction is compared to explicit versus implicit processes or social role behavior versus tropisms (Bornstein, 2015; Bornstein, Chapter 1, this volume). It follows that self-report findings often seem to be at variance with the results of Rorschach testing (Mihura et al., 2013). It has been demonstrated that individuals are not fully able to describe themselves accurately and often not fully willing to be forthright and truthful (Galione & Oltmanns, 2014). Conversely, Viglione (1999) in a review of the literature about Rorschach validity and utility concluded that the evidence suggests that the Rorschach is most helpful in assessment contexts in which the respondent is not fully able or willing to provide this sought-after accurate picture. Indeed, this seems to be particularly the case when concerns about self-presentation are high (Nosek, 2005), as in a CCE.

Assessment That Applies to Novel, Stressful, Private Circumstances

The Rorschach has specific advantages in assessing disintegrating families in the custody evaluation context. In divorces and custody disputes, parents are under considerable strain and are required to improvise—i.e., make decisions and solve problems without the habits, conventions, or scripts that usually tell them how to behave, as they gradually navigate the transition to a new kind of stability. The Rorschach task shares many features with the challenges faced by divorcing parents: It presents novel, ambiguous, yet provocative stimuli and requires impromptu decision-making under stressful conditions. It usually elicits anxiety in the respondent about how he or she is performing and what that performance has revealed about him or her as a parent. Thus it reveals implicit motives, needs, and traits where fixed social role expectations are relaxed or absent (McClelland, Koestner, & Weinberger, 1989) and as they unfold under stress and over time (Viglione & Meyer, 2008). Thus one can make the inference that the behaviors codified and observed in the Rorschach examination situation generalized to similar conditions in life, per behavioral theory (Viglione & Rivera, 2003; 2012). In short, the Rorschach task tends to reveal how people behave spontaneously in stressful circumstances.

In custody evaluations, one wants to develop some understanding of how people behave behind closed doors, away from public scrutiny, in their most intimate family relationships. The Rorschach provides some clues to such behavior, because it is particularly well-suited to predicting how people are most likely to behave in intimate contexts (Finn, 2011; Shapiro, Leifer, Marton, & Kassem, 1990).

Assessment That Exposes Contradictory Behavior

The Rorschach helps to clarify when a parent's self-understanding or self-presentation requires further investigation. A parent who describes himself as self-confident and assertive in interviews and on self-report testing but scores at the ninety-fifth percentile on Oral-Dependent Language (a well-validated, Rorschach measure of implicit dependency; Bornstein & Masling, 2005) is revealing something he may not be aware of about himself. Another parent who insists that she tries to avoid conflict and searches for "win-win solutions" but is passive-aggressive about following test instructions (Prompts and Pulls; Pr, Pu) and produces a Rorschach protocol with validated scores that show a deficit in representations of cooperative interactions (Cooperative Movement; COP) and a surfeit of representations of destructive or coercive relationships (Mutuality of Autonomy Pathology; MAP), defensive superiority (Personalized Knowledge Justification; PER), aggressive preoccupations (Aggressive Contents and Aggressive Movement; AGC, AGM), and oppositional characteristics (Space Reversal; SR) is probably not the team player she presents herself to be, at least when she is not under public scrutiny.

Assessment That Provides Psychologically Meaningful Context

The Rorschach is also helpful in contextualizing findings about respondents. In addition to formal coding, Rorschach responses occur in response to differing conditions, including the changing features of particular inkblot stimuli ("card pull"); affective and defensive reactions to just previous Rorschach responses (sequence); changing emotional reactions to the test situation and to the examiner; and thematic preoccupations or internal conflicts stimulated by certain cards. In interpreting Rorschach responses, examiners are encouraged to take note of how particular scores and test behaviors appear to be influenced by such contextual factors. This sometimes makes it possible to engage in "if-then" interpretations (Mischel & Shoda, 1995). For example, "If the respondent becomes stimulated by content that reminds her of a prior traumatic experience, she shows signs of emotional constriction and the quality of her reality testing begins to falter." The richness of Rorschach interpretation consists in the interplay between nomothetic and idiographic, as well as between trait-based and dynamic, perspectives.

As a standardized behavioral task, the most valid Rorschach inferences are those in which the behaviors observed and coded in the microcosm of the task generalize to parallel mental, verbal, perceptual, and interactive behaviors in the external environment. By having litigants show something rather than just say something about themselves, it is possible to observe motives, traits, and coping patterns *in vivo*, permitting rich, multifaceted, and contextualized inferences (Erard, this volume; Erard & Viglione, 2014; Viglione & Rivera, 2003, 2012). For example, here is a Rorschach response from a custody evaluation:

> **Here they are characters from Peter Pan with feathers in their hair,[1] staring at each other in wonderment: "Is it really you? What do I see?" They are peering into each other—"What's real here?" They can't tell which is real and which is the true reflection.[2]**

This response demonstrates, both thematically and in the formal coding, a diffuse, foggy, incoherent, preoccupied (though not especially distorted) sense of self. It was given by a father who (backed by a generous family trust fund) had rarely stuck with a job or educational plan throughout his life. He often gave the impression of a middle-aged man who, like Peter Pan and his "lost boy" companions, had never grown up. He had dropped in and out of his children's lives and had reinvented himself over and over. The court had wondered if he might be too narcissistic to manage consistent parenting.

Here is another response from a custody case:

> **A Popsicle stick . . . don't know if I'm hungry . . . caught my eye . . . 2 Popsicles, divided, you could break them apart.[3]**

This response is evocative of oral dependency (also supported by the formal coding with ODL) and experiences of emotional distance and loss. It was given by a mother who had pursued an affair to escape from a marriage she described as cold, unaffectionate, and loveless.

Assessment That Reveals Interpersonal Styles

Every Rorschach administration involves an interpersonal transaction. Responses are requested by one person (the examiner) and given directly to the examiner by another person (the respondent), and during the Clarification Phase, a kind of dialogue about those responses ensues between them. Depending on individual inclinations, the respondent may behave bashfully and diffidently, arrogantly and highhandedly, anxiously and warily, boldly and ostentatiously, conscientiously, impulsively, helplessly, and so on in negotiating this transaction. Along with the nomothetic features of their responses and idiopathic elements of the response content, such behavior can be revealing about how respondents spontaneously construe interactions with others.

Assessment That Can Address Key Questions

Thus the Rorschach can help address many important questions about parents of the sort that judges would like to answer in deciding custody disputes or developing parenting plans, such as

- How are they likely to hold up in stressful and emotionally painful circumstances?[4]
- Can they respond with warmth, sensitivity, and empathy to children's emotional demands?[5]
- Are their expectations of themselves and others realistic?[6]
- Can they distinguish clearly between their own and their children's needs (Johnston, Walters, & Oleson, 2005a)?[7]
- Do they have sufficient interpersonal skills for effective co-parenting?[8]
- Are they prone to violence or suicide?[9]

The Rorschach is one of a small number of personality tests that are suitable for use with school-age children. Moreover, the ability to use a single test from early childhood through old age offers an advantage in terms of understanding the interpretation of the variables across the lifespan and for understanding the correlates of development on the test (Stanfill, Viglione, & Resende, 2013a, 2013b). The following are some representative questions that the Rorschach may be helpful in answering about children in custody cases:

- How mature is their cognitive and social judgment in appraising their home environment[10] (Erard, 2005)?
- Are they emotionally resilient or fragile?[11]
- Are they showing signs of harm from current family dynamics?[12]
- Is their estrangement from a parent associated with poor social reality testing[13] (see Johnston, Walters, & Olesen, 2005b)?

- Does this look more like a response to current stress or a developmental delay[14] (Roseby, 1995)?
- How independent and adaptable is this child likely to be in a setting of rapidly shifting routines and environments (Erard, 2005)?[15]

Finally, the Rorschach may prove to be useful in the essential task of assessing the match between parents' dispositions and psychological resources and the needs of their children. Rorschach results provide meaningful insights into respondents' interpersonal styles and capacities (Stricker & Healy, 1999). Comparing the parents' Rorschach findings with each other and with those of the children, particularly with respect to interpersonal functioning, may elucidate family dynamics (Calloway, 2005).

Limitations of Performance-Based Testing

For all of its advantages in child custody evaluations, the Rorschach should not be used on its own. It is important to know something about how people understand themselves—that alone is an important aspect of personality functioning (Mihura & Graceffo, 2014). Much of an individual's daily behavior may reflect his or her conscious self-appraisal and may show few signs of those difficulties that show up on the Rorschach, which concerns itself more with less observable, implicit tendencies and motives. Hence people's thoughts, feelings, and behaviors, when available to introspection and conscious self-management, are likely to be better described by self-report tests than by the Rorschach (see Cogswell & Emmert, 2014). Self-report instruments may be most pertinent to describing what people are like: when operating within habitual social roles and conventions, when interacting with others within prescribed routines, when reflecting and reporting on their thoughts and feelings, or when making deliberate decisions according to consciously held values. But conversely, when people are behaving impulsively, adapting to novel situations, engaging wholeheartedly in intimate exchanges, responding to unanticipated stresses or provocations, or exhibiting character traits observable to others over time, Rorschach descriptions may capture more of the relevant psychological processes and behaviors. Generally speaking, predictive validity is usually maximized by using a combination of implicit and explicit measures (Back, Schmukle, & Egloff, 2009).

The Role of R-PAS in Addressing Rorschach Controversies

Controversies over the Rorschach have been well publicized. In particular, John Exner's Comprehensive System (CS; Exner, 2002) norms have been vigorously challenged as overpathologizing (Erickson, Lilienfeld, & Vitacco, 2007; Hunsley & DiGiulio, 2001; Meyer, Erdberg, & Shaffer, 2007; Viglione & Hilsenroth, 2001; Viglione & Meyer, 2008; Viglione & Giromini, 2015; Wood, Nezworski, Garb, & Lilienfeld, 2001). In addition, many traditional CS Rorschach variables have poor support in the empirical literature (Jørgensen, Andersen, & Dam, 2000; Mihura, et al., 2013; Nezworski & Wood, 1995). Also, when the standard CS administration is used in court-ordered evaluations, defensive respondents often produce short records, which have low reliability and are difficult to interpret (Exner, 2002).

Fortunately, many such concerns have been effectively addressed with the development of the Rorschach Performance Assessment System® (R-PAS®; Meyer et al., 2011). R-PAS was developed when the dominant system of the twentieth century, John Exner's Comprehensive System (CS; 2003), was essentially frozen in place after Exner's death in 2006. The decision by Exner's estate not to support any further changes in the CS represented a very serious problem, because a strong empirical foundation that evolves with emerging research is critical for both clinical and forensic applications according to contemporary professional standards. Indeed, John Exner had clearly recognized and embraced this point. Between the introduction of the CS in 1974 and 2006, the system underwent four major revisions and many smaller adjustments, leading to many changes in administration rules, variable selection, scoring indices, and interpretive principles. Members of the Rorschach Research Council (RRC), Exner's scientific advisory board, believed that Rorschach-based assessment needed to continue to evolve with new research and technical refinements (see Erard, Meyer, & Viglione, 2014). Four of the six current RRC members (joined by the first author) designed R-PAS as a clinically rich, evidence-based, logically transparent, internationally focused, and user-friendly system available for applied practice. The goal of R-PAS is to continue to solidify the scientific groundwork begun by the CS for using the Rorschach while focusing on its unique contribution to assessment.

R-PAS Innovations Help Standardize Practice and Improve Validity

R-PAS improves on the CS by using adult and child normative reference data that have been derived from large, international samples, which more accurately represent the typical scores of nonpatients than the previous CS norms. The system seeks to align interpretation with the currently available evidence base by focusing on the published empirical evidence (Mihura et al., 2013), a survey of experienced clinicians (Meyer, Hsiao, Viglione, Mihura, & Abraham, 2013), and analyses of the response process (i.e., the psychological operations believed to be involved in producing a particular response feature).[16] R-Optimized administration procedures limit error associated with the number of responses (R) and help keep the length of records in the interpretive "sweet spot" (Meyer et al., 2011; Reese, Viglione, Giromini, 2014; Viglione et al., 2014). Detailed guidance on administration, coding, and interpretation with extensive examples is provided to minimize variation across examiners.

Other R-PAS Advantages

R-PAS also offers a number of additional advantages in child custody evaluations. Records distorted by abnormal response sets (e.g., those that are defensively guarded or withholding) can be corrected to some extent using a procedure called Complexity Adjustment, which permits test users to estimate what the scores would have looked like if the test had been taken with an average level of engagement. Scoring for R-PAS Form Quality, an essential variable for assessing whether a respondent understands self and others realistically and conventionally and is able to make sound judgments based on objective facts, is based on not only the frequency of particular responses, but also their accuracy as rated by 569 judges from around the world rating over 13,000 response objects, with approximately 5,000 of these objects included in R-PAS Form Quality tables. Results from R-PAS records results are organized according to the strength of the evidence and presented graphically in a manner that is understandable to the intelligent layman. Finally, like the CS before the passing of John Exner, R-PAS is subject to ongoing validation and refinement through an active, ongoing research program—reflecting the kind of commitment to the scientific method and peer review that helps ensure legal admissibility.[17]

THE ART OF MULTIMETHOD PERSONALITY ASSESSMENT

Viewing test results in the context of data from other assessment instruments often provides important insights, particularly when one attends carefully to the nature of the method that produced the responses (Mihura & Graceffo, 2014). For example, an elevated MMPI-2 Scale 8 may say more about insecurity and feelings of estrangement than psychosis if it occurs in the context of an average-level Thought and Perception Composite (TP-Comp) score on R-PAS (see Erard, 2005). Because TP-Comp is more of a direct performance measure of thought disorder than Scale 8, whereas the latter is both an indirect and more heterogeneous scale, one can be reasonably confident that the MMPI-2 is not showing sensitivity to a subtle psychotic process that the Rorschach is missing.[18] On the other hand, in the context of a clinically significant elevation on the Personality Assessment Inventory SUI scale (a direct measure of self-attributed suicidal ideation), a score that is average or below on the Rorschach Suicide Concerns Composite (SC-Comp) should not be used to cast doubt on the presence of suicidal ideation, although this seeming discrepancy may indicate that the respondent differs in some important ways from many people who actually commit suicide. In still other cases, a notable discrepancy between self-report and Rorschach scores may help differentiate and integrate multiple perspectives. For example, a mother's self-description as shy and unassertive, accompanied by elevations on Space Reversal (an R-PAS indicator of oppositionality or resistance to influence) and Aggressive Contents, may point to an area of ambivalence or unresolved conflict (Cogswell & Emmert, 2014) and could help to explain why the father might see her so differently than she sees herself (Mihura & Graceffo, 2014). More detailed guidelines for integrated interpretation of self-report and Rorschach results are available in work by Finn (1996), Smith and Finn (2014), and Ganellen (1996). In general, both self-report and performance assessment instruments are required to cover the full range of relevant constructs (Bornstein, 2015; Erdberg, 2008; Mihura, 2012).

Child Custody Litigants and the Rorschach

We sought to obtain a child custody sample that had been administered the Rorschach using R-PAS as part of a child custody or parenting time evaluation and to compare their data to a CS sample, for which similar custody data were published in 2008 (Singer, Hoppe, Lee, Olesen, & Walters, 2008).

The 2008 CS Sample

Singer et al. (2008) collected, scored, and analyzed Rorschach data from 728 child custody litigants (CCLs), using the Comprehensive System (CS). Those authors used the CS normative data as a comparison. While the CCL group provided a normative number of responses, there were some distinguishing features, consistent with some other clinical literature, that described child custody litigants. The question remains whether using the CS norms might have led to characterizing this group as more problematic or pathological than is actually the case.

Singer et al.'s CS CCLs looked markedly constricted and showed deficits in coping thought to be an indication of challenges in interpersonal functioning. They were noted to have problem-solving difficulties, inconsistent coping efforts, unpredictable behavior, and an uncertain self-image. Some used fantasy versus constructive problem-solving efforts, were ruminative, and did not consider their feelings or intuition. Others were highly expressive and action-oriented and used a trial-and-error approach. They used their own experiences to justify their responses in a defensive manner or as a way to show their superiority, indicative of self-focus and challenges in hearing the perspective of others.

When examining this group's processing of affect, stress tolerance, and self-control, the CS group of CCLs showed limited psychological resources and appeared to be situationally and chronically stressed. They had difficulties with frustration tolerance and impulse control. With respect to self-perception and object relations, the group was either self-absorbed or compared themselves negatively to others, with nearly one-third having a reflection response and more than 40% with negative self-concepts. They showed difficulty in reflecting upon their own behavior and challenges with empathy. Their capacity to engage in and anticipate cooperative activities with other was also impaired. Many were hypervigilant.

Finally, in regard to cognitive style, ideation, mediation, and processing, the Singer et al.'s CS CCLs showed impaired reality testing, distortions in their perceptions of others, and challenges with affectively charged boundaries. Additionally, some parents showed illogical thinking.

The Current R-PAS Sample

The current sample consisted of 376 child custody litigants (CCLs). This sample was collected by experienced child custody evaluators from a number of states between 2011 and 2015. CCLs from California, Michigan, and Texas were included. The sample was equally divided between men and women. The average age was 41 years (SD= 8.9) and, on average, the group had some college education (M = 15.5, SD = 3.1). The protocols were scored using R-PAS (Meyer et al., 2011). The differences between some of these scores and those from similar variables in the CS sample are striking. A detailed comparison will follow a description of the R-PAS data.

Reliability Issues

To assess interrater coding reliability, 28 pairs of protocols that were legibly transcribed and for which locations were documented were drawn from the sample and independently recoded by one or another of the authors, who were blind to the original coding. Variables were selected based on their importance for interpretation so that the variables from Summary Scores and Profile Pages 1 and 2 were used.[19]

We calculated intraclass correlation (ICC) for 62 variables. This chance-corrected statistic is recognized as appropriate for Rorschach interrater reliability at the protocol level (Meyer et al., 2002; Viglione, Blume-Marcovici, Miller, Giromini, & Meyer, 2012). In a smaller sample, such as our 28 records, any single variable (especially low base rate variables with few values) might include substantial error in the ICC estimate of reliability. Thus reliability estimates may be over- or underestimated for individual variables. However, the overall reliability, even if it is to some degree underestimated because of low base rates and more approximate, should be evident in the summary data.

The median and mean correlations were 0.77 and 0.74, respectively. The range for excellent reliabilities is greater or equal to 0.75, with good reliability in the range of 0.60 to 0.74. Thus, overall, the reliability of the coding in this sample is likely good to excellent, but there were some notable exceptions with respect to particular variables.

Reliability estimates involving FQ- determinations were disproportionately poor, with ICCs for FQ-% at 0.29 and WD-% at 0.31, and WSumCog scores were less reliable than expected (ICC = 0.42). In contrast, the FQo% ICC was in the excellent range at 0.76. Thus, part of the FQ reliability was weak, whereas another aspect was in the excellent range. Accordingly, when evaluating judgment, perception, adaptation, and reality testing solely on the basis of the normative data in this sample, it may be best to focus on FQo%. In addition, the reliability data would support EII-3 above the TP-Comp (which significantly weights FQ-%) in evaluating the overall level of disturbance.

Contributors to the current sample had varying amounts of training and experience with R-PAS at the time of testing, particularly in coding the oldest cases in the sample, which date back to 2011 when the R-PAS manual was just being published. In addition, because most examiners were primarily concerned with preserving just enough information to facilitate their own coding shortly after administering the test (i.e., no review or research project was anticipated at the time), documentation of precise response locations in the verbatim protocol and on the location sheets was variable in quality and clarity, leading to ambiguities in re-coding. This may be especially true of FQ coding in that it requires knowing how a response content is mapped on the card location.

The chief differences in coding FQo and FQ- is that FQo objects are well-known and listed in the FQo tables, whereas FQ- responses are idiosyncratic and often unlisted there. FQo responses are mostly unambiguous and are based on a very large amount of research data for R-PAS FQ ("tabled" FQ determinations). On the other hand, many FQ- determinations are based on examiner judgments. Non-tabled FQ judgments by any two raters are likely to correlate at about .20 to .25 depending on the technical statistical routines (Meyer et al., 2011). Using the guidance provided by the FQ tables through finding the object or by extrapolation from the shapes in the FQ table greatly increases FQ determination accuracy and interrater agreement. When examiners based their FQ coding decisions on personal judgment rather than use of the tables or clearly justified extrapolations from them, FQ coding becomes more mistake-prone and less reliable.

In research and teaching, it has been apparent that former CS users who are transitioning to R-PAS sometimes do not scrutinize the FQ tables for matches and similarly shaped objects, such that they do not fully follow the extrapolation guidelines detailed in the R-PAS manual. (Although these guidelines had also been recommended for the CS [Viglione, 2002, 2010], Exner himself never included them in any official CS publication.) Thus, a carryover from CS FQ coding practices may have contributed to R-PAS FQ coding problems and resulting ICC problems. The threshold for coding objects as FQ- (rather than FQo or FQu) is much more stringent than in the CS. Thus R-PAS FQ- objects tend to be more distorted than CS, and many that were coded FQ- in the CS are now FQu or even FQo in R-PAS (Meyer et al., 2011).

Consistent with the R-PAS FQ research (Meyer et al., 2011), one can formulate answers corresponding to FQ- and FQu to the examiner judgment question, "Can I see it quickly and easily at the designated blot location?" In R-PAS, the FQ- answer is, "Not really. I don't really see that. Overall it does not match the blot area." In contrast, the FQu answer is, "A little. If I work at it, I can sort of see it." In other words, marginal CS FQ- responses are FQu in R-PAS. This translates grossly to about nearly half of the FQ- CS responses now being FQu in R-PAS.

Comparison of Custody Reference Data to R-PAS Nonpatient Norms

The following interpretive domains are discussed regarding these litigants: Administration Behaviors and Observations, Engagement and Cognitive Processing, Perception and Thinking Problems, Stress and Distress, and Self and Other Representation. Where discrepancies from R-PAS nonpatient norms are mentioned, statistically significant differences are emphasized (see Table 7.1).

Administration Behaviors and Observations

Although it is not unusual for CCLs to be cautious in their approach to self-report instruments (Bagby, Nicholson, Buis, Radnovich, & Fidler, 1999; Bathurst, Gottfried, & Gottfried, 1997; Posthuma & Harper, 1998; Siegel, 1996; Strong, Greene, Hoppe, Johnston & Olesen, 1999), the litigants in this sample did not need much encouragement to provide the

Table 7.1: R-PAS Normative Reference Values for CCE's

Page 1	Domain/Variable	N	M	SD	Min	5%ile	25%ile	Med	75%ile	95%ile	Max
Administration Behaviors & Observations											
	Pr	376	97.5	12.8	89	89	89	89	104	123	142
	Pu	376	99.9	9.7	96	96	96	96	96	117	144
	CT	376	100.2	13.4	86	86	86	98	110	126	134
Engagement & Cognitive Processing Complexity											
	R	376	100.5	14.0	61	77	91	101	110	124	142
	F%**	376	99.3	11.3	60	83	92	99	107	117	134
	Blend*	376	97.2	14.7	56	74	86	97	108	121	136
	Sy	376	102.2	14.7	56	74	86	97	108	121	136
	MC	376	101.0	15.2	73	73	91	102	110	128	143
	MC-PPD	376	101.5	13.9	68	75	92	101	112	124	139
	M	376	98.5	14.2	64	74	95	98	113	123	138
	M/MC	355	100.9	13.9	68	75	92	101	112	124	139
	(CF+C)/SumC**	286	100.2	14.7	56	74	89	101	109	119	141
			103.8	14.5	71	71	91	100	113	125	137
Perception & Thinking Problems											
	EII-3	376	102.1	14.4	69	77	91	99	110	123	135
	TP-Comp**	376	104.8	14.3	75	75	94	104	113	126	126
	WSumCog**	376	103.0	17.9	64	73	90	101	115	128	143
	SevCog	376	100.2	16.8	64	80	93	103	117	142	142
	FQ-%**	376	105.5	16.0	79	79	92	102	113	133	148
	WD-%**	376	104.8	11.2	94	94	94	94	113	123	144

FQo%*	376	96.2	16.7	78	78	78	92	106	114	143	143
Popular**	376	96.6	15.8	82	82	82	92	106	115	134	143
Stress & Distress											
m*	376	101.9	13.8	68	74	74	85	97	105	120	142
Y**	376	102.7	15.3	56	73	73	88	96	103	126	142
MOR*	376	98.0	13.4	84	84	84	97	97	113	125	146
SC-Comp*	376	102.1	14.0	85	85	85	85	99	114	126	148
Self & Other Representation											
ODL%**	376	94.0	13.6	86	86	86	86	100	110	123	146
SR	376	97.9	16.0	64	72	72	91	104	112	127	143
MAP/MAHP**	376	88.1	15.4	74	74	74	74	96	106	118	143
PHR/GPHR	342	100.2	12.9	87	87	87	87	87	102	122	141
M-*	376	102.7	17.5	72	72	72	72	81	99	123	123
AGC**	376	91.7	16.1	75	75	75	87	100	111	131	136
V-Comp*	376	102.0	11.1	95	95	95	95	95	113	123	143
H	376	99.2	13.7	74	74	74	86	94	100	120	132
COP**	376	105.9	14.3	61	79	79	92	101	113	124	137
MAH	376	102.6	14.8	75	75	75	88	98	106	123	139
Page 2											
Engagement & Cognitive Processing											
W%*	376	104.2	14.5	88	88	88	88	102	111	134	148
Dd%**	376	94.4	14.0	90	90	90	90	105	116	134	142
SI	376	98.1	14.9	69	82	82	92	103	115	130	143
IntCont	376	100.6	13.5	75	75	75	82	95	104	115	135
Vg%*	376	97.6	16.6	74	74	74	86	96	111	127	143
V	376	101.0	14.1	81	81	81	93	100	112	124	138
FD	376	101.0	13.4	86	86	86	86	96	106	123	148

(Continued)

Table 7.1: Continued

Domain/Variable	N	M	SD	Min	5%ile	25%ile	Med	75%ile	95%ile	Max
R8910%**	376	96.5	11.8	92	92	92	92	109	126	140
WSumC	376	101.2	13.6	88	88	88	104	115	122	145
C	376	101.0	10.8	62	79	92	95	104	115	138
Mp/(Ma+Mp)	253	101.6	14.0	70	78	92	99	111	122	148
Perception & Thinking Problems										
FQu%	376	100.1	10.7	95	95	95	95	114	124	148
Stress & Distress										
PPD**	376	102.7	15.3	75	75	89	104	113	130	130
YTVC***	376	102.1	13.8	64	79	91	99	110	125	143
Cblend*	376	102.0	13.2	91	91	91	91	107	126	145
C***	376	102.2	14.5	67	77	94	103	112	127	146
CritCont%**	376	95.7	14.8	73	81	91	100	112	130	142
Self & Other Representation										
SumH	376	98.4	13.2	91	91	91	91	107	126	145
refl*	376	102.3	13.0	84	84	97	105	111	124	148
NPH/SumH	325	99.4	15.3	70	70	86	96	106	122	148
p/(a+p)	365	99.8	14.7	70	75	90	99	111	122	137
AGM	376	99.9	14.6	63	77	91	99	106	122	146
T	376	101.0	11.9	95	95	95	95	113	128	148
PER**	376	110.0	15.6	65	76	88	99	111	127	127
An	376	99.2	14.7	70	75	90	99	111	122	137

*p < 0.05, *p < 0.01

Note: Ns less than 376 signify proportions, which are not calculated if there are less than four total coded responses in the denominator. Statistical contrasts to the R-PAS adult normative reference sample used the descriptive data and Ns in the R-PAS manual (Meyer et al.). By definition, M of 100 and SD of 15 were assumed.

requested number of responses per card (Pr, M = 97.5), nor did they show difficulties in inhibiting their output (Pu, M= 99.9). CCLs in this regard did not appear guarded or uncooperative, nor did they seem to have trouble following the test instructions. Their card turning, which would suggest, on the positive side, an indication of curiosity or flexibility and on the negative side, an indication of compulsive, hostile, defiant, suspicious or anxious behavior, was also in the average range (CT, M = 100.2).

Engagement and Cognitive Processing

While one might consider that these litigants could appear superficially cooperative, but show poor engagement with the test, the findings from this domain indicate that their productivity and engagement were average (R, M = 99.3; Complexity, M = 100.5). From a validity perspective, these scores indicate that most of these custody respondents using the R-Optimized administrative procedure are providing enough information to interpret and are sufficiently involved in the task. Thus we do not see short, impoverished records as a means of avoiding scrutiny in the evaluation. Moreover, the R-PAS R-Optimized administration technique is working in that short records are very infrequent. The mean number of responses is approximately 23 per record, with a standard deviation of about 3.

Indeed, they do not demonstrate the sort of detached, simplistic processing that may be expected of someone trying to conceal psychopathology. Rather they are actually a little more likely than most people to show a meaningful personal investment in their observations and to make significant connections among their experiences (F%, M = 97.2; Blend, M = 102.2; Sy, M = 101). It may be that during an emotional period in the lives, they are paying particular attention to the details and nuances of their experience and are treating even seemingly small matters as significant.

There is nothing remarkable about the psychological resources and coping abilities that are shown on average by this litigant group. Their resources and adaptive capacity (MC, M = 101.5; MC-PPD, M = 100.2) appear to be adequate. That is, they are likely to have enough resources to manage the stress they are experiencing. Their approach to problem solving involves a balanced combination of deliberate planning and trial-and-error improvisation (M/MC, M = 100.2). They do not usually rely too much on escapist fantasy (Mp/Ma + Mp, M = 101.6).

In general, this group shows an average level of overall emotional reactivity (WSumC, M = 101.2, C, M = 101). However, they tend to express their feelings and impulses with somewhat more drama and intensity than most people (CF+C/SumC, M = 103.8). Perhaps to protect themselves from excessive emotional display or impetuous actions, they are somewhat more likely to avoid situations with strong emotional demands (R8910%, M = 96.5).

Their cognitive processing may lean toward drawing broad generalizations from limited experience, while overlooking idiosyncratic details (W%, M = 104.2; Dd%, M = 94.4), but at the same time, they do not show evidence of responding in an impressionistic and vague manner (Vg%, M = 97.6). They do not appear to be overly self-critical, but they demonstrate an average ability to think reflectively about their own and others' behavior (FD, M = 101; V, M = 101).

Perception and Thinking Problems

The biggest challenge noted in this group appears to be with making realistic, undistorted appraisals of their experience and environment (FQ-%, M = 105.5, SD = 16.7 and WD-%, M = 104.8, SD = 15.8; note that FQo%, a more reliably coded variable in this sample, is also significantly low, M = 96.2). This group tends to be rather individualistic in their interpretation of everyday situations and problems and may have some unconventional attitudes (P, M = 96.6, SD = 15.3). The somewhat elevated Thought and Perception Composite (TP-Comp, M = 104.8, SD = 16.8) may be a reflection of mildly impaired reality testing and judgment among some individuals, a function of the variability in coding/re-coding of minus responses, or the result of immature or ineffective reasoning (WSumCog, M = 103, SD = 16). However, the CCLs did not show an elevated number of instances of seriously disturbed thinking (SevCog, M = 100.2), and the more reliably coded EII-3, an indicator of overall adaptive or pathological psychological functioning, was not significantly elevated (EII, M = 102.6).

Stress and Distress

Given the amount of stress that is usually associated with custody litigation, it is not surprising that there are several indicators of internal strain. In Table 7.1, seven of the nine Stress and Distress variables on Page 1 and Page 2 are significantly higher than the R-PAS normative data. There are elevated scores reflecting tension or activation that is outside of conscious control, helpless insecurity, gloominess, and overall stress (m, M = 101.9; Y, M = 102.7; C', M = 101.0; PPD, M = 102.7; YTVC', M = 102.1) and a slight uptick in self-destructive or suicidal risk (SC-Comp, M = 102.1, SD = 16). Probably because the pain of the divorce and worries about loss of access to children tarnish experiences that would ordinarily be pleasant or joyful, there are more color-shading blends (CBlend, M = 102).

Morbid content, often an indication of depression or an experience of feeling damaged or under attack, and Critical Contents, which are often indicative of traumatic stress or the deterioration of coping strategies, are lower than expected (MOR, M = 98; CritCont%, M = 95.7), but this is probably the result of avoidance of giving obviously negative content responses as a form of impression management. Generally speaking, content scores are more easily manipulated as part of an impression management strategy to appear more socially acceptable than are structural variables (Benjestorf, Viglione, Lamb, & Giromini, 2013; Ganellen, 2008; Schultz, Chapter 3, this volume).

Self and Other Representation

As may be expected among people who are engaged in high-stakes litigation with intimate enemies, there are some tendencies to project negative motives onto other people and to be hypervigilant against possible threats (M-, M = 102.7; V-Comp = 102.0). They may also be somewhat more likely to place their own needs ahead of others (r, M = 102.3). They appear to be substantially less dependent on other people (and perhaps thus more willing to try to go it alone as parents; ODL, M = 94.0). They also show low numbers of Space Reversal responses, which may suggest a lack of creativity or healthier expressions of self-assertiveness and an indication of a lack of flexibility in their problem solving (SR, M = 97.9).

CCLs in our sample provide very little evidence on the test of their aggressive concerns (AGC, M = 91.7). On the contrary, they show elevations in the number of Cooperative responses (COP, M = 105.9), representations of healthy, mutually beneficial interactions (MAP/MAHP, M = 88.1, SD = 17.5; MAH, M = 102.6), and positive-themed, realistic representations of other people (PHR/GPHR, M = 100.2, SD = 16.1). Such findings might be thought surprising given the challenges this group has with cooperatively coming to agreements about their children, the difficulties that are evident in co-parenting, and the allegations that are levied against each other. The best explanation is probably not that they have superior interpersonal skills and attitudes, but rather that they have some ability to skew their response content to emphasize positive representations and interactions and minimize negative ones in order to look psychologically healthy.

Finally, they can either be quite defensive (justifying their views by their own personal knowledge, experience, or authority) or notably inclined toward bringing experiences from their personal and family lives into the testing (PER, M = 110). In custody testing, it is advisable to review responses coded PER to determine the nature of the self-reference (e.g., defensive self-enhancement or emphasis on one's children). The CCLs show an average degree of interest in other people (SumH, M = 98.4), and despite their reluctance to share their children with each other, they do not seem to show an exceptionally strong desire for interpersonal closeness and affection (T, M = 101).[20]

Comparison of CS and R-PAS Data

While a point-by-point comparison of the current sample and the 2008 CS sample is beyond the scope of this chapter and may not be possible, as some of the scores in the CS are no longer calculated and various non-CS scores are found in R-PAS, the R-PAS data seems to depict a mostly psychologically healthier group of litigants. This is not surprising, as the CS norms tend to overpathologize in several areas (see for example, Meyer et al., 2007; Viglione & Giromini, 2015). The groups are most alike in their challenges with perceiving themselves and other people realistically and arriving at rational judgments, but some caution must be applied to the R-PAS Form Quality results because of reliability issues described earlier. Both samples attempt to justify their responses with their own experience, but our R-PAS sample is not so cognitively and emotionally constricted. Both groups mix deliberative and improvisational approaches to solving problems, but where this is interpreted as a problematic in the CS, this is not the case in R-PAS. Signs of implicit distress, indicative of anxiety, irritation, sadnesss, or helplessness trouble both groups, but these problems appear more pronounced in the CS data.

With respect to self and object representations, the R-PAS group offers more seemingly healthy responses, suggesting an interest in cooperative interactions, but with the same level of distortions in their interpersonal relationships. There is also a tendency toward self-protective vigilance in both groups. Issues related to self-absorption are present in both groups, but more pronounced in the CS group.

Conclusion

Multimethod personality assessment is a valuable means of gathering evidence about key questions concerning parents' and children's capacities, inclinations, and behaviors in child custody evaluations. Rorschach testing offers incremental validity to findings from self-report instruments. When used in a battery including broadband self-report tests, Rorschach testing provides an opportunity to observe personality in action, as well as what people say about themselves. It introduces fresh insights about unacknowledged, peremptory inclinations and reactions, particularly in novel and stressful circumstances and in intimate and family settings. It also contextualizes descriptions of people in terms of the situations or provocations that lead to particular emotions and behavior, reveals interpersonal styles, and often provides access to information that may have been otherwise concealed by impression management.

The Rorschach Performance Assessment System® (R-PAS®; Meyer et al., 2011) is an evidence-based, internationally focused, user-friendly system that extends Exner's original CS philosophy of preserving the best practices and variables from previous Rorschach systems and generating and continually adapting to developments in research and practice. R-PAS has introduced several important innovations and refinements in Rorschach administration, scoring, and interpretation, which make it more valid and useful in multimethod forensic assessment. These include administrative rules designed to keep the number of responses within a meaningfully interpretable range; detailed administration, scoring, and interpretive guidance to reduce examiner variability; more accurate and representative adult and child normative reference data; variable selection based on the best available evidence; the use of complexity adjustment to compensate for inadequate or excessive engagement with the test; and the use of graphical displays of Standard Scores and percentiles to make it easy to show and explain clinically significant scores to a judge or other intelligent layperson.

R-PAS data concerning 376 CCLs (see Table 7.1), contributed by eight custody evaluators in private practice, dating from shortly after the system was introduced, showed good to excellent overall coding reliability, which is reassuring given that there was no formal vetting of level of training or experience for these examiners and that many were still in the process of making the transition from the CS. At the same time, greater than expected chance-corrected inconsistency in some scores, mostly involving FQ- and related scores (but not FQo), may have reflected some carry over from habitual CS patterns of coding and some inconsistencies in the documentation of response locations.

The R-PAS CCL sample looked less troubled in several respects than an earlier CS sample (Singer et al., 2008). To a large extent, this may be explained by differences in R-PAS norms (which are based on norms yielding less pathologizing interpretations than the CS), but it is also possible (judging from R-PAS data on Complexity and F%) that R-PAS administration led to more meaningful engagement in the testing process, which revealed more about available coping resources.

Much has been found with MMPI-2 and MMPI-2-RF data from custody cases (Bagby et al., 1999; Bathhurst et al., 1997; Kauffman et al., 2015; Posthuma & Harper, 1998; Strong et al., 1999), the R-PAS CCL sample showed mostly small or subtle differences between custody litigants and the normative reference sample. However, whereas on the self-report tests nearly all discrepancies from the normative reference group made custody litigants look "healthier," for the most part, the CCLs only looked healthier on R-PAS on certain scores that are particularly face valid and thus susceptible to deliberate manipulation (i.e., content-based scores). In some other respects, the CCLs in the R-PAS sample looked somewhat more troubled, as we will now describe.

The key findings from an analysis of small, but statistically significant, discrepancies between the CCL data and R-PAS normative data appear to be that the CCL sample looked very much like the standard nonpatient R-PAS norms, except for some possible judgment and reasoning problems; some indications of increased stress and distress; and some interpersonal difficulties associated with self-centeredness, projective defenses, and hypervigilance, as well as a notable tendency to emphasize representations associated with positive impressions (e.g., COP, MAH, GHR) and personal experiences (PER) and to minimize representations associated with negative impressions (AGC, MOR, Critical Contents). Custody evaluators using the Rorschach in multimethod assessment are cautioned to bear in mind that because of the influence of such attempted impression management, some content-based scores may be distorted in a healthy direction and to consider this in interpreting Rorschach data in these cases.

Notes

1 J.M. Barrie, the author of *Peter Pan*, called these motherless waifs, "The Lost Boys."

2 R-PAS coding: VII. D2 (H),NC Sy o P Ma,r FAB1 PH

3 R-PAS coding: VI. v W Sy NA—F ODL

4 Look at EII-3, MC—PPD; defenses, breakdowns, and recoveries in sequence analysis.

5 Look at T, M frequency and quality, F% (high), COP, MAH, CF+C/Sum C, V-Comp.

6 Look at FQ-, M-, Non-pure H/Sum H.

7 Look at PER, M-, r, F% (very high or low), behavior with the examiner.

8 Look at COP, PHR/GPHR, MAP/MAHP, Pure H, complexity, interaction with examiner.

9 Look at SR, AGC & AGM, MAP, CF+C/SumC, S-Comp, Vg, violent and self-destructive themes and imagery.

10 Look at FQo%, TP-Comp, PHR/GPHR, MAP/MAHP, M- and M quality, and NPH/SumH.

11 Look at MC—PPD, EII-3, and recovery in sequence analysis.

12 Look at EII-3, PPD, PTI, and CritCont.

13 Look at V-Comp, M-, PTI, and PHR/GPHR.

14 Look at m and Y, CritCont, MC, and complexity.

15 Look at EII-3, ODL, p/(p + a), F%, SR, and complexity.

16 For example, it is hypothesized that attributing human movement to static images (coded on the Rorschach as M) involves the use of imagination to animate what is seen and an operation of projecting one's own actions or experiences into someone else. This hypothesis has received confirmation from EEG studies that demonstrate an association between M responses and *mu* suppression, reflecting the activity of mirror neurons (Giromini, Porcelli, Viglione, Parolin, & Pineda, 2010; Porcelli, Giromini, Parolin, Pineda, & Viglione, 2013). With this conceptual basis, along with numerous clinical studies showing expected associations between M responses and pertinent empirical correlates, M is interpreted as reflecting a capacity for imagination, mentalization, deliberate action, and empathic identification.

17 For detailed discussions concerning the admissibility of expert testimony based on R-PAS findings, see Erard & Viglione (2014) and Erard, Meyer, & Viglione (2014); but see Gurley, Sheehan, Piechowski, & Gray (2014) and Kvisto, Gacono, & Medoff (2013).

18 One limitation of this reasoning comes up in the case of a well-encapsulated delusional disorder without associated thinking disturbance. In this context, MMPI-2 Scale 6 may actually be more sensitive to the problem than the Rorschach (see Khadivi, Chapter 6, this volume).

19 Proportions are not calculated by the R-PAS online program when there are fewer than four scores in the proportion, so that there were missing data for these scores. To retain 28 pairs of protocols for these seven proportion scores, we used those proportion subcomponents available in data. For example, for the MAH to MAP proportion (MAH/MAHP) both MAH and MAP were analyzed. When both subcomponents were not available, we substituted the numerator and denominator (e.g., CF+C and SumC separately for CF+C/SumC).

20 In interpreting T, its low base rate in CS and R-PAS normative samples should be recognized (Meyer et al., 2007; 2011). T = 0 is normative, with about half of individuals with the CS and R-PAS having no T. Thus, T = 0 should not be counted a deficit, even if it may be associated with a higher likelihood of interpersonal distancing relative to higher levels of T.

References

Ackerman, M. J., & Pritzl, T. B. (2011). Child custody evaluation practices. *Professional Psychology: Research and Practice, 28*, 137–145.

American Psychological Association. (2010). Guidelines for child custody evaluations in family law proceedings. *American Psychologist, 65*(9), 863–867.

Archer, E. M., Hagan, L. D., Mason, J., Handel, R., & Archer, R. P. (2012). MMPI-2-RF characteristics of custody evaluation litigants. *Assessment, 19*(1), 14–20.

Association of Family and Conciliation Courts. (2006). *Model standards of practice for child custody evaluation.* Retrieved from http://www.afccnet.org/Portals/0/ModelStdsChildCustodyEvalSept2006.pdf

Back, M. D., Schmukle, S. C., & Egloff, B. (2009). Predicting actual behavior from the implicit and explicit self-concept of personality. *Journal of Personality and Social Psychology, 97*(3), 533–548.

Bagby, R. M., Nicholson, R. A., Buis, T., Radovanovic, H., & Fidler, B. J. (1999). Defensive responding on the MMPI-2 in family custody and access evaluations. *Psychological Assessment, 9*(3), 205–211.

Bathurst, K., Gottfried, A. W., & Gottfried, A. E. (1997). Normative data for the MMPI-2 in child custody litigants. *Psychological Assessment, 9*(3), 205–211.

Benjestorf, S. T., Viglione, D. J., Lamb, J. D., & Giromini, L. (2013, May 27). Suppression of aggressive Rorschach responses among violent offenders and nonoffenders. *Journal of Interpersonal Violence, 28*, 2981–3003. doi:10.1177/0886260513488688

Blais, M. A., Hilsenroth, M. J., Castlebury, F., Fowler, J. C., & Baity, M. R. (2001). Predicting DMS-IV cluster B personality disorder criteria from MMPI-2 and Rorschach data: A test of incremental validity. *Journal of Personality Assessment*, 76(1), 150–168.

Bornstein, R. F. (2015). Personality assessment in the diagnostic manuals: On mindfulness, multiple methods, and test score discontinuities. *Journal of Personality Assessment*, 97(5), 446–455.

Bornstein, R. F., & Masling, J. M. (2005). The Rorschach oral dependency scale. In R. F. Bornstein & J. M. Masling (Eds.), *Scoring the Rorschach: Seven validated systems* (pp. 135–157). Mahwah, NJ: Lawrence Erlbaum Associates.

Bow, J. (2006). Review of empirical research on child custody practice. *Journal of Child Custody*, 1(3), 23–50.

Brodzinski, D. M. (1993). On the use and misuse of psychological testing in child custody evaluations. *Professional Psychology: Research and Practice*, 24, 213–219.

Calloway, G. C. (2005). The Rorschach: Its use in custody evaluations. *Journal of Child Custody*, 2(1–2), 153–158.

Cogswell, A., & Emmert, N. (2014). Multimethod assessment of implicit and explicit processes. In C. J. Hopwood and R. F. Bornstein (Eds.), *Multimethod clinical assessment* (pp. 150–174). New York: Guilford.

Emery, R. E., Otto, R. K., & O'Donahue, W. T. (2005). A critical assessment of child custody evaluations: Limited science and a flawed system. *Psychological Science in the Public Interest*, 6(1), 1–29.

Erard, R. E. (2005). What the Rorschach can contribute to child custody and parenting time evaluations. *Journal of Child Custody*, 2(1/2), 119–142.

Erard, R. E., Meyer, G. J., & Viglione, D. J. (2014). Setting the record straight: Comment on Gurley, Sheehan, Piechowski, & Gray (2014) on the admissibility of the Rorschach Performance Assessment System (R-PAS) in court. *Psychological Injury and Law*, 7, 165–177.

Erard, R. E., & Viglione, D. J. (2014). The Rorschach Performance Assessment System (R-PAS) in child custody evaluations. *Journal of Child Custody*, 11, 159–180.

Erdberg, P. (2008). Multimethod assessment as a forensic standard. In C. B. Gacono & F. B. Evans (Eds., with N. Kaser-Boyd & L. A. Gacono), *The handbook of forensic Rorschach assessment* (pp. 561–566). New York: Routledge.

Erickson, S. K., Lilienfeld, S. O., & Vitacco, M. J. (2007). A critical examination of the suitability and limitations of psychological tests in family court. *Family Court Review*, 45, 157–174.

Evans, F. B., & Schutz, B. M. (2008). The Rorschach in child custody and parenting plan evaluations: A new conceptualization. In C. B. Gacono & F. Barton Evans (with N. Kaser-Boyd & L. A. Gacono, Eds.), *The handbook of forensic Rorschach assessment* (pp. 233–254). New York: Routledge.

Exner, J. E. (2002). *The Rorschach: A comprehensive system: Basic foundations and principles of interpretation* (Vol. 1, 4th ed.). Hoboken, NJ: Wiley.

Finn, S. E. (1996). Assessment feedback integrating MMPI-2 and Rorschach findings. *Journal of Personality Assessment*, 67, 543–557.

Finn, S. E. (2011). Journeys through the valley of death: Multimethod psychological assessment and personality transformation in long-term psychotherapy. *Journal of Personality Assessment, 93*(2), 123-141.

Gacono, C. B., Evans, F. B., & Viglione, D. J. (2002). The *Rorschach in forensic practice. Journal of Forensic Psychology Practice, 2*, 33-54.

Galione, J., & Oltmanns, T. F. (2014). Introduction to multimethod clinical assessment. In C. J. Hopwood & R. F. Bornstein (Eds.), *Multimethod clinical assessment* (pp. 21-50). New York: Guilford Press.

Ganellen, R. J. (1996). *Integrating Rorschach and the MMPI-2 in personality assessment.* Mahwah, NJ: Erlbaum.

Ganellen, R. J. (2008). Rorschach assessment of malingering and response sets. In C. B. Gacono & F. Barton Evans (Eds., with N. Kaser-Boyd & L. A. Gacono), *The handbook of forensic Rorschach assessment* (pp. 89-120). New York: Routledge.

Giromini, L., Porcelli, P., Viglione, D. J., Parolin, L., & Pineda, J. A. (2010). The feeling of movement: EEG evidence for mirroring activity during the observations of static, ambiguous stimuli in the Rorschach cards. *Biological Psychology, 85*, 233-241.

Gurley, J. R., Sheehan, B. L., Piechowski, L. D., and Gray, J. (2014). The admissibility of the R-PAS in court. *Psychological Injury and Law, 7*, 9-17.

Hildebrand, M., & de Ruiter, C. (2008). Psychological assessment with the Rorschach and MMPI-2 in a forensic psychiatric hospital. *Rorschachiana, 29*, 151-182.

Hopwood, C. J., & Bornstein, R. F. (Eds.), (2014). *Multimethod clinical assessment.* New York: Guilford Press.

Hunsley, J., & DiGiulio, G. (2001). Norms, norming, and clinical assessment. *Clinical Psychology: Science and Practice, 8*, 378-382.

Johnston, J. R., Walters, M. G. F., & Oleson, N. W. (2005a). Clinical ratings of parenting capacity and Rorschach protocols of custody-disputing parents: An exploratory study. *Journal of Child Custody, 2*(1-2), 159-178.

Johnston, J. R., Walters, M. G. F., & Olesen, N. W. (2005b). Is it alienating parenting, role reversal, or child abuse? A study of children's rejection of a parent in custody disputes. *Journal of Emotional Abuse, 5*, 191-218.

Jørgensen K., Andersen, T. J., Dam, H. (2000). The diagnostic efficiency of the Rorschach Depression Index and the Schizophrenia Index: A review. *Assessment, 3*, 259-280.

Kauffman, C. M., Stolberg, R., & Madero, J. (2015). An examination of the MMPI-2-RF (Restructured Form) with the MMPI-2 and MCMI-III of child custody litigants. *Journal of Child Custody, 12*(2), 129-151.

Kvisto, A. J., Gacono, C., & Medoff, D. (2013). Does the Rorschach meet standards for forensic use? Considerations with introducing a new Rorschach coding system. *Journal of Forensic Psychology Practice, 13*(5), 380-410.

McCann, J. T., Flens, J. R., Campagna, V., Collman, P., Lazzaro, T., & Connor, E. (2001). The MCMI-III in child custody evaluations: A normative study. *Journal of Forensic Psychology Practice, 1*, 27-44.

McClelland, D. C., Koestner, R., & Weinberger, J. (1989). How do self-attributed and implicit motives differ? *Psychological Review, 96*, 690-702.

Melton, G. B., Petrila, J., Poythress, N. G., & Slobogin, C. (2007). *Psychological evaluations for the courts: A handbook for mental health professionals and lawyers* (3rd ed.). New York: Guilford.

Meyer, G. J. (1999). The convergent validity of MMPI and Rorschach scales: An extension using profile scores to define response and character styles on both methods and a reexamination of profile scores to define response and character styles on both methods and a reexamination of simple Rorschach response frequency. *Journal of Personality Assessment, 78*, 104–129.

Meyer, G. J., Erdberg, P., & Shaffer, T. W. (2007). Towards international normative reference data for the Comprehensive System. *Journal of Personality Assessment, 89*, S201–S216.

Meyer, G. J., Finn, S. E., Eyde, L. D., Kay, G. G., Moreland, K. L., Dies, R. R., Eisman, E. J., Kubiszyn, T. W., & Reed, G. M. (2001). Psychological testing and psychological assessment: A review of evidence and issues. *American Psychologist, 56*(2), 128–165.

Meyer, G. J., Hilsenroth, M. J., Baxter, D., Exner, J. E., Jr., Fowler, J. C., Piers, C. C., & Resnick, J. (2002). An examination of interrater reliability for scoring the Rorschach Comprehensive System in eight data sets. *Journal of Personality Assessment, 78*, 219–274.

Meyer, G. J., Hsiao, W.-C., Viglione, D. J., Mihura, J. L., & Abraham, L. M. (2013). Rorschach scores in applied clinical practice: A survey of perceived validity by experienced clinicians. *Journal of Personality Assessment, 95*, 351–365.

Meyer, G. J., Viglione, D. J., Mihura, J. L., Erard, R. E., & Erdberg, P. (2011). *Rorschach Performance Assessment System: Administration, coding, interpretation, and technical manual*. Toledo, OH: Rorschach Performance Assessment System, LLC.

Mihura, J. L. (2012). The necessity of multiple test methods in conducting assessments: The role of the Rorschach and self-report. *Psychological Injury and Law, 5*, 97–106.

Mihura, J. L., & Graceffo, R. A. (2014). Multimethod assessment and treatment planning. In C. J. Hopwood and R. F. Bornstein (Eds.), *Multimethod clinical assessment* (pp. 285–318). New York: Guilford.

Mihura, J. L., Meyer, G. J., Dumitrascu, N., & Bombel, G. (2013). The validity of individual Rorschach variables: Systematic reviews and meta-analyses of the Comprehensive System. *Psychological Bulletin, 139*, 548–605.

Mischel, W., & Shoda, Y. (1995). A cognitive-affective system theory of personality: Reconceptualizing situations, dispositions, dynamics, and invariance in personality structure. *Psychological Review, 102*(2), 246–268.

Nezworski, M. T., & Wood, J. M. (1995). Narcissism in the comprehensive system for the Rorschach. *Clinical Psychology: Science and Practice, 2*, 179–199.

Nosek, B. A. (2005). Moderators of the relationship between implicit and explicit evaluation. *Journal of Experimental Psychology: General, 134*, 565–584.

Porcelli, P., Giromini, L., Parolin, L., Pineda, J. A., & Viglione, D. J. (2013). Mirroring activity in the brain and movement determinant in the Rorschach test. *Journal of Personality Assessment, 95*, 444–456.

Posthuma, A. B., & Harper, J. F. (1998). Comparison of MMPI-2 responses of child custody and personal injury litigants. *Professional Psychology: Research and Practice, 29*, 437–443.

Reese, J., Viglione, D. J., & Giromini, L. (2014). A comparison between comprehensive system and an early version of the Rorschach Performance Assessment System administration with outpatient children and adolescents. *Journal of Personality Assessment, 96*, 515–522. doi:10.1080/00223891.2014.889700

Roseby, V. (1995). Uses of psychological tests in a child-focused approach to child custody evaluations. *Family Law Quarterly, 28*, 97–110.

Sellbom, M., & Bagby, R. M. (2008). Response styles on multiscale inventories. *Clinical Assessment of Malingering and Deception, 3*, 182–206.

Shapiro, J. P., Leifer, M., Marton, M. W., & Kassem, L. (1990). Multimethod assessment in sexually abused girls. *Journal of Personality Assessment, 55*, 234–238.

Siegel, J. C. (1996). Traditional MMPI-2 validity indicators and initial presentation in custody evaluations. *American Journal of Forensic Psychology, 14*, 55–63.

Singer, J., Hoppe, C. F., Lee, S. M., Olesen, N. W., & Walters, M. G. (2008). Child custody litigants: Rorschach data from a large sample. In C. Gacono and B. Evans (Eds., with N. Kaser-Boyd & L. A. Gacono), *The handbook of forensic Rorschach assessment* (pp. 445–464). New York: Routledge.

Smith, J. D., & Finn, S. E. (2014). Integration and therapeutic presentation of multimethod assessment results: An empirically supported framework and case example. In C. J. Hopwood and R. F. Bornstein (Eds.), *Multimethod clinical assessment* (pp. 403–425). New York: Guilford.

Stanfill, M. L., Viglione, D. J., & Resende, A. C. (2013a). Measuring psychological development with the Rorschach. *Journal of Personality Assessment, 95*, 174–186. doi:10.1080/00223891.2012.740538

Stanfill, M. L., Viglione, D. J., & Resende, A. C. (2013b). Correction to: Measuring psychological development with the Rorschach. *Journal of Personality Assessment, 95*, 435. doi:10.1080/00223891.2013.779563

Stricker, G., & Healy, B. D. (1999). Projective assessment of object relations: A review of the empirical literature. *Psychological Assessment: A Journal of Consulting and Clinical Psychology, 2*, 219–230.

Strong, D. R., Greene, R. L., Hoppe, C., Johnston, T., & Olesen, N. (1999). Taxometric analysis of impression management and self-deception on the MMPI-2 in child-custody litigants. *Journal of Personality Assessment, 73*(1), 1–18.

Viglione, D. J. (1999). A review of recent research addressing the utility of the Rorschach. *Psychological Assessment, 11*, 251–265.

Viglione, D. J. (2002). *Rorschach coding solutions: A reference guide for the Comprehensive System*. San Diego: Author.

Viglione, D. J. (2010). Rorschach coding solutions: A reference guide for the Comprehensive System (2nd ed.). San Diego: Author.

Viglione, D. J., Blume-Marcovici, A. C., Miller, H. L., Giromini, L., & Meyer, G. (2012). An inter-rater reliability study for the Rorschach Performance Assessment System. *Journal of Personality Assessment, 94*(6), 607–612. doi:10.1080/00223891.2012.684118

Viglione, D. J., & Giromini, L. (2015, April 9). International versus Comprehensive System Rorschach norms for children, adolescents, and adults. *Journal of Personality Assessment*. Advance online publication. doi:10.1080/00223891.2015.1136313

Viglione, D. J., & Hilsenroth, M. (2001). The Rorschach: Facts, fiction, and future. *Psychological Assessment, 13*, 452–471.

Viglione, D. J., & Meyer, G. J. (2008). An overview of Rorschach psychometrics for forensic practice. In C. B. Gacono & F. Barton Evans (with N. Kaser-Boyd & L. A. Gacono Eds.), *The handbook of forensic Rorschach assessment* (pp. 21–53). New York: Routledge.

Viglione, D. J., Meyer, G., Jordan, R. J., Converse, G. L., Evans, J., MacDermott, D., & Moore, R. (2014, August 7). Developing an alternative Rorschach administration method to optimize the number of responses and enhance clinical inferences. *Clinical Psychology & Psychotherapy*. Advance online publication. http://dx.doi.org/10.1002/cpp.1913

Viglione, D. J., & Rivera, B. (2003). Assessing personality and psychopathology with projective tests. In J. R. Graham & J. A. Naglieri (Eds.), *Comprehensive Handbook of Psychology: Assessment Psychology* (Vol. 10, pp. 531–553). New York: Wiley.

Viglione, D. J., & Rivera, B. (2012). Performance assessment of personality and psychopathology. In I. B. Weiner (Ed.-in-Chief), J. R. Graham, & J. A. Naglieri (Vol Eds.), *Comprehensive handbook of psychology: Assessment psychology* (2nd ed., Vol. 10, pp. 600–621). Hoboken, NJ: John Wiley & Sons.

Weiner, I. B. (1999). What the Rorschach can do for you: Incremental validity in clinical applications. *Assessment, 6*, 327–339.

Weiner, I. B. (2005). Integrative personality assessment with self-report and performance-based measures. In S. Strack (Ed.), *Handbook of personology and psychopathology* (pp. 317–331). Hoboken, NJ: Wiley.

Wood, J. M., Nezworski, T. M., Garb, H. N., & Lilienfeld, S. O. (2001). Problems with the norms of the Comprehensive System for the Rorschach: Methodological and conceptual considerations. *Clinical Psychology: Science and Practice, 8*(3), 397–402.

CHAPTER 8

MADNESS, MAYHEM, AND MURDER
A Comparative Rorschach Case Study of Methamphetamine Psychosis and Paranoid Schizophrenia
Marvin W. Acklin

INTRODUCTION: METHAMPHETAMINE PSYCHOSIS

Clinical and forensic psychologists working in the legal system encounter individuals with psychiatric and legal issues associated with methamphetamine abuse or dependence. Methamphetamine use is the cause of social, economic, and legal pathologies and psychiatric comorbidity, and it has a strong association with criminal violence. There is a substantial prevalence of psychosis with meth dependence, consistently described as a toxic paranoid-hallucinatory state. Since first described in the 1950s, methamphetamine psychosis (MAP) has been described as indistinguishable from paranoid schizophrenia. Hawaii, one of the first places in the United States to experience the crystal meth epidemic, has a history of highly publicized, grisly homicides and case law on mental states associated with MAP. Methamphetamine's unique pharmacology challenges conventional legal notions of criminal responsibility and, ultimately, treatment or confinement after disposition.

This chapter addresses the history of methamphetamine epidemics in Japan, the United States, and worldwide as well as methamphetamine pharmacology, phenomenology, neurobiology, and clinical/diagnostic issues. In order to address the long vexing differential diagnosis of MAP and schizophrenia, a Rorschach clinical case study will examine two cases utilizing the Rorschach Performance Assessment System® (R-PAS®). The neurobiology of violence and forensic issues related to MAP and criminal responsibility will be considered in closing.

Amphetamine and Methamphetamine Epidemics

Methamphetamine was first synthesized from ephedrine in 1893 by a Japanese chemist, six years after the discovery of amphetamine. In 1919, crystallized methamphetamine was synthesized by reducing ephedrine using red phosphorus and iodine, providing the basis for widespread production. Methamphetamine was not produced in significant quantities in the U.S. domestic market until the 1960s, when the first methamphetamine "epidemic" appeared on the West Coast.

The Japanese military used amphetamine and methamphetamine extensively during World War II. Following the dumping of military stores of methamphetamine on the open market during reconstruction of the country, there was a sharp increase in the number of methamphetamine users. The peak of the epidemic occurred in 1954 when the number of methamphetamine users was estimated between 550,000 and 1,000,000 (Sato, Numachi, & Hamamura, 1992). Approximately 220,000 methamphetamine psychoses were reported during the 1945–1955 epidemic (Yui, Ikemoto, Ishiguro, & Goto, 2000). Meth use spread to construction workers, truck drivers, and other blue-collar workers, students, housewives, and office workers. In Japan, polysubstance use is rare. Methamphetamine is used primarily by intravenous injection without any other substance such as hallucinogens, cannabis, cocaine, opiates, or alcohol.

Since the drug was uncontrolled and publicly available, Japan's first epidemic continued until 1957. Synthetic methamphetamine produced by a domestic pharmaceutical company was distributed in 100% pure ampules on the open market and injected intravenously by users. More than 55,000 persons were arrested for drug-related crimes, and the estimated number of methamphetamine abuse cases was over half a million (Fukushima, 1994; Yui, Ikemoto, Ishiguro, & Goto, 2000). After enactment of the Stimulant Drug Control Law in 1951 prohibiting the use and possession of methamphetamine and the Mental Health Act that permitted involuntary treatment of chronic users (Anglin, Burke,

Perrochet, Stamper, & Dawud-Noursi, 2000), methamphetamine abuse dramatically subsided.

Methamphetamine abuse in Japan began to rise again from about 1970 and the second epidemic peaked in 1984. The second epidemic was characterized by promotion by Japanese gangsters. Heinous crimes by methamphetamine abusers increased and became a serious social problem. The third epidemic, which continues today, began in 1995. The third epidemic was characterized by the entry of Iranian drug dealers into the Japanese market. The Japanese were among the first to encounter methamphetamine challenges to insanity statutes (Fukushima, 1994).

The low incidence of comorbid substance use in Japan permitted investigators to observe the sequence of now well-recognized psychiatric symptoms induced by methamphetamine without modification by other drugs. Clinical investigation revealed three core characteristics of methamphetamine abuse/dependence: (a) progressive qualitative alteration of mental symptoms from a nonpsychotic to a pre-psychotic to a severely psychotic state, (b) enhanced vulnerability to relapse of psychosis after cessation of drug intoxication, and (c) very long duration of the vulnerability to relapse (Yui, Ikemoto, Ishiguro, & Goto, 2000; Ujike & Sato, 2004). Japan's unique circumstance revealed that longer, more frequent consumption of methamphetamine-induced psychosis at a high rate increased susceptibility to relapse due to subsequent consumption, aggravated spontaneous relapse without drug ingestion, and created a poorer long-term prognosis.

In the United States, amphetamine was sold over the counter as a nasal decongestant and asthma inhaler (also commonly used in England) until 1959, with an associated black market of illegally diverted pharmaceutical methamphetamine. Popular with motorcycle gangs in California in the mid-1960s, the drug became popular among the general population. A surge of crystal methamphetamine ("ice") use hit Hawaii in the 1980s, imported from Asia. In the 1990s, ice use was rampant in Hawaii. It was used by extended kinship networks, including entire families, co-workers, and neighborhoods (Anglin, Burke, Perrochet, Stamper, & Dawud-Noursi, 2000). Eventually, clandestine laboratories (including both super labs and "Beavis and Butthead" labs) spread across the United States, creating a wave of violence, trafficking, child endangerment, chemical hazards, and criminal justice system impacts that continues today.

Prevalence/Worldwide and United States

Methamphetamine abuse and dependence has developed into a worldwide problem. Methamphetamine is the second most popular illicit drug worldwide, with an annual global prevalence estimated at 0.4%. The United Nations Office on Drugs and Crime estimated that 290 tons of methamphetamine were synthesized in 2005, which is equivalent to 2.9 billion 100 mg doses. Epidemiological data suggest that methamphetamine use in 2005 was highest among 18- to 25-year-olds. Use of the drug is common in Asia, Oceania, and North America. Annual prevalence among adults is 14% in the Philippines, 3.2% in Australia, and 0.8% in the United States. In an Internet study designed to model U.S. population norms (Durell, Kroutil, Crits-Christoph, Barcha, & Van Brunt, 2008), the estimated lifetime prevalence of methamphetamine use among 18- to 49-year-olds was 0.6%. About half a million Americans had used methamphetamine in the previous month. A 2008 United Nations Office on Drugs and Crime World Drug Report (United Nations, 2008) estimated that there were approximately 25,000,000 abusers of methamphetamine worldwide, exceeding that of cocaine and heroin. A recent national survey on drug use and health estimated 105,000 new methamphetamine users in the United States in 2010, which was down from triple this level early in the decade. According to the 2012 National Household Survey on Drug Abuse, approximately 1.2 million people reported past-year use of methamphetamine and 440,000 reported using it in the previous month (Substance Abuse and Mental Health Services Administration, 2013).

Methamphetamine abuse is strongly associated with crime. In one survey, the percentage of male arrestees was highest in Honolulu (40%), followed by Phoenix (38%), San Diego (36%), and Los Angeles (29%); Zorick, Rad, Rim, & Tsuang, 2008). Methamphetamine use has had a major impact on the legal system. It is associated with self-reported violent criminal behavior and recidivism among parolees, with 82% of methamphetamine users returning to custody within 12 months.

Methamphetamine

Methamphetamine belongs to the class of substituted phenylethylamines (Shulgin, 1978). It is related to other dimethylphenylethylamines as a positional isomer of compounds that share the common chemical formula $C_{10}H_{15}Ni_{1}$. S-methamphetamine hydrochloride is a white or translucent crystal and is referred to commonly as "ice" or "crystal meth." Crystal methamphetamine may be eaten, snorted, injected, or—in the preferred manner in the United States—vaporized in a glass pipe. Compared to amphetamine, methamphetamine has longer half-life, passes more readily through the blood-brain barrier into the central nervous system, and potentiates greater effects on the central nervous system.

At low-to-moderate doses used in clinical experiments, methamphetamine responses include arousal, reduced fatigue, euphoria, positive mood, accelerated heart rate, elevated blood pressure, pupil dilation, increased temperature, reduced appetite, and short-term improvement in cognitive domains, including sustained attention. High-dose intravenous methamphetamine administration evokes marked positive subjective responses, followed by the onset of psychotic symptoms. A series of studies has examined experimentally induced stimulant psychosis (e.g., Angrist & Gershon, 1970). High-dose experiments using amphetamine indicate that psychosis may be introduced in subjects without previous psychosis based on dosage and duration of use.

Low-to-moderate doses of methamphetamine cause cognitive changes, including increased arousal and alertness, and improved attention and concentration, particularly evident in subjects who are sleep deprived. Affective changes include decreased appetite and increased libido, increased confidence, and elevated mood. Higher doses of methamphetamine cause dysphoria due to excessive stimulation; symptoms are evident as restlessness and anxiety, and are associated with tremors and dyskinesia. In cases of binge drug use, which may last over a period of days, the euphoric effects of the drug diminish over time, while dysphoria and compulsive behavior increases, with the latter known as "tweaking." Binge users may exhibit highly focused and repetitive behaviors such as "punding," the stereotyped handling, sorting, and dissembling of objects. Binge use of methamphetamine has been reported to induce sleeplessness, hallucinations, and paranoia associated with irritability and unprovoked aggression.

The clinical literature has been consistent in indicating that methamphetamine psychosis (MAP) refers to paranoid-hallucinatory states induced by the drug, which are indistinguishable from the positive symptom picture of acute paranoid schizophrenia. Regular methamphetamine use is also associated with a high incidence of chronic psychotic symptoms. The most common signs of MAP are hallucinations, delusions, and ideas of reference. Delusions of persecution, as well as ideas of reference and of mind reading are common. Pre-psychotic abnormal experiences, such as delusional moods or ideas of reference, are seen first and then shift to a psychotic state of potent delusions, delusions of reference, persecution, poisoning, and auditory visual hallucinations.

Methamphetamine abuse and dependence is associated with significant psychiatric comorbidity. In one treatment study (Salo, Flower, Kielstein, Leamon, Nordahl, & Galloway, 2011), 28.6% had primary psychotic disorders—23.8% of which were substance-induced—13% had methamphetamine-induced delusional disorders, and 11% had methamphetamine-induced hallucinations. Substantial percentages of methamphetamine users reported symptoms of paranoia (64% of males and 67% of females) and 40% of males and 47% of females reported illusions or hallucinatory-like states such as "imagining someone calling your name." Among a sample of 170 Japanese methamphetamine users affected by psychosis, 59% recovered from psychosis within 30 days, but symptoms persisted for more than one month among 41%, including 28% expressing symptoms after more than six months abstinence (Yui, Ikemoto, Ishiguro, & Goto, 2000). These findings have contributed to a long-standing controversy over whether MAP triggers a primary psychosis or has neurotoxic factors that precipitate chronic psychosis (Bramness, Gundersen, Guterstam et al., 2012).

Latency between the initial use and onset of psychosis varies from weeks to 20 years based on dose of methamphetamine, frequency of consumption, route of administration, circumstances of abuse, and individual vulnerability to psychosis. It is accepted that vulnerability to relapse of MAP develops during methamphetamine abuse (Yui, Ikemoto, Ishiguro, & Goto, 2000). Longer methamphetamine abuse can induce a spontaneous relapse due to unspecified stressors, such as jail detention without methamphetamine consumption (Sato, Chen, Akiyama, & Otsuki, 1983; Sato, Numachi, & Hamamura, 1992). Spontaneous relapse may also occur after severe insomnia or heavy alcohol consumption. The longer the duration of methamphetamine abuse, the worse the prognosis for psychosis relapse.

Long-term use of methamphetamines by humans results in a host of medical problems (Panenka, Procyshyn, Lecomte, MacEwan, Flynn et al., 2013). These include severe cardiovascular complications related to chronic hypertension and cardiovascular disease, such as angina, arrhythmias, valvular disease, hemorrhagic/ischemic strokes, and a high incidence of myocardial infarction. Chronic methamphetamine use is associated with malnourishment and can result in "meth mouth," a dental condition associated with severe decay and loss of teeth. Chronic users experience formication, the feeling of insects crawling on or under the skin. Skin lesions are commonly observed in methamphetamine users as a result of the compulsive scratching that accompanies drug use. Lesions frequently become infected, resulting in bacterial cellulitis, bacteremia, and sepsis in some cases. Methamphetamine use is associated with impairment in neuropsychological performance corresponding with frontal striatal and limbic abnormalities. Principal neurocognitive impairments appear to occur in the domains of executive functioning, learning, episodic memory, speed of information processing, motor skills, working memory, and perceptual narrowing (Scott, Woods, Matt, Meyer, Heaton et al., 2007).

Users typically recover from MAP within one week, or one month at the longest: the "transient type" of MAP. Recovery from MAP may sometimes be delayed to over one month, or occasionally over six months: the "prolonged or persistent" type. Longer and heavier abuse of methamphetamine delays recovery and worsens the prognosis for recovery. Vulnerability to relapse of psychosis developed during meth abuse does not seem to decrease over time.

Long-term use of methamphetamine has severe psychosocial consequences. Similar to other forms of addiction, methamphetamine use impairs executive neurocognitive function and results in poor coping skills, including disorganized lifestyle and interpersonal difficulties. These effects may be particularly evident in methamphetamine users, as chronic methamphetamine use causes irritability, aggression, and impulsivity. These factors strongly impact social activities such as employment and housing, as well as social support. For example, in one urban study of methamphetamine users, 28% were homeless and another 48% lived in sheltered or transitional housing (Panenka, Procyshyn, Lecomte, MacEwan, Flynn et al., 2013).

Amphetamine and Methamphetamine Psychosis: Classic Studies

Connell's classic monograph (1958) described amphetamine psychosis in England, which was largely the result of asthma inhaler abuse. Connell's study of 42 amphetamine-associated psychosis cases concluded that psychosis associated with amphetamine usage was much more frequent than would be expected from reports in the literature. The clinical picture is primarily a paranoid psychosis with ideas of reference, delusions of persecution, and auditory/visual hallucinations in a setting of clear consciousness. There are no physical signs of diagnostic amphetamine intoxication, and the mental picture may be indistinguishable from acute or chronic paranoid schizophrenia. Connell considered amphetamine a true "hallucinogen," since it can produce a psychosis with hallucinations after a single large dose. Connell found that patients with amphetamine psychosis typically recovered within a week. Connell was concerned about whether amphetamine psychosis was a transient condition, or triggered a latent schizophrenia. Connell observed that patients whose psychoses persisted after cessation of drug influence should be considered probable schizophrenics. He noted that a considerable number of patients with amphetamine psychosis were ultimately diagnosed as schizophrenics.

A second classic in the MAP literature is an Australian study (Bell, 1965). In a case of 14 inpatients with MAP, 100% of the cases had persecutory delusions, and a significant number of cases had delusions of influence and auditory hallucinations. Psychotic episodes typically resolved within 7-10 days. Only two cases involved reports of schizophrenic thought disorder. Bell believed that amphetamine intoxication can precipitate the onset of a schizophrenic episode. Bell found that clinically, amphetamine psychosis and paranoid schizophrenia were indistinguishable. All of his patients had delusions of persecution, auditory hallucinations, and disturbed behavior and affect.

Bell observed two distinct groups of patients. The "non-schizophrenic" subjects had psychotic disorders that cleared within ten days of the withdrawal of amphetamine. They did not exhibit schizophrenic thought disorder. It was not uncommon for them to experience vivid visual hallucinations. The other group of subjects suffered psychoses that lasted for months, and all the characteristics of their illness, including the presence of thought disorder and the relative absence of visual hallucinations, were typical of schizophrenia. Bell concluded that amphetamine intoxication could precipitate the onset of a schizophrenic episode. He noted that two distinctive features of amphetamine psychosis are the prominence of visual hallucinations in some cases and the absence of formal thought disorder in all cases. Bell argued that amphetamine should be considered a "psychotomimetic" substance since it produces a "model schizophrenia."

Some of the most influential studies of MAP are from Japan. In two comprehensive and influential studies of MAP (Sato, Chen, Akiyama, & Otsuki, 1983; Sato, Numachi, & Hamamura, 1992), researchers noted the striking similarities between the symptoms of MAP and paranoid schizophrenia that have been widely discussed since Connell's pioneering work (1958), including prominent persecutory delusions, Schneiderian first-rank symptoms, including auditory hallucinations, while the sensorium remained clear. They observed that MAP has been proposed as a pharmacological model for schizophrenia. They reported characteristic clinical features of the paranoid psychotic state including the recurrence of psychosis after a prolonged period of abstinence by a few reinjections or even a single one in an amount less than that used in the past and that small doses of D2 receptor antagonist haloperidol had a potent prophylactic effect on the acute exacerbation following meth reuse. They also noted important differences from Connell on the clinical course and duration of the psychosis after cessation of methamphetamine use.

The most prominent symptoms were delusions with persecutory and jealous content in both the initial and relapse psychotic episodes. Some patients also had bizarre delusions of being controlled, thought broadcasting, or thought insertion. Auditory hallucinations tended to be comments, often threatening, on their behaviors and/or thoughts. Loosening of associations was found in 19% of the patients during the initial psychotic episode and in 18.8% of the patients during the relapse psychotic episode. These Japanese researchers observed the prevalence and strong similarity of psychotic symptoms in both acute and relapse states. Methamphetamine relapse induced a paranoid psychotic state almost identical to the initial psychosis, characterized by abundant paranoid delusions, frequently accompanied by auditory hallucinations, bizarre ideas, e.g., delusions of being controlled, thought broadcasting, thought insertion, and thought withdrawal, combined with loosening of associations. Although Bell (1965) reported that visual hallucinations predominate auditory hallucinations, Sato et al. (1992) found that auditory hallucinations, with voices commenting on behavior, were prominent, while the sensorium remained clear. Concerning the progressive evolution of the paranoid psychotic state, behavioral activation and euphoric effects diminished with repeated use of amphetamine, while psychotic symptoms were progressively enhanced.

Pharmacology and Neurobiology of Methamphetamine Psychosis

Methamphetamine is a psychomotor stimulant with potent physiological effects on peripheral and central systems, resulting in both physical and psychological effects, including hyperarousal, euphoria, irritability, and insomnia (Perry, Sprock, Schaible, McDougall, Minassian, Jenkins, & Braff, 1995; Amgrist, Corwin, Bartlik, & Cooper, 1987). The CNS effects of methamphetamine are mediated mainly by stimulation of the monoaminergic dopamine, norepinephrine, and serotonin systems. Acute effects of methamphetamine modulate dopamine release at two main molecular substrates on dopamine neuronal terminals: the vesicular monoamine transporter-2 (VMAT-2) and the plasmalemal dopamine transporter (DAT). Levels of specific monoamines increase in a regionally dependent manner. The psychological effects of methamphetamine resemble those of other amphetamines and vary depending on both the method of administration and the amount of drug used. The fastest onset of effects occurs after either smoking or injecting methamphetamine, whereupon near-instantaneous, drug-induced psychological effects are experienced. Oral ingestion produces a delayed onset of psychological effects and reduces bioavailability of methamphetamine. The similarities in MAP and schizophrenia have made amphetamine a primary psychotomimetic model agent in schizophrenia research. It is likely that the resemblance is caused by the altered function of mesolimbic dopamine systems and prefrontal cortical function.

One of the most characteristic features of methamphetamine is neural "sensitization," also called behavioral sensitization or reverse tolerance phenomenon (Hseih, Stein, & Howells, 2014; Ujike & Sato, 2004), where lower doses of repeated methamphetamine exposure have been shown to produce behavioral effects that best model psychosis by indicators such as increased locomotion, hallucinatory behaviors in the case of non-human primates, pre-pulse inhibition deficits, latent inhibition deficits, and other cognitive effects. The recurrence of psychotic symptoms after cessation of the drug suggests that "amphetamine users undergo a long lasting change in physiology that produces an increased susceptibility to relapse/symptom reemergence" (Featherstone, Kapur, & Fletcher, 2007,

p. 1558). While studies in the methamphetamine sensitization model of psychosis are extensive, few have examined the effects of chronic methamphetamine exposure on the cortical GABAminergic system.

Methamphetamine use in humans leads to a plethora of structural and metabolic central nervous system changes. Chronic exposure to methamphetamine can result in neuropsychological deficits (Jacobs, Fujii, Schiffman, & Bello, 2008; Scott, Woods, Matt, Meyer, Heaton et al., 2007). It is increasingly clear that chronic methamphetamine use does not affect all aspects of cognition equally. This may be due to the differential distribution of monoamines in the brain, which serve as the substrate for neurotoxicity. The most consistent and severe changes include impairments in memory, attention, and executive function.

The sum of clinical studies suggests that methamphetamine dependence is associated with brain function that is required for "top down" control of behavior (Baicy & London, 2007). Brain imaging studies note significant abnormalities in cortical and limbic systems, including deficits in markers of dopaminergic and serotonergic transmitter systems. There is reasonably strong evidence that genetic variation in neurotransmitter systems and in neurodevelopment is associated with risk for MAP. These findings, coupled with the findings that repeated methamphetamine treatment directly sensitizes dopamine receptors in the nucleus accumbens and ventral tegmental area, and reduces striatal dopamine transporter, strongly suggest that the enhanced striatal dopamine neurotransmission plays an important role in methamphetamine-induced behavioral sensitization. The role of corticolimbic dysregulation has significant implications for anger, hostility, and violence, factors that are directly related to dysfunction in the prefrontal cortex, causing insufficient inhibitory control of the amygdala. Amygdala hyperreactivity to perceived threats acts synergistically with impaired inhibitory control, which leads to violence and aggressive behavior (Baicy & London, 2007).

Neuropsychologists have studied corticolimbic deficits extensively. Scott et al. (2007) conducted a meta-analysis of the neurocognitive effects of methamphetamine abuse and dependence showing deficits in episodic memory, executive functions, information processing speed, motor skills, language, and visual constructional abilities. Neuroimaging studies have revealed that methamphetamine can cause neurodegenerative changes in the brains of human addicts, including persistent decreases in the level of dopamine transporters in the orbitofrontal context, dorsolateral prefrontal cortex, and caudate-putamen.

In a meta-analysis of 18 studies, Jacobs, Fujii, Schiffman, and Bello (2008) examined neurocognitive functions in schizophrenia and MAP. Neurocognitive test scores for participants with paranoid schizophrenia (N = 20) and MAP (N = 19) were obtained from hospital records and compared. Impairments of episodic memory, executive functions, information processing speed, motor skills, language, and visuo-constructional skills were noted. Contrary to predictions, no significant differences were found between the groups in any neurocognitive domain. Rather both groups seemed to perform consistently with what might be expected for schizophrenia. The observed pattern of performance across both groups suggests that the similarities and shared presentation features between MAP and paranoid schizophrenia extend to neurocognition and point to a common underlying pathophysiology.

In addition to the acute effects of methamphetamine intoxication and psychosis, chronic use has been linked to neurotoxicity. These findings have been documented in human and animal models (Zorick, Rad, Rim, & Tsuang, 2008). Chronic meth use is associated with a 20% to 33% decrease in DA transporter binding and receptor density and reduced density in orbifrontal and bilateral amygdalae, correlated with length of use and psychiatric morbidity measures. While some chronic users demonstrate DA transporter recovery and increased DA receptor density, persistent decreases in striatal and nucleus accumbens DA metabolism has been found after a year of abstinence. In a study of Hawaiian meth users, persistent focal perfusion deficits in frontal, temporal, and parietal lobes were associated with violent and aggressive behavior. These deficits are thought to be associated with reduced 5-HT transporter density, serotonin being a neurotransmitter associated with inhibitory controls (Buffenstein, Heaster, & Ko, 1999).

Using MRI from 20 MAP patients and 20 healthy controls, Orikabe et al. (2011) found significant gray matter volume reductions with both the amygdala and hippocampus bilaterally in subjects with MAP compared with controls. The prominent relative volume reduction in amygdala rather than in hippocampus could be a relatively specific characteristic of MAP, since previous studies have shown significant volume reductions less frequently in the amygdala and hippocampus in other psychoses such as schizophrenia.

Methamphetamine Psychosis: Predisposing and Recovery Factors

Predisposing Factors

Chen et al. (2003) attempted to characterize methamphetamine users and to examine the relationship of premorbid personality, social functioning, and other psychiatric disorders to MAP. Their MAP patients presented a clinical picture that mimicked the positive symptoms of schizophrenia: 85% had auditory hallucinations, 71% persecutory delusions, 63% delusions of reference. They concluded that premorbid schizoid or schizotypal personality traits predisposed methamphetamine users to develop psychosis.

Broad-spectrum psychopathology may also play an important role in premorbid vulnerability to meth psychosis and chronic MAP. Pre-existing psychopathology has been linked to MAP vulnerability. Akiyama, Saito, and Shimoda (2011) found that 24% of MAP subjects suffered from a variety of affective, anxiety, and psychotic disorders prior to their first methamphetamine use, indicating vulnerability to chronic MAP. These findings suggest the presence of a psychotic diathesis in methamphetamine users. Exposure to threatening and stressful life events during previous methamphetamine use may elicit sensitization of the noradrenergic mechanisms to subsequent mild stress leading to spontaneous recurrences in subjects with previous meth psychosis. Salo et al. (2008) found significant positive correlations between frequency of MAP episodes and scores on the Wender Utah Rating Scale (WURS), a scale that retrospectively measures childhood attention function and hyperactivity. Findings indicated a relationship between measures of early attention and hyperactivity and the emergence of psychotic episodes in individuals who abuse methamphetamine heavily in adulthood and reach criteria for dependence.

Family psychiatric history has been found to be a risk factor for MAP. Salo, Fassbender, Buonocore, and Ursu (2013) found that methamphetamine-dependent subjects with a familial history of psychiatric disorders reported that they experienced psychotic episodes more frequently than those methamphetamine-dependent subjects without a family history of psychiatric illness, emphasizing a neurobiological vulnerability to the emergence of MAP symptoms.

Linkages between MAP and prior and concurrent drug abuse have been also been explored (Kuzenko et al., 2011). They examined substance abuse histories in a community sample of 2,588 adolescent and young adults in Munich Germany as predisposing factors in the development of psychosis. The main finding of the study was that in adolescents and young adults, use of cocaine, amphetamine, and/or psychedelics was associated with a heightened lifetime risk of psychotic symptoms.

Recent neuroimaging studies have linked the neurobiology of MAP and developmental factors implicated in emotional regulation. Amygdala volume has been hypothesized to be adversely affected by childhood maltreatment (Dean, Kohno, Hellemann, & London, 2014). In their longitudinal study of 503 males, Pardini, Raine, Erickson, and Loeber (2014) found that men with lower amygdala volume have long-standing history of aggression and psychopathic features. Studies of emotional reactivity consistently show amygdala hyperresponsivity to fearful and threatening images, particularly faces, in adults with a history of maltreatment. Individuals with a history of maltreatment reliably demonstrated differential amygdala hyperactivity and other limbic areas during presentation of threatening stimuli. Investigators examined histories of childhood maltreatment and resting state functional connectivity of the amygdala with fMRI imaging in 15 abstinent methamphetamine-dependent subjects. As expected, childhood maltreatment was positively associated with resting state connectivity between the amygdala and various areas of the right cerebral hemisphere, cerebellum, and brainstem. The study found reduced conductivity between limbic and cortical regions in individuals with a history of maltreatment relative to those reporting no maltreatment. Adults with a history of maltreatment exhibited volumetric deficits in the prefrontal cortex, hippocampus, corpus callosum, and cerebellum. Furthermore, individuals who reported maltreatment exhibited abnormalities in activation of the dorsolateral prefrontal cortex (PFC) and interior cingulate cortex during tests of working memory and inhibitory control. These important corticolimbic factors and their linkages to violence will be discussed further later in this chapter.

Recovery and Relapse Factors

Distinguishing between patients who quickly recover from MAP (transient type) and those with a prolonged psychosis (persistent type) has been a major focus of clinical investigation. A subset of abstinent meth-dependent patients develops chronic psychosis even after long-term cessation of stimulant use. Akiyama and colleagues (2011) examined a sample of incarcerated defendants with heavy histories of methamphetamine use with the hypothesis that a significant percentage of individuals would demonstrate chronic psychosis despite long-term supervised abstinence in the medical unit setting of the prison, contrary to the typical transient phenomena and rapid remission following detoxification. Several reports indicate that pre-existing schizophrenia may precipitate chronic meth psychosis. They concluded that pre-existing schizophrenia and premorbid schizoid/schizotypal personality traits with a family history of schizophrenia among the first-degree relatives may predispose users to protracted psychotic symptoms.

Factors associated with persistent psychotic symptoms after abstinence were also examined in 295 individuals with methamphetamine abuse over a period of six months for patterns of methamphetamine and other substance use (Lecomte et al., 2013). Individuals with methamphetamine abuse and psychotic symptoms were assessed at baseline and then monthly for symptoms and substance use for six months. Analyses revealed two trajectories of the individuals with positive symptoms, with one group presenting with persistent psychotic symptoms (30% of the sample). Those with persistent psychosis were significantly older, had more severe psychotic symptoms, had misused methamphetamine for more years, had more antisocial personality traits, and had more sustained depressive symptoms. Strongest predictors of the persistent psychosis group demonstrated a dose dependent relationship between methamphetamine and psychosis, including more severe psychotic symptoms, longer use of methamphetamine, and sustained depressive symptoms. In a cohort study of 42,212 patients with methamphetamine-related conditions, the meth cohort had significantly higher odds of subsequently receiving a diagnosis of schizophrenia than cocaine, opioid, and alcohol groups (Callaghan, Cunningham, Allebeck, Arenovich, Sajeev et al., 2012).

With respect to the differential diagnosis of schizophrenia and substance-induced psychosis in the DSM-5 (American Psychiatric Association, 2013), the diagnosis of schizophrenia is made when there are at least two (or more) of the following criteria, each present for a significant portion of time during a one-month period: 1) delusions; 2) hallucinations, disorganized speech (e.g., frequent derailment or incoherence); and 3) grossly disorganized or catatonic behavior, negative symptoms (diminished emotional expression or avolition). Continuous signs of the disturbance must persist for at least six months and the disturbance is not attributable to the physiological effects of a substance (e.g., a drug of abuse). Individuals with substance/medication-induced psychotic disorder may present with symptoms characteristic of schizophrenia, but the substance-induced psychotic disorder can usually be distinguished by the chronological relationship of substance use to the onset and remission of the psychosis in the absence of substance use. Evidence of an independent psychotic disorder could include the following: 1) symptoms persist for a substantial period of time (e.g., about one month) after the cessation of acute withdrawal or severe intoxication, or 2) there are other signs of an independent, non-substance-induced psychotic disorder (e.g., a history of recurrent non-substance/medication-related episodes).

The Psychopharmacology of Methamphetamine Psychosis and Schizophrenia: Model Psychoses

Since the discovery of LSD's "psychotomimetic" properties in the early 1950s, investigators have proposed and studied a variety of chemical and animal models for schizophrenia and psychosis (Curran, D'Souza, Robbins, & Fletcher, 2009; Hollister, 1968). Similarities in the phenomenology of hallucinogenic drugs and primary endogenous psychoses have been of intense interest since the 1950s. Various drugs, including hallucinogens and amphetamine and methamphetamine in particular (Bell, 1965; Carhart-Harris, Brugger, Nutt, & Stone, 2013; Connell, 1958; Gonzales-Maeso & Sealfon, 2009; Janowsky & Risch, 1979; Snyder, 1973), have been proposed as pharmacological models for schizophrenia. "Clinical descriptions indicate the presence of psychedelic-like states with disturbances of visual perception, synesthesias, alterations of time and space perception and ecstatic-transcendental feelings during the incipient endogenous psychotic episodes" (Gouzoulis-Mayfrank et al., 1998, p. 400; Vollenweider, Vollenweider-Scherperhuyzen, Babler, Vogel, & Hell, 1998).

Experimental models of laboratory-induced psychosis have a fascinating and controversial history. The major neuropharmacological theories of schizophrenia have their origins in studies of the effects of drugs of abuse (Murray, Paparelli, Morrison, Marconi, & Di Forti, 2013). The notion that administration of psychoactive drugs can produce effects resembling symptoms of schizophrenia has both adherents and outspoken critics (Hollister, 1962; Snyder, 1973). There has been controversy about the extent to which effects induced by drugs can model the complex, diverse range of cognitive, emotional, and behavioral symptoms of the endogenous psychoses. Originally focused on the "dopamine theory of schizophrenia, increasingly sophisticated investigations have addressed the potential of drugs with prominent dopaminergic, serotonergic, glutamatergic, or cannabinoid actions" (Steeds, Carhart-Harris, & Stone, 2015). Early laboratory studies of amphetamine intoxication and experimentally induced psychosis found that the "induction of an amphetamine-sensitized state reproduces many of the deficits associated with schizophrenia, especially those most closely associated with positive symptoms" (Featherstone, Kapur, & Fletcher, 2007, p. 1566). Although drug-induced psychotic symptoms may not meaningfully model the complex and diverse disorders called schizophrenia, the mental changes induced by different psychotomimetics have continuing significant potential in delineating the pathophysiology of psychoses particularly with respect to pharmacological and endogenous dopamine sensitization mechanisms (Hermens et al., 2009; Howes & Kapur, 2009; Srisurapanont et al., 2011; Ujike, 2002).

Schizophrenia has long been considered a "dopamine disorder" based on the psychosis-inducing effects of dopamine-releasing drugs, such as amphetamine, and the anti-psychotic efficacy of the score of drugs that block the dopamine D2 receptor (Insel, 2010). Positron-Emission Tomography (PET) studies have suggested that hyperactivity of dopaminergic transmission is present in schizophrenia (Laruelle & Abi-Dargham, 1999). Amphetamine-induced dopamine release in the striatum, DOPA decarboxylase activity, and D2 receptor density in the striatum appears to be elevated in patients with schizophrenia, compared to normal controls. PET studies confirm hyperfrontality in both chronic and never-medicated, first-episode schizophrenia patients, which is associated with negative symptoms (Wong & Van Tol, 2003).

There have been several prospective, controlled studies in which amphetamine psychosis was experimentally induced in non-schizophrenic drug users (e.g., Griffith, Oates, & Cavanaugh, 1968; Angrist & Gershon, 1970; Angrist, Sathananthan, Wilk, & Gershon, 1974). These studies indicated that amphetamine psychosis can be induced in non-schizophrenic subjects. Researchers have used the relative prevalence of thought disorder; the degree of affective drive, lability, and blunting; as well as the type of hallucinations experienced to argue both in support of and against the presumption that similarities exist between amphetamine psychosis and schizophrenia. Janowsky and Risch (1979) found Schneider's first-rank symptoms in experimentally induced amphetamine psychosis in a number of subjects. Schneider's first-rank symptoms were found in at least 7, or possibly 10, of 15 cases, i.e., in 46%–66% of the subjects. They argued that the frequent occurrence of Schneider's first-rank symptoms and schizophrenia-discriminating symptoms in cases of experimentally induced amphetamine psychosis and non-schizophrenic subjects lends credence to the possibility that amphetamine-induced psychosis is a pharmacologic parallel of the schizophrenic state.

Advances in the understanding of brain neurotransmitter systems have enabled sophisticated emergent neurobiological models of schizophrenia (Steeds, Carhart-Harris, & Stone, 2015). Recent research investigated the relative strengths of dopaminergic, glutamatergic, serotonergic, cannabinoid, GABAminergic, cholinergic, and opioid pharmacological models of schizophrenia, comparing neurochemical findings of schizophrenia supporting the models and considering the effects of the candidate drugs in humans and contrasting evidence from animal models. The psychostimulants—amphetamine and cocaine—increase synaptic levels of dopamine and exacerbate psychotic episodes in people with existing schizophrenia (Laruelle & Abi-Dargham, 1999). The dopaminergic theory provides an explanation for some of the positive delusional syndromes of psychosis due to overactive mesolimbic dopaminergic transmission. Increasing evidence, however, suggests that serotonin may also be implicated. Novel atypical antipsychotics have potent antagonistic action at 5-H2 T receptors, and classic indolamine hallucinogens, which interfere with the serotonin system, can elicit schizophrenia-like symptoms in humans (Vollenweider, Vollenweider-Scherpenhuyzen, Babler, Vogel, & Hell, 1998).

Positive symptoms induced by amphetamines and cocaine include auditory hallucinations, thought disorder, and grandiose delusions, and chronic amphetamine users have been found to score highly on the Positive and Negative Syndrome Scale (PANSS). Dopaminergic psychostimulants provide a good model of the paranoid psychosis of schizophrenia but do not accurately mimic the cognitive or negative symptom domains. Currently, there remains no single coherent hypothesis for the pathogenesis of schizophrenia.

Other stimulants and hallucinogens have been examined in relation to schizophrenia. Both cocaine and phencyclidine (PCP) psychosis, for example, present a spectra of symptoms that can be found in schizophrenia (Erard, Luisada, & Peele, 1980). Phenomenologically, PCP and cocaine provoke delusions. The human psychoactive effects of PCP and LSD-25 include perceptual disturbances, sensory processing, cognition changes, changes in brain metabolism, and self-representation. PCP psychosis produces paranoid delusions, delusions of physical power, and transcendental delusions. In contrast, cocaine psychosis has been described as distinguishable from schizophrenia by the absence of flat affect, self-limited nature, presence of psychomotor agitation, and an insistent search for communication rather than avoidance of contact. Both stimulant-induced and PCP-induced psychoses have been proposed as models for the idiopathic psychosis of schizophrenia (Rosse et al., 1994). PCP-induced psychosis was less associated with suspiciousness and more associated with delusions of physical power, altered sensations, and unusual experiences. PCP-induced psychosis has been proposed as a better drug-induced model of schizophrenia than stimulant-induced psychosis because PCP psychosis induces a wider range of symptoms of schizophrenia, including not only positive symptoms, but negative symptoms as well. Overall, a preponderance of evidence indicates that the schizophrenia-related psychosis elicited by LSD-like drugs results from the drug complexing with postsynaptic cortical 5-HT 2A receptors.

Vollenweider, Vollenweider-Scherpenhuyzen, Babler, Vogel, and Hell (1998) corroborated suggestions of similarities between the early and acute stages of schizophrenia and the psychological effects of indoleamine-derived hallucinogens such as psilocybin and LSD. In particular, the finding that psilocybin-produced derealization and depersonalization associated with heightened mood, euphoria, grandiosity, and visual hallucinations is consistent with the observation that the earliest affective changes in incipient schizophrenia are often pleasurable and that visual, as opposed to auditory hallucinations, occur with higher prevalence in the first break than chronic schizophrenics. They found that psilocybin-induced psychosis could be completely prevented by either the atypical neuroleptic and mixed 5 HT 2/D2 antagonist risperidone or by the 5-HT 2 antagonist ketaserin, but not by the typical neuroleptic D2 antagonist haloperidol. Classical neuroleptics (e.g. Haldol or Thorazine) enhance rather than ameliorate LSD-induced psychosis. The classic amphetamine-induced model of psychosis has generally been used to assess the actions of typical antipsychotics, such as haloperidol, whose efficacy appears to be attributable to dopamine antagonism.

The particular malignance of MAP, characterized by bizarre hallucinations, paranoia, and violence, is most likely due to the predominance of dopaminergic neural mechanisms (similar to paranoid schizophrenia) and contrasts strongly with psychedelic experiences of psilocybin users. Psilocybin users described their experiences in religious terms, as ineffable, positive, life-changing experiences (Griffiths, Johnson, & Richards, 2011; Griffiths, Richards, McCann, Jesse, 2006; MacLean, Johnson & Griffiths, 2011). This appears to be directly related to the psychopharmacology and neurobiology of psilocybin, a serotonin 1A/2A/2C receptor agonist, enhances positive mood and attenuates recognition of negative facial expression and reduces neural responses to negative stimuli, including amygdala reactivity (Kometer, Schmidt, Bachmann, Studereus, Seifritz, & Vollenweider, 2012; Kraehenmann, Preller, Scheidegger, Pokorny, Bosch, Seifritz, & Vollenweider, 2015).

MAP Phenomenology: The Paranoid-Hallucinatory State

The phenomenology of psychosis in general and MAP in particular has been of interest to clinical investigators, including the development of standardized assessments of altered states on consciousness (Dittrich, 1998; Leamon et al., 2010). While the phenomenology of the psychoses is a topic too broad for coverage here, recent interest in a classification of psychotic symptoms including rare or atypical symptoms throws light on the unique, terrifying phenomenology of MAP (Ghaffari-Nejad, Ziaadini, Saffari-Zadeha, Kheradmand, & Pouya, 2014). Although euphoria is commonly reported by methamphetamine users before the onset of psychotic symptoms, MAP is almost uniformly described as a malignant psychosis—a toxic paranoid-hallucinatory state—characterized by paranoia and terror (Ujike & Sato, 2004). To assess psychotic phenomenology, investigators (Leamon et al., 2010) administered the Methamphetamine Experience Questionnaire to 274 methamphetamine-dependent subjects: 45% of subjects first experienced paranoia with methamphetamine use. Auditory hallucinations were the most frequently reported type of hallucination (67%), followed by visual (63%) and tactile (37%). Paranoid experiences were very distressing to subjects. A considerable number of subjects (37%) reported acting on their paranoia by obtaining a weapon, 11% reported using a weapon, and 15% had attacked others.

Multiple investigations have attempted to differentiate psychotic symptoms in MAP and schizophrenia. Harris and Batki (2000) compared the symptom profile of patients with cocaine- or amphetamine-induced psychosis and the relationship between the type and severity of psychotic symptoms and the type and intensity of emergency interventions required. PANSS scores indicated that in comparison to schizophrenic patients, MAP patients had a high level of positive symptoms and a moderately low (but still substantial) level of negative symptoms. All subjects had persecutory delusions, 89% had delusions of reference, 53% had grandiose delusions, 32% had somatic delusions, and 95% had bizarre delusions. Ninety-five percent had auditory hallucinations. The findings support previous reports of the predominance of positive symptoms in stimulant-induced psychosis but also that stimulant psychosis can mimic a broader range of schizophrenic symptoms, including substantial negative and bizarre symptoms.

Panenka et al. (2013) characterized drug use and associated mental illness in a predominately methamphetamine-using population in the urban setting of Vancouver, British Columbia. Consistent with other reports, psychotic symptoms were common among participants in their study. Both methamphetamine users and schizophrenic patients showed similar levels of psychosis for positive symptoms, which included delusions, grandiosity, suspiciousness, and hallucinations. By contrast, the methamphetamine users had lower scores than the schizophrenia patients on negative symptoms, which included variables such as blunted affect, thought disorganization, and social withdrawal. Methamphetamine users had higher scores than schizophrenic patients on affective symptoms such as hostility, anxiety, and depression. These observations indicate that methamphetamine-induced psychosis shares both similarities and differences with schizophrenia, which may have important implications with regards to diagnosis and treatment.

Sociodemographic and anamnestic variables also seem to be useful to clinicians because a personal or familial history of psychiatric disorders and poor premorbid functioning suggest a primary psychosis, whereas the presence of antisocial features and suicidal ideation is more frequent in the substance-induced psychoses. In a comprehensive study of MAP in Thailand, Srisurapanont et al. (2003) found negative psychotic symptoms in a substantial minority of patients (21.4% of 168 methamphetamine psychotic patients) with various ethnicities. Methamphetamine psychotic patients had more severe positive symptoms, i.e., delusions, hallucinations, incoherent speech, depression, and anxiety. They found a lifetime prevalence of specific psychotic symptoms ranging from 23% to 88%: Persecutory delusions were most prevalent followed by both visual and auditory hallucinations. The authors found three typologies based on endorsement of patterns of 14 psychotic symptoms experienced by methamphetamine-dependent individuals. Consistent with previous observations, all three typologies featured persecutory delusions. The authors estimated that 30% of people diagnosed with a stimulant-induced psychosis will be re-diagnosed with schizophrenia within eight years. Urging a modern version of the amphetamine model of psychosis, the authors support using MAP as a human model for studying the onset and course of schizophrenia.

In contrast to investigations that emphasize the similarities, Rosenthal and Miner (1997) derived a statistical model that distinguished between substance-induced psychosis and schizophrenia in patients who had both psychoactive substance use disorders and prominent delusions or hallucinations. Formal thought disorder and bizarre delusions significantly predicted the diagnosis of schizophrenia. The pattern of presenting symptoms and clinical history differentiated patients with MAP due to substance use disorders from those whose psychosis was due to schizophrenia. Thought disorder and bizarre delusions were major criterion subsets of schizophrenia, but not of substance use disorders. More specifically, patients with schizophrenia were preferentially sensitive to methylphenidate-induced increases in BRPS positive symptoms, hostility, and suspiciousness compared to non-schizophrenic controls (Sharma, Javaid, Pandey, Janicak, & Davis, 1991)—the result of post synaptic dopaminergic sensitivity. Using single photon emission computerized tomography, Laruelle, Abi-Dargham, Van Dyck, Gil, D'Souza et al. (1996) measured amphetamine-induced dopamine release in 15 schizophrenic patients. Increased binding of specific D_2 was observed in schizophrenic patients with emergence or worsening of positive symptoms.

A classification taxonomy of psychotic symptoms may be of some value in the disambiguation of schizophrenia and MAP. Seven different paranoid-hallucinatory syndromes of schizophrenia have been identified in cross-cultural studies: religious grandiosity, low perception syndrome, coenesthetic hypochondria syndromes, apocalyptic guilt syndrome, persecutory syndrome, poisoning syndrome, and delusional jealousy (Stompe et al., 2007). Iranian investigators sought to identify phenomenological differences between methamphetamine-induced psychotic symptoms and schizophrenic symptoms. Their qualitative study aimed to explain the psychotic experience of patients with amphetamine-induced psychosis using the descriptive phenomenological method (Ghaffari-Nejad et al., 2014). The analysis was performed according to the seven-stage Colaizzi method (a qualitative methodology for descriptive phenomenology). Patients with methamphetamine-induced psychosis presented more rare psychotic symptoms, even ones that have not been reported before, than typically encountered in other psychoses. These include oneiroid states, scene hallucinations, Capgras and Cotard's syndromes, somatic delusions, lycanthropy, conditional transmogrification, synesthesias, and formication.

Psychological Assessment of MAP

Research on the use of psychodiagnostic methods to differentiate schizophrenia and MAP is quite limited. A literature search of the PSYCINFO database yielded no studies with search terms "methamphetamine" and "Rorschach." Perry and colleagues (1995) examined single-dose amphetamine intoxication in 22 normal undergraduates using Rorschach anxiety and thought disorder variables (Ego Impairment Index). They found that a single dose of amphetamine in normal subjects increased stress and anxiety indicators, but not thought disorder indicators on the Rorschach.

There is a limited body of studies examining the Rorschach and psychedelic drugs (e.g., Barr, Langs, Holt, Goldberger, & Klein, 1972; Bercel, Travis, Olinger, & Dreikurs, 1956; Levine, Abramson, Kaufman, Markham, & Kornetsky, 1955). Early studies noted the similarity between psychedelics and schizophrenia. Rorschach responses were regarded by some to be similar to those of schizophrenics, while appearing to others to be more like acute exogenous psychosis. Almost every observer commented upon the increased tendency toward concrete thinking (Hollister, 1964).[1] The literature includes two papers in which Rorschach test data are considered in relation to amphetamine use, both cited in Weiner (1964). Some Rorschach test findings indicate that amphetamine use produces increased responsivity and emotionality, but no decrease in reality testing capacity. Weiner suggested that further validity studies of Rorschach indices of emotionality and reality testing may contribute significantly to early differentiation of amphetamine psychosis from paranoid schizophrenic reactions. Clearly, this is an area that deserves further investigation.

METHAMPHETAMINE PSYCHOSIS AND VIOLENCE

The association between MAP and violence has been noted from the earliest accounts in the psychiatric literature. Ellinwood (1971) described 13 cases of individuals who committed homicide while intoxicated with amphetamines. In most of these cases, the events leading to the homicidal act were directly related to amphetamine-induced paranoid thinking, panic, emotional lability, or lowered impulse control. In 6 of 13 cases, paranoia was the primary condition during the homicide. Three persons with low tolerance took large amounts of amphetamines over a period of a few hours; all three developed paranoid panic states.

A study of the amphetamine trade in Oklahoma City in the 1960s described bizarre violence associated with amphetamines parties. During the Japanese epidemic of amphetamine abuse, 31 out of 60 convicted murderers had some connection with misuse of amphetamines (Fukushima, 1994). The three phases leading to violent conduct follow a sequence of chronic amphetamine use, acute changes in the individual state of emotional arousal, and situational factors that trigger the specific events leading to the act of violence. The phase of chronic methamphetamine abuse sets the stage, and includes changes in the individual's frame of mind including suspiciousness, paranoid thinking, and fearful regard of the environment.

Typologies of drug use and violence have been proposed (Boles & Miotto, 2003; Hoaken & Stewart, 2003): psychopharmacological violence, systemic violence, and economic compulsive violence. Four explanations have been offered regarding the relation of psychostimulants and violence: a) psychostimulant users could have an inherent propensity to engage in aggressive behavior, b) aggression is a result of psychostimulant withdrawal, c) aggressive behavior is a means to gain access to psychostimulants, and d) psychostimulants can induce/exacerbate psychotic symptoms, which increases the likelihood of violent behavior. It is the fourth explanation that is primarily considered in this chapter.

Tyner & Fremouw (2008) critically examined the empirical literature on methamphetamine use and violence. Their review served to clarify the relation of methamphetamine and violence by critically examining existing literature on methamphetamine and violence from 1975 to 2005. The population covered by this literature was representative of the worldwide epidemiology of methamphetamine. Included were samples from Japan, Thailand, Hawaii, and California, where methamphetamine use is regarded as problematic. Their comprehensive review elaborated on methamphetamine and its epidemiology, consequences of use, and relation to violence. Approximately half of adult probationers, a third of state prisoners, and a quarter of federal prisoners report being intoxicated at the time of the offense. Of all adult arrestees in the United States, at least half test positive for one or more drugs at the time of detainment. Almost a third of victims of violent crime perceived the perpetrator to be under the influence of drugs at the time of the offense.

Incidence of aggression and violence was studied in 1,060 methamphetamine users in a multi-site outpatient treatment study (Zweben et al., 2004). They reported high levels of problems controlling anger and violent behavior, with a correspondingly high frequency of assault and weapons charges. Measures indicated increased frequency of violent behavior or crimes, assault, use of weapons, and self-assessment of difficulty controlling angry behavior or anger: 43% reported they had problems controlling their violent behavior, with a disproportionately elevated number of assault and weapons incidents. A study of 39 methamphetamine-abstinent dependent users and controls examined aggression and alexithymia (Payer, Lieberman, & London, 2011). Methamphetamine-dependent participants self-reported more aggression and alexithymia than control participants and perpetrated aggression more following provocation.

McKetin, McLaren, Lubman, and Hides (2008; see also McKetin, McLaren, Riddell, & Robins, 2006) examined MAP and violence in a sample of 71 methamphetamine users experiencing psychotic symptoms. They noted that the main symptoms of MAP are persecutory ideation and hallucinatory experiences (auditory and visual), and described a clinical presentation strikingly similar to acute paranoid schizophrenia. Methamphetamine-related psychiatric admissions were more likely to be associated with aggressive behavior than other psychiatric admissions. Methamphetamine-related homicides strongly suggest a link with paranoia brought on by the drug (citing Ellinwood, 1971). Using the Brief

Psychiatric Rating Scale, 23% of participants had experienced a clinically significant symptom of psychosis in the past year and 27% of participants reported pathological hostility during the preceding year.

There appears to be a dose-related increase in violent behavior during periods of methamphetamine use that is largely independent of the violence risk associated with psychotic symptoms. McKetin et al. (2014) found a clear dose-response increase in violent behavior when participants were using methamphetamine compared to when they were not using the drug. Although psychotic symptoms significantly exacerbated the risk of violent behavior, the relationship between methamphetamine use and violent behavior was largely independent of psychotic symptoms, suggesting a direct relationship between the drug and violent behavior. From a public health point of view, the findings indicate that violence is a key harm associated with methamphetamine use.

Stretsky (2009) examined the relationship between methamphetamine use and homicide, using the National Household Survey on Drug Abuse and the Survey of Inmates in State and Federal Correctional Facilities. The main exposure measure was methamphetamine, and the main outcome measure was homicide. The results suggest that the odds of committing a homicide are nearly nine times greater for an individual who uses methamphetamine. More important, the association between methamphetamine use and homicide persists even after adjusting for alternative drug use, sex, race, income, age, marital status, previous arrest, military experience, and education level. Methamphetamine was the only drug use variable that was strongly correlated with homicide. Of 205 frequent methamphetamine users who resided in Los Angeles, California, 26% of the study respondents said they were violent (defined as any form of deliberate physical harm inflicted on another individual) under the influence of methamphetamine. The association between methamphetamine use and homicide is for methamphetamine users who report using methamphetamine within the previous month (odds ratio 13.87).

COMPARATIVE CASE STUDY OF MAP HOMICIDE VERSUS PARANOID SCHIZOPHRENIA

Introduction

This study compared Rorschach test protocols of two individuals referred for diagnostic assessments: one individual diagnosed with schizophrenia, paranoid type, and the other with methamphetamine dependence and methamphetamine-induced psychotic disorder. Of special interest was the degree to which the test protocols could be distinguished on critical Rorschach indicators of psychosis.

The Rorschach assessment of psychotic disorders rests on a robust behavioral science foundation, which has been largely exempt from attacks by Rorschach method critics (Acklin, 1999). The Rorschach Inkblot Test is of particular value in relation to the problems with self-report where individual may attempt to underreport, exacerbate, or malinger psychopathology. Hermann Rorschach noted the characteristic aspects of "schizophrenic" thinking in his seminal monograph (1942). Rorschach observed boundary disturbances and combinatory thinking frequently noted in psychotic records, including the contamination response (Schwartz & Lazar, 1984), observing that schizophrenics "give many interpretations in which confabulation, combination, and contamination are mixed in together." Rapaport referred to "deviant verbalizations" as indicative of thought disturbance (e.g., fabulized combinations, confabulations, and contaminations), the examination of which was "the highway for investigating disorders of thinking" (cited in Kleiger, 1999, p. 46).

Exner developed the Comprehensive System (CS) for the Rorschach after reviewing and integrating the splintered Rorschach scoring approaches extant in the late 1960s (Exner, 1969). Exner (1974) gathered a group of codes for unusual verbalizations, known as Special Scores, which became the basis for several variable clusters reflecting perceptual and thinking disturbances: Deviant Verbalizations (DV), Deviant Responses (DR), Incongruous Combinations (INCOM), Fabulized Combinations (FABCOM), Contaminations (CONTAM), and Autistic Logic (ALOG), which are weighted and summarized in a single score: the WSum6. The WSum6 serves as a gross measure of the amount of thought disorder present in the record. Combining the Special Scores with several other variables associated with psychosis led to a composite index to detect "schizophrenia" (the Schizophrenia Index [SCZI]: M-, weighted Special Scores, low X+% and F + %, CF + C, high X-%, and the absence of whole human responses) (Exner, 1993). The SCZI showed reasonably good clinical sensitivity, but also a rather high false-positive rate. Examiners using the SCZI to identify schizophrenia were warned to be alert to the distinct possibility of obtaining a false positives. In

1990, Exner added Level 1 and Level 2 distinctions to responses, based on their degree of deviancy, which improved the discriminatory power of the SCZI Index. Later, these levels and other refinements were used in converting the SCZI in the Comprehensive System by the Perceptual-Thinking Index (PTI; Exner, 2000), which reduced the false-positive rate and focused on the identification of psychosis in general, not just schizophrenia. A PTI of three or greater usually identifies serious adjustment problems attributable to ideational dysfunction. Recent international studies have confirmed the PTI as a discriminating variable in psychosis (e.g., Benedik, Coderl, Bon, & Smith, 2013). Biagiarelli et al. (2015) demonstrated validity of the Comprehensive System PTI with the Positive and Negative Syndrome Scale (PANSS), finding that X-% significantly correlated with negative symptoms, WSum6 with thought disorder, and M- with delusions. Smith and colleagues (2001) validated the PTI in children and adolescents findings that M- was a particularly robust indicator of thought disorder. Hilsenroth and colleagues (2007) demonstrated the strong similarity of Exner's SCZI and PTI (r = 0.96), robust interrater reliability, strong discriminant validity, and accuracy in the classification of psychotic disorders.

The Rorschach Performance Assessment System™ (R-PAS™; Meyer, Viglione, Mihura, Erard, & Erdberg, 2011) was introduced to correct mounting criticism of the Comprehensive System's psychometric problems and to continue to incorporate new research into Rorschach assessment. The Comprehensive System (CS) PTI was converted using a weighted regression formula into the Thought-Perception Composite (TP-Comp) as a measure of perceptual and thinking problems for R-PAS. It has been shown to be associated with everyday behavior and social functioning in schizophrenia (Moore, Viglione, Rosenfarb, Patterson, & Mausbach, 2013; Viglione, Giromini, Gustafson, & Meyer, 2014). Dzamonia-Ignjatovic, Smith, Jocic, and Milanovic (2013) compared CS and R-PAS psychosis variables, finding that both were effective in differentiating schizophrenic from non-schizophrenic patients but that the R-PAS TP-Comp and the Ego Impairment Index (EII-3; a composite measure of thought disturbance and psychological impairment) had better predictive power. A recent Taiwanese study demonstrated the validity of R-PAS indices in the classification of psychosis and incremental validity of R-PAS perception and thinking variables over CS counterparts (Su, Viglione, Green, Tam, Su, & Chang, 2015).

Hypotheses

It was hypothesized, based on the common perception that schizophrenia and MAP are indistinguishable, that the two Rorschach protocols would not be distinguishable on primary R-PAS indicators of psychosis. Of particular interest were components of the Perception and Thinking Problems section of the R-PAS results page, which includes a set of variables associated with both psychosis and everyday and social functioning in schizophrenia (Moore, et al., 2012). Among these, the EII-3 was a specific focus.

The following variables were also examined: TP-Comp (composed of six variables), WSumCog and SevCog (measures of thought disorder), Distorted Form Quality Percent and Common Area Distorted Form Quality Percent (FQ-% and WD-%; both measures of arbitrary perception, which has been implicated in negative symptoms of schizophrenia), and FQo% and Populars (both measures of conventional perception). Several additional variables were examined which have shown value in the discrimination of psychosis: the Vigilance Composite (V-Comp), Critical Contents% (CritCont%), M-, and human representation variables from the Self and Other Representations cluster.

Method

Both records were administered according to the R-Optimized administration instructions and scored according to the R-PAS scoring manual (Meyer, et al., 2011). Standard Scores, percentile ranks, and +/-1SD difference scores were examined. Information in the case studies is camouflaged to protect the identity of the participants.

Case 1: Mr. PS

PS was referred by a local psychiatrist for a psychological evaluation to provide a differential diagnosis and treatment recommendations.

Mr. PS was a single, 39-year-old Caucasian man, the second of three children of a physician. His parents commented, "We've been worried about him since he was three." He struggled academically in elementary school, especially on his refusal to do homework, but excelled in math and was enrolled at a very young age in mathematics in an elite California state university. He was always very quiet, undisclosive, sometimes unintelligible, and emotionally unexpressive. His mother remarked that he never got angry. Intelligence testing done at an unspecified age reportedly yielded an IQ of 153.

He earned a bachelor's degree in computer science in 1995 and obtained a master's degree in 1997, but did not invite his parents to the latter graduation. His first job with a software company ended after 18 months with his being laid off. He estimated that he has had ten jobs in 20 years. Most recently, he was recruited to work at a large Internet company. In April 2012, his mother learned inadvertently that he had been fired the previous March. He was unable to explain why he had been fired; he vaguely alluded to a poor work attitude. He has remained unemployed since then.

During his sister's recent wedding, his parents, alarmed at his recent weight gain and overall deteriorated appearance, and concerned about his declining vocational and financial status, invited him to come home to allow him to regroup. This did not occur. He spent a lot of time in his room, with the door locked, and apparently slept a lot. He did not engage with his family but reportedly went out in the evening to play chess in a local park. For years, he failed to answer phone calls or e-mails.

On at least one occasion, his mother was unable to get a response at his apartment. On other occasions, when visiting she found his living space a shambles of boxes, old documents, and unopened mail. Although he traditionally visited home for Christmas, he failed to do so from 1998 to 2000. At one point during that time, he called his mother in the middle of the night to report, "I think dad is gay," apparently based on his father's habit of playfully pinching his behind. On another occasion at 2003, he abruptly appeared at his sister's, having driven from San Diego to Sacramento, to report excitedly, "Something's wrong ... I'm not thinking straight!"

Over the years, his parents have made abortive attempts to obtain an explanation for his peculiar behavior, but these have had the character of guessing or grasping at straws. For example, several years ago, after reading reports of delayed effects of concussions, his father arranged for a neuropsychological evaluation that was begun but not completed. The testing psychologist, puzzled, wondered if he had Asperger's syndrome. Most recently, the possibility of ADHD was raised, which was the basis for the referral to the psychiatrist.

During the interview, Mr. PS was described as overweight and casually dressed. He was pleasant and cooperative, with a relative lack of emotional expression. He was extremely vague, although his thought processes did not seem disordered. At the end of the interview, the psychiatrist reported that he felt he knew very little about him and would gain little from further questioning. Mr. PS and his parents agreed to the psychological evaluation with the rationale that testing might lead to some intervention that could improve his life. The psychiatrist posed the query, "The question is what is his diagnosis in the broadest sense?"

Mr. PS was examined over a two-day period, since he had traveled from an outer island to Honolulu. His mother, who accompanied him, provided collateral information. Although he was continuously cooperative, he demonstrated minimal interaction with the examiner and a very flat affect. At the time of the examination, he was taking no medications.

Results of Psychological Testing: MMPI-2

This is a valid MMPI-2 protocol with a Welsh code of 6*8"2'70+-459–1/3:F'+-/:LK#. Mr. PS's MMPI-2 validity profile demonstrated elevated F (T = 79) and F_B (T = 87) scales, indicating significant levels of psychopathology, accompanied by very low L (T = 39), K (T = 35), and S (T = 34), indicative of an overreporting response set, likely associated with psychological deterioration and collapse. The PSY-5 scales, Content, and Content Component scales indicate the presence of Psychoticism (T = 85), Negative Symptoms (T = 70), Bizarre Mentation (T = 74), and Psychotic Symptomatology (T = 95). His Paranoia subscales are elevated, especially Persecutory Ideas (T = 94). Mr. PS's 682 code type, along with a prominent "paranoid valley," is commonly seen in paranoid schizophrenic individuals (Friedman, Lewak, Nichols, & Webb, 2001). Mr. PS is likely moody, hostile (ANG2: Irritability T = 71), withdrawn, negativistic, emotionally inappropriate, uncomfortable around people, and spends much of his time, as his parents report, alone and self-absorbed in fantasy. His relations with his family are seriously troubled (Family Discord T = 65). Significant thinking problems are present including unrealistic ideas, misinterpretations, or frank delusions. He is likely to be perceived by others as odd, unusual or bizarre. He demonstrates a significant apathy syndrome (Mental Dullness T = 76, Brooding T = 70, Lack of Drive T = 77, Submissiveness T = 72). He endorsed a large number of critical items reflecting anxiety, depression, hostility, persecutory ideas, family conflict, and deviant beliefs.

Mr. PS was administered the Schedule for Nonadaptive and Adaptive Personality second edition (SNAP-2) to augment the assessment data. He scored low on desirability (T = 40), high on deviance (T = 71), with significant elevations on mistrust (T = 65), self-harm (T = 69), detachment (T = 75), paranoid (T = 67), schizotypal (T = 65), schizoid (T = 81), and depressive diagnostic (T = 76) scales. The SNAP-2 appeared to present a valid and accurate picture of Mr. PS's mental health status.

Results of Psychological Testing: R-PAS

Mr. PS's Rorschach profile indicates serious problems in thinking clearly and perceiving people, and his environment accurately (EII-3 SS = 143, 99th PR; TP-Comp SS = 142, 99th PR). Profile scales show severe disturbances in thought processes that are most indicative of psychotic-level lapses in conceptualization, reasoning, communication, or thought organization (WSumCog SS = 148, 99th PR). Mr. PS's distortion and misinterpretation are strongly associated with reality disturbance and psychopathology, indicative of poor judgments or unconventional behavior.

Internal imagery and preoccupations overwhelm Mr. PS's ability to process and interpret external reality. He may describe things in a mistaken, distorted, overly personalized way that others will not understand. These distortions and reality disturbance occurs even in perceptual situations that are common and familiar (WD-% SS = 143, 99th PR).

Mr. PS's profile suggests a highly problematic understanding of self and others (SumH 75, 5th PR). He sees himself and others in a distorted, illogical, unrealistic, and partial manner. He has serious difficulty understanding other people as complex whole individuals (PHR/GPHR SS = 136, 99th PR). He views himself and others in unrealistic or fantastical ways. The findings suggest a tendency to identify with fantasy characters from popular culture or with Mr. PS's own idiosyncratic fantasy life.

Overall, Mr. PS's Rorschach profile shows elevations on several measures of thought disorder. Additionally, he appears to be highly vigilant in a manner that is consistent with paranoid thinking (V-Comp SS = 118, 89th PR). He appears to have lapses in cognitive processes, in both the representation of self and others and perception and thinking problems (EII-3 SS = 143, 99th PR). His thought patterns are not likely due to immaturity but rather an inefficient and idiosyncratic way of thought processing (Populars SS = 80, 9th PR; FQo% SS = 85, 16th PR). In his interactions with others, Mr. PS shows difficulty mentalizing and understanding others. He has notable problems in his internalized sense of others. He has serious problems in recognizing and appreciating others' points of view in problems and situations, which often leads to misreading and misunderstanding. Mr. PS's distortions and misinterpretations are strongly associated with reality disturbance and psychopathology, often leading to poor judgments or unconventional behavior.

Mr. PS's DSM-IV clinical diagnosis of schizophrenia, paranoid type, was consistent with his history, clinical presentation, and psychological evaluation findings, particularly his R-PAS findings.

Case 2: Mr. MAP

MAP was referred by the public defender for a psychological evaluation to assess his competence to stand trial and take criminal responsibility in the context of prosecution for a grisly murder.

Mr. MAP was charged with murder in the second degree in the death of a 34-year-old male. The decedent's body was dismembered into seven parts separated by six circumferential incised wounds; 49 additional sharp-force injuries to various body parts were also present. The medical examiner observed 46 sharp-force injuries to the lower and upper neck and upper extremities, including injuries to lungs and liver, and three sharp-force injuries to the pelvic area and proximal thighs. The decedent's dismembered body parts were discovered in a shallow grave in suburban Honolulu. Other body parts were found in a state of decomposition on an adjacent hillside. The decedent's toxicological analysis revealed the presence of methamphetamine, amphetamine, tetrahydrocannabinol, ethanol, and a by-product of nicotine. Cause of death was determined to be the result of multiple sharp-force injuries.

Mr. MAP is a married, 47-year-old man, born on the West Coast. He was raised in Southern California, graduated from high school, and received a master's degree in 1997. He obtained a real estate broker's license. He had an extensive history of methamphetamine and other hallucinogen use. This included several psychiatric hospitalizations for methamphetamine-induced psychosis. He had an initial psychotic episode in 1972, following heavy methamphetamine use. He had further psychiatric treatment in the 1990s, including several rehab experiences, all organized around methamphetamine dependence.

He reports that he typically experiences hallucinations when under the influence of crystal methamphetamine. He sees and hears things, even when not using drugs, and has become accustomed to his hallucinations. In 2011 and 2012, he began using "bath salts" (amphetamine-like substances that cause an agitated delirium and violent behavior) in addition to methamphetamine, which he thinks precipitated a psychotic episode in fall 2012. He reportedly made a trip to Hawaii in 2012: "All I thought about was methamphetamine. I was hooked on methamphetamine. I had a methamphetamine addiction."

Mr. MAP came to Hawaii with his wife to acquire a condo residence for vacation rental. The work involved leasing a suitable condo unit and rehabbing and decorating the unit as a vacation rental. His wife left while he was supposed to do the work. Instead, he went on a methamphetamine binge. He found online listings on Craigslist of people advertising marijuana and established contact with street dealers in Waikiki. He reports that during the time he was supposed to be rehabbing the condominium unit, "My personal drives went wild." He says that he and the decedent engaged in cross-dressing. He recalls that he bought clothing items from the adult store within walking distance of the condo. "Mainly I did it, I wanted girls there to amplify it . . . he was showing that he was a psycho. I was playing the female role." He imagined that he was "a powerful, beautiful woman." He was using methamphetamine every day, cross-dressing, and partying with the street dealer and his male and female friends. While he was staying in the condo, people came over to party at all hours of the day and night. Mr. MAP was "all dressed up" in women's clothes. He notes that the decedent had street connections: "Low life in Waikiki."

The eleventh floor condo overlooked Waikiki. As time went on, he began to feel "trapped" in the condo: "There was this guy who was acting psychotic. We got a warning about the noise; we had to cut down." He thought he could read the decedent's thoughts: "We had a psychic connection." He states, "We had many conversations ideas having to do with aliens, earth and air, friction, and carried ongoing psychic conversations." Gradually, "I became in fear of my life." He reports that he heard a voice in the decedent's head telling him to kill me. "I thought maybe it was the government. I thought he was supposed to kill me." He described the absurdity of the situation: "The guy was big, muscular. I was dressed down as a woman. I had a limited way out; he had my keys." He reports an increasing, brooding sense of doom: "I was afraid. I knew he had a knife; once I tried to run out of the unit, he stopped me. I thought he was trying to kidnap me; he was guarding the front door. I thought I was being kidnapped by a guy with a knife." He took down a large mirror from the wall, which he was going to use as a shield to "confuse my attacker." He barricaded himself on the lanai of the condo unit with the mirror: "I was in a defensive position." That day he thought he was having a stroke; he felt like he "was a priest in hell. All of these devils were assaulting me; he [the decedent] was one of the demons. Satan was trying to kill me." He reports that he was hearing voices, hallucinating. Late in the afternoon, the decedent was asleep in the guest room. "I didn't have a weapon. I broke the mirror and took a shard of glass. I put a towel around it, went into the guestroom; he was reclining with his knife. I tried to grab the knife. I stabbed him in the neck; he came at me. I stabbed him with the knife in the torso."

He says following the murder, he wandered around Waikiki in a paranoid fog. "I didn't know what to do." He wondered if he should call the police. He dismembered the body with tools purchased at Home Depot, put the dismembered body parts in the condo refrigerator, and then left for ten days to the mainland. While on the mainland, he entered a drug rehab program under pressure from his family. In the interim, the dismembered body was in the condo refrigerator. It was difficult getting the body to fit into the refrigerator. He took out the inside of the refrigerator so the body would fit.

He describes the "overall thing was a bizarre scene amplified by meth." He thought he was under surveillance by the government. He got information from a website called Godlike Productions, and was concerned about being "on their radar." He had fantasies of being an "intergalactic diplomat." He describes dismembering the body as "surreal." The whole experience was surrounded by hallucinations. Before killing the decedent, "I had an ongoing awareness that he had a knife." He drove 20 miles away and tried to dispose of the body parts, but the ground was very hard. About ten days later, a man walking his dog near a cemetery about 20 miles away noticed a partially buried body and called police, who recovered the dismembered body from two shallow graves.

Mr. MAP was examined over a two-day period at the local jail where he was in pre-trial custody. He was taking no medications. He appeared to be irritable, with a flat, negative affect, with continuing complaints of auditory hallucinations and many bizarre ideas. He was observed to be a ragged, undernourished man with an edgy, hostile attitude, who nevertheless complied with the psychological evaluation

Results of Psychological Testing: MMPI-2

Mr. MAP responded to all items on the MMPI-2. His profile is consistent with the Welsh Code of 4*86"9'7+2-015/3:F***"'+-/:*LK#*. The grossly elevated F (T = 120), FB (T = 92), and FP (T = 94) suggested an overreporting response set, which, as in all forensic examinations raises concerns about faking bad. On the other hand, his very low L (T = 39), K (T = 39), and S (T = 30) suggest significant deterioration and psychological collapse. The 486 code type is consistent with serious psychopathology, including a "paranoid valley" (Friedman, Lewak, Nichols, & Webb, 2001) commonly encountered in individuals with paranoid schizophrenia. Elevated Psychopathic Deviancy (T = 90) and Hypomania (T = 72) reflect a picture of tense agitation. On the MMPI-2 Restructured Clinical Scales, Content Scales, PSY-5, Harris Lingoes subscales, and Content Component Scales, a picture of florid psychopathology is presented: Ideas of Persecution (T = 88), Dysfunctional Negative Emotionality (T = 75), Aberrant Experiences (T = 83), and Hypomanic Activation (T = 63), Bizarre Mentation (T = 98), Psychoticism (T = 107), and Persecutory Ideas (T = 112). He elevated on measures of cynicism (RC T = 80), substance use (AAS T = 70), and family discord (FAM T = 69).

Mr. MAP was administered the MCMI-III as a supplemental measure: He scored very high on Disclosure (BR = 92), Dependent (BR = 91), Antisocial (BR = 91), Drug Dependence (BR = 107), and Delusional Disorder (BR = 102).

Results of Psychological Testing: R-PAS

Mr. MAP's responses on the R-PAS reveal a markedly high degree of disturbance. His extremely high score on the TP-Comp score (SS = 142, 99th PR) reveals a level of thinking and reality testing disturbances that would typically be found in individuals with drug-induced psychotic disorders or schizophrenic disorders. His WSumCog score (SS = 148, 99th PR) is extremely high and provides further evidence of disturbed and disordered thinking. He likely has difficulty in reasoning, communication, and thought organization. His extremely elevated SevCog score (SS = 148, 99th PR) indicates severe disruption in thought processes that are typically most indicative of psychotic-level lapses in conceptualization, reasoning, communication, or thought organization. His high proportion of Color dominant responses [(CF+C)/SumC = 126, 96th PR] indicate very poor emotional controls and the likelihood of explosive emotional reactivity.

Interpersonally, his abundance of responses involving Aggressive Content (SS = 120, 91st PR) and Aggressive Movement (SS = 110, 75th PR) indicates an identification with power, aggressiveness, and dangerousness. He may also fear elements in his environment and vacillate between fears of attack and urges to assault others. He has difficulty understanding people as complex and whole individuals, as indicated by his difficulty in representing whole humans in his responses. His low COP score (SS = 88, 21st PR) indicates that he also views relationships as non-supportive and uncooperative.

His extremely high score on CritCont% (SS = 140, 99th PR) draws on a range of codes reflecting response imagery that is often censored or inhibited in general social interactions. It was developed as a measure of ego lapse or failure to censor problematic imagery. This score presents three possibilities to consider 1) a history of trauma and propensity for dissociation; 2) the presence of crude or primitive cognitions that suggest a failure of censorship (as in borderline or psychotic states); 3) exaggeration and malingering by expressing crude, dramatic, or disturbing imagery on the test in an effort to be shocking (Ganellen, Wasyliw, Haywood, & Grossman, 1996).

Mr. MAP's DSM-IV clinical diagnosis, based on the history, clinical presentation, and psychological evaluation, was methamphetamine dependence in early sustained remission in controlled environment, and methamphetamine-induced psychotic disorder with hallucinations and delusions. The wounds suffered by the decedent, 49 sharp-force stab wounds, clearly indicative of "overkill," suggests a frenzied fatal assault consistent with affective violence and rage-type murder (Cartwright,

2002). At the time of the commission of the homicide, his cognitive and volitional capacities were substantially impaired due to chronic voluntary methamphetamine intoxication.

In order to compare the two Rorschach records, selected R-PAS indicators are listed in Table 8.1, with particular interest in the Perception and Thinking and Self and Other Representation clusters in order to demonstrate similarities and differences between the two clinical presentations.

Mr. PS and Mr. MAP differed on responses, prompts, and pulls, but not on card turning. The records demonstrate similar levels of complexity. Of the 15 psychotic indicators, 11 of the variables were indistinguishable using a -1/+1 SD difference (MAP/MAHP could not be compared, because Mr. PS's record did not contain codable responses). On all of the major psychosis indicators, both records show severe thought disturbance and impaired reality testing. Of the three remaining variables, Mr. MAP's record indicates higher Populars, M- (an indicator of delusional processes), and Critical Contents. Both records reflect presence of thought disorder indicators, uniformly poor perceptual accuracy and objection relations, and high levels of hypervigilance, which essentially "red line" test perceptual and thinking indicators.

Conclusions

Comparison of Rorschach psychosis indicators reflect insignificant differences, supporting the well documented similarity in the phenomenology of schizophrenia and MAP. Both protocols indicate severe impairments in perception and thinking. All of the R-PAS psychosis indicators are positive for both cases, which are well established in the Rorschach literature, and were extremely high in both. At least for the primary R-PAS indicators for disturbed thinking, including impaired reality testing and thought disorder, the two protocols were indistinguishable. Similarly, the MMPI-2's were indicative of psychosis (with a notable sociopathic character features observed in Mr. MAP's clinical profile). As noted by previous commentators (Hollister, 1962; Rosenthal & Miner, 1997), given similarities of clinical presentation, extra-Rorschach indicators, most notably the clinical and substance history, would be critical in differential diagnosis.

Table 8.1: Comparison of R-PAS MAP and Paranoid Schizophrenia Indicators[2]

Domain/Variables		Mr. PS		Mr. MAP		Diff
		SS	PR	SS	PR	−1SD/+1SD
Administrative Behaviors						
	Prompts	89	24	104	62	+⟩
	Pulls	96	40	116	86	+⟩
	Card Turning	86	18	86	18	o
Responses		102	55	92	30	⟨+
Complexity		92	30	98	45	o
Perception and Thinking Problems						
	EII-3	143	>99	143	>99	o
	TP-Comp	142	99	142	99	o
	WSumCog	148	>99	148	>99	o
	SevCog	144	>99	144	>99	o
	FQ-	143	>99	143	>99	o
	WD-%	143	>99	143	>99	o
	FQo%	85	16	87	20	o
	P	80	09	103	94	+⟩
	MAP/MAHP	NA	—	123	94		
	PHR/GHR	136	99	133	99	o
	M-	95	36	123	94	+⟩
	V-Comp	118	89	121	92	o
	CritCont%	86	17	140	>99	+⟩
Self and Other Representation						
	SumH	109	74	113	81	o
	NPH/SumH	127	96	122	93	o

The Psychobiology of Violence

Two major types of human aggressive behavior have been distinguished (Meloy, 2006). The first, "affective" violence is characterized by intense emotional arousal, like anger/or fear, in response to a perceived threat. The second type of aggression, "instrumental" or "predatory" violence is aggressive behavior with reduced emotional reactivity, which looks premeditated and deliberate. Affective aggression is exhibited in all mammalian species and appears to be mediated through the amygdala-hypothalamus-periaqueductal gray ("basic threat system"), regulated by several regions of the frontal cortex, and the orbital, medial, and ventrolateral frontal cortex (Blair, 2012). Serotonin facilitates prefrontal cortical regions, such as the orbital frontal cortex (OFC) and anterior cingulate cortex (ACC), which are involved in modulating and suppressing the emergence of aggressive behaviors primarily by acting on serotonin 5-HT2 receptors (Siever, 2008). Gabaminergic reactivity and GABA receptors also reduce subcortical reactivity; therefore, reduced gabaminergic activity can increase aggression. Raine and colleagues (1998) used PET scans to distinguish affective and predatory murderers findings that affective murderers have lower prefrontal activity and higher subcortical activity than comparisons. Predatory murderers have prefrontal level similar to nonclinical comparisons, but excessive subcortical activity. Analysis of the mechanism of inducing reactive aggression in mammals in response to a threat provides experimental evidence linking the aggression and fear (Blair, 2012). These findings have been validated in a variety of clinical syndromes with increased risk of aggression, e.g., intermittent explosive disorder (Coccaro, McCloskey, Fitzgerald, & Phan, 2007), PTSD, and borderline personality disorder (Silva, Derecho, Leong, Weinstock, & Ferrari, 2001).

The emotional substrates of impulsive or affective aggression implicate the amygdala, hippocampus, hypothalamus, anterior cingulate cortex, insular cortex, ventral striatum, and other interconnected corticolimbic structures. The amygdala is activated in situations that connote threat and general negative affect (Davidson, Putnam, & Larson, 2000; Pardini, Raine, Erickson, & Loeber, 2014). Mechanisms for the suppression of negative emotion operate through an inhibitory connection from regions of the prefrontal cortex, probably the OFC to the amygdala. Serotonin-rich tracts in the prefrontal cortex are implicated in emotion regulation. These are regions of the brain that are inversely associated with activation of the amygdala. Thus impulsive, affective aggression may be the product of emotion regulation failure, particularly in threat situations. Stimulation and lesion studies using fMRI have confirmed the role of the amygdala and paralimbic prefrontal regions including the dorsal and ventral/orbital/medial prefrontal cortex. Coccaro and colleagues (2007, 2011) demonstrated a link between amygdala-OFC dysfunction and impulsive aggression in subjects with intermittent explosive disorder (IED), finding exaggerated amygdala and diminished OFC reactivity to faces conveying (anger) in IED subjects relative to controls. In summary, the inability to regulate negative emotion may result from impairment in the capacity of the PFC to inhibit emotional activation arising from subcortical structures (Seo, Patrick, & Kennealy, 2008).

In addition to cortical-limbic findings in aggression, neuromodulatory hypotheses have emerged linking the interactions of canonical neurotransmitters dopamine, serotonin, and GABA. Several studies implicated D2 receptor subtype in the mesocortical 5-HT receptor subtypes have emerged to be significant targets for anti-aggressive interventions (de Almeida, Ferrari, Parmigiani, & Miczek, 2005). Amphetamine's affinity for dopaminergic function has been linked to a level of aggressive social behavior (Seo et al., 2008). The limbic dopamine system is involved in the preparation, execution, and consequences of aggressive acts. Serotonin hypofunction may represent a biochemical trait that predisposes individuals to impulsive aggression with dopamine hypofunction contributing in an additive faction to serotonergic deficit.

It seems clear in this review that pharmacological, neurocognitive, and possibly premorbid factors predispose methamphetamine psychotics to experiences of extreme negative affect, bizarre hallucinations and other perpetual distortions, psychotic paranoia, impaired emotional regulation, and associated violence. Strong neuroanatomical linkages between schizophrenia, MAP, and violence, largely focused on dopaminergic factors, are clear.

It is worth mentioning in this context that a diagnosis of schizophrenia significantly increases the risk for homicidal offending when compared to the general population (Naudts & Hodgins, 2006), especially in those with comorbid histories of substance abuse or a stable pattern of antisocial offending (Fazel, Buxrud, Ruchkin, & Grann, 2010).

In a 25-year study of Austrian homicides (Schanda, Knecht, Schreinzer, Stompe, Ortwein-Swoboda, Waldhoer, 2004), schizophrenia was associated with an increased likelihood of homicide: 6-fold in men, 26-fold in women, in the latter 19-fold even after age adjustment. In men (63.4%), there was a predominance of paranoid schizophrenia and in women (47%), a predominance of paranoid and schizoaffective subtypes. Comorbid alcohol use/dependence additionally increased odds of homicidal offending. A study from the Russian Federation found significantly increased odds for commission of homicide in schizophrenic offenders (N = 133; Golenkov, Large, Nielssen, & Tsymbalova, 2011). Murderers were predominantly paranoid schizophrenics (78%), with delusions of persecution and auditory hallucinations, who stabbed family members (51%) and acquaintances (43%). Alcohol intoxication was reported in 45% at the time of homicide. On the other hand, Skeem and colleagues, analyzing data from the MacArthur Violence Risk Assessment Study (Skeem, Kennealy, Monahan, Peterson, & Appelbaum, 2016), qualified the association between psychosis and violence. They found that psychosis sometimes foreshadows violence for a fraction of high-risk individuals ("Psychosis immediately precedes violence for about a fifth of this group's incidents," p. 48). They recommend that delusions and hallucinations be targeted for violence prevention.

Meth psychosis is best described as a toxic paranoid-hallucinatory state. In considering linkages between meth psychosis and violence, however, situational factors must be considered, which form the immediate precipitants for violence. It is important to adopt a context-specific approach in which the immediate context of homicide events (intoxication and situational dynamics) is integrated with the background context (trajectories and lifestyles of offenders and victims, antecedents to events, and broader sociocultural factors). This implicates the indirect relationship between intoxication and homicide, whereby the circumstance of intoxication interacts with particular individual, situational, and sociocultural variables to enhance the likelihood of fatal violence (Miles, 2012).

Neuropsychodynamics of Paranoid Rage Murder

Recent developments in psychoanalytic theory, in combination with the neuroscience findings reviewed earlier, permit a heretofore impossible integration of psychodynamics and neurobiology in understanding violence. Psychoanalysts have been particularly interested in distinguishing between "affective (reactive, impulsive, emotional, hot-blooded, self-perseverative) and predatory (instrumental, cold-blooded, premeditated), with relatively distinctive behavioral manifestations and neurobiological underpinnings" (Fonagy, 2003; Meloy, 1988; Raine et al., 1998; Meloy, 2006; Yakeley & Meloy, 2012, p. 237). Affective aggression is linked to threat and anxiety, activated by frustration or threat from an internal/external object (Blair, 2012). Particular interest has been focused on "rage-type murder," defined as a murderous act triggered by a sudden, primitive explosive affective state (Cartwright, 2002). Cartwright notes that rage-type murder suddenly erupts when there is a collapse in a fragile defensive system (the "narcissistic exoskeletion") and attributes all types of violence as expressions of unbearable states of mind. Rather than a simply diffuse, objectless affective discharge, full-fledged rage "always reveals an underlying conscious or unconscious fantasy that includes a specific relation between an aspect of the self and an aspect of a significant other" (Kernberg, 1992, p. 22). Rage at the most primitive level of object relations removes an imminent source of extreme psychic pain, erupting as "a defensive response to the threat of self-annihilation with the aim of destroying the perceived annihilator" (Cartwright, 2002, p. 25). In a similar vein, Glasser (1998) considered "self-perseverative" violence as a primary response triggered by any threat to the physical or psychological self.

> Such threats may be external, and could include attacks on a person's self-esteem, frustration, humiliation, or an insult to an ideal to which the person is attached . . . The violence response is fundamental, immediate, and aimed at eliminating the source of danger.
> (Yakeley & Meloy, 2012, p. 232)

Yakeley and Meloy note that "Affective violence and Glasser's self-perseverative violence are virtually synonymous" (p. 235).

Four decades of research have implicated the primary role of dopamine in the phenomenology of schizophrenia and MAP, reflected in animal studies and efficacy of D2 receptor antagonist medications such as haloperidol. The review cited earlier demonstrates that violent behavior is mediated through corticolimbic and neuromodulatory processes, including serotoninergic and GABA inhibitory interneurons in the prefrontal cortex. Cortical-limbic function has been shown to be central in the interpretation of sensory stimuli and potential for danger. Paranoia appears to be the central factor in methamphetamine violence. Substance-induced, rage-type murder appears to be driven by paranoia. Aggravated limbic arousal associated with threat and impaired prefrontal functioning results in affective aggressives misinterpreting environmental and situational stimuli as dangerous and threatening, which in turn results in "inappropriate, unreasoned violent behavior that is, in effect, a pre-emptive strike against a perceived threat" (Raine et al., 1998; Crowe & Blair, 2008). All of these neurobiological factors overlap in schizophrenia, MAP, and the violent loss of self-regulation, creating a potent combination for psychotic violence.

Legal and Forensic Issues in the Differential Diagnosis of MAP

The unique psychopharmacology and neurobiology of MAP poses significant challenges to the legal system with respect to questions of criminal responsibility, voluntary intoxication, and the insanity defense. Insanity statutes focus on cognitive and volitional factors in determining an individual's criminal responsibility (Bourget, 2013). In cases of MAP, where there is commission of a homicide, it is frequently the case that individuals can be shown to be substantially impaired with respect to their cognitive or volitional capacities. The criminal law, however, does not excuse behavior based on "voluntary" or "self-induced" intoxication. Based on neurobiological sensitization processes described earlier, however, it is clear that some individuals continue to experience a methamphetamine-induced psychotic disorder after active metabolites of the drug have vanished from their body. These would be considered to be the "persistent" versus "transient" types of MAP.

This raises the perennial and still unresolved question about the relationship between MAP and primary psychoses such as schizophrenia (Fazel, Langstrom, Hjern, Grann, & Lichtenstein, 2009). Further, it raises the complicated issue about criminal responsibility where an individual is psychotic due to a substance-induced psychosis, but not intoxicated: so-called settled insanity (Feix & Wolber, 2007; Meloy, 1992). Settled insanity as a legal theory and criminal defense has provoked intense debate and legal controversy. Various states have adopted different positions on the issue, specifically whether self-induced intoxication satisfies tests for the insanity defense.

It should not be surprising that MAP-associated violence is shocking or bizarre. Methamphetamine's potent neurobiological, psychopharmacological, and psychodynamic characteristics aggravates the capacity for violence, giving expression to the most primitive and destructive human impulses.

Notes

1 Curiously, hypotheses that Rorschach protocols from schizophrenic- and LSD-25-induced psychoses would contain more manifestations of primary process were not supported (Barr et al., 1972; Silverman; Lapkin, & Rosenbaum, 1962).

2 Complete R-PAS data: Responses, Results Pages, and Location sheets may be found at www.hawaiiforensicpsychology.com.

References

Acklin, M. W. (1999). Behavioral science foundations of the Rorschach Test: Research and clinical applications. *Assessment, 6*(4), 319-324.

Akiyama, K., Saito, A., & Shimoda, K. (2011). Chronic methamphetamine psychosis after long-term abstinence in Japanese incarcerated patients. *The American Journal on Addictions, 20*(3), 240-249.

American Psychiatric Association (2013). *Diagnostic and Statistical Manual of Mental Disorders, 5th edition (DSM-5)*. Washington, DC: American Psychiatric Association.

Anglin, M. D., Burke, C., Perrochet, B., Stamper, E. W., & Dawud-Noursi, S. (2000). History of the methamphetamine problem. *Journal of Psychoactive Drugs, 32*(2), 137-141.

Angrist, B. M., Corwin, J., Bartlik, B., & Cooper, T. (1987). Early pharmacokinetics and clinical effects of oral d-amphetamine in normal subjects. *Biological Psychiatry, 22*, 1357-1368.

Angrist, B. M., & Gershon, S. (1970). The phenomenology of experimentally induced amphetamine psychosis—Preliminary observations. *Biological Psychiatry, 2*, 95-107.

Angrist, B. M., Sathananthan, G., Wilk, S., & Gershon, S. (1974). Amphetamine psychosis: Behavioral and biochemical aspects. *Journal of Psychiatric Research, 11*, 13-23.

Baicy, K., & London, E. D. (2007). Corticolimbic dysregulation and chronic methamphetamine abuse. *Addiction, 102*, 5-15.

Barr, H. L., Langs, R. J., Holt, R. R., Goldberger, L., & Klein, G. S. (1972). *LSD: Personality and experience*. New York: Wiley-Interscience.

Bell, D. S. (1965). Comparison of amphetamine psychosis and schizophrenia. *British Journal of Psychiatry, 111,* 701-707.

Benedik, E., Coderl, S., Bon, J., & Smith, B. L. (2013). Differentiation of psychotic from nonpsychotic inpatients: The Rorschach perceptual thinking index. *Journal of Personality Assessment, 95*(2), 141-148.

Bercel, N. A., Travis, L. E., Olinger, L. B., Dreikurs, R. (1956). Model psychoses induced by LSD-25 in normals. II. Rorschach test findings. *AMA Archives of Neurology and Psychiatry, 75,* 612-618.

Biagiarelli, M., Roma, P., Comparelli, A., Andrados, P., Di Pomponio, I., Corigiliano, V., Curto, M., . . . Ferracuti, S. (2015). Relationship between the Rorschach Perceptual Thinking Index (PTI) and the Positive and Negative Syndrome Scale (PANSS) in psychotic patients: A validity study. *Psychiatry Research, 225,* 315-321.

Blair, R. J. R. (2012). Considering anger from a cognitive neuroscience perspective. *Wiley Interdisciplinary Reviews. Cognitive Science, 3*(1), 65-74.

Boles, S. M., & Miotto, K. (2003). Substance abuse and violence: A review of the literature. *Aggression and Violent Behavior, 8,* 155-174.

Bourget, D. (2013). Forensic considerations of substance-induced psychosis. *Journal of the American Academy of Psychiatry and the Law, 41,* 168-173.

Bramness, J. G., Gundersen, O., Gutersam, J., et al. (2012). Amphetamine-induced psychosis - A separate diagnostic entity or primary psychosis triggered in the vulnerable. *BMC Psychiatry, 12,* 221-228.

Buffenstein, A., Heaster, A., & Ko, P. (1999). Chronic psychotic illness from methamphetamine. *American Journal of Psychiatry, 156,* 662.

Callaghan, R., Cunningham, J., Allebeck, P., Arenovich, T., Sajeev, G., Remington, G., . . . Kish, S. (2012). Methamphetamine use and schizophrenia: A population-based cohort study in California. *American Journal of Psychiatry, 169*(4) 389-396.

Carhart-Harris, R. L., Brugger, S., Nutt, D. J., & Stone, J. M. (2013). Psychiatry's next top model: cause for a re-think on drug models of psychosis and other psychiatric disorders. *Journal of Psychopharmacology, 27*(9), 771-778.

Cartwright, D. (2002). *Psychoanalysis, violence, and rage-type murder: Murdering minds.* New York: Brunner-Routledge.

Chen, C. K., Lin, P. C., Sham, D., Ball, D., Loh, E. W., Hsiao, C., Chiang, Y,. . . Murray, R. (2003). Premorbid characteristics and co-morbidity of methamphetamine users with and without psychosis. *Psychological Medicine, 33,* 1407-1414.

Coccaro, E. F., McCloskey, M. S., Fitzgerald, D. A., & Phan, K. L. (2007). Amygdala and orbitofrontal reactivity to social threat in individuals with impulsive aggression. *Biological Psychiatry, 62,* 168-178.

Coccaro, E. F., Sripada, C. S., Yanowitch, R. N., & Phan, K. L. (2011). Corticolimbic function in impulsive aggression. *Biological Psychiatry, 69,* 1153-1159.

Connell, P. H. (1958). *Amphetamine psychosis.* London: Chapman & Hall.

Crowe, S. L., & Blair, R. J. R. (2008). The development of antisocial behavior: What can we learn from functional neuroimaging studies? *Development and Psychopathology, 20,* 1145-1159.

Curran, H. V., D'Souza, D. C., Robbins, T. W., & Fletcher, P. (2009). Modelling psychosis. *Psychopharmacology, 206,* 4, 513-514.

Davidson, R. J., Putnam, K. M., & Larson, C. L. (2000). Dysfunction in the neural circuitry of emotion regulation—A possible prelude to violence. *Science, 289,* 591-594.

de Almeida, R., Ferrari, P., Parmigiani, S., & Miczek, K. (2005). Escalated aggressive behavior: Dopamine, serotonin, and GABA. *European Journal of Pharmacology, 526,* 51-64.

Dean, A. C., Kohno, M., Hellemann, G., & London, E. D. (2014). Childhood maltreatment and amygdala connectivity in methamphetamine dependence: A pilot study. *Brain and Behavior, 4*(6), 867-876.

Dittrich, A. (1998). The standardized psychometric assessment of altered states of consciousness in humans. *Pharmacopsychiatry, 31,* 80-84.

Durell, T. M., Kroutil, L. A., Crits-Christoph, P., Barcha, N., & Van Brunt, D. L. (2008). Prevalence of nonmedical methamphetamine use in the United States. *Substance Abuse Treatment, Prevention, and Policy, 3,* 1-10.

Dzamonia-Ignjatovic, T., Smith, B. L., Jocic, D., & Milanovic, M. (2013). A comparison of new and revised Rorschach measures of schizophrenic functioning in a Serbian clinical sample. *Journal of Personality Assessment, 95*(5), 471-478.

Ellinwood, E. H. (1971). Assault and homicide associated with amphetamine abuse. *American Journal of Psychiatry, 127*(9), 90-96.

Erard, R., Luisada, P., & Peele, R. (1980). The PCP psychosis: Prolonged intoxication or drug-precipitated functional illness. *Journal of Psychedelic Drugs, 12*(3-4), 235-250.

Exner, J. E. (1969). *The Rorschach systems.* New York: Grune & Stratton.

Exner, J. E. (1974). *The Rorschach: A comprehensive system Volume 1.* New York: Wiley.

Exner, J. E. (1993). *The Rorschach: A comprehensive system Volume 1* (3rd Ed.). New York: Wiley.

Exner, J. E. (2000). *2000 Alumni Newsletter.* Asheville, NC: Rorschach Workshops.

Fazel, J. M., Langstrom, N., Hjern, A., Grann, M., & Lichtenstein, P. (2009). Schizophrenia, substance abuse, and violent crime. *Journal of the American Medical Association, 31*(9), 2016-2023.

Fazel, S., Buxrud, P., Ruchkin, V., & Grann, M. (2010). Homicide in discharged patients with schizophrenia and other psychoses: A national case-control study. *Schizophrenia Research, 123,* 263-269.

Featherstone, R. E., Kapur, S., & Fletcher, P. J. (2007). The amphetamine-induced sensitized state as a model of schizophrenia. *Progress in Neuro-Psychopharmacology & Biological Psychiatry, 31,* 1556-1571.

Feix, J., & Wolber, G. (2007). Intoxication and settled insanity: A finding of not guilty by reason of insanity. *Journal of the American Academy of Psychiatry and the Law, 35,* 172-182.

Fonagy, P. (2003). Toward a developmental understanding of violence. *British Journal of Psychiatry, 183,* 190-192.

Friedman, A., Lewak, R., Nichols, D., & Webb, J. (2001). *Psychological Assessment with the MMPI-2,* (2nd ed.). Mahwah, NJ: Lawrence Erlbaum Associates.

Fukushima, A. (1994). Criminal responsibility in amphetamine psychosis. *The Japanese Journal of Psychiatry and Neurology, 48,* 1-4.

Ganellen, R. J., Wasyliw, O. R., Haywod, T. W., & Grossman, L. S. (1996). Can psychosis be malingered on the Rorschach? An empirical study. *Journal of Personality Assessment, 66*(1), 65-80.

Ghaffari-Nejad, A., Ziaadini, H., Saffari-Zadeha, S., Kheradmand, A., & Pouya, F. (2014). A study of the phenomenology of psychosis induced by methamphetamine: A preliminary research. *Addiction Health, 6*(3/4), 105-110.

Glasser, M. (1998). On violence: A preliminary communication. *The International Journal of Psychoanalysis, 79*, 887-902.

Golenkov, A., Large, M., Nielssen, O., & Tsymbalova, A. (2011). Characteristics of homicide offender with schizophrenia from the Russian Federation. *Schizophrenia Research, 133*, 232-237.

Gonzales-Maeso, J., & Sealfon, S. C. (2009). Psychedelics in schizophrenia. *Trends in Neurosciences, 32*(4), 225-232.

Gouzoulis-Mayfrank, E., Habermeyer, E., Hermle, L., Steinmeyer, A. M., Kunert, H. J., & Sass, L. (1998). Hallucinogenic drug induced states resemble acute endogenous psychoses: Results of an empirical study. *European Psychiatry, 13*, 399-406.

Griffith, J. J., Oates, J., & Cavanaugh, J. (1968). Paranoid episodes induced by drugs. *Journal of the American Medical Association, 205*, 39.

Griffiths, R. R., Johnson, M. W., & Richards, W. A. (2011). Psilocybin occasioned mystical-type experiences: Immediate and persisting dose-related effects. *Psychopharmacology, 218*(4), 659-665.

Griffiths, R. R., Richards, W. A., McCann, U., & Jesse, R. (2006). Psilocybin can occasion mystical-type experiences having substantial and sustained personal meaning and spiritual significance. *Psychopharmacology, 187*, 268-283.

Harris, D., & Batki, S. L. (2000). Stimulus psychosis: Symptom profile and acute clinical course. *The American Journal on Addictions, 9*, 28-37.

Hermens, D., Lubman, D., Ward, P., Naismith, S., & Hickie, I. (2009). Amphetamine psychosis: a model of studying the onset and course of psychosis. *MJA, 1904*, S22-S25.

Hilsenroth, M. J., Eudell-Simmons, E. M., DeFife, J. A., & Charnas, J. (2007). The Rorschach Perceptual Thinking Index (PTI): An examination of reliability, validity, and diagnostic efficiency. *International Journal of Testing, 7*(3), 269-291.

Hoaken, P. N. S., & Stewart, S. H. (2003). Drugs of abuse and the elicitation of human aggression. *Addictive Behaviors, 28*, 1533-1554.

Hollister, L. (1962). Drug-induced psychoses and schizophrenic reactions, a critical comparison. *Annals of the New York Academy of Sciences, 96*, 80-88.

Hollister, L. (1964). Chemical psychoses. *Annual Review of Medicine, 15*, 203-214.

Hollister, L. (1968). *Chemical psychoses: LSD and related drugs.* Springfield, IL: Charles C. Thomas.

Howes, O. D., & Kapur, S. (2009). The dopamine hypothesis of schizophrenia: Version III—The final common pathway. *Schizophrenia Bulletin, 235*(3), 549-562.

Hsieh, J. H., Stein, D. J., & Howells, F. M. (2014). The neurobiology of methamphetamine-induced psychosis. *Frontiers in Human Neuroscience, 8*, 1-12.

Insel, T. R. (2010). Research Perspective: Rethinking schizophrenia. *Nature, 468*, 187-193.

Jacobs, E., Fujii, D., Schiffman, J., & Bello, I. (2008). An exploratory analysis of neurocognition in methamphetamine-induced psychotic disorder and paranoid schizophrenia. *Cognitive Behavioral Neurology, 21*(2), 98–103.

Janowsky, D. S., & Risch, C. (1979). Amphetamine psychosis and psychotic symptoms. *Psychopharmacology, 65*, 73–77.

Kernberg, O. F. (1992). *Aggression in personality disorders and perversions.* London: Yale University Press.

Kleiger, J. H. (1999). *Disordered Thinking and the Rorschach : Theory, Research, and Differential Diagnosis.* New York: Routledge.

Kometer, M., Schmidt, A., Bachmann, R., Studereus, E., Seifritz, E., & Vollenweider, F. X. (2012). Psilocybin biases facial recognition, goal directed behavior, and mood state toward positive relative to negative emotions through different serotonergic subreceptors. *Biological Psychiatry, 72*, 898–906.

Kraehenmann, R., Preller, K. H., Scheidegger, M., Pokorny, T., Bosch, O., Seifritz, E., & Vollenweider, F. X. (2015). Psilocybin-induced decrease in amygdala reactivity correlates with enhanced positive mood in healthy volunteers. *Biological Psychiatry, 78*, 572–581.

Kuzenko, N., Sareen, J., Beesdo-Baum, K., Perkonigg, A., Hofer, M., Simm, J., Lieb, R., ... Wittchen, H. (2011). Associations between use of cocaine, amphetamines, or psychedelics and psychotic symptoms in the community sample. *Acta Psychiatrica Scandinavica, 123*, 466–474.

Laruelle, M., & Abi-Dargham, A. (1999). Dopamine as the wind of the psychotic fire: New evidence from brain imaging studies. *Journal of Psychopharmacology, 13*(4), 358–371.

Laruelle, M., Abi-Dargham, A., Van Dyck, C., Gil, R., D'Souza, C. D., Erdos, J., ... Innis, R. (1996). Single photon emission computerized tomography imaging of amphetamine-induced dopamine release in drug-free schizophrenic patients. *Proceedings of the National Academy of Sciences, 93*, 9235–9240.

Leamon, M. H., Flower, K., Salo, R. E., Salo, R., Nordahl, T., Kransler, H., & Galloway, G. (2010). Methamphetamine and paranoia: the methamphetamine experience questionnaire. *The American Journal on Addictions, 19*, 155–168.

Lecomte, T., Mueser, K. T., MacEwan, W., Thornton, A., Buchanan, T., Bouchard, V., Goldner, E., & Honer, W. (2013). Predictors of persistent psychotic symptoms in persons with methamphetamine abuse receiving psychiatric treatment. *The Journal of Nervous and Mental Disease, 201*(12), 1085–1089.

Levine, A., Abramson, A., Kaufman, M. R., Markham, S., & Kornetsky, C. (1955). Lysergic acid diethylamide (LSD-25): XIV. Effect on personality as observed in psychological tests. *The Journal of Psychology, 40*, 351–366.

MacLean, K. A., Johnson, M. W., & Griffiths, R. R. (2011). Mystical experiences occasioned by the hallucinogen psilocybin leads to increases in the personality domain of openness. *Journal of Psychopharmacology, 25*(11), 1453–1461.

McKetin, R., Lubman, D. I., Najman, J. M., Dawe, S., Butterworth, P., & Baker, A. L. (2014). Does methamphetamine use increase violent behavior? Evidence from a prospective longitudinal study. *Addiction, 109*, 798–806.

McKetin, R., McLaren, J., Lubman, D. I., & Hides, L. (2008). Hostility among methamphetamine users experiencing psychotic symptoms. *The American Journal on Addictions, 17*, 235-240.

McKetin, J., McLaren, J., Riddell, S., & Robins, L. (2006). The relationship between methamphetamine use and violent behavior. *Crime and Justice Bulletin, 97*, 1-16.

Meloy, J. R. (1988). Violent and homicidal behavior in primitive mental states. *Journal of the American Academy of Psychoanalysis, 16*, 381-394.

Meloy, J. R. (1992). Voluntary intoxication and the insanity defense. *The Journal of Psychiatry & Law, 20*(4), 439-457.

Meloy, J. R. (2006). Empirical basis and forensic application of affective and predatory violence. *Australian and New Zealand Journal of Psychiatry, 40*, 529-547.

Meyer, G., Viglione, D., Mihura, J., Erard, R., & Erdberg, P. (2011). *Rorschach Performance Assessment System: Administration, coding, interpretation, and technical manual*. Toledo, OH: Rorschach Performance Assessment System, LLC.

Miles, C. (2012). Intoxication and homicide: A context-specific approach. *British Journal of Criminology, 52*, 870-888.

Moore, R. C., Viglione, D. J., Rosenfarb, I. S., Patterson, T. L., & Mausbach, B. T. (2013). Rorschach measures of cognition relate to everyday and social functioning in schizophrenia. *Psychological Assessment, 25*(1), 253-263. doi: 10.1037/a0030546.

Murray, R. M., Paparelli, A., Morrison, P., Marconi, A., & Di Forti, M. (2013). What can we learn about schizophrenia from studying the human model, drug-induced psychosis? *American Journal of Medical Genetics, 162B*, 661-670.

Naudts, K., & Hodgins, S. (2006). Neurobiological correlates of violent behavior among persons with schizophrenia. *Schizophrenia Bulletin, 32*(3), 562-572.

Orikabe, L., Yamasue, H., Inoue, H., Takayanagi, Y., Mozue, Y., Sudo, Y., Ishii, T., ... Kasai, K. (2011). Reduced amygdala and hippocampal volumes in patients with methamphetamine psychosis. *Schizophrenia Research, 132*, 183-189.

Panenka, W. J., Procyshyn, R. M., Lecomte, T., MacEwan, G., Flynn, S., Honer, W., & Barr, A. (2013). Methamphetamine use: A comprehensive review of molecular, preclinical and clinical findings. *Drug and Alcohol Dependence, 129*, 167-179.

Pardini, D., Raine, A., Erickson, K., & Loeber, R. (2014). Lower amygdala volume in men is associated with childhood aggression, early psychopathic traits and future violence. *Biological Psychiatry, 75*(1), 73-80.

Payer, D. E., Lieberman, M. D., & London, E. D. (2011). Neural correlates of affect processing and aggression in methamphetamine dependence. *Archives of General Psychiatry, 68*(3), 278-282.

Perry, W., Sprock, J., Schaible, D., McDougall, A. M., Jenkins, M., & Braff, D. (1995). Amphetamine on Rorschach measures in normal subjects. *Journal of Personality Assessment, 64*(3), 456-465.

Raine, A., Meloy, J. R., Bihrle, S., Stoddard, K., LaCasse, L., & Buchsbaum, M. (1998). Reduced prefrontal and increased subcortical brain functioning assessed using positron emission tomography and predatory and affective murderers. *Behavioral Sciences and the Law, 16*, 319-332.

Rorschach, H. (1942). *Psychodiagnostics*. New York: Grune & Stratton.

Rosenthal, R. N., & Miner, C. R. (1997). Differential diagnosis of substance-induced psychosis with schizophrenia in patients with substance use disorders. *Schizophrenia Bulletin, 23*(2), 187-193.

Rosse, R. B., Collins, J. P., Fay-McCarthy, M., Alim, T. N., Wyeth, R. J., & Deutsch, S. I. (1994). Phenomenologic comparison of the idiopathic psychosis of schizophrenia and drug-induced cocaine and phencyclidine psychoses: a retrospective study. *Clinical Neuropharmacology, 17*(4), 359-369.

Salo, R., Fassbender, C., Buonocore, M. H., & Ursu, S. (2013). Behavioral regulation in methamphetamine abusers: an fMRI study. *Psychiatry Research: Neuroimaging, 211*(3), 234-238.

Salo, R., Fassbender, C., Iosif, A. M., Ursu, S., Leamon, M. H., & Carter, C. (2013). Predictors of methamphetamine psychosis: History of ADHD-relevant childhood behaviors and drug exposure. *Psychiatry Research, 210*, 529-535.

Salo, R., Flower, K., Kielstein, A., Leamon, M., Nordahl, T., & Galloway, G. (2011). Psychiatric comorbidity in methamphetamine dependence, *Psychiatry Research, 186*, 356-361.

Salo, R., Nordahl, T. E., Leamon, M. H., Natsuaki, Y., Moore, C., Waters, C., & Carter, C. (2008). Preliminary evidence of behavioral predictors of recurrent drug-induced psychosis in methamphetamine abuse. *Psychiatry Research, 157*, 273-277.

Sato, M., Chen, C. C., Akiyama, K., & Otsuki, S. (1983). Acute exacerbation of paranoid state after long-term abstinence in patients with previous methamphetamine psychosis. *Biological Psychiatry, 18*(4), 429-440.

Sato, M., Numachi, Y., & Hanamura, T. (1992). Relapse of paranoid psychotic state in methamphetamine model of schizophrenia. *Schizophrenia Bulletin, 18*(1), 115-122.

Schanda, H., Knecht, G., Schreinzer, D., Stompe, T., Ortwein-Swoboda, G., & Waldhoer, T. (2004). Homicide and major mental disorders: A 25 year study. *Acta Psychiatrica Scandinavica, 1110*, 98-107.

Schwartz, F., & Lazar, Z. (1984). Contaminated thinking: A specimen of the primary process. *Psychoanalytic Psychology, 1*(4), 319-334.

Scott, J. C., Woods, S. P., Matt, G. E., Meyer, R. A., Heaton, R. K., Atkinson, J. H., & Grant, I. (2007). Neurocognitive Effects of Methamphetamine: A Critical Review and Meta-analysis. *Neuropsychology Review, 17*, 275-297.

Seo, D., Patrick, C., & Kennealy, P. J. (2008). Role of serotonin and dopamine system interactions in the neurobiology of impulsive aggression and its comorbidity with other clinical disorders. *Aggression & Violent Behavior, 13*(5), 383-395.

Sharma, R. P., Javaid, J. L., Pandey, G. N., Janicak, P., Davis, J. M. (1991). Behavioral and biochemical effects of methylphenidate in schizophrenic and non-schizophrenic patients. *Biological Psychiatry, 30*(5), 459-466.

Shulgin, A. T. (1978). *Chapter 6: Psychotomimetic drugs: Structure-activity relationships. Handbook of Psychopharmacology, Volume 11: Stimulants*. New York: Plenum Press.

Siever, L. J. (2008). Neurobiology of aggression and violence. *American Journal of Psychiatry, 165*(4), 429-442.

Silva, J. A., Derecho, D. V., Leong, G. B., Weinstock, R., & Ferrari, M. M. (2001). A classification of psychological factors leading to violent behavior in posttraumatic stress disorder. *Journal of Forensic Sciences, 30*, 316.

Silverman, L. H., Lapkin, B., & Rosenbaum, I. S. (1962). Manifestations of primary process thinking in schizophrenia. *Journal of Projective Techniques, 26*, 117-127.

Skeem, J., Kennealy, P., Monahan, J., Peterson, J., & Appelbaum, P. (2016). Psychosis uncommonly and inconsistently precedes violence among high-risk individuals. *Clinical Psychological Science, 4*(1), 40-49.

Smith, S. R., Baity, M. R., Knowles, E. S., & Hilsenroth, M. J. (2001). Assessment of disordered thinking in children and adolescents: the Rorschach Perceptual-Thinking Index. *Journal of Personality Assessment, 77*, 3, 447-463.

Snyder, S. H. (1973). Amphetamine psychosis: A "model" schizophrenia mediated by cathecolamines. *American Journal of Psychiatry, 1340*(1), 61-67.

Srisurapanont, M., Ali, R., Marsden, J., Sunga, A., Wada, K., & Monteiro, M. (2003). Psychotic symptoms in methamphetamine psychotic in-patients. *International Journal of Neuropsychopharmacology, 6*(4), 347-352.

Srisurapanont, M., Jarusuraisin, N., Kittirattanapaiboon., P, Kao, U. (2011). Treatment for amphetamine dependence and abuse. *Cochrane Database of Systematic Reviews*, Issue 4. Art. No.: CD003022.

Steeds, H., Carhart-Harris, R. L., & Stone, J. N. (2015). Drug models of schizophrenia. *Therapeutic Advances in Psychopharmacology, 5*(1), 43-58.

Stompe, T., Bauer, S., Karakula, H., . . . Gschaider, S. (2007). Paranoid-hallucinatory syndromes in schizophrenia: Results of the International Study on Psychotic Symptoms. *World Cultural Psychiatry Review, 1*(3-4), 63-68.

Stretsky, P. B. (2009). National case-control study of homicide offending and methamphetamine use. *Journal of Interpersonal Violence, 24*, 911-924.

Su, W., Viglione, D., Green, E., Tam, W. C., Su, J., & Chang, Y. (2015). Cultural and linguistic adaptability of the Rorschach Performance Assessment System as a measure of psychotic characteristics and severity of mental disturbance in Taiwan. *Psychological Assessment, 27*(4), 1273-1285.

Substance Abuse and Mental Health Services Administration (2013). *Results from the 2012 National survey on drug use and health: Summary of national findings*. NSDUH Series H-46, HHS Publication No. (SMA) 13-4795. Rockville, MD: Substance Abuse and Mental Health Services Administration.

Tyner, E. A., & Fremouw, W. J. (2008). The relation of methamphetamine use and violence: A critical review. *Aggression and Violence Behavior, 13*, 285-287.

Ujike H. (2002). Stimulant-induced psychosis and schizophrenia: The role of sensitization. *Current Psychiatry Reports, 4*(3), 177-184.

Ujike, H., & Sato, M. (2004). Clinical features of sensitization to methamphetamine observed in patients with methamphetamine dependence and psychosis. *Annals of the New York Academy of Sciences, 1025*, 279-287.

United Nations (2008). 2008 World Drug Report. Retrieved from https://www.unodc.org/documents/wdr/WDR_2008/WDR_2008_eng_web.pdf

Viglione, D., Giromini, L., Gustafson, M. L., & Meyer, G. J. (2014). Developing continuous variable composites for Rorschach measures of thought problems, vigilance, and suicide risk. *Assessment, 21*(1), 42-49.

Vollenweider, F. X., Vollenweider-Scherperhuyzen, M., Babler, A., Vogel, H., & Hell, D. (1998). Psilocybin induces schizophrenia-like psychosis in humans via a serotonin-2 agonist action. *Cognitive Neuroscience, 17*(1), 3897-3902.

Weiner, I. B. (1964). Differential diagnosis of amphetamine psychosis. *Psychiatric Quarterly, 38,* 707–716.

Wong, A. H. C., & Van Tol, H. H. M. (2003). Schizophrenia: From phenomenology to neurobiology. *Neuroscience and Biobehavioral Reviews, 27,* 269–306.

Yakeley, J., & Meloy, J. R. (2012). Understanding violence: The psychoanalytic thinking matter? *Aggression & Violent Behavior, 17,* 229–239.

Yui, K., Ikemoto, S., Ishiguro, T., & Goto, K. (2000). *Studies of amphetamine or methamphetamine psychosis in Japan.* Annals of the New York Academy of Science. Walden, MA: Wiley.

Zorick, T. S., Rad, D., Rim, C., & Tsuang, J. (2008). An overview of methamphetamine-induced psychotic syndromes. *Addictive Disorders & Their Treatment, 7*(3), 143–156.

Zweben, J. E., Cohen, J. B., Christian, D., Galloway, G., Salinardi, M., Parent, D., & Iguchi, M. (2004). Psychiatric symptoms in methamphetamine users. *The American Journal on Addictions, 13,* 181–190.

Part III

Special Topics

Chapter 9

COLLABORATIVE/ THERAPEUTIC ASSESSMENT IN MULTIMETHOD FORENSIC EVALUATIONS

Bruce L. Smith and F. Barton Evans

Introduction

One of the most exciting innovations in recent clinical practice has been the development of Collaborative/Therapeutic Assessment, commonly abbreviated C/TA[1] (Finn & Tonsager, 1997; Finn, 2007). This approach to psychological assessment seeks to break down the boundary between assessment and psychotherapy by a planned use of the assessment as a therapeutic intervention. Finn and Tonsager (1997) contrast information-gathering and therapeutic modes of assessment and note that a) in the former the goal is the accurate diagnosis of the client and the facilitation of communication between professionals, whereas in the latter the goal is for the client to develop new understandings of herself; b) in therapeutic assessment, the assessor is a participant-observer as opposed to an "objective observer"; c) in therapeutic assessment, the tests are seen as tools to increase empathy so that the assessor may better access the client's inner life rather than standardized samples of behavior for nomothetic comparison; and d) in therapeutic assessment, the focus is more on the client's subjective experience rather than on the scores themselves (p. 397). Research has demonstrated the superiority of C/TA in terms of client satisfaction, compliance with post-assessment recommendations, and initial alliance in subsequent psychotherapeutic relationships (Poston & Hanson, 2010).

By contrast, assessment in forensic contexts operates with significantly different parameters. The consumer of the forensic assessment is rarely the person being assessed, but some third party (court, attorney, hearing board, etc.); the goal is an unbiased appraisal of the client's psychological condition and an answer to specific psycholegal questions, and the role of the assessor is typically seen as a dispassionate objective observer. Indeed, it is the neutrality of the examiner that is seen as the *sine qua non* of forensic evaluations. In addition, it is frequently believed that forensic assessors must maintain a high index of suspicion, as examinees often have powerful motivation to present themselves in particular ways. One of the main elements of a competent forensic evaluation is the assessment of malingering, whether positive or negative. Thus a C/TA within the context of forensic assessment would seem to be an oxymoron. Despite this, the integration of some principles from C/TA into forensic practice is precisely what we are going to argue for in this chapter.

Are Principles of C/TA and Forensic Assessment Fundamentally Incompatible?

The prevailing ethos in forensic psychology is that all things "therapeutic" are fundamentally incompatible with forensic assessment. Greenberg and Shuman's (1997) classic paper on this matter goes so far as to state that there is an irreconcilable conflict between therapeutic and forensic roles. They outline ten fundamental differences between therapeutic and forensic roles, which as general statements are fundamentally sound. Yet, upon closer scrutiny, elements of C/TA challenge prevailing assumptions in forensic psychology and can be critical in providing a more fully informed forensic opinion. Further, as we will demonstrate, in certain areas of forensic practice, these elements of C/TA can be useful in assisting resolution of legal matters to the benefit of the litigant, attorneys, triers of fact, and relevant social agencies.

Greenberg and Shuman's (1997) article has been taken up as an almost canonical position in the forensic psychology literature in large part because of its emphasis on establishing good practice boundaries. Yet, in its well-placed fervor for clarity, an important assumption about the nature of the personality assessment process, whether clinical or forensic, has gone unexamined. Under the heading, "Cognitive Set and Evaluative Attitude of Each Expert," Greenberg and Shuman assert that the clinical assessor is "supportive, accepting, empathic," whereas the forensic assessor is "neutral, objective, detached" (p. 52). As any well-trained psychodynamic assessor knows, the cognitive set and evaluative attitude cannot be so neatly pigeonholed. Whether or not the forensic assessor chooses to recognize it, he or she is a participant-observer during the forensic assessment, and therefore a purely detached position is not only a realistic impossibility but also eschews critical evidence of great value to the final forensic opinion. It is good to remember that Sullivan's (1954) development of the concept of participant-observation was indeed an application of common anthropological and sociological research methods of his era (see also Sullivan, 1953) and an early model for both clinical and forensic applications.

Further, the Greenberg and Shuman's delineation of clinical assessment as "empathic" and forensic assessment as "detached" creates unanticipated problems in the personality assessment process. In the psychoanalytic literature, Lipton (1977) astutely opined that psychoanalysis's neutral and detached stance might iatrogenically contribute to the increased numbers of schizoid and narcissistic clients reported. In a similar context, Wiegert (1970) expanded the psychoanalytic concept of neutrality to one of benevolent neutrality in which empathic attunement co-exists with observant neutrality. The point here is that, especially in some areas of forensic practice, detachment can lead to an emotionally aloof stance that creates a subtle hindrance to the level of compassionate engagement necessary for a comprehensive understanding of the client in both forensic and clinical contexts. As Evans (2005) posited, true neutrality in forensic practice is where the assessor strives at the same time to be totally skeptical *and* totally open. As practiced by many forensic examiners, maintaining a position of only skepticism and suspicion is therefore fundamentally biased, and the value of personality tests as de-biasing is undercut by an all-too-wary and negative predisposition toward disbelief.

To expand upon the foregoing a bit further, it is good to recall Schafer's classic study of the interpersonal dynamics in psychological testing (1954). He articulated four different roles that the psychological assessor typically embodies: the voyeuristic, the autocratic, the oracular, and the saintly. Each of these roles calls forth a reciprocal role on the part of the examinee. Significantly, Schafer pointed out that elements of the test data may at times primarily reflect these reciprocal role relationships rather than aspects of the examinee's enduring personality.

Problems with Detached Forensic Psychological Assessment

As one of us has articulated in previous publications (Smith, 1990, 2005), strict neutrality is a myth. The transference-countertransference dynamics in any psychological interview are such that the examiner is pulled into reciprocal role relationships with the subject in ways that are often outside of awareness. The point here is that a strict inquisitorial approach is not, in fact, neutral. Whereas an approach that stresses empathy with the examinee runs the risk of over-identification and a loss of objectivity, a strictly detached stance runs the opposite risk: that the examiner is experienced as an adversarial interrogator. Given this, we believe that an ongoing examination of the examiner's inevitable countertransference should be an integral part of the evaluation process. To illustrate, in cases in which the examinee has suffered severe trauma or mistreatment, there may be a tendency on the part of the examiner to empathize to the exclusion of any balancing skepticism. On the other hand, some examinees may be so off-putting either by their manner in the interview, or the nature of the behavior that brought them there, for which the examiner may be unconsciously inclined to view them—and their test data—in the most negative light possible. The process of self-examination can serve both to de-bias the examiner and as an additional source of information about the examinee (see, for example, Pickar, 2008; Pickar & Erard, 2008).

It may be helpful here to unpack the concept of C/TA and separate the *collaborative* from the *therapeutic* aspects. Although there is a growing interest in what has been called "therapeutic jurisprudence" (Dickie, 2008; Madsen & Holmberg, 2015), and we will argue for the incorporation of some therapeutic principles in forensic evaluations, it is our position that even in examinations in which there is no therapeutic component, the evaluation process can still be collaborative. Collaborative assessment (Fischer, 1985/1994) conceptualizes the assessment process as a collaboration between client and assessor in which each bring their special knowledge to the endeavor. The assessor brings her expertise in psychology and in the use of assessment instruments; the client brings his knowledge of his history and his subjective experience. It is our contention that by collaborating with the examinee in a forensic examination, not only will the process be less traumatizing for the examinee but also it will be likely to yield a more accurate assessment. Too frequently, in our experience, forensic examiners who are overly concerned with maintaining strict "neutrality" conduct examinations as if they were depositions, and the examinee is treated as if she were a hostile witness, as in the following example:

> Ms. A was an attractive, 40-year-old woman, who had suffered extreme sexual harassment at a male-dominated workplace. Explicit pornographic pictures and videos had been sent to her cell phone and co-workers had frequently come up behind her and simulated sexual acts and made various vulgar sexual comments to and about her in public. After some months of this, during which time the management of her company refused to take action, she left work on stress disability and subsequently resigned when she received no reassurances that the conduct would be stopped. She then sued her employer for sexual harassment, sexual discrimination, and constructive discharge.
>
> Ms. A alleged willful and negligent infliction of emotional harm and was subjected to two psychological evaluations, one each by defense and plaintiff experts. Complicating the case was the fact that Ms. A's sister, from whom she had been largely estranged, committed suicide a few weeks after Ms. A left work on disability. Thus one of the tasks of the forensic psychological evaluations was to parcel out the effects of the workplace stress from those of her sister's suicide.
>
> The defense expert, Dr. B, conducted a "by the book" evaluation, in which her interview of the plaintiff was highly structured. Ms. A reported feeling that Dr. B was conducting a cross-examination and did not understand her. She likened it to "another deposition." Indeed, by rigidly adhering to an interview schedule, she failed to gain a full picture of Ms. A's experience.
>
> Dr. B asked Ms. A to enumerate her "symptoms" as a result of the harassment. She then repeated the process for the "symptoms" following Ms. A's sister's suicide. Based on a comparison of the two symptom lists, Dr. B opined that Ms. A's symptoms were largely similar (anxiety, depression, insomnia, loss of appetite), with the single exception that "grief" was mentioned for the suicide and not for the workplace harassment. She then concluded that although Ms. A had suffered emotional distress from both events, since loss of a loved one was a more serious event and the sister's suicide had engendered an additional symptom, it was the more significant causal event.

By contrast, the plaintiff's expert (BLS) approached the evaluation from a more collaborative perspective, inviting Ms. A to discuss her experiences in her own words and in her own way. She was able in this instance to elaborate on the nature of her estrangement from her sister, the differences between her responses to the two stressors, and especially how her stress over the workplace harassment had rendered her much less capable of dealing with the death of her sister. This added perspective enabled the plaintiff's psychologist to more fully understand and explain the effects of the workplace harassment on Ms. A's emotional state. In addition, this perspective buttressed the psychological test findings from both self-report instruments and the Rorschach, both of which showed high levels of anxiety and situational stress, but only moderate sadness. We would argue that in this instance, a "neutral, objective" approach clearly yielded inferior information and led to a faulty conclusion.

Not only does a more collaborative approach increase the likelihood of a more revealing interview, but research has shown that it increases the quantity and quality of the yield from psychological tests as well (see Evans, 2005; Hanson & Poston, 2011; Poston & Hanson, 2010.)

It should also be borne in mind that many—if not most—litigants who are evaluated by psychologists have suffered trauma of one sort or another. This is true almost by definition of plaintiffs in civil cases who have put their psychological condition at issue; it is certainly true for immigration cases in which the petitioner is seeking asylum, and it is even the case for many criminal defendants who have been frequently victimized themselves. Part of a forensic evaluation inevitably requires the retelling of painful traumatic events. As is known, telling one's story of trauma can be a healing experience or a re-traumatizing one depending on how the story is received by the listener (see Herman, 1992/2015).

As noted by Evans (2005) and Mollica, Wyshak, & Lavelle (1987), maintaining the balance of skepticism and empathy is critical when working with survivors of torture and other victims of psychological trauma. As Evans (2005) stated,

> A lack understanding of the impact of skepticism and disbelief in the interpersonal realm can potentially—and substantially—skew information gathered in a forensic assessment. Based on the work of Mollica and his colleagues (Mollica, Wyshak, & Lavelle, 1987; Mollica, Caspi-Yavin, Bollini, Truong,

Tor, & Lavelle, 1992) with Indochinese refugees, such skepticism can in fact be absolutely toxic to torture victims and others who have suffered from interpersonal violence (see also Kassindja & Miller, 1998; Herman, 1992). On the other hand, psychopathic individuals are often quite highly adept at interpersonal maneuvers designed to neutralize skepticism (Hare, 1993). Naturally, an attitude of unquestioning belief and acceptance of what we are told, what we also call naivety, is equally problematic in forensic assessment.

Skepticism and detachment, unbalanced by empathy and respect for the forensic evaluee, is itself a fundamentally non-neutral position.

With this said, what elements of C/TA may lend themselves in particular to enhanced forensic practice? Of the C/TA elements cited in the introduction, three stand out as suitable for adaptation to forensic practice: 1) the assessor as participant-observer, as opposed to an "objective, detached observer"; 2) personality tests as "empathy magnifiers" that access the client's inner world (rather than simply as standardized samples of behavior for nomothetic comparison), with a focus more on the client's subjective experience rather than scores by themselves; and 3) the use of C/TA style assessment results feedback such as "extended inquiry" to clarify forensic findings. These principles, unmoored from their therapeutic ancestry, can provide a corrective to a detached, skeptical, and, ultimately, biased forensic stance.

Introducing BETAssessment™

In order to better distinguish current Therapeutic Assessment, therapeutic assessment, and Collaborative/Therapeutic Assessment treatment models from a more generic approach to assessment that incorporates the aforementioned three principles, we introduce the term, "BETAssessment™," which stands for Building Empathy through Assessment. We have chosen to introduce this term in order to distinguish an approach that, while incorporating Collaborative/Therapeutic Assessment principles, does not adhere to any specific model of therapeutic assessment currently being practiced. BETAssessment™ systematically includes the client and assessor, forensic or clinical, as active participants in the assessment process, collaborating wherever possible with mutually agreed upon goals, and incorporating many C/TA principles applicable across nearly all personality assessment contexts.

Principle 1: Forensic Assessor as Participant-Observer

While this principle was discussed earlier in terms of the impact of detached, skepticism in forensic assessment, it is a fundamental aspect of both C/TA and interpersonal psychodynamic approaches (see Sullivan, 1954) to assessment that the assessor is aware that she or he both participates in the assessment and impacts the behavior of the person evaluated. An important finding in the C/TA literature is that a "neutral," detached stance can heighten already high suspicion in examinees and lead to less accurate findings, while a collaborative stance on the part of the assessor decreases the frequency of invalid protocols in self-report instruments (Aschieri, Finn. & Gazale, 2011). Of course, it is important to think of the kind of forensic setting. This approach may have limited value in certain forensic contexts, such as criminal court. On the other hand, there are case examples of child custody/parenting plan evaluations (see Evans, 2012) and termination of parental rights assessments in which a collaborative hybrid approach yielded rich Minnesota Multiphasic Personality Inventory-2 (MMPI-2; Butcher et al., 2001) and Rorschach findings, as well as enduring and satisfying resolutions. The following case illustrates this principle:

> Ms. T was a 21-year-old mother, whose nearly one-year-old son was placed into foster care by Child Protective Services (CPS) following a report that she was unable to care competently for her baby. She was in a highly abusive marriage and, after numerous unsuccessful attempts at separating from her husband, had fallen into a deep depression, engaging in polysubstance abuse, oversleeping, and socially withdrawing to the degree that friends were concerned about the baby. Her own extended family was unresponsive and unsupportive. Ms. T described a long family history of chaotic relationships, physical abuse, and physical abandonment of her at age 16. She reported a history of drug and alcohol abuse beginning at age 13, though quite interestingly, she remained sober during her pregnancy. CPS had already petitioned successfully to terminate parental rights (TPR) of the father and was now in similar proceedings with the mother. Ms. T was engaged in divorce proceedings from the father.
>
> Further, the foster parents of her child had become highly attached to him and had also petitioned for adoption contingent on the TPR proceedings. The assessor (FBE) was asked by the court to provide a parenting

fitness evaluation addressing questions about ongoing vulnerability to substance abuse and mental disorder, strengths and weaknesses in parenting capacity, and recommendations about possible unification of the mother and son. The assessor reached an agreement with CPS and the court to provide the assessment report in the form of a letter to the judge and Ms. T. When Ms. T was asked what question she would like answered by the forensic assessment, she angrily demanded, "Why are they keeping me from my baby?"

Ms. T's psychological testing revealed no elevated clinical scales on the Personality Assessment Inventory (Morey, 1991), but did show mild elevations on subscales indicating possible psychological trauma (ARD-T = 70) and negative relationships (BOR-N = 65). Her Trauma Symptom Inventory (TSI) showed no clinical elevations and indeed no scores over T-50. On the other hand, her Abusive Behavior Observation Checklist (Dutton, 1992) was indicative of pervasive sexual, emotional, and physical abuse in her marriage. Unsurprisingly, the Rorschach yielded a 22-response protocol with an avoidant style (L = 1.75), consistent with a shutdown presentation seen in PTSD (van der Kolk & Ducey, 1989). Further, she showed limited coping resources (EA = 5), was overwhelmed with stressful life events (D = -3), perhaps even chronically so (AdjD = -1). Especially important was her interpersonal inadequacy and tendency to be incompetent in managing social relationships (CDI = 5), as well as an orientation to life in which aggression was seen as natural and expected (AgC = 6). On the other hand, there were no gross problems with reality testing or thought disorder (PIT = 0). Overall, her Rorschach suggested a very inadequate and overwhelmed young woman, consistent with her recent traumatic marriage and long-term traumatic background.

At the beginning of the second session summarizing and discussing the results of the forensic assessment, Ms. T added the following questions, "Should I let my son stay with foster parents? I love him and want him to be with me." Together we reframed the question as, "What is the most caring thing to do for your son?" After discussing this, Ms. T stated, "I am not sure if I can really give him what he is getting. He is very close to his foster parents." The examiner in returned replied, "You love your son so much that you want what is best for him even if it is painful for you, and you are really puzzled about what to do." Two days later, CPT called the examiner to share that Ms. T decided to sign an order allowing for her son to be adopted by his foster parents and had worked out an arrangement with them where she could get regular visitation with him. A follow-up a year later revealed that Ms. T remained proud of her decision and was now in a committed relationship with a reliable man with a stable, close-knit family. This case illustrates how a C/TA-informed approach can turn a potentially acrimonious conflict in which there are winners and bitter losers into one in which the parties can achieve a resolution that is best for all concerned.

Principle 2: Personality Tests as "Empathy Magnifiers"

Finn (2007) described psychological tests as "empathy magnifiers," by which he meant that, rather than viewing them as means to arrive at the "objective truth" of the client's personality, he saw them as serving to better enable the assessor to "get in their client's shoes" (p. 38). In forensic assessment, this enables the assessor to understand the litigant's subjective experience, which is often a crucial component of the overall evaluation. Of course, this must be reconciled with the more objective empirical data in drawing conclusions about the specific questions for the assessment. The Rorschach, as a relatively unstructured task with a free associative component that evokes images from the subject's own internal world, is uniquely suited to allow for this kind of empathic knowledge, as the following example illustrates:

> Ms. E was a 21-year-old South American woman seeking political asylum. She had entered the United States illegally, after fleeing her home country because of threats on her life. She had been kidnapped and held for two days by a guerrilla group along with four other young women. During her captivity, she was repeatedly beaten and sexually assaulted. She was able to escape with the aid of a sympathetic guerrilla, but felt that she was not safe remaining at home, as she learned that all of the other victims had been slain. The Immigration and Naturalization Service (now Immigration and Customs Enforcement) has a high index of suspicion for asylum seekers, and it was decided that a psychological evaluation would be useful in order to determine if her current state was consistent with the experiences she was claiming.
>
> Although the story she told to the examiner (BLS) was consistent with her accounts in previous interviews, she was somewhat dispassionate in her retelling. It was through the Rorschach, however, that the true horror of her experiences came through. Her Rorschach protocol revealed a woman who was flooded with affect and pain. She had a D-score of -3 and an AdjD of -1.

Five inanimate movement responses (m) suggested a sense that her life felt to her as if it were spinning out of control. Her Experience Balance (EB) was pervasively extratensive, and she had an FC:CF+C ratio of 1:7. All of these are signs of trauma according to research findings (Armstrong & Lowenstein, 1990; van der Kolk & Ducey, 1984, 1988). An Affective Ratio (Afr) of 0.29 indicated that avoidance was her primary coping mechanism. Most striking of all, however, was her Trauma Content Index (TCI), which was 0.91. The TCI (Armstrong, 1991) is the ratio of primitive and distressing contents (i.e., An, Bl, Sx, MOR, and AG) to R. Non-traumatized subjects generally have a TCI below 0.25, whereas a TCI above 0.40 is considered highly elevated. It is clear from these data that Ms. E was being flooded with disturbing images.

As clear as the structural data were, it was through Ms. E's verbalizations that the true power of her experience came through. Her first response of "bat," led her to say, "I'm scared of bats," suggesting some loss of distance from the card. On Card II, she saw in order, "blood," "a bleeding heart," and "a vagina bleeding, completely destroyed." Card III included the response "2 people...ripping a heart out," and Card IV was "a monster, like a terrorist." So it went throughout the protocol, one image of aggression or sexual violence after another. On Card VI, for instance, she saw another "damaged vagina," actually seeing the achromatic card as having red blood and dark hair. Finally, on Card X, she saw "hell," with various animals falling into fire or an abyss. This protocol, disturbing as it was, enabled the examiner to empathize with Ms. E's horror and her struggle to cope with her experience. Although the evaluation was conducted in English, Ms. E had an interpreter present in case she had difficulties in her second language. The experience of the Rorschach was so powerful that the interpreter herself began to weep.

Given the evidence from the psychological evaluation as well as confirmatory accounts from her home country, Ms. E easily won her case and was granted asylum. Given the nature of her traumatic history, the evaluation could easily have been seriously re-traumatizing; however, the empathic approach enabled her to tell her story and reveal her personality in an atmosphere of safety. Indeed, following the resolution of the immigration case, Ms. E chose to begin psychotherapy with the examiner—a treatment that lasted several months and was considered successful.

In other instances, the forensic assessor may find that other psychological issues are more important in explaining the plaintiff's emotional suffering in a personal injury case. Such findings can lead to feelings of shame in the plaintiff for having misattributed current psychological concerns. The following is a case where a BETAssessment™ focus on using psychological tests as empathy magnifiers to provide forensic results served as a bridge between the results of the forensic assessment and an outcome that led to a resolution of emotional issues not directly connected to the litigation itself.

Ms. F was a 28-year-old woman who was referred for an evaluation as part of a personal injury case. She had suffered a severed Achilles tendon and other lower leg injuries in a work-related accident. Although she eventually made a full recovery from the injuries, she was severely disabled for some time. As a result, she could not work for many months. In addition—and importantly—Ms. F was an athlete, and her inability to run or work out was extremely distressing to her. She began to show symptoms of a major depression.

Ms. F had a history of depression that first manifested during her freshman year in college. She was forced to take a year off in order to recover, and subsequently she experienced another episode around the time she graduated. Significantly, she was highly identified with her father, who had lost his job in early middle age and had sunk into a chronic depression of his own. Her mother wound up having to support the family with a small family business, as her father was not able to secure employment again. It was clear from the evaluation that Ms. F's identification with her father was contributing to her depression after the injury, in that she unconsciously feared that she, too, would be unable to work again.

The Rorschach results were consistent with a diagnosis of depression, and supported the aforementioned interpretation. Her protocol had 4 C' responses and 4 MOR responses, suggestive of depression and feeling damaged, and 7 Animal Movement responses (FM), suggestive of unmet need states. Furthermore, the content of her actual responses showed a repetitive pattern of "spoiled" answers, in which an initially upbeat image is changed into one that is damaged or depressed. For example, a response featuring a butterfly is elaborated as follows: "The wings are down, so it looks threatening or submissive.... maybe it wants to take me down with it." Her most revealing answer to Card VIII was, "A man with a long face, a sad face ... like he's mourning." Other elements of the Rorschach, however, indicated a robust personality structure with more than adequate resources. The evaluator was able to conclude that Ms. F had an episode of depression that was clearly triggered by the injury. Once she recovered physically, she was able to gain employment and resume her athletic pursuits, and her depression lifted. In consultation with the evaluator, her attorney decided not to pursue special emotional damages as part of her lawsuit.

Following the decision not to pursue emotional damages, the evaluator met with Ms. F to provide feedback on the assessment. She was told that she had indeed been depressed, but that her depression was not simply a cyclical mood shift, nor was it only a result of PTSD, but rather reflected her identification with her father and her fear that she might end up like him. This interpretation resonated with her and accomplished two goals. In the first place, it helped her to accept the fact that her emotional state would not be part of the lawsuit, and second, provided her with a focus to pursue in individual psychotherapy. Making sense of her depression was immensely relieving to her and provided a benefit from the forensic evaluation over and above its role in the litigation.

Principle 3: Use of C/TA Feedback to Clarify Forensic Findings

One of the central concepts of forensic psychology is the integration of multiple sources of information, generally clinical interview, collateral data, and psychological testing results. This "three-legged stool" of information provides a basis for arriving at a fuller picture of evaluees' overall personality by sifting through confirming and disconfirming sources. C/TA feedback can form a bridge to further explore puzzling aspects of forensics assessment findings.

For example, a veteran claiming disability compensation for posttraumatic stress disorder (PTSD) may report severe and disabling symptoms on clinical interview, reciting his symptoms in what appears to be a rote or emotionless manner. Face valid measures of PTSD such as the PTSD Checklist (PCL: Weathers et al., 1993) and the Mississippi Combat-Related PTSD Scale (MISS: Keane, Caddell, & Taylor, 1988) indicate severe levels of PTSD. On the other hand, the VA medical records and other corroborative records may show no prior diagnosis or treatment of PTSD and numerous prior negative Primary Care-PTSD screenings (Ouimette, Wade, Prins, & Schohn, 2008) with no symptoms endorsed. MMPI-2 testing shows a pattern of PTSD exaggeration common in compensation-seeking veterans (Gold & Frueh, 1999; Tolin, Steenkamp, Marx, & Litz, 2010). In many psycholegal arenas, it would be tempting simply to opine that there is insufficient evidence of PTSD due to military service. Yet, as Worthen & Moering (2011) note, VA disability law of equipoise directs the Compensation and Pension (C&P) psychologist and benefits adjudicator to give the veteran the "benefit of the doubt" in arriving at opinions, which essentially means that only 50% certainty is necessary for a positive finding.

Two cases with seemingly similar psychological assessment findings are used to illustrate the important of C/TA feedback in forensic assessment:

> Veteran Mr. A claimed severe and debilitating PTSD symptoms on his original application for C&P. His scores on face valid measures of PTSD were in the severe range. Although his score on the F scale of the MMPI-2 was significantly elevated and in most cases would make the test appear to be invalid, it was not in a range where overreporting could be reliably differentiated from extreme distress (see Franklin et al., 2002) and the Fp scale was not significantly elevated. His 14-response Rorschach was marginally interpretable at best, with a very high Lambda and a few elevations on other scores, more consistent with a defensive than an avoidant presentation (see van der Kolk & Ducey, 1989). His Trauma Content Index (TCI; Armstrong & Lowenstein, 1990) was not elevated, and there was no other content or thematic repetition suggestive of traumatic preoccupation. The VA medical records indicated no diagnosis or treatment of PTSD or other mental disorder and included seven negative PC-PTSD screens over the past 11 years, the most recent being about one year earlier. His interview was frequently vague about the experience and effects of his purported PTSD symptoms, but he endorsed every PTSD symptom on the Clinician Administered PTSD Scale (CAPS: Blake et al., 1995). Additionally, he failed to provide good examples of each traumatic symptom, which triggers concerns about possible malingering. At the end of the assessment, the evaluator (FBE) shared that he wondered if the veteran could help him clear up a disparity in the findings, noting that the veteran had never claimed any PTSD symptom on any VA record and, in fact, had given seven negative PTSD screens. After a somewhat uncomfortable discussion, during which the assessor normalized compensation-seeking behavior, the veteran revealed that he was recently retired, was having trouble making ends meet, and heard at a bar at a local veterans' organization that getting a PTSD disability payment was easy. The veteran then voluntarily withdrew his C&P claim and no report was placed in his file.

Veteran Mr. B was assessed for his original claim for C&P. His scores on face valid measures of PTSD were in the mild to moderate range. His score on the F scale of the MMPI-2 was significantly elevated, though not invalid, and the Fp scale was not significant. His 17-response Rorschach indicated an avoidant presentation (see van der Kolk & Ducey, 1989). While it showed an elevated Lambda, there were breakthrough, "color shock" responses of blood and morbid content on Cards II and III, followed by a shutting down of response richness in the cards that followed. His TCI was 0.30. The VA medical records indicated no diagnosis or treatment of PTSD or other mental disorder and included four negative PC-PTSD screens over the past ten years, the most recent being several years earlier. He was seen initially with his wife, who nearly always accompanied him to all his VA medical visits. The veteran was hesitant to report symptoms during his interview, and the assessor requested to see the veteran alone for the last part of his interview. He then endorsed numerous (but not all) PTSD symptoms on the CAPS and provided good examples for each symptom, which is indicative of accurate reporting. At the end of the assessment, the assessor shared that he wondered if the veteran could help him clear up a disparity in the findings, noting that the veteran had never claimed any PTSD symptom on any VA record and in fact had given four negative PTSD screens. The veteran revealed that he had been unwilling to discuss or endorse his war-related symptoms with his wife present, as she was not in good health and he did not want to worry her. He explained that he only recently applied for service-connected C&P benefits for long-standing back problems and PTSD, because his symptoms of both made it difficult for him to continue working in his self-employed business. The veteran's explanation was sufficient to remove the assessor's doubt and led to an extended discussion about the merits of seeking treatment for PTSD. A follow-up revealed that the veteran later received service-connected benefits for PTSD and actively sought treatment for the disorder.

The Rorschach in Multimethod Forensic BETAssessment™

As has been reported previously, the Rorschach is an important element in forensic evaluations because it provides incremental validity over interview and self-report data (Erdberg, 2008; Gacono & Evans, 2008), is generally considered to be less subject to conscious manipulation (Ganellen, 2008), and accesses aspects of the individual's functioning generally outside of awareness (Bornstein, 2011). The presented cases are intended to illustrate how the Rorschach may provide incremental validity above self-report instruments. The access to implicit personality processes is in turn vital to a more accurate and empathic understanding of the individual being assessed in both forensic and clinical settings. As such, the Rorschach is especially suited to address split-off affect states that are outside the respondent's awareness and therefore difficult to discuss (Finn, 2007) as in the cases presented earlier. As a result, use of the Rorschach is especially useful in BETAssessment™.

Summary

The challenge for the forensic assessor is to go beyond the surface presentation of the examinee in order to fully answer the forensic questions, while at the same time avoiding traumatizing or re-traumatizing her. In this chapter, we have presented a model for conducting C/TA-informed forensic evaluations that we believe allows for an objective evaluation of the examinee's state of mind, while at the same time maintaining empathy for her. We have explicated the rationale for this approach, which we term BETAssessment™, drawn from both interpersonal psychodynamic theory and the research literature. Within this model, the Rorschach holds a unique and vital place as an instrument that can provide both examiner and examinee insight into heretofore unknown or unacknowledged aspects of the examinee's personality. We believe that this model holds promise for the conduct of accurate and humane forensic evaluations.

Note

1 While the term therapeutic assessment is used broadly, Stephen Finn and the Therapeutic Assessment Institute prefer to reserve the specific term "Therapeutic Assessment" with upper case "T" and "A" for the specific model promulgated by them (Finn, 2007). Out of respect for Finn's wishes, we will use the term Collaborative/Therapeutic Assessment (C/TA) to avoid confusion.

References

Armstrong, J. (1991). The psychological organization of multiple personality disordered patients as revealed in psychological testing. *Psychiatric Clinics of North America, 14,* 533–546.

Armstrong, J., & Lowenstein, R. (1990). Characteristics of patients with multiple personality and dissociative disorders on psychological testing. *Journal of Nervous and Mental Disease, 174,* 448–454.

Aschieri, F., Finn, S. E., & Gazale, M. F. (September, 2011). *Openness of clients on tests as a result of constructing a collaborative relationship: A study with the MMPI-2*. Paper presented at the annual meeting of the Italian Psychological Association, Catania, Sicily, as part of a symposium, "Collaborative Assessment: Clinical and Research Aspects," F. Aschieri, Chair.

Blake, D. D., Weathers, F. W., Nagy, L. M., Kaloupek, D. G., Gusman, F. D., Charney, D. S., & Keane, T. M. (1995). The development of a clinician-administered PTSD scale. *Journal of Traumatic Stress, 8*(1), 75–90.

Bornstein, R. F. (2011). From symptom to process: How the PDM alters goals and strategies in psychological assessment. *Journal of Personality Assessment, 93*, 142–150.

Butcher, J., Dahlstrom, W. G., Graham, J., Tellegen, A., & Kaemmer, B. (2001). *Minnesota Multiphasic Personality Inventory-2 (MMPI-2)*, Minneapolis: University of Minnesota Press.

Dickie, I. (2008). Ethical dilemmas, forensic psychology, and therapeutic jurisprudence. *Thomas Jefferson Law Review, 30*, 455–461.

Dutton, M. A. (1992). *Empowering and healing the battered woman: A model for assessment and intervention*. New York: Springer.

Erdberg, P. S. (2008). Multimethod assessment as a forensic standard. In C. B. Gacono, F. B. Evans (Eds.) & N. Kaser-Boyd, L. A. Gacono (Collaborators), *The LEA series in personality and clinical psychology. The handbook of forensic Rorschach assessment* (pp. 561–566). New York: Routledge/Taylor & Francis Group.

Evans, F. B. III. (2005). Trauma, Torture, and Transformation in the Forensic Assessor. *Journal of Personality Assessment, 84*(1), 25–28. http://dx.doi.org/10.1207/s15327752jpa8401_06

Evans, F. B. III. (2012). Therapeutic assessment alternative to custody evaluation: An adolescent whose parents could not stop fighting. In S. E. Finn, C. T. Fischer & L. Handler (Eds.), *Collaborative/therapeutic assessment: A casebook and guide* (pp. 357–378). Hoboken, NJ: John Wiley.

Finn, S. E. (2007). *In our clients' shoes: Theory and techniques of therapeutic assessment*. New York: Routledge.

Finn, S. E., & Tonsager, M. E. (1997). Information-gathering and therapeutic models of assessment: Complementary paradigms. *Psychological Assessment, 9*(4), 374–385.

Fischer, C. T. (1985/1994). *Individualizing psychological assessment*. New York: Routledge.

Franklin, C., Repasky, S., Thompson, K., Shelton, S., & Uddo, M. (2002). Differentiating overreporting and extreme distress: MMPI-2 use with compensation-seeking veterans with PTSD. *Journal of Personality Assessment, 79*(2), 274–285.

Gacono, C. B., & Evans, F. B. (Eds.). (2008). *The LEA series in personality and clinical psychology: The handbook of forensic Rorschach assessment* (N. Kaser-Boyd & L. A. Gacono, Collaborators). New York: Routledge/Taylor & Francis Group.

Ganellen, R. J. (2008). Rorschach assessment of malingering and defensive response sets. In C. B. Gacono, F. B. Evans (Eds.) & N. Kaser-Boyd, L. A. Gacono (Collaborators), *The LEA series in personality and clinical psychology: The handbook of forensic Rorschach assessment* (pp. 89–119). New York: Routledge/Taylor & Francis Group.

Gold, P. B., & Frueh, C. B. (1999). Compensation-seeking and extreme exaggeration of psychopathology among combat veterans evaluated for posttraumatic stress disorder. *Journal of Nervous and Mental Disease, 187*(11), 680-684.

Greenberg, S. A., & Shuman, D. W. (1997). Irreconcilable conflict between therapeutic and forensic roles. *Professional Psychology: Research and Practice, 28*(1), 50-57. http://dx.doi.org/10.1037/0735-7028.28.1.50

Hanson, W. E., & Poston, J. M. (2011). Building confidence in psychological assessment as a therapeutic intervention: An empirically based reply to Lilienfeld, Garb, and Wood (2011). *Psychological Assessment, 23*(4), 1056-1062.

Hare, R. D. (1993). *Without conscience: The disturbing world of the psychopaths among us.* New York: Guilford.

Herman, J. (2015). *Trauma and recovery: The aftermath of violence—from domestic abuse to political terror.* New York: Basic Books.

Herman, J. L. (1992). *Trauma and recovery: The aftermath of violence—from domestic abuse to political terror.* New York: Basic Books.

Kassindja, F., & Miller, L. M. (1998). *Do they hear you when you cry?* New York: Delta.

Keane, T. M., Caddell, J. M., & Taylor, K. L. (1988). Mississippi Scale for Combat-Related Posttraumatic Stress Disorder: Three studies in reliability and validity. *Journal of Consulting and Clinical Psychology, 56*, 85-90. doi:10.1037/0022-006X.56.1.85

Lipton, S. D. (1977). The advantages of Freud's technique as shown in his analysis of the Rat Man. *The International Journal of Psychoanalysis, 58*(3), 255-273.

Madsen, K., & Holmberg, U. (2015). Interviewees' psychological well-being in investigative interviews: A therapeutic jurisprudential approach. *Psychiatry, Psychology and Law, 22*(1), 60-74. doi.org/10.1080/13218719.2014.918083

Mollica, R. F., Caspi-Yavin, Y., Bollini, P., Truong, T., Tor, S., & Lavelle, J. (1992). The Harvard Trauma Questionnaire: Validating a cross-cultural instrument for measuring torture, trauma, and posttraumatic stress disorder in Indochinese refugees. *Journal of Nervous and Mental Disease. 180*, 111-116.

Mollica, R. F., Wyshak, G., & Lavelle, J. (1987). The psychosocial impact of war trauma and torture among Southeast Asian refugees. *American Journal of Psychiatry, 144*, 1567-1572.

Morey, L. (1991). *The Personality Assessment Inventory.* Tampa, FL: Psychological Assessment Resources.

Ouimette, P., Wade, M., Prins, A., & Schohn, M. (2008). Identifying PTSD in primary care: Comparison of the Primary Care-PTSD Screen (PC-PTSD) and the General Health Questionnaire-12 (GHQ). *Journal of Anxiety Disorders, 22*(2), 337-343.

Pickar, D. B. (2008). Countertransference and the child custody evaluator. *Journal of Child Custody, 4*(3-4), 45-67.

Pickar, D. B., & Erard, R. E. (2008). Countertransference bias in child custody evaluations is just a horse of a different color: A rejoinder to Martindale and Gould. *Journal of Child Custody, 4*(3-4), 77-89.

Poston, J. M., & Hanson, W. E. (2010). Meta-analysis of psychological assessment as a therapeutic intervention. *Psychological Assessment, 22*(2), 203-212.

Schafer, R. (1954). *Psychoanalytic interpretation in Rorschach testing.* New York: Grune & Stratton.

Smith, B. (1990). The origins of interpretation in the countertransference. *Psychoanalytic Psychology*, 7(supl.), 89-104.

Smith, B. (2005). The observer observed: Discussion of papers by Evans, Finn, Handler, and Lerner. *Journal of Personality Assessment, 84*, 33-36.

Sullivan, H. S. (1953). *The interpersonal theory of psychiatry*. New York: WW Norton & Company.

Sullivan, H. S. (1954). *The psychiatric interview*. New York: WW Norton & Company.

Tolin, D. F., Steenkamp, M. M., Marx, B. P., & Litz, B. T. (2010). Detecting symptom exaggeration in combat veterans using the MMPI-2 symptom validity scales: A mixed group validation. *Psychological Assessment, 22*(4), 729-736.

van der Kolk, B. A., & Ducey, C. P. (1984) Clinical implications of the Rorschach in posttraumatic stress disorder. In B. A. van der Kolk (ed). *Post-traumatic stress disorder: Psychological and biological sequelae* (pp. 30-42). Washington, DC: American Psychiatric Press.

van der Kolk, B. A., & Ducey, C. P. (1989). The psychological processing of traumatic experience: Rorschach patterns in PTSD. *Journal of Traumatic Stress, 2*(3), 259-274.

Weathers, F., Litz, B., Herman, D., Huska, J., & Keane, T. (October, 1993). *The PTSD Checklist (PCL): Reliability, validity, and diagnostic utility*. Paper presented at the Annual Convention of the International Society for Traumatic Stress Studies, San Antonio, TX.

Weigert, E. (1970). *The courage to love: Selected papers of Edith Weigert, M.D.* New Haven, CT: Yale University Press.

Worthen, M. D., & Moering, R. G. (2011). A practical guide to conducting VA compensation and pension exams for PTSD and other mental disorders. *Psychological Injury and Law, 4*(3-4), 187-216.

Chapter 10

USING THE CS IN AN R-PAS WORLD

Multimethod Forensic Assessment with the Exner Comprehensive System

F. Barton Evans

The Rorschach Inkblot Method (RIM; Rorschach, 1942) is a uniquely valuable assessment method in clinical and forensic practice, which evaluates implicit aspects of personality functioning that are frequently untapped by more widely used self-report inventories (Bornstein, 2002, 2011; Mihura, 2012). The RIM is the most commonly used (Archer, Buffington-Vollum, Stredny & Handel, 2006) and well-validated performance-based assessment method in forensic settings (Gacono & Evans, 2008). When used within a contemporary, empirically based scoring and interpretive system, the RIM has been found to meet evidentiary standards necessary for use in court (Erard, 2012; McCann & Evans, 2008; Meloy, 2008; Ritzler, Erard, & Pettigrew, 2002a, 2002b) and has been found to be useful in both clinical and forensic settings (Status of the Rorschach, 2005). The Rorschach is especially valuable in forensic settings because 1) the RIM was not devised to be content valid and rests on completely different assumptions than is the case for a questionnaire or self-report test (Bornstein, 2011), and 2) RIM interpretation is based on a large body of empirical research connecting particular types of responses validly to important external benchmarks (Mihura, Meyer, Dumitrascu, & Bombel, 2013). Combined with self-report measures with substantial validity, the RIM offers a distinctly different way of assessing characteristics that provide incremental validity over self-report methods (see Weiner, 2013). Because forensic psychological assessment is particularly sensitive to distortions resulting from response style, the RIM also offers an assessment approach that is often much less vulnerable to distortion than self-report methods (Ganellen, 2008; Schultz, this volume).

The purpose of this chapter is to provide a guide for experienced users of the Exner Comprehensive System (CS: Exner, 2003; Exner & Erdberg, 2005) to navigate in forensic settings now that there is a new and alternative system for the RIM. The advent of the Rorschach Performance Assessment System® (R-PAS®: Meyer, Viglione, Mihura, Erard, & Erdberg, 2011) and its incorporation of important new empirical findings that have been published since the fifth and final revision of the Exner Comprehensive System (Exner, 2001) can provide assistance for experienced forensic CS users who either have not chosen to adopt R-PAS or have ongoing forensic assessments while preparing to learn R-PAS. This chapter will explore the use of the CS in forensic assessment, including recommendations for evidence-based modifications found in R-PAS to update current CS practice. In my opinion, incorporating new empirical findings into current CS practice clearly stands in the tradition of John Exner's remarkable and long-standing legacy of revising the CS when warranted by sufficient new research findings, as evidenced by his four major revisions between his initial publication of the CS (Exner, 1974) and his last (Exner, 2001). Naturally, it is also always incumbent upon all forensic RIM assessors to keep abreast of cutting-edge RIM research.

Why Continue to Use the CS?

For many years, the CS was the only well developed and widely accepted empirical system of administration, scoring, and interpretation of the RIM sufficient for routine use in evaluations for the courts. The CS combined the best elements of several prior systems and blended the RIM's interpretative richness (e.g., Lerner, 1998, 1991) with "dust bowl empiricism" (Exner, 1974). Although it came under intense challenge by a group of academics generally untrained in the instrument (see Garb, 1999; Garb, Wood, Lilienfeld, & Nezworski, 2002; Lilienfeld, Wood, & Garb, 2001; Hunsley & Bailey, 1999; Wood, Nezworski, & Stejskal, 1996; Ziskin,1995), most of their criticisms were refuted by others in the forensic assessment literature (see Gacono & Evans, 2008 for a comprehensive review of these issues). A well-researched statement by the Board of Trustees of the Society for Personality Assessment concluded that the Rorschach CS was empirically grounded and beneficial when properly used in both clinical and forensic settings (Status of the Rorschach, 2005).

One salutary consequence of the relentless critical challenges faced by the Rorschach several years ago was that they served to provoke the most active review of the validity and reliability of the CS since Exner's original work, most notably the outstanding Rorschach meta-analyses by Mihura, Meyer, Dumitrascu, and Bombel (2013). As will be discussed later, the Rorschach meta-analyses, the Composite International Reference Values (CIRV), and other research findings now incorporated into R-PAS other modifications and improvements to the already impressive empirical foundation of the CS. Recommendations later in this chapter will address these important empirical findings, which can (and in many cases should) be assimilated into the present-day CS forensic practitioner's practice.

With this background in mind, there are three principal reasons for experienced CS users to feel confident in maintaining an ethical, evidenced-based use of Exner's system: 1) a legitimate preference for the CS by experienced forensic Rorschach practitioners, 2) the use of the CS as an internationally preferred system, and 3) cautions and critiques raised about the current acceptability of the R-PAS in forensic settings.

Experienced Forensic CS Users

There are several reasons why experienced forensic CS users may decide to continue to use the CS. First, and most obviously, because they have honed their expert skills in using the CS system for years, experienced forensic psychologists may continue using the CS to provide expert forensic opinions. These forensic assessors have honed their expert skills in using this system for years. They may not wish to shift to a new system, but rather choose to update their use of the CS with more recent research from both systems, per standard forensic practice. Learning a new system such as R-PAS may also entail time, expense, and even some initial conceptual interference that may be counterproductive for a busy forensic practice. Although the American Psychological Association

Ethical Standard 9.08b states: "Psychologists do not base such decisions or recommendations on tests and measures that are obsolete and not useful for the current purpose" (American Psychological Association, 2010), there is nothing to suggest that CS-based approaches are obsolete if used in the context of new R-PAS and CS-based research findings recommended later in this chapter.

Additionally, the continued utilization of the CS allows ready incorporation of ongoing research in the United States and around the world from RIM databases gathered using the CS. Examples include recent CS-based publication of Iranian CS norms (Hosseininasab, Mohammadi, Weiner, & Delavar, 2015) and the forthcoming analysis of a sample of over 750 CS RIM protocols of VA veterans over 20 years, evaluating the longitudinal predictive validity of CS indices in predicting suicide and longevity (A. C. Horn, personal communication, February 16, 2016). These and other research findings may aid in the ongoing upgrade of the empirical basis of the RIM and will support continued CS-based forensic use incorporating these findings.

Further, some CS practitioners may be cautious about adopting a new RIM methodology, based on a view that R-PAS does not yet have a long history and substantial forensic literature beyond its CS underpinnings to aid the forensic practitioner.

International Forensic CS Users

While, as Erard, Meyer, and Viglione (2014) note, R-PAS training is broadly international and has been adopted increasingly by many non-North American RIM practitioners, the CS continues to be actively used around the world (Piotrowski, 2015b), even as training in the RIM declines in the United States (Piotrowski, 2015a; Ready & Veague, 2014). In response to the changing times, the Comprehensive System International Rorschach Association (CSIRA) was formed as a forum to encourage training, practice, and research in the CS.

It is unclear whether CSIRA or other organizations will successfully revive CS research and find ways to incorporate R-PAS empirical advances, though the normative research by Hosseininasab et al. (2015) shows promise in this regard. A larger task will be finding a way to incorporate new research and changes into the CS-based practice, given the copyright restrictions currently prohibiting modifications to the CS

Structural Summary. An example of CS-based practice transcending the formal CS Structural Summary includes Tibon-Czopp and Weiner's (2016) CS-based approach, which includes recently developed scales not part of the CS such as the Ego Impairment Index (Perry & Viglione, 1991), the Reality-Fantasy Scale (Tibon, Handelzalts & Weinberger, 2005), and two new scores, the Complexity Index and the AdjDMD (the Adjusted D-score minus the D-score; Tibon-Czopp & Weiner, 2016). It is worthy of note that the structural summary in the Tibon-Czopp/Weiner book does not include the CS Intellectualization Index and the Obsessive Index, which have not fared well in validity studies.

Critiques of Testimony Based on R-PAS in Forensic Settings

R-PAS is not without its critics, and even has its detractors. The publication of the Special Section on the Rorschach in *Psychological Injury and Law* (Evans, 2012) introduced to the forensic literature new possibilities provided by the R-PAS for forensic assessment. While strongly supporting the development of the R-PAS, Khadivi and Evans (2012) raised questions about its current use in forensic settings. First, they cited concerns about the lack of independent research examining the validity of the R-PAS as a whole, apart from its CS research roots, with no head-to-head research studies comparing both systems. Second, they queried whether R-Optimized administration is a modification of its CS administrative roots or whether it makes R-PAS a different test than the CS. Third, they noted the lack of independently gathered normative and clinical samples using the new R-PAS administrative procedures. Erard's (2012) article in the same Rorschach Special Section presented compelling evidence responding to these concerns.

Similarly to Khadivi and Evans (2012), Kivisto, Gacono, and Medoff (2013) questioned whether the R-PAS R-Optimized administrative procedure has rendered the CS and R-PAS non-equivalent. They were also concerned about the use of norms based on the international normative sample (Meyer, Erdberg, & Shaffer, 2007), which were modified to simulate the R-Optimized procedure, instead of using entirely new non-patient or clinical normative samples gathered while using R-PAS administration procedure. Taking a more strident tone than Khadivi and Evans and leaning heavily on McCann and Evans's (2008) analysis of why the

CS is admissible in court, they took issue with Erard's (2012) conclusions about the admissibility of R-PAS. While Kvisto et al. (2013) raised provocative questions, it should be noted that they relied to a large degree on still unpublished 1992 papers concerning the sensitivity of changes in standard CS administration, while failing to cite the peer-reviewed study by Dean, Viglione, Perry, and Meyer (2007), showing promise about maintaining CS validity using an early version of the R-Optimized procedure. Subsequently, as will be discussed later in this chapter, Viglione et al. (2015) demonstrated that the current R-Optimized Rorschach procedure reduced error associated with variability in R and enhanced the validity of clinical inferences. This study provides important empirical evidence that addresses the concerns of Khadivi and Evans (2012) and Kivisto, Gacono, and Medoff (2013) about use of the R-Optimized administration procedure.

Finally, while it is beyond the scope of this chapter to fully summarize, Gurley, Sheehan, Piechowski, and Gray (2014) presented an extensive critique regarding the admissibility of the R-PAS in forensic practice. This critique did not add substantively to the points already raised by Khadivi and Evans (2012) and Kivisto, Gacono, and Medoff (2013). The response by Erard et al. (2014) carefully corrected the Gurley et al.'s (2014) many legal, psychometric, and research misconceptions. Nonetheless, well-prepared forensic RIM assessors using either a CS-based or R-PAS system may wish to familiarize themselves with this article and the response to it.

In conclusion, the position of this chapter in informing forensic RIM practitioners of disagreements within the professional community in no way should be seen as an attempt to invalidate the points raised by Erard (2012) and Erard, Meyer, and Viglione (2014) concerning the admissibility of R-PAS. These points of disagreement will hopefully provide grist for the intellectual mill of personality assessment usage in forensic RIM practice, which has been so productive in the past to CS and R-PAS development. It is recommended that the continued use of the CS in forensic practice should be undertaken with appropriate modifications recommended in the following section. With this in mind, the current use of either the CS or the R-PAS in forensic practice rather serves as offering alternative approaches, similar to those choosing to use the MMPI-2 over the MMPI-RF in forensic practice.

Updating the CS

So how can a CS forensic practitioner prepare for an increasingly R-PAS world? The following are four recommended ways in which forensic psychologists can overcome some of the empirical problems with the CS itself, which has not been formally revised by Rorschach Workshops for over 15 years.

Mihura et al. (2013) Meta-Analyses

As stated earlier, RIM critics stimulated perhaps the most active review of the validity and reliability of RIM variables since Exner's (1974) original CS, most notably the remarkably comprehensive Rorschach meta-analyses by Mihura, Meyer, Dumitrascu, and Bombel (2013). These meta-analyses reviewed 68 major variables in the CS, using modern meta-analytic procedures and found five levels of strength of validity support. These findings ranged in strength from Excellent ($r > 0.33$ for 14 variables) to Absence of Evidence (no published studies found for 12 variables since 1974). Thirty-nine variables achieved at least modest validity. Variables with excellent validity, not surprisingly, included Human Movement (M), Experience Actual (EA), Sum of Shading (SumShd), Inanimate Movement (m), D-score, Anatomy plus X-ray (An+Xy), synthesized responses (DQ+), most Form Quality variables (X+%, WDA%, X- %/XA%), Sum of Special Scores (Sum/WSum6), Level 2 Special Scores, the Perceptual Thinking Index (PTI), and the Suicide Constellation (S-Con). Table 10.1 summarizes the findings of the meta-analyses.

Also supporting the special value of the RIM as a performance-based measure and its utility in multimethod assessment, the meta-analyses convincingly demonstrated that valid CS scores were much more strongly correlated with externally assessed criteria such as behavioral observations, observer ratings, and psychiatric diagnosis than with self-assessed criteria, such as self-report measures. The importance of the RIM in assessing implicit personality functioning and providing incremental validity over self-report methods in forensic settings has been well discussed by Mihura (2012).

The findings of the Mihura et al. (2013) meta-analyses have now become an essential resource for current, well-prepared RIM practitioners when presenting Rorschach findings in court, regardless of whether

Table 10:1 Strength of the Validity Evidence for Rorschach Comprehensive System (CS) Variables

Level of Support	Controls & Situational Stress	Affective Features	Interpersonal & Self-Perception	Information Processing	Cognitive Mediation & Ideation	Indices
Excellent ($r \geq 0.33$, $p < 0.001$; thus FSN > 50)	M EA SumShd m D-Score		An+Xy	DQ+	X+% WDA% X-%/XA% Sum/WSum6	PTI S-Con
Good ($r \geq 0.21$, $p < 0.05$, FSN ≥ 10)	R Lambda WSumC SumY	FC:CF+C Blends SumC' Afr	COP MOR SumT H/H:NPH GHR Fr+rF	Zf	Lv2 P	
Modest ($p < 0.05$; $r \geq 0.21$, FSN < 10 or $r = 0.15$–0.20; FSN ≥ 10)	es		PER PHR SumV	DQv PSV	Xu% M-	DEPI CDI
Little ($p < 0.05$; $r < 0.15$ or FSN < 10) to None ($p > 0.05$)	FM[a] AdjD EB Style FM+m EBPer EB: Ambitent	S Pure C CP SumC':WSumC	AGM[a] Food[a] Isol Indx a:p 3r+(2)/R FD Human Cont.	Zd W:M W:D:Dd	S- Mnone 2AB+Art+Ay	HVI
Absence of Evidence (Studies = 0)						OBS

[a] = Little Support

This table is Copyright 2012 by Rorschach Performance Assessment System, LLC (R-PAS®), and it is based on data that were subsequently published in Table 3 of "The Validity of Individual Rorschach Variables: Systematic Reviews and Meta-analyses of the Comprehensive System," by J. L. Mihura, G. J. Meyer, N. Dumitrascu, and G. Bombel, 2013, *Psychological Bulletin*, *139*, p. 570. Copyright 2012 by American Psychological Association. Reprinted with permission of R-PAS.

they use the CS or R-PAS. In response to Mihura at al. (2013), even staunch RIM critics have acknowledged the validity of a number of CS variables (Wood, Garb, Nezworski, Lilienfeld & Duke, 2015; see also a reply by Mihura, Meyer, Dumitrascu, & Bombel, 2015). In my opinion, forensic practitioners proceed at their peril in providing expert testimony on treasured, but empirically non-supported, CS variables, such as the Intellectualization Index and the Obsessive Index, or place too much emphasis on such weakly supported variables as EB style or Pure C in their conclusions. Although Rorschach variables not found valid in the meta-analyses are not necessarily inadmissible in an expert opinion, the forensic RIM assessor bears the heavy burden of providing a clear basis for these variables' use beyond just their inclusion in the CS.

International Reference Norms

Shaffer, Erdberg, and Meyer (2007) published a Special Supplement on international norms in the *Journal of Personality Assessment*. This monumental project included 21 adult samples from 17 countries and 19 child and adolescent samples from ten widely distributed European countries, three South American countries, Israel, Japan, and Australia, as well as the United States. They determined that the total adult sample was sufficiently coherent to warrant pooling of the respective results to create Composite International Norms, later renamed the Composite International Reference Values (CIRV), thus creating Rorschach CS norms that generalized across languages, cultures, and sampling strategies. Comparing CIRV norms with Exner's (2007) sample, they determined that the CIRV differed from the Exner CS norms in nearly one-third of all variables, revealing that the Exner CS norms show a bias toward more pathological interpretations. On the basis of this comparison, they wrote, "However, Exner's samples also appeared to have healthier looking Form Quality scores, less general disturbance, more Color and resources, and better human representations than did the other international samples" (p. 337). They concluded with a recommendation for the use of CIRV reference data as a corrective in interpreting CS variables. Although there has been controversy about the applied use of the CIRV (see Ritzler & Sciara, 2009), in three research studies of interpretive validity and addressing critical concerns about sample collection, Meyer, Shaffer, Erdberg, and Horn (2015) provide strong corroboration for the use of CIRV over the Exner CS norms. They strongly urged adoption of the CIRV for making interpretive inferences in clinical practice, a recommendation that is even more important in forensic settings, where the demand for a substantial empirical foundation for expert opinions is higher.

The research on CIRV is compelling and suggests that, for those assessors continuing to use of the CS in forensic settings, at the very least, they need to take these international reference data into account. For those CS assessors who continue to be skeptical of the new research or have become used to the Exner CS norms, a defensible interpretive strategy could be to use both the Exner reference sample and the CIRV as ways to guide inferences regarding deviations from what is normal for individuals. On the other hand, given the growing research on the problems with the Exner CS norms, failure to utilize the CIRV may lead to overly pathological interpretations for about one-third of CS variables and therefore could easily open the assessor to significant challenge from a well-prepared attorney. One drawback for those untrained in the R-PAS is that coding must adhere to the new R-PAS practice rather than CS coding rules. With that said, this author has found that learning R-PAS coding is a natural extension of CS coding, only with clearer scoring criteria, in turn enhancing coding reliability.

R-Optimized Administration

Another strategy used by the R-PAS system that varies considerably from CS practice is R-Optimized administration. In an article written nearly 25 years ago, Meyer (1992) raised a critical concern about the impact of response frequency (R) on the validity of other CS variables, noting: "R is consistently and highly correlated with many other Rorschach scores" (p. 232). In this article, he explored the possibility of introducing greater structure into Rorschach administration to control for the many problems associated with too high or too low R and to "sharpen the Rorschach's ability to assess and predict important aspects of personality" (p. 231). However, Meyer also acknowledged the potential difficulties that might arise from developing a more structured administration in order to limit R. Subsequently, Meyer and his colleagues (Dean, Viglione, Perry, & Meyer, 2007) successfully experimented with a method to optimize the response range for increasing CS validity, which led ultimately to the R-Optimized administration procedure.

For those unfamiliar with R-Optimized administration, the purpose is to aim for a range of R between 18 and 28, which empirically constitutes the "sweet spot" of valid interpretation of R-PAS as well as CS variables. Before administering the RIM, the assessor asks for "two ... maybe three, responses" to each card. During the test, the assessor prompts for a second response to each RIM card, when only one is given, and requests the card to be returned after four responses. As noted earlier, Khadivi and Evans (2012) raised concerns, not dissimilar to Meyer's (1992), about what might be lost with the shift from a more open-structured RIM to the more strictly prescriptive R-Optimized administration procedure. They wondered how this approach would affect the RIM interpretation. They supported the gathering of normative and clinical samples using the R-Optimized administration procedure and comparing these findings to the R-Optimized modeled norms using the CS administration. Recent research by Viglione et al. (2015) addressed these and other concerns, listing among the advantages of R-Optimized administration 1) the elimination of overly short or excessively long records, which often lack reliability and validity; 2) better psychometric properties; and 3) virtual eradication of the cumbersome requirement for re-administration because of inadequate R.

While many clinicians may continue to regret the loss of a more open-structured administration, the better psychometric properties of the R-Optimized administration, as well as ease of administration, warrants serious consideration by CS users. R-Optimized administration offers considerable advantage to forensic assessors, especially with unmotivated forensic respondents, as they are more likely to provide a validly interpretable record by better controlling for adequate R. As research has strongly indicated, there is increased reliability and validity of the RIM production when R is controlled, thus adopting R-Optimized administration in the forensic context should be carefully considered. Further, it is relatively easy to incorporate into CS-based practice. Naturally, forensic examiners will want to prepare for concerns regarding questions about whether the use of the R-Optimized administration constitutes a different test and therefore potentially inapplicable for CS norms. Assessors wishing to adopt the R-Optimized administration may wish to carefully review Erard (2012) and Erard, Meyer, and Viglione (2014), and also keep abreast of the growing empirical literature in preparing for such questions under cross-examination.

Use of Empirically Supported Non-CS Scales

Bornstein and Masling (2005b) were instrumental in re-introducing empirically supported RIM scales not included in the CS, which helped open the door for inclusion of several valuable scales in forensic assessment. Other scales from forensically relevant populations have also been introduced (e.g., Gacono & Meloy, 1994/2013). A number of non-CS scales have substantial empirical support, but forensic assessors who limit RIM analysis to CS variables may not be acquainted with these potentially useful independent scales. Indeed, as I recall from several of the last annual Rorschach Workshops Advanced Seminars, there was lively debate about the use of several of these scales up until the time of John Exner's death.

Fortunately, the empirical sturdiness of several such scales, including Aggressive Content (AgC: Gacono & Meloy, 1994/2013, Kivisto & Swan, 2013), the Rorschach Oral Dependency scale (ROD: Bornstein & Masling, 2005a; Masling, Rabie, & Blondheim, 1967), Mutuality of Autonomy (MOA: Fowler & Erdberg, 2005; Urist, 1977), the Ego Impairment Index (EII: Perry & Kinder, 1992), and the Trauma Content Index (TCI: Armstrong & Lowenstein, 1990; Brand, Armstrong, Loewenstein, & McNary, 2009) were deemed sufficiently valid to be included in R-PAS, albeit using somewhat different names and some small adjustments and specifications. The use of these five scales is highly recommended, as they add an extra dimension covering important implicit psychological processes that are not available in the CS and difficult to assess with other evidence-based clinical instruments.

CONCLUSION

There is compelling evidence for the value of comprehensive, multi-method assessment that integrates self-report and performance-based methods, as illustrated by Hopwood and Bornstein (2014) and Mihura (2012) and throughout this book. Especially in forensic settings (Gacono & Evans, 2008), the RIM has long-proven value, especially in terms of tapping implicit personality processes and providing incremental validity over self-report methods. In terms of its history of empirical sturdiness and admissibility in psycholegal settings, the RIM has no peer in the performance-based assessment of personality. While it was perhaps an unfortunate decision to maintain the copyrighted CS Structural Summary as it was left at the time of John Exner's death, there is nothing to prevent the continued evolution and improvement of the RIM under the rubric of "CS-based" approaches or through a new system such as R-PAS.

The developers of R-PAS have risen to the challenge of improving the RIM and have offered an important extension of the CS tradition, while providing new and vital research showing more than ever the value of the RIM. Seasoned forensic evaluators using the CS may feel that the jury is not yet in on R-PAS as a whole, but at least four empirical improvements upon which the R-PAS is built provide important advances for the RIM. As such, all forensic RIM users need to take R-PAS developments into serious consideration. At least two of the advances, the use of the Mihura et al. (2013) meta-analyses and the CIRV, are, in my opinion, essential for all RIM users and need to be incorporated into CS practice. Given the commonalities between the CS and the R-PAS, an attitude of open and friendly debate and challenge will likely accelerate the further development of the RIM in multimethod forensic psychological assessment.

References

American Psychological Association (2010). *Ethical principles of psychologists and code of conduct*. Retrieved from http://www.apa.org/ethics/code/principles.pdf

Archer, R. P., Buffington-Vollum, J. K., Stredny, R. V., & Handel, R. W. (2006). A survey of psychological test use patterns among forensic psychologists. *Journal of personality assessment, 87*(1), 84–94.

Armstrong, J., & Lowenstein, R. (1990). Characteristics of patients with multiple personality and dissociative disorders on psychological testing. *Journal of Nervous and Mental Disease, 174*, 448–454.

Bornstein, R. F. (2002). A process dissociation approach to objective-projective test score interrelationships. *Journal of Personality Assessment, 78*, 47–68.

Bornstein, R. F. (2011). From symptom to process: How the PDM alters goals and strategies in psychological assessment. *Journal of Personality Assessment, 93*, 142–150.

Bornstein, R. F., & Masling, J. M. (2005a). The Rorschach Oral Dependency Scale. In R. F. Bornstein & J. M. Masling (Eds.), *The LEA series in personality and clinical psychology. Scoring the Rorschach: Seven validated systems* (pp. 135–157). Mahwah, NJ: Lawrence Erlbaum Associates.

Bornstein, R. F., & Masling, J. M. (Eds.). (2005b). *Scoring the Rorschach: Seven validated systems*. New York: Routledge/Taylor & Francis Group.

Brand, B. L., Armstrong, J. G., Loewenstein, R. J., & McNary, S. W. (2009). Personality differences on the Rorschach of dissociative identity disorder, borderline personality disorder, and psychotic inpatients. *Psychological Trauma: Theory, Research, Practice, and Policy, 1*(3), 188–205. http://dx.doi.org/10.1037/a0016561

Dean, K. L., Viglione, D. J., Perry, W., & Meyer, G. J. (2007). A method to optimize the response range while maintaining Rorschach comprehensive system validity. *Journal of Personality Assessment, 89*(2), 149–161. http://dx.doi.org/10.1080/00223890701468543

Erard, R. E. (2012). Expert testimony using the Rorschach Performance Assessment System in psychological injury cases. *Psychological Injury and Law, 5*, 122–134.

Erard, R. E., Meyer, G. J., & Viglione, D. J. (2014). Setting the record straight: Comment on Gurley, Sheehan, Piechowski, and Gray (2014) on the admissibility of the Rorschach Performance Assessment System (R-PAS) in court. *Psychological Injury and Law, 7*(2), 165–177. http://dx.doi.org/10.1007/s12207-014-9195-x

Evans, F. B. (2012). Introduction: To Practice Matters Special Section on the Rorschach. *Psychological Injury and Law, 5*(2), 95–96. http://dx.doi.org/10.1007/s12207-012-9133-8

Exner, J. E., Jr. (1974). *The Rorschach: A comprehensive system.* Oxford, England: John Wiley.

Exner, J. E., Jr. (2001). *Rorschach® Structural Summary & Workbook* (5th ed.). Lutz, FL: PAR, Inc.

Exner, J. E., Jr. (2003). *Basic foundations and principles of interpretation. The Rorschach: A comprehensive system* (4th ed.). Hoboken, NJ: John Wiley.

Exner, J. E., Jr. (2007). A new U.S. adult nonpatient sample. *Journal of Personality Assessment, 89*, S1, S154–S158. http://dx.doi.org/10.1080/00223890701583523

Exner, J. E., Jr., & Erdberg, P. (2005). *Advanced interpretation, Vol. 2. The Rorschach: A comprehensive system* (3rd ed.). Hoboken, NJ: John Wiley.

Fowler, J. C., & Erdberg, P. (2005). The Mutuality of Autonomy Scale: An implicit measure of object relations for the Rorschach Inkblot Method. *South African Rorschach Journal, 2*(2), 3–10.

Gacono, C. B., & Evans, F. B. (Eds.). (2008). *The LEA series in personality and clinical psychology. The handbook of forensic Rorschach assessment* (N. Kaser-Boyd & L. A. Gacono, Collaborators). New York: Routledge/Taylor & Francis Group.

Gacono, C. B., & Meloy, J. R. (1994/2013). *The Rorschach assessment of aggressive and psychopathic personalities.* New York: Routledge/Taylor & Francis Group.

Ganellen, R. J. (2008). Rorschach assessment of malingering and defensive response sets. In C. B. Gacono, F. B. Evans (Eds.) & N. Kaser-Boyd, L. A. Gacono (Collaborators), *The LEA series in personality and clinical psychology. The handbook of forensic Rorschach assessment* (pp. 89–119). New York: Routledge/Taylor & Francis Group.

Garb, H. N. (1999). Call for a moratorium on the use of the Rorschach Inkblot Test in clinical and forensic settings. *Assessment, 6*(4), 313–315.

Garb, H. N., Wood, J. M., Lilienfeld, S. O., & Nezworski, M. T. (2002). Effective use of projective techniques in clinical practice: Let the data help with selection and interpretation. *Professional Psychology: Research and Practice, 33*, 454–463.

Gurley, J. R., Sheehan, B. L., Piechowski, L. D., & Gray, J. (2014). The admissibility of the R-PAS in court. *Psychological Injury and Law, 7*(1), 9–17. http://dx.doi.org/10.1007/s12207-014-9182-2

Hopwood, C. J., & Bornstein, R. F. (Eds.). (2014). *Multimethod clinical assessment*. New York: Guilford Publications.

Hosseininasab, A., Mohammadi, M. R., Weiner, I. B., & Delavar, A. (2015). Rorschach Comprehensive System data for a sample of 478 Iranian children at four ages. *Journal of Personality Assessment, 97*(2), 123–135. http://dx.doi.org/10.1080

Hunsley, J., & Bailey, J. M. (1999). The clinical utility of the Rorschach: Unfulfilled promises and an uncertain future. *Psychological Assessment, 11,* 266–277.

Khadivi, A., & Evans, F. B. (2012). The brave new world of forensic Rorschach assessment: Comments on the Rorschach Special Section. *Psychological Injury and Law, 5*(2), 145–149. http://dx.doi.org/10.1007/s12207-012-9134-7

Kivisto, A. J., Gacono, C., & Medoff, D. (2013). Does the R-PAS meet standards for forensic use? Considerations with introducing a new Rorschach coding system. *Journal of Forensic Psychology Practice, 13*(5), 389–410. http://dx.doi.org/10.1080/15228932.2013.838106

Kivisto, A. J., & Swan, S. A. (2013). Rorschach measures of aggression: A laboratory-based validity study. *Journal of Personality Assessment, 95,* 38–45.

Lerner, P. M. (1991). *Psychoanalytic theory and the Rorschach*. Hillsdale, NJ: Analytic Press.

Lerner, P. M. (1998). *Psychoanalytic perspectives on the Rorschach*. Mahwah, NJ: Analytic Press.

Lilienfeld, S. O., Wood, J. M., & Garb, H. N. (2001). What's wrong with this picture? *Scientific American, 284*(5), 80–87.

Masling, J., Rabie, L., & Blondheim, S. H. (1967). Obesity, level of aspiration, and Rorschach and TAT measures of oral dependence. *Journal of Consulting Psychology, 31*(3), 233–239. http://dx.doi.org/10.1037/h0020999

McCann, J. T., & Evans, F. B. (2008). Admissibility of the Rorschach. In C. B. Gacono, F. B. Evans (Eds.) & N. Kaser-Boyd, L. A. Gacono (Collaborators), *The LEA series in personality and clinical psychology. The handbook of forensic Rorschach assessment* (pp. 55–78). New York: Routledge/Taylor & Francis Group.

Meloy, J. R. (2008). The authority of the Rorschach: An update. In C. B. Gacono, F. B. Evans (Eds.) & N. Kaser-Boyd, L. A. Gacono (Collaborators), *The LEA series in personality and clinical psychology. The handbook of forensic Rorschach assessment* (pp. 79–87). New York: Routledge/Taylor & Francis Group.

Meyer, G. J. (1992). Response frequency problems in the Rorschach: Clinical and research implications with suggestions for the future. *Journal of Personality Assessment, 58*(2), 231–244. http://dx.doi.org/10.1207/s15327752jpa5802_2

Meyer, G. J., Erdberg, P., & Shaffer, T. W. (2007). Toward international normative reference data for the Comprehensive System. *Journal of Personality Assessment, 89*(Suppl1), S201–S216. http://dx.doi.org/10.1080/00223890701629342

Meyer, G. J., Shaffer, T. W., Erdberg, P., & Horn, S. L. (2015). Addressing issues in the development and use of the Composite International Reference Values as Rorschach norms for adults. *Journal of Personality Assessment, 97*(4), 330–347. http://dx.doi.org/10.1080/00223891.2014.961603

Meyer, G. J., Viglione, D. J., Mihura, J. L., Erard, Robert E., & Erdberg, P. (2011). *Rorschach Performance Assessment System: Administration, coding, interpretation, and technical manual.* Toledo, OH: Rorschach Performance Assessment System, LLC.

Mihura, J. L. (2012). The necessity of multiple test methods in conducting assessments: The role of the Rorschach and self-report. *Psychological Injury and Law, 5,* 97-106.

Mihura, J. L., Meyer, G. J., Dumitrascu, N., & Bombel, G. (2013). The validity of individual Rorschach variables: Systematic reviews and meta-analyses of the Comprehensive System. *Psychological Bulletin, 139,* 548-605.

Mihura, J. L., Meyer, G. J., Dumitrascu, N., & Bombel, G. (2015). Standards, accuracy, and questions of bias in Rorschach meta-analyses: Reply to Wood, Garb, Nezworski, Lilienfeld, and Duke (2015). *Psychological Bulletin, 141,* 250-260.

Perry, G. G., & Kinder, B. N. (1992). Susceptibility of the Rorschach to malingering: A schizophrenia analogue. In C. D. Spielberger & J. N. Butcher (Eds.), *Advances in personality assessment,* Volume 9 (pp. 127-140). Hillsdale, NJ: Lawrence Erlbaum.

Perry, W., & Viglione, D. J. (1991). The Ego Impairment Index as a predictor of outcome in melancholic depressed patients treated with tricyclic antidepressants. *Journal of Personality Assessment, 56,* 487-501.

Piotrowski, C. (2015a). On the decline of projective techniques in professional psychology training. *North American Journal of Psychology, 17,* 259-265.

Piotrowski, C. (2015b). Projective techniques usage worldwide: A review of applied settings 1995-2015. *Journal of the Indian Academy of Applied Psychology, 41*(3), 9-19.

Ready, R. E., & Veague, H. B. (2014). Training in psychological assessment: Current practices of clinical psychology programs. *Professional Psychology: Research and Practice, 45*(4), 278-288.

Ritzler, B., Erard, R., & Pettigrew, G. (2002a). Protecting the integrity of Rorschach expert witnesses: A reply to Grove and Barden (1999) re: The admissibility of testimony under Daubert/Kumho analyses. *Psychology, Public Policy, and Law, 8*(2), 201-215.

Ritzler, B., Erard, R., & Pettigrew, G. (2002b). A final reply to Grove and Barden: The relevance of the Rorschach Comprehensive System for expert testimony. *Psychology, Public Policy, and Law, 8*(2), 236-246.

Ritzler, B., & Sciara, A. (2009). *Rorschach Comprehensive System international norms: Cautionary notes.* Retrieved from http://www.rorschachtraining.com

Rorschach, H. (1942). *Psychodiagnostics: A diagnostic test based on perception* (P. Lemkau & B. Kronenberg, Trans.). Berne, Switzerland: Huber. (Original work published 1921).

Shaffer, T. W., Erdberg, P., & Meyer, G. J. (2007). Introduction to the JPA Special Supplement on International Reference Samples for the Rorschach Comprehensive System. *Journal of Personality Assessment, 89,* S1, S2-S6. http://dx.doi.org/10.1080/00223890701629268

The Status of the Rorschach in Clinical and Forensic Practice: An Official Statement by the Board of Trustees of the Society for Personality Assessment. (2005). *Journal of Personality Assessment, 85*(2), 219-237. http://dx.doi.org/10.1207/s15327752jpa8502_16

Tibon, S., Handelzalts, J. E., & Weinberger, Y. (2005) Using the Rorschach for exploring the concept of transitional space within the political context of the Middle East. *International Journal of Applied Psychoanalytic Studies, 2*(1), 40-57.

Tibon-Czopp, S., & Weiner, I. B. (2016). *Rorschach assessment of adolescents: Theory, research, and practice.* New York: Springer-Verlag.

Urist, J. (1977). The Rorschach test and the assessment of object relations. *Journal of Personality Assessment, 41,* 3-9.

van der Kolk, B. A., & Ducey, C. P. (1989). The psychological processing of traumatic experience: Rorschach patterns in PTSD. *Journal of Traumatic Stress, 2,* 259-274.

Viglione, D. J., Meyer, G., Jordan, R. J., Converse, G. L., Evans, J., MacDermott, D., & Moore, R. (2015). Developing an alternative Rorschach administration method to optimize the number of responses and enhance clinical inferences. *Clinical Psychology & Psychotherapy, 22*(6). 546-558. http://dx.doi.org/10.1002/cpp.1913

Weiner, I. B. (2013). Assessment of personality and psychopathology with performance-based measures. In K. F. Geisinger, B. A. Bracken, J. F. Carlson, J.-I. C. Hansen, N. R. Kuncel, S. P. Reise & M. C. Rodriguez (Eds.), *APA handbook of testing and assessment in psychology* (Vol. 2): *Testing and assessment in clinical and counseling psychology* (pp. 153-170). http://dx.doi.org/10.1037/14048-010

Wood, J. M., Garb, H. N., Nezworski, M. T., Lilienfeld, S. O., & Duke, M. C. (2015). A second look at the validity of widely used Rorschach indices: Comment on Mihura, Meyer, Dumitrascu, and Bombel (2013). *Psychological Bulletin, 141*(1), 236-249. http://dx.doi.org/10.1037/a0036005

Wood, J. M., Nezworski, M. T., & Stejskal, W. J. (1996). The Comprehensive System for the Rorschach: A critical examination. *Psychological Science. 7,* 3-10.

Ziskin, J. (1995). Challenging personality testing: The Rorschach & other projective methods (pp. 823-884). In J. Ziskin (Ed.), *Coping with psychiatric and psychological testimony, Vol. 2* (5th ed.). Los Angeles, CA: Law and Psychology Press.

INDEX

Note: figures and tables are denoted with italicized page numbers; end note information is denoted with an n and note number following the page number.

Achievement Striving 71, *72*
Administrative Behaviors and Observations 48, 173–4, 225, *226*, 229, *279*
age, R-PAS® norms reflecting 51–4, *53*, 56–7, 223
aggression: methamphetamine psychosis and 243, 244, 245, 246, 255, 262, 265–70, 274–86; neuropsychodynamics of paranoid rage murder and 283–5; PAI assessment of 133, 134, 137–8; psychobiology of violence and 281–3; violence risk assessments of 199, 203–5
Aggressive Content 37, 59, 62, 73, 178, 215, 221, 278, 327
Aggressive Movement 73, 179, 215, 278; alcohol use *see* substance use
Anatomy content 60, 179
antisocial behavior: methamphetamine psychosis and 262; PAI assessment of 133, 134, 137
anxiety/anxiety disorders: impression management of 108, 109; methamphetamine psychosis and 262, 263; PAI assessment of 137–8; PAI-Rorschach integrated assessment of 154–6; R-PAS® scoring relative to 50

Beck Depression Inventory 7, 114
behavioral indices 8

BETAssessment®: assessor as participant-observer in 304–6; as Collaborative/Therapeutic Assessment 153, 303–12; forensic finding clarification via feedback from 309–11; overview of 303, 312; PAI-Rorschach integrated results inquiry in line with 153; personality tests as 'empathy magnifiers' in 306–9; Rorschach in 153, 304, 305, 306–9, 310–12
bipolar disorder, impression management of 103
Blood content 60
Boll, Thomas 29
borderline personality disorder 281
Brief Psychiatric Rating Scale 266–7

child custody evaluations (CCEs): art of multimethod personality assessment for 221; child custody litigant samples for 222–3; child custody litigant *vs.* nonpatient norms comparison for 225–32, *226–8*; Collaborative/Therapeutic Assessment in 304–6; contextualized findings in 215–16; contradictory behavior assessed in 214–15; "Guidelines for Child Custody Evaluations in Family Law Proceedings" on 211; impression management detection in 117, 212–14;

333

interpersonal style assessed in 216–17, 218; key questions addressed in 217–18; limitations of performance-based testing for 218–19; "Model Standards of Practice for Child Custody Evaluation" on 211; multimethod approach importance in 212–19, 221, 233–5; novel, stressful, and private circumstances assessed in 214; overview of 210–11, 233–5; personality testing contributions to 211–12; reliability considerations in 223–5; Rorschach for 117, 213–36, 304, 305; R-PAS® use in 215, 216, 219–35; self-report tests in 212–13, 218, 221, 234, 304, 305

clinical interviews, psychotic offender evaluation using 198, 199

Cognitive Codes 42, 43, 46, 176, 270, 278

Collaborative/Therapeutic Assessment (C/TA): assessor as participant-observer in 297, 299, 303, 304–6; BETAssessment® as 153, 303–12; collaboration, specifically, in 300–2; compatibility of C/TA and forensic assessment 298–9, 303; forensic finding clarification via feedback from 303, 309–11; in multimethod forensic assessments 297–312; overview of 297–8, 312; PAI-Rorschach integrated results inquiry in line with 153; personality tests as 'empathy magnifiers' in 297, 303, 306–9; problems with forensic assessment vs. 300–3; Rorschach in 153, 304, 305, 306–9, 310–12

Color Dominance Proportion 60, 71, 278

competency evaluations: impression management in 103; psychotic offender evaluations including 201–3

Composite International Reference Values (CIRV) 324–5

Comprehensive System see Exner Comprehensive System

Comprehensive System International Rorschach Association (CSIRA) 319

constructive tests 7–8

Cooperative Movement (COP) 119, 172, 178, 215, 278

criminal issues: crime, violence and meth use 243, 244, 245, 246, 255, 262, 265–70, 274–86; criminal responsibility evaluations 200–1; criminological model of malingering 95–6; insanity evaluations related to 196, 200–1, 285–6; psychotic offender evaluations related to 194–207; United Nations Office on Drugs and Crime 245

Critical Content 73, 172, 177, 231, 270, 278

CS (Comprehensive System) see Exner Comprehensive System

custody evaluations see child custody evaluations

Daubert standard (*Daubert v. Merrell Dow Pharmaceuticals*, 1993) 11–12, 75, 76

depression/depressive disorders: Collaborative/Therapeutic Assessment of 308–9; impression management of 103, 105, 109, 114–15, 164; methamphetamine psychosis and 262, 263; PAI assessment of 137, 139, 155; PAI-Rorschach integrated assessment of 155; personal injury evaluations of 164, 308–9; Rorschach/R-PAS® assessment of 50, 149, 155, 308–9

diagnosis: *Diagnostic and Statistical Manual* for 78, 195–6; *International Classification of Diseases* for 78; of MAP and paranoid schizophrenia 242, 256–7, 262, 267–8, 274, 278, 280, 285–6; PAI assessment data use in 138–40; of psychotic offenders 194–207; R-PAS® data limitations for making 78

Diffuse Shading 176

dissociation: impression management of 115; personal injury evaluation of 183, 185n5; Rorschach assessment of 149, 151

drug use see substance use

Early Memories Procedure 8

educational level, R-PAS® norms reflecting 51–4, 53, 223

Ego Impairment Index (EII) 37, 60, 64, 74, 176, 230, 264, 269, 273, 327

Engagement and Cognitive Processing 48, 70, 174–5, 226, 227–8, 229–30

Erard, Robert E. 30

Erdberg, Philip 29, 30

ethnicity, R-PAS® norms reflecting 51–3, 53

Exner, John E. 29–30, 63–4, 79, 219, 268, 317

Exner Comprehensive System: clinical and forensic practice Rorschach scoring

via 28–30, 316–28; composite variables in 41–5; Constellation Indices in 41–2; construct validity of 67–9, 73–4; empirically supported non-CS scales *vs.* 327; examiner variability associated with 33–4; experienced forensic users of 318–19; Hypervigilance Index (HVI) in 41, 45; impression management detection via 113, 114; international forensic users of 319–20; international reference norms *vs.* 38, 39, 54–5, 220, 324–5; learning and interpretation challenges with 46–8; MAP and schizophrenia evaluations in 268–9; meta-analyses of 322–4, *323*; multimethod forensic assessment continued use of 316–28; norms and normative anchors in 38–41, 54–5, 220, 324–5; perceptual accuracy indices in 34–5; Perceptual Thinking Index (PTI) in 41, 43, 74, 269; prior research application to 63–4; protocol simplicity or complexity adjustments in 48–51; psychotic offender evaluations using 195, 197; reasons for continued use of 317–21; reliability of 58–62, 223–5; response variability errors associated with 31–2, 62–3, 325–6; Rorschach Research Council on 29–30; R-PAS® addressing psychometric limitations of 31–51, 219–21, 325–8; R-PAS® comparison in child custody evaluations 222–35; R-PAS® critiques and continued use of 320–1; R-PAS® replacing 30–1, 76; Schizophrenia Index (SCZI) in 43, 114, 268–9; Suicide Constellation (S-CON) in 41, 44–5; updating 29–30, 322–7; variable interpretation in 36–8
Explosion content 60
externalizing disorders, PAI assessment of 137

Federal Rules of Evidence (FRE), on legal admissibility 12
Fire content 60
Fowler, Christopher 29
Frye standard (*Frye v. United States*, 1923) 11, 75, 76

gender: PAI demographics related to 134; R-PAS® norms reflecting 51–3, *53*, 56, 223
Greene, Roger 29

Hilsenroth, Mark 29
Historical-Clinical-Risk Management-20 (HCR-20) 203–4
Holtzman Inkblot Test 7
Human Movement (M) 46, 172, 174–5, 177, 235n16
Human Representations (H) 172–3, 177, 270
Hypervigilance Index (HVI) 41, 45

immigration evaluations: background information for 142–4; Collaborative/Therapeutic Assessment in 306–7; extended inquiry in 153–4; forensic referral question and legal issues in 141–2; outcome of 156; PAI findings, specifically, for 145–7, *146–8*; PAI-Rorschach integration in 141, 152–3, *153*; psychological opinions regarding exceptional hardship from 154–6; Rorschach findings, specifically, for 149, 151–2, 306–7
impression management: child custody evaluations detecting 117, 212–14; coaching on psychological tests for 96–8, 100, 102, 103, 105–6, 109, 110, 114, 116–17; cost-benefit analysis assumption in 96; dimensional models of 93–4; MCMI-III for detecting 110–11; M-FAST for detecting 102–3; MMPI-2 for detecting 93, 104–6; motivations to malinger and 95–6; multimethod approach to detecting 117–20; overview of 92–3, 120–1; PAI for detecting 50, 107–9, 135–6, 145–7, *148*; performance-based testing for detecting 112–20; personal injury evaluation detecting 103, 164; prevalence of malingering and 94–5; psychotic offender evaluation detecting 199; Rorschach for detecting 97, 112–17, 213–14; self-report instruments for detecting 50, 93, 98–112, 117–20, 135–6, 145–7, *148*, 164, 199, 212–13; SIMS for detecting 100–2, 164; SIRS/SIRS-2 for detecting 93, 98–100, 164, 199; underreporting in 98, 103, 105–6, 108–9, 111, 116, 117, 135–6, 212–13
Inanimate Movement (m) 77, 176, 307
informant reports 8
insanity evaluations 196, 200–1, 285–6
intellectual disability, impression management of 101

335

Intellectualized Content 175
intermittent explosive disorder (IED) 281, 282
International Classification of Diseases 78
interpersonal traits: PAI assessment of 138; Rorschach assessment of 216-17, 218
in vivo behavior, Rorschach measure of 26-8
Item Response Theory (IRT) 133, 134

Journal of Personality Assessment 38, 324

legal admissibility: Daubert standard for 11-12, 75, 76; FRE Rule 702 on 12; Frye standard for 11, 75, 76; of psychological assessments 11-12; of R-PAS® based testimony 75-6, 221, 321
Level 1 Fabulized Combinations 60
Level Incongruous Combinations 60

malingering: adaptational model of 96; coaching on psychological tests for 96-8, 100, 102, 103, 105-6, 109, 110, 114, 116-17; cost-benefit analysis assumption on 96; criminological model of 95-6; dimensional models of 93-4; false imputation as 94; MCMI-III for detecting 110-11; M-FAST for detecting 102-3; mild, moderate, and severe 93; MMPI-2 for detecting 93, 104-6; motivations for 95-6; multimethod approach to detecting 117-20; PAI for detecting 107-9, 136; pathogenic model of 95; prevalence of 94-5; pure *vs.* partial 94; Rorschach for detecting 97, 112-17; self-report instruments for detecting 93, 98-112, 117-20; SIMS for detecting 100-2; SIRS/SIRS-2 for detecting 93, 98-100; *see also* impression management
MAP *see* methamphetamine psychosis (MAP) evaluations
MCMI-III/IV *see* Millon Clinical Multiaxial Inventory-III/IV
methamphetamine psychosis (MAP) evaluations: amphetamine and methamphetamine epidemics necessitating 243-4; Brief Psychiatric Rating Scale in 266-7; case history and referral questions in 270-2, 274-7; classic studies involving 248-51; crime, violence and meth use links in 243, 244, 245, 246, 255, 262, 265-70, 274-86; definition and description of methamphetamine for 245-8; differential diagnosis of MAP and schizophrenia in 242, 256-7, 262, 267-8, 274, 278, 280, 285-6; legal and forensic issues in 285-6; Methamphetamine Experience Questionnaire in 261; method used in 270; MMPI-2 in 272-3, 277; neuropsychodynamics of paranoid rage murder in 283-5; overview of 242-3; paranoid-hallucinatory states in 246-7, 249-50, 261-4, 265, 266-7, 275-7, 283; paranoid schizophrenia-MAP comparative case study using 267-86; paranoid schizophrenia-MAP similarities in 242, 246, 249-50, 251, 253, 254, 256-61, 262-4, 267-86; pharmacology and neurobiology of MAP for 251-3; Positive and Negative Syndrome Scale in 259, 262, 269; predisposing factors for MAP in 254-5, 256; prevalence of meth abuse and 245; psychobiology of violence in 281-3; psychopharmacology of MAP and schizophrenia in 257-61; recovery and relapse factors in 246, 250, 251, 255-7; Rorschach for 243, 264-5, 267-70, 273-4, 277-80; SNAP-2 in 273
Meyer, Gregory 29, 30
M-FAST *see* Miller Forensic Assessment of Symptoms Test
Mihura, Joni 29, 30, 322-4
Miller Forensic Assessment of Symptoms Test (M-FAST) 102-3, 199
Millon Clinical Multiaxial Inventory-III/IV(MCMI-III/IV) 110-11, 163, 213, 277
Minnesota Multiphasic Personality Inventory(-2) (MMPI/MMPI-2): child custody evaluations using 213, 221, 234; Collaborative/Therapeutic Assessment using 304, 309-11; complexity scores of 48; construct validity of 10, 64, 65, 66, 70; diagnostic hypothesis developed from 138-9; impression management detection via 93, 104-6; MAP and schizophrenia evaluations using 272-3, 277; paranoid criteria from 45; personal injury evaluations using 163, 165, 169-70; prior research application to

64; psychotic offender evaluation using 198–9; PTSD assessment using 309–11; Rorschach integration with *153*
MMPI/MMPI-2 *see* Minnesota Multiphasic Personality Inventory(-2)
mood disorders, impression management of 99–100, 103, 105, 108, 109, 114–15, 164; *see also* anxiety/anxiety disorders; depression/depressive disorders
Morbid Content 72, 73, 77, 176–7, 231
M Proportion (MProp) 172–3
multimethod forensic assessments: in child custody evaluations (*see* child custody evaluations); Collaborative/Therapeutic Assessment in 297–312; Exner Comprehensive System for (*see* Exner Comprehensive System); in immigration evaluations (*see* immigration evaluations); impression management detection via (*see* impression management); in methamphetamine psychosis and schizophrenia evaluations 242–85; opportunities and challenges of 3–17; in personal injury evaluations 103, 163–85, *188–93*, 308–9; Personality Assessment Inventory-Rorschach integration in 131–57; psychotic offender evaluations as 194–207; Rorschach in (*see* Rorschach Inkblot Method; Rorschach Performance Assessment System®)
Mutuality of Autonomy Health 59, 60, 62, 178
Mutuality of Autonomy Pathology 59, 60, 62, 73, 215
Mutuality of Autonomy Scale (MOA) 37, 58, 65, 327

NEO Personality Inventory 7, 8
Non-Pure H Proportion (NPH/SumH) 172, 178
norms: adult 51–5, *53*; child and adolescent 56–7; child custody evaluation comparison of 225–32, *226–8*; Exner Comprehensive System norms 38–41, 54–5, 220, 324–5; Form Quality standards for 57–8; international reference norms 38, 39, 52, 54–5, 220, 324–5; normative anchor improvements 38–41, 220; R-PAS® norms 38–41, 51–8, *53*, 220, 223, 225–32, *226–8*

opportunities and challenges of multimethod assessments: clinical utility of test results 11; convergences and divergences in test results 8–10; legal admissibility of test results 11–12; mono- *vs.* multimethod assessments 4–6, 12; overview of 3–4, 12–15; process-based classification of tests 6–8; Rorschach and self-report data contrast 12–15; scientific *vs.* adversary system evaluation 15–17; testing *vs.* assessment distinction 4–5; validity of test scores 10–11
Oral Dependency Language 59, 62, 177, 215, 216

PAI *see* Personality Assessment Inventory
paranoid conditions: MAP paranoid-hallucinatory states as 246–7, 249–50, 261–4, 265, 266–7, 275–7, 283; neuropsychodynamics of paranoid rage murder 283–5; PAI assessment of 137–8; paranoid schizophrenia as 242, 246, 249–50, 251, 253, 254, 256–61, 262–4, 267–86; psychotic offender evaluations of 202; Vigilance Composite (V-Comp) on 45
PCP psychosis 260
PDS (Posttraumatic Stress Diagnostic Scale) 168–9
Perception and Thinking Problems 48, 70, 176, *226–7*, *228*, 230, 270, *279*
Perceptual Thinking Index (PTI) 41, 43, 74, 269
Perry, William 29
personal injury evaluations: case background and interview highlights for 166–7; case illustration of 165–84; Collaborative/Therapeutic Assessment in 308–9; idiographic findings in 179–83; impression management in 103, 164; MMPI-2/MMPI-2-RF use in 163, 165, 169–70; multimethod forensic assessment for 103, 163–85, *188–93*, 308–9; nomothetic findings in 171–9; PDS use in 168–9; personal injury litigation requiring 160–5; psychosocial history for 167–8; PTSD assessment in 164, 166–7, 168–70, 179–84; questions to be answered in 161–2; referral questions for 168; Rorschach/R-PAS® use in 165, 170–84, *188–93*, 308–9;

337

self-report tests in 163–4, 165, 168–70; summarizing results of 183–4
Personality Assessment Inventory (PAI): case study of Rorschach and 141–56; child custody evaluations using 221, 305; clinical scales in 137; Collaborative/Therapeutic Assessment using 153, 305; construct validation framework for 132–5; content validity in 140–1; development of 131; diagnostic hypothesis developed from 138–40; immigration evaluations using 141–56; impression management detection via 50, 107–9, 135–6, 145–7, *148*; interpersonal scales in 138; interpretive guidelines for, in forensic practice 138–40; personal injury evaluations using 163; psychotic offender evaluation using 198; Rorschach integration with 131, 140–57, *146–8, 150–1, 153*; as self-report test 7; Structural Summary of 139–40; supplemental indicators in 138, *148*; treatment consideration scales in 137–8; underreporting on 108–9, 135–6; validity scales in 135–6, 140–1, *148*
Personal Justification Responses (PER) 172
Personal Knowledge Justification 60, 179, 215
Populars 60, 270, 274
Positive and Negative Syndrome Scale (PANSS) 259, 262, 269
Posttraumatic Stress Diagnostic Scale (PDS) 168–9
posttraumatic stress disorder (PTSD): Collaborative/Therapeutic Assessment of 309–11; impression management of 99–100, 103, 104–5, 109, 115, 164; Mississippi Combat-Related PTSD Scale on 309; personal injury evaluations of 164, 166–7, 168–70, 179–84; Posttraumatic Stress Diagnostic Scale measuring 168–9; psychobiology of violence in 281; PTSD Checklist on 309; Rorschach assessment of 310–11
Potentially Problematic Determinants 177
psilocybin-induced psychosis 260–1
psychogenic non-epileptic seizures, impression management of 101

psychological assessments: behavioral indices in 8; clinical utility of 11; coaching on, for impression management 96–8, 100, 102, 103, 105–6, 109, 110, 114, 116–17; Collaborative/Therapeutic Assessment as 297–312; constructive tests in 7–8; construct validity of 10–11; convergences and divergences in test results for 8–10; informant reports in 8; legal admissibility of 11–12; maximal *vs.* typical performance measures with 26–8; multimethod (*see* multimethod forensic assessments); process-based classification of tests in 6–8; Rorschach in (*see* Rorschach Inkblot Method); scientific *vs.* adversary system evaluation of 15–17; self-report tests in (*see* self-report tests); standardized tasks in 25–6, 28; stimulus attribution tests in 7, 13–15; testing *vs.* assessment distinction for 4–5
Psychological Injury and Law 75, 320
psychotic disturbances: impression management of 99–100, 101, 103, 104–5, 108, 109, 114, 199; methamphetamine psychosis as 242–85; PAI assessment of 137; psychotic offender evaluations for 194–207; R-PAS® validity on 73–5; schizophrenia as (*see* schizophrenia); Thought and Perception Composite (TP-Comp) on 41, 42–4, 74
psychotic offender evaluations: case studies of 196–7, 199, 200–1, 202–3, 204–5; clinical interviews in 198, 199; competency evaluations in 201–3; core psychotic symptom assessment in 197; court diversion and treatment planning using 206–7; criminal responsibility evaluations in 200–1; impression management detection in 199; insanity evaluations as 196, 200–1; multimethod forensic assessment Rorschach use for 198–9; overview of 194–5; Rorschach for 194–207; self-report tests in 198–9; sentencing evaluations in 205; strengths and limitations of Rorschach in psychosis assessment for 197–8; unique role of Rorschach in psychosis assessment for 195–7; violence risk assessments in 199, 203–5

INDEX

PTSD *see* posttraumatic stress disorder
PTSD Checklist 309

Qualitative and Structural Dimensions of Object Representations 7–8

Reflections (r) 172–3, 174, 178
reliability, R-PAS® interrater or coding 58–62, 223–5
Repeatable Battery for Assessment of Neuropsychological Status (RBANS) 205
Rorschach, Hermann 24–5, 268
Rorschach examiners: R-PAS® examiner variability limits 33–4; R-PAS® interrater reliability of 58–62, 223–5; training of 61–2
Rorschach Inkblot Method (RIM): child custody evaluations using 117, 213–36, 304, 305; coaching and available information on 97, 116–17; Collaborative/Therapeutic Assessment using 153, 304, 305, 306–9, 310–12; examiners using (*see* Rorschach examiners); Exner Comprehensive System scoring of (*see* Exner Comprehensive System); immigration evaluations using 141–56, 306–7; impression management detection with 97, 112–17, 213–14; limitations of 197–8, 218–19; MAP and schizophrenia evaluations using 243, 264–5, 267–70, 273–4, 277–80; multimethod forensic assessments using (*see* multimethod forensic assessments); personal injury evaluations using 165, 170–84, *188–93*, 308–9; Personality Assessment Inventory integration with 131, 140–57, *146–8, 150–1, 153*; psychotic offender evaluations using 194–207; reasons for using 23–30; Rorschach Research Council on 29–30, 31, 63, 79, 219; R-PAS® scoring of (*see* Rorschach Performance Assessment System®); self-report data combined with, for multimethod assessments 117–20, 131–57; self-report data contrast to 12–15, 27, 112; as stimulus attribution test 7, 13–15; structural summary and supplemental scores in *150–1*
Rorschach Oral Dependency Scale (ROD) 37, 58, 327

Rorschach Performance Assessment System® (R-PAS®): Achievement Striving in 71, *72*; Administrative Behaviors and Observations in 48, 173–4, 225, *226*, 229, *279*; Aggressive Content in 37, 59, 62, 73, 178, 215, 221, 278, 327; Aggressive Movement in 73, 179, 215, 278; Anatomy content in 60, 179; Blood content in 60; child custody evaluations using 215, 216, 219–35; clarification phase standardization in 33–4; Cognitive Codes in 42, 43, 46, 176, 270, 278; Color Dominance Proportion in 60, 71, 278; Complexity and Complexity-Adjusted scores in 48–51, 54, 60, 70, 112–13, 171–2, 174–5, *192–3*, 220, *279*; composite variable improvements in 41–5; construct validity of individual variables in 62–70; construct validity studies of 70–5, *72*; Cooperative Movement in 119, 172, 178, 215, 278; correlational studies of validity of 73–5; Critical Content in 73, 172, 177, 231, 270, 278; critiques of 320–1; Diffuse Shading in 176; easier learning and interpretation via 46–8; Ego Impairment Index in 37, 60, 64, 74, 176, 230, 264, 269, 273, 327; Engagement and Cognitive Processing in 48, 70, 174–5, *226, 227–8*, 229–30; examiner variability limited with 33–4; Exner Comprehensive System *vs.* (*see* Exner Comprehensive System); experimental studies of validity of 70–3, *72*; Explosion content in 60; Fire content in 60; forensic setting use of 75–8; Form Quality (FQ) tables in 34–5, 42–3, 57–8, 220, 224–5; Human Movement in 46, 172, 174–5, 177, 235n16; Human Representations in 172–3, 177, 270; idiographic findings in 179–83; impression management detection via 112–13; Inanimate Movement in 77, 176, 307; initial results scan in 172–3; Intellectualized Content in 175; legal admissibility of 75–6, 221, 321; Level 1 Fabulized Combinations in 60; Level Incongruous Combinations in 60; limitations of 76–8; MAP and schizophrenia evaluations using 243, 269–70, 273–4, 277–80; meta-analyses of validity of 64–70; Morbid Content in 72, 73, 77, 176–7, 231; M Proportion in 172–3; Mutuality of Autonomy

Health in 59, 60, 62, 178; Mutuality of Autonomy Pathology in 59, 60, 62, 73, 215; nomothetic findings in 171–9; Non-Pure H Proportion in 172, 178; normative anchor improvements in 38–41, 220; norms in 38–41, 51–8, *53*, 220, 223, 225–32, *226–8*; online scoring program with 42, 236n19; Oral Dependency Language in 59, 62, 177, 215, 216; overview of 79; Perception and Thinking Problems in 48, 70, 176, *226–7, 228*, 230, 270, *279*; perceptual accuracy indices updated in 34–5; personal injury evaluations using 165, 170–84, *188–93*, 308–9; Personal Justification Responses in 172; Personal Knowledge Justification in 60, 179, 215; Populars in 60, 270, 274; Potentially Problematic Determinants in 177; prior research application to 62–4; protocol simplicity or complexity adjustments in 48–51; psychometric foundations of 23–80; psychometric limitations addressed by 31–51, 219–21, 325–8; psychotic offender evaluations using 195, 197; reasons for Rorschach use, generally 23–30; reasons for R-PAS use, specifically 30–1; Reflections in 172–3, 174, 178; reliability in 58–62, 223–5; response variability errors limited with 31–2, 62–3, 325–6; R-optimized administration of 32, 33, 39–40, 62–3, 220, 229, 270, 320–1, 325–6; Self and Other Representations in 48, 70, 177–9, *227, 228*, 231–2, 270, *279*; Sex content in 60; Space Integration in 38, 59, 60, 71, 175; Space Reversal in 38, 59, 62, 172–3, 177, 215, 221, 231; standard score profiles in 47–8; Stress and Distress in 48, 70, 71–2, 77, 176–7, *227, 228*, 230–1; Suicide Concern Composite (SC-Comp) in 41, 44–5, 77, 177, 221, 231; summarizing results of 183–4; Sum of all Human Representations in 172–3, 178; Sum of Shading in 77, 176; Synthetic Whole responses in 60, 71; Texture in 119, 179, 236n20; Thought and Perception Composite (TP-Comp) in 41, 42–4, 74, 176, 221, 230, 269, 270, 273, 277–8; Trauma Content Index in 149, 177, 307, 310–11, 327; Vagueness in 60, 175; validity check via 171–2; variable interpretation alignment with validity evidence in 36–8; Vigilance Composite (V-Comp) in 41, 45, 172–3, 178–9, 270, 273; Vista in 72, 172–3, 175, 177; Weighted Sum of Cognitive Codes in 176, 270, 273, 278; Weighted Sum of Color in 46, 60, 71, *72*, 174–5

Rorschach Prognostic Rating Scale 58

Rorschach Research Council 29–30, 31, 63, 79, 219

R-PAS® *see* Rorschach Performance Assessment System®

Schedule for Nonadaptive and Adaptive Personality-2 (SNAP-2) 273

schizophrenia: impression management of 100, 101, 103, 104–5, 109, 114; MAP and paranoid schizophrenia 242, 246, 249–50, 251, 253, 254, 256–61, 262–4, 267–86; PAI assessment of 139; PCP psychosis and 260; psilocybin-induced psychosis and 260–1; psychotic offender evaluations for 196–7, 199; R-PAS® Complexity score with 49; R-PAS® interrater reliability with 59–60; R-PAS® validity on 74–5; Schizophrenia Index (SCZI) on 43, 114, 268–9; violence and 282–3, 284–5

Self and Other Representations 48, 70, 177–9, *227, 228*, 231–2, 270, *279*

self-report tests: Beck Depression Inventory as 7, 114; broadband personality measures as 103–12; child custody evaluations use of 212–13, 218, 221, 234, 304, 305; Collaborative/Therapeutic Assessment using 153, 304, 305, 309–11; impression management detection via 50, 93, 98–112, 117–20, 135–6, 145–7, *148*, 164, 199, 212–13; malingering-specific instruments as 98–103; MAP and schizophrenia evaluations using 272–3, 277; MCMI-III/IV as 110–11, 163, 213, 277; M-FAST as 102–3, 199; MMPI/MMPI-2 as 10, 45, 48, 64, 65, 66, 70, 93, 104–6, 139, *153*, 163, 165, 169–70, 198–9, 213, 221, 234, 272–3, 277, 304, 309–11; NEO Personality Inventory as 7; PAI as 7, 50, 107–9, 131–57, 163, 198–9, 221, 305; PDS as 168–9; personal injury evaluations using 163–4, 165, 168–70; psychological assessment use of, generally 4, 6–7, 12–15, 27; psychotic offender evaluation use of 198–9; Rorschach combined with, for multimethod assessments 117–20,

131–57; Rorschach contrast to 12–15, 27, 112; SIMS as 100–2, 164; SIRS/SIRS-2 as 93, 98–100, 164, 199; validity of 10, 64, 65, 66, 70, 98–112, 103–4, 118–19, 132–6, 140–1, 164
Sex content 60
Shedler-Westen Assessment Procedure 8
somatoform disorders: impression management of 105; PAI assessment of 137
Space Integration (SI) 38, 59, 60, 71, 175
Space Reversal (SR) 38, 59, 62, 172–3, 177, 215, 221, 231
Standards for Educational and Psychological Testing 5, 6
stimulus attribution tests 7, 13–15
Stress and Distress 48, 70, 71–2, 77, 176–7, 227, 228, 230–1
Structured Interview of Reported Symptoms-2 (SIRS/SIRS-2) 93, 98–100, 164, 199
Structured Inventory of Malingered Symptomatology (SIMS) 100–2, 164
substance use: methamphetamine psychosis from 242–85; PAI assessment of 138; PCP psychosis from 260; psilocybin-induced psychosis from 260–1
suicide/suicide ideation: MAP and 262; PAI assessment of 138–9; Suicide Concern Composite (SC-Comp) on 41, 44–5, 77, 177, 221, 231; Suicide Constellation (S-CON) on 41, 44–5
Sum of all Human Representations (SumH) 172–3, 178
Sum of Shading 77, 176
Synthetic Whole responses 60, 71

Texture 119, 179, 236n20
Thematic Apperception Test (TAT) 7, 113
Thought and Perception Composite (TP-Comp) 41, 42–4, 74, 176, 221, 230, 269, 270, 273, 277–8
thought dysfunction: PAI assessment of 137; Perception and Thinking Problems on 48, 70, 176, 226–7, 228, 230, 270, 279; perceptual accuracy indices on 34–5; Perceptual Thinking Index on 41, 43, 74, 269; Thought and Perception Composite on 41, 42–4, 74, 176, 221, 230, 269, 270, 273, 277–8; *see also* psychotic disturbances
Trail-Making Test (TMT) 9

Trauma Content Index (TCI) 149, 177, 307, 310–11, 327
trauma responses: Collaborative/Therapeutic Assessment of 300–3, 306–7; extended inquiry on 153–4; impression management of 115; PAI assessment of 137; Rorschach/R-PAS® assessment of 50, 115, 149, 177, 306–7, 310–11, 327; Trauma Symptom Inventory on 305; *see also* posttraumatic stress disorder
Trauma Symptom Inventory (TSI) 305

United Nations: demographic and normative data from 52, 53; Office on Drugs and Crime 245

Vagueness 60, 175
validity: construct validity of psychological assessments 10–11; convergent 64; correlational studies of R-PAS® 73–5; discriminant 64, 133–4; experimental studies of R-PAS® 70–3, 72; impression management detection via validity scales 98–112, 118–19; meta-analyses of R-PAS® 64–70; PAI construct validation framework 132–5; PAI content validity 140–1; PAI validity scales 135–6, 140–1, 148; R-PAS® as validity check 171–2; R-PAS® construct validity of individual variables 62–70; R-PAS® variable interpretation alignment with validity evidence 36–8; self-report test 10, 64, 65, 66, 70, 98–112, 103–4, 118–19, 132–6, 140–1, 164
Vigilance Composite (V-Comp) 41, 45, 172–3, 178–9, 270, 273
Viglione, Donald 29, 30
violence *see* aggression; criminal issues
Vista (V) 72, 172–3, 175, 177
Visual-Motor Gestalt Test 8

Wechsler Intelligence Scale IV (WAIS-IV) 205
Weighted Sum of Cognitive Codes 176, 270, 273, 278
Weighted Sum of Color 46, 60, 71, 72, 174–5
Weiner, Irving 29
Wender Utah Rating Scale (WURS) 254
workers' compensation cases, impression management in 103, 105

341